CONTESTED COMMUNITIES

A book in the series

COMPARATIVE AND INTERNATIONAL

WORKING-CLASS HISTORY

General Editors:

Andrew Gordon / Harvard University

Daniel James / Duke University

Alexander Keyssar / Duke University

Thomas Miller Klubock

CONTESTED COMMUNITIES

Class, Gender, and Politics in Chile's

El Teniente Copper Mine, 1904–1951

Duke University Press   Durham and London   1998

© 1998 Duke University Press

All rights reserved

Printed in the United States of America on acid-free paper ∞

Typeset in Bembo by Tseng Information Systems, Inc.

Library of Congress Cataloging-in-Publication

Data appear on the last printed page of this book.

CONTENTS

PREFACE

On a cold winter night in 1991, immersed in research for this book, I accompanied close to two hundred copper miners as they marched through the streets of Rancagua, the city below the El Teniente mine, to protest the recently elected democratic government's plans to expand foreign investment in new copper enterprises and thus initiate the incremental privatization of an industry nationalized in 1971 by the socialist government of Salvador Allende. The mood that night was subdued and markedly different from that of miners in strikes and protests during the four decades preceding the military coup of 1973, when thousands of workers and their family members would routinely take to the streets in community-wide mobilizations. The march was noticeable for the small number of protesters and the absence of women from workers' families, and it reflected profound changes in the Chilean economy, society, and politics that had undermined miners' militant traditions of labor activism and strong community ties since the 1973 military coup of Augusto Pinochet. The unified working-class community and cohesive mining workforce that had been created during one stage of the internationalization of capital following the First World War was now being rent asunder by transformations in Chile's insertion into the global economy.

In this book I chart the construction of a permanent working-class community in Chile's export mining sector in response to North American capital's requirements for a trained and stable labor force. I examine changes in both men's and women's lives provoked by this new stage in capitalist economic development. As many writers have observed, "globalization" is both shaped by ideologies of gender and structures gender relations through the international division of labor, the organization of labor markets, and the ordering of household production. In Chile, North American capital employed gendered social welfare and labor policies in order to reorganize relations between men and women and everyday forms of sociability to conform to the model of the male-headed nuclear family, redefining working-class masculinity and femininity in terms of the ideology of female domesticity. The logic of economic development and capital accumulation was articulated with an autonomous, but related, logic of power based on gendered social hierarchy. Thus, the community and class identities forged during this process of capitalist development in the mining export sector were informed by new arrangements of gender.

Globalization is not an inevitable or inexorable process. The ways in which local societies are integrated into the international capitalist system are shaped as much by internal social, political, and cultural configurations of forces as by international structures of trade and circulation. This study shows that capital's strategies are played out on terrain molded by forms of social life shaped by gender, as well as internal patterns of class relations and state formation. In Chile, both men and women struggled against the reorganization of their economic and social lives according to the dictates of foreign capital in the export sector. They asserted control over both their labor and their social-sexual lives. But, even as they resisted radical changes in their patterns of everyday life, men and women came to identify with new gendered concepts of work and family and built a stable community of male-headed households in response to the initiatives of North American capital.

The formation of a permanent working-class community in the export sector was articulated with the process of state formation in Chile following the First World War. The development of an activist state and corporatist labor relations system after 1930 buttressed the North American company's corporate welfare policies; male workers were provided new guarantees, such as the right to unionize and a "family wage," while women had the right to male workers' wages and benefits. At the same time, the state's regulation of labor relations, the legitimization of a new set of rights in both corporate and state social welfare programs, and the development of nationalist languages of citizenship offered workers new resources in their conflicts with foreign capital. Men and women drew on the strength of their community and a sense of gendered rights to a family wage, backed by the state, to confront the power of the North American mining company in El Teniente. Thus, the process of capital accumulation in Chile's foreign-controlled export sector and the power of the North

American mining company was limited, modified, and challenged by the formation of an activist and interventionist state and forms of working-class mobilization, rooted in new structures of community and shaped by new definitions of gender, citizenship, and class.

The 1973 military coup in Chile transformed Chile's social and political landscape. The regime dismantled the corporatist system of labor relations established during the 1930s and unleashed a campaign of terror against organized labor and the Left. In addition, the military government embarked on a radical policy of economic restructuring according to the tenets of neoliberal, free-market ideology. Chile's insertion into the world economy was redrawn as the military dictatorship opened the economy to trade and investment. Whereas the copper-driven export economy had created the conditions for a stable working-class community organized around male-headed nuclear families, in the new free market, labor was (under)valued for its flexibility and mobility. The state-run copper company began to employ private subcontractors who could provide cheap, nonunion, temporary labor. In addition, liberalization created new export economies, mostly in the fruit, forestry, and fishing industries, that required a part-time and inexpensive labor force. Today, Chile's fruit exporters employ female workers at low wages, provide few benefits, and actively prevent the unionization of the workforce. Neoliberal economic restructuring in Chile, as in many Latin American countries, has eroded the structure of the working-class, male-headed nuclear family by increasing low-paying "feminized" jobs and eliminating jobs that provided male workers a family wage. The dismantling of state social programs and protections and the repression of organized labor under the dictatorship only accelerated and exacerbated this process. In El Teniente, working-class men and women no longer enjoy the forms of community solidarity or closely knit family ties that had been the basis for the development of a powerful labor movement until 1973.

By tracing the emergence of a dynamic labor movement in the copper industry during the first half of the century, I do not seek to romanticize working-class resistance but to learn from the strengths and weaknesses of past challenges fashioned by working people to the march of capitalism. Thus, I explore the dialectical process in which transformations in the process of capital accumulation and the structure of the global market destroyed old arrangements of class and gender, while forging a unified community that provided the basis for a militant working-class politics committed to socialist change and to the nationalization of the foreign-owned copper industry. In addition, I analyze the tensions, fractures, and contradictions in working-class culture and politics before 1973. The resilient community identity and robust labor politics of the mining enclave masked fundamental inequalities between men and women; indeed, the strength of workers' challenge to the authority of North American capital was predicated on the subordination of women within the nuclear family. As was clear during that rainy night in 1991, to confront Chile's new role in the global market and a hegemonic discourse of neoliberalism, advocated by the stewards of the transition to democracy as avidly as by the ideologues of the military regime, the men and women of the El Teniente mining community will have to imagine and build new forms of community based on shifting definitions of work, class, and gender.

ACKNOWLEDGMENTS

Many people have contributed to the making of this book. Writing it has made me more aware than ever that intellectual work takes place through debate and conversation and within communities of all sorts.

At Yale University I had the good fortune to study with Emilia Viotti da Costa, a brilliant teacher and historian. Professor da Costa's intellectual engagement and critical insight were a constant source of inspiration and guidance. Daniel James introduced me to the study of Latin American labor history and has been a valued teacher and friend. I have learned a great deal from our many discussions and from his pathbreaking writings in the fields of labor and gender history. I am grateful to have had the opportunity to study with David Montgomery, whose work in labor history has been a constant reference and who provided valuable comments from the book's beginnings as a doctoral dissertation.

I would also like to acknowledge two teachers who played a role early on in shaping my interest in intellectual labor. Robert Kaplan's high school philosophy seminars showed me how exciting intellectual inquiry could be. I continue to draw on insights gained in Paul Jefferson's classes in political theory and intellectual history both in high school and at Haverford College.

The two readers of the manuscript for Duke University Press, Jeffrey Gould and John French, provided extremely valuable criticisms and suggestions for revisions. I have not always taken their suggestions, but this book is much the better for their engaged readings. I am especially grateful to John French, who read the lengthy manuscript twice with meticulous care and provided extraordinarily detailed and generous comments.

In Chile, the Department of History of the Universidad de Santiago de Chile (USACh) provided me institutional support and affiliation. I particularly thank Julio Pinto Vallejos for his help and friendship. His own work in Chilean history and his critical comments on my research have been very important to this project.

I owe a large debt of gratitude to the staffs of various archives in Chile, including the Biblioteca Nacional and Archivo Nacional in Santiago, the Conservador de Bienes y Raíces in Rancagua, and the Registro Civil in Machalí. The Office of Public Affairs (Asuntos Públicos) of CODELCO-Chile, División El Teniente, facilitated my access to company personnel files and documents left behind by the former Braden Copper Company and allowed me to publish here photographs of El Teniente's early history.

Paola Fernández transcribed a number of the oral histories cited in the book and performed some of the interviews under my direction. I thank her for her invaluable assistance.

This book could never have been completed without the help and support of the many members of El Teniente's mining community who spent countless hours talking with me. From the beginning, it was clear that those with whom I spoke understood the importance of history to the world of everyday politics. While this history probably diverges in many ways from the histories they would have written, I hope that this book can, in some measure, repay them for the warmth with which they received me and can also contribute to their ongoing struggles. I have listed in the bibliography many of the people who generously agreed to be interviewed, but I especially thank the leadership of the mine's eight unions, particularly the largest, the Sindicato Industrial Sewell y Mina, for their support. The members of the Círculo Social Sewell provided hospitality and valuable assistance. I am grateful for the friendship and help of Daniel Silva and Domingo Quintero, from whom I have learned a tremendous amount.

A number of people read different parts of the manuscript and provided important comments. Heidi Tinsman has been a good friend and intellectual interlocutor. Her readings of drafts of the dissertation and manuscript were invaluable. Kenneth Andrien, a fine historian and excellent colleague, read the manuscript twice and each time offered helpful suggestions for revisions. Barbara Weinstein and Gilbert Joseph also read parts of the manuscript, and I am very grateful for their insightful comments.

Over the years I have learned much from a community of historians loosely associated with the Latin American Labor History Conference, where I have presented pieces of this work in the form of papers and where I have found vigorous and stimulating intellectual exchange.

I benefited greatly from the editorial support and guidance of Valerie Millholland of Duke University Press and from the book's masterly copy-editor, Nancy J. Malone. Ron McLean of Ohio State University produced the maps for the book. All photos are courtesy of CODELCO-Chile, División El Teniente.

Material support came from a number of sources. An initial research trip to Chile was funded by a summer research grant from the Yale University Center for International and Area Studies. Later research and writing were funded by a Center for International and Area Studies Henry Hart Rice fellowship and a Yale University Robert M. Leylan Fellowship. In addition, I received financial support in the form of research grants for two additional trips to Chile from Montana State University and Ohio State University. My first four years of graduate school were funded by a Jacob K. Javits fellowship from the U.S. Department of Education.

It is difficult to acknowledge adequately the many different contributions of my parents, Dorothy Miller and Daniel Klubock, my sister, Katharine Klubock, and my grandmother Jean Miller to this book. I am thankful to each for their love and support and for their abiding commitment to building a just society, which continually renews my faith in the possibility of a better world.

Finally, I thank Sandhya Shukla for her love and companionship. I have learned a great deal during our years together; her wisdom, political commitment, and humor have made her a true partner in this project.

INTRODUCTION

In April 1983, the national union of the Chilean copper miners, under independent leadership for the first time in a decade, called for a general strike in Chile's copper mines and for a day of national protest against the military regime of Augusto Pinochet. The following month, workers in El Teniente, the world's largest underground copper mine, paralyzed production for twenty-four hours in an illegal work stoppage. In response to the copper miners' call, tens of thousands of workers and poor people (*pobladores*) came together to demand democracy and to protest the military regime's use of force to suppress workers' organizations and demands, as well as the regime's new "labor plan" and free-market economic policies. This explosion of mass protest signaled the reemergence of an independent national labor movement and popular civilian opposition to military rule after almost a decade of repression.

Women from the El Teniente mining community played a prominent role in the 1983 strike and protests. They marched and battled the military in the streets, organized collective soup kitchens for the families of workers fired for striking, and banged empty pots and pans in rejection of the regime's combination of brutal repression and harsh neoliberal economic restructuring. Women's participation in political and labor struggles had been a feature of life in the El Teniente mining camps for decades. Miners' wives had joined their husbands on picket lines and formed their own political committees and organizations in the mining camps since the emergence of an independent union movement during the late 1930s. Following the election of the left-center Popular Front coalition in 1938, miners' unions built a powerful challenge to the authority of the mine's North American proprietor, the Kennecott Copper Company's subsidiary, the Braden Copper Company, based on mining families' tight

Provinces

1. Aconcagua
2. Aisén
3. Antofagasta
4. Arauco
5. Atacama
6. Bío Bío
7. Cautín
8. Chiloé
9. Colchagua
10. Concepción
11. Coquimbo
12. Curicó
13. Linares
14. Llanquihue
15. Magallanes
16. Malleco
17. Maule
18. Nuble
19. O'Higgins
20. Osorno
21. Santiago
22. Talca
23. Tarapacá
24. Valdivia
25. Valparaíso

Chile

N

Iquique

Antofagasta ● **3**

● **5**

La Serena ●
11

Valparaíso ● **1**
25
21 ★Santiago
9 Rancagua
19
17 **12**
10 **13** **22**
Concepción ● **18**
4
Lebu ● **16** ● **6**
7
Valdivia ● **24**
14
20
Ancud ●
8

2

SCALE IN MILES
0   100   200

15

community ties and the mobilization of both men and women in labor struggles.

Copper mining communities have played a prominent role in Chilean history since the decade of the 1930s, when copper replaced nitrates as the motor of the Chilean economy. Because of copper's central role in the Chilean economy, supplying over 80 percent of Chile's foreign earnings by the early 1970s, miners have had an enormous impact on national events. Given the almost constant strike activity in Chile's major Chuquicamata and El Teniente copper mines from 1938 to 1970, miners occupied a pivotal position in the growing political movement that sought to wrest control of the mines from their North American owners, the Kennecott and Anaconda Copper Companies. Miners' unions, led by militants of the Socialist and Communist Parties, also provided an important base for the increasingly radical labor movement of the 1960s and the election of socialist Salvador Allende's Popular Unity coalition (UP) in 1970.

The scant social scientific literature on Chilean copper miners has focused on the question of whether miners constitute one of Chile's most militant and radical groups of workers or compose a labor aristocracy fighting to preserve their entitlements and advantageous position in the national economy. Studies of copper miners have sought to shed light on the apparently perplexing paradox of miners' class consciousness.[1] In the context of almost constant legal and illegal strike activity during the three decades leading up to the election of Allende, copper miners were heralded as the inheritors of the radical traditions of their predecessors in the nitrate mines, where, in the traditional labor historiography, the Chilean labor movement and the Left are said to have been born. This analysis of the copper miners reflects a more general literature that argues that in enclave economies workers achieve a level of militancy not found in other sectors of the economy as a result of the close, unmediated contact and conflict between labor and capital and the isolation and homogeneity of the mining community.[2]

Yet, after a strike of mostly white-collar, Christian Democratic workers in the El Teniente mine in 1973 that contributed to the demise of Allende's socialist experiment, sociologists began to stress copper miners' privileged status as a high-paid labor elite.[3] Social scientists argued that workers employed in modern sectors of Latin American economies are more skilled and enjoy higher income levels and benefits and are thus separated from

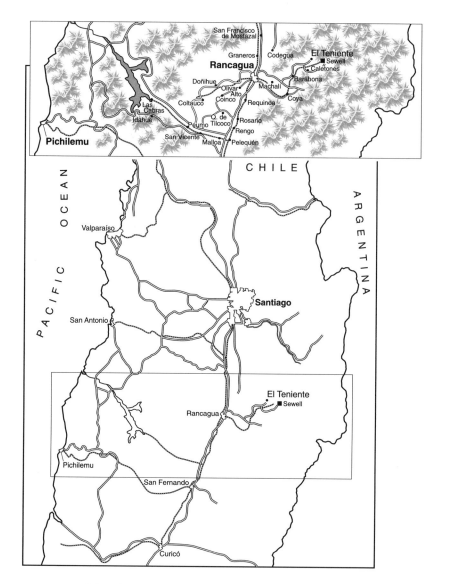

Rancagua and the El Teniente Mine

the less skilled, poorly paid workers in other sectors of the economy.[4] These writers held that workers in the "advanced" capitalist sectors of dependent economies are concerned with social mobility and the mainte-nance of their privileged standard of living and are unreceptive to appeals for solidarity with other sectors of the working class.[5] Chilean copper miners have thus been characterized as the embodiment of the unique revolutionary traditions of the Chilean working class or as a labor aris-tocracy concerned with immediate economic demands and social ascen-sion. Ironically, both of these models of the copper miners' conscious-ness have been inferred from the structural conditions and location of the copper mines. In addition, both the "vanguard" and "labor aristocracy" approaches propose normative models of class consciousness that obscure the complicated and contradictory forms of miners' everyday culture and political practice forged in the specific historical contexts of workplace, home, and community.

In this book I seek to avoid the constraints of this binary opposition by exploring the historical experiences of the El Teniente copper miners from the beginning of the twentieth century, when the mine went into operation, to the 1950s. I integrate structuralist concerns with politics, the composition of the labor force, the structure of the labor market and industry, and the labor process, with the new labor history's focus on working-class subjectivity and agency. To understand miners' conscious-ness, culture, and politics, I focus on the process of class formation, the transformation of a population of itinerant laborers into a settled and trained workforce in a modern capitalist enterprise. Building a permanent labor force in the copper mine involved a fundamental restructuring of the social relations and cultural worlds within which the men and women who migrated to the mine in search of work conducted their every-day lives. Working-class men and women developed their class identity through their struggles to build new forms of community in response to initiatives by both North American capital and the state to establish a dis-ciplined and stable labor force in the rapidly expanding copper industry.

Rather than accept a model of consciousness and identity as reduc-ible to social-structural location or variables, I understand working-class political consciousness and everyday forms of culture to be produced in the tensions, conflicts, and mutual appropriations that define the process of hegemony building. Raymond Williams, in his discussion of Antonio

Gramsci, argues that hegemony is constituted through "structures of feeling," the symbolic arrangements through which formal ideology shapes everyday experiences, thoughts, and values. The Gramscian use of hegemony focuses on the naturalization of social systems of appropriation, production, and reproduction through the extension of dominant ideologies into the "cultural unconsciousness" that orders and makes sense of social reality at the level of everyday common sense, "what goes without saying," or what Pierre Bourdieu refers to as "habitus."[6] This understanding of hegemony calls our attention to the interplay of ideology, politics, and the informal cultural worlds of day-to-day life and underlines the importance of examining the dialectical relationship between ordinary people's "structures of feeling" and political identity and practice.

The naturalization of dominant ideologies and social relations in the patterns of daily life is not a unilinear, unmediated, or uncontested process. As Williams argues, hegemony does not "just passively exist as a form of dominance. It has to be renewed, recreated, defended, and modified. It is also continually resisted, limited, altered, challenged by pressures not at all its own."[7] Working-class subjectivity and political identity must be understood, then, in the tensions, contradictions, and relations between ideology, social realities, and everyday forms of cultural and political practice. In the case of El Teniente, I argue, working-class men and women drew on and appropriated elements of elite ideologies, as well as traditions of working-class culture rooted in the nineteenth century, to shape counterhegemonic strategies, to build their own collective identity, and to critique the harsh social realities of work and life in the mine and its camps.

In this sense, the political consciousness of the mining community was hybrid; the structures of feeling and political culture of the community were composed by often competing and contrasting ideological formations and by the interpenetration of both class and nonclass discourses and practices.[8] Miners' political culture did not reflect an autonomous or univocal working-class identity, dictated by the structural circumstances of their labor. Rather, working-class men and women built their sense of class and community from the cultural resources at their disposal; elements drawn from the ideologies of employers, the state, middle-class social reformers, and organized labor and the Left shaped both miners' everyday forms of sociability and their political identity. The mining community elaborated what Williams calls "practical wisdom" or "common sense" in the context of the shifting balance of resistance and accommodation to the pressures and ideological initiatives of the state and employers. The result was forms of cultural and political practice defined by tension and contradiction.

Despite the profound impact of capitalist economic development on gender relations and women's role in early labor movements, historians have tended to ignore the role of gender in shaping working-class culture and politics in Latin America. In their focus on the transformation of peasants and artisans into miners or industrial workers, the separation of workers from the means of subsistence, the deskilling of labor, the introduction of new production techniques, and the development of the scientific management of the labor process, labor historians have written about class as homogeneous, unified, and implicitly masculine. By eliding gender's role in working-class formation, historians have naturalized the masculinization of labor and class identity and have neglected women's role in the process of proletarianization. They have also ignored the ways in which working-class formation was structured by gender ideologies and involved the reorganization of relations between men and women and social constructions of masculinity and femininity.[9]

I argue that the process of class formation in the copper mines must be understood as a "gendered" process in which formal gender ideologies and informal norms, values, and practices surrounding sexuality shaped working-class structures of feeling and political consciousness.[10] A number of feminist scholars have argued that sexual difference may have biological standing, but its social and cultural form, organization, and meaning is historical and in a constant process of elaboration. Gender is, then, the historical process of ordering and organizing the social construction of sexual difference.[11] This implies that a "gendered" history must focus on working-class masculinity and femininity, treating both men and women as "gendered" historical subjects; it must also explore the ways in which working-class politics and subjectivity are shaped by social practices and hierarchies based on the arrangement of power surrounding sexuality.

In El Teniente, I argue, the material social relations and symbolic universe that defined the cultural worlds of the mining camps during the process of proletarianization were organized along the axis of gender, as well as the axis of class. Managerial practices, state policies, and workers' responses were played out on the field of gender and sexuality. Proletarianization in the mine involved a reorganization of the gendered division of labor and redefinition of masculinity and femininity. Rather than separate variables, gender and class composed interlocking organizations of social power and cultural meaning in the mining camps. Hegemony was constituted by the process in which class relations were produced and reproduced in articulation with the organization of sexuality and the construction of gender. Thus, an analysis of the forms of working-class politics and culture produced in the mining camps must account for the ways in which new arrangements of gender were naturalized during the process of proletarianization and the ways in which men and women sought control and meaning in their lives, not just in the sphere of work and wages, but in the worlds of sexuality, family, and community as well.

The first three chapters of this book examine the transformation of a transient population of migrant, single male and female workers into a stable working-class community built on the foundation of the male-headed nuclear family from the early years of copper production beginning in 1904 until the late 1930s. In Chapter 1 I focus on the development of the North American mining enterprise, the origins of El Teniente's early workforce, and mine workers' strategies of resistance to proletarianization. Anthropologists have shown how miners and peasants in Latin America employed autonomous village traditions to judge the exploitative social relations of agrarian or industrial capitalism and then acted collectively to transform them. Such writers as June Nash and Michael Taussig have demonstrated that the reinvention of Andean cultural practices in the Bolivian tin mines allowed workers to build an image of the past with which they condemned the conditions of work and life they confronted in the mines.[12] Chilean copper miners had no common peasant traditions or community structures to draw on as they confronted the grim social realities of labor in a modern capitalist enterprise. Most miners came from diverse origins and had been part of a transient labor force that traveled the length of the country in search of employment. Mine workers in El Teniente deployed the traditions of mobility of nineteenth-century itinerant peons (*peones*) to resist pressures to conform to new rhythms of discipline and work in the copper industry. The migration of male workers was accompanied by a parallel movement of single women to the El Teniente copper mine and to the informal settlements (*callampas*) on the outskirts of the mine's camps in search of wage labor in domestic service and in an underground economy of bars and brothels. Men and women established informal sexual/romantic relationships and participated together in a tumultuous everyday culture. Drinking, fighting, and the expression of an unruly sense of masculine virility shaped the contours of miners' opposition to company and state authority.

In Chapter 2, I examine how, following the First World War, the copper company combined rigorously repressive labor policies backed by sympathetic Chilean governments and local elites with a program of corporate social welfare with which it hoped to eliminate workers' disruptive forms of sociability, transience, and labor militancy. I trace shifting international corporate strategies and the gendered nature of North American capital's social and labor policies. Corporate welfare programs in the El Teniente mine focused on the regulation of sexuality as the cornerstone of cultural reform and labor discipline. The North American company located the source of workers' instability in the fluid world of working-class gender relations and prescribed the "modern" nuclear family and the domestic space, drawn from a middle-class ideal, as an antidote to male and female workers' transience and disorderly habits. These corporate welfare policies resonated at the national level to the interest of Chilean social reformers in establishing social and labor legislation in response to the labor upheavals of the 1919 postwar recession.

Chapter 3 is concerned with the formation of a permanent working-class community in the mining camps and the elaboration of a leftist labor tradition rooted in the history of the northern nitrate mines following the 1930–1932 world recession. I explore how the world economic crisis and domestic social and economic dislocations created the conditions for the formation of a stable working-class community. The international economic crisis dealt a final blow to the nitrate industry that had fueled Chilean economic development since the late nineteenth century. Many former nitrate miners found work in the copper mine and brought with them the experiences of labor conflict and leftist political activism gained in the northern desert. With the inducements provided by the North American company's corporate welfare system, men and women started to marry and form families with greater frequency. As they began

to make their lives in the mining camps during the 1930s, the labor traditions of the north supplied a coherent, shared symbolic past that served as
the basis for the developing community identity of the mining families.

In Chapter 4 I describe the role played by the state in the gendered process of working-class formation in El Teniente. Between 1938 and 1947
a series of coalition governments, including the Chilean Popular Front,
headed by the Radical Party (PR) and including, at varying times, the
Chilean Communist (PC) and Socialist (PS) Parties, implemented labor reforms, provided support for the urban labor movement, and established
welfare programs at the state level. Workers were able to reap the benefits
of the new system of labor relations by using their organizational power to
strike and force the Braden Copper Company to sign collective contracts
that provided wage increases, pensions, cost-of-living raises, and a special
subsidy for workers with families. The coalition governments also provided copper workers new languages of nationalism, democracy, and citizenship that they could use to express their interests in conflicts with the
foreign copper company. The miners drew on the rhetoric of democracy
and citizenship in their struggles with the copper company, reading "class-
specific" intonations into Popular Front ideology and producing their own
militant version of the Popular Front's imagined national community. The
Popular Front reproduced the Braden Copper Company's corporate welfare program at the state level by engaging in similar projects of moral and
cultural reform. In the copper mines, the Socialist and Communist Parties
and the miners' union embarked on campaigns to reform "disruptive"
forms of working-class sociability. Like the company, the miners' union
also focused on the family as the arena in which a "proletarian morality"
would be formed. The social projects of the Left, organized labor, and
the Popular Front thus overlapped with the North American copper company's gendered corporate welfare strategies of social and moral reform.[13]

Chapters 5, 6, and 7 provide an examination of the ways in which the
men and women who settled in El Teniente accommodated to the new
order of social relations in the modern copper industry, while crafting
strategies of resistance to the emergent regimes of class and gender. In
Chapter 5 I explore the tensions between accommodation and resistance
in the workplace, positing that the hegemony of the labor process and
organization of work was established on a field of power defined by gender. Inside the mine, workers built a combative work culture based on an

intense sense of masculine pride and self-assertion. Codes of honor and manhood defined solidarities within work crews and provided the basis for collective action in wildcat section strikes. At the same time, driven by a system of incentives and work bonuses, miners began to locate masculine pride in their capacity for hard physical labor, work skills, and high earnings. Miners' sense of manhood thus provided the basis for both informal forms of opposition to company authority and workers' adaptation to the company's demands for production and the organization of the labor process. In addition, the masculinization of labor reaffirmed male workers' sense of patriarchical authority and naturalized the sexual division of labor and women's subordination within the household.

Chapter 6 focuses on male workers' forms of everyday culture outside the mine. Miners sought to assert control over their nonwork lives in such social practices as drinking, gambling, and illicit sex, in which they reproduced their masculine work identity and workplace solidarities and expressed opposition to company authority. At the same time, the promise of social mobility and the ideal of middle-class respectability disseminated in the company's welfare programs shaped the development of a new form of working-class masculinity in the mining camps. Male workers who participated in company-sanctioned cultural activities found masculine affirmation in a sense of middle-class respectability. Social and cultural institutions, however, established forms of social solidarity that could be mobilized during labor conflicts as workers sought to make the company's paternalist promises of social mobility material reality. Ultimately, both forms of workers' cultural practice created the basis for styles of opposition which coincided in defining public space as a male domain and which thus contributed to the masculinization of class identity and politics.

In Chapter 7 I discuss women's responses to the shifting terrain of gender in the mining camps. Single women who worked as domestic servants and maids often sought to maintain their sexual and economic autonomy by engaging in multiple informal relationships with men based on the exchange of sex, service, and companionship for money and goods. Yet, pushed by the low pay of work as domestic servants and the strict regulatory regime established by the company and the state and pulled by the inducement of the economic and social security of marriage, women increasingly settled in the mining camps and formed families, redefining their femininity in terms of their position as housewife and mother.

Women invoked the dominant moral codes of the emergent gender ideology of female domesticity and appealed to company and state agencies to assert a measure of control over their families' resources and their relationships with their husbands. Restricted to the household, excluded from public space, and increasingly identified with their families, married women employed hegemonic notions of appropriate female behavior and respectability to construct a language of rights to economic security and social welfare for themselves and their children. This sense of gendered rights could be mobilized in both conflicts with their husbands and confrontations with the company and state.

Chapter 8 describes how the newly formed mining families established tight community ties that laid the basis for a powerful union movement during the 1940s. Although men and women increasingly conformed to the new arrangements of work and family life in El Teniente, the settling of a permanent workforce in the mine did not lead to labor peace. Male workers and their wives looked to the state and the company welfare system to satisfy their rights to a decent living. But to fulfill their aspirations to a better life — to make the promises of citizenship, social welfare, and middle-class respectability material reality — men and women also turned to collective action. In combative strike movements throughout the 1940s, miners phrased their conflicts with the company and the state in terms of their perceived rights to protection from the galloping cost of living and arbitrary firings, as well as to social benefits for their families. Miners' unions drew strength from the intimate ties that bound their families and community together around a set of common interests and in opposition to a shared enemy. Women's dependence on their husband's wages and on the copper company for a series of benefits brought them together with men in collective movements. Women drew on their duties as wives and mothers and their new sense of rights to make demands for their families' welfare.

In Chapter 9 I chart the growing combativeness of the miners' strikes, which exposed the limits of the Popular Front's reformist social and economic program and the crevices in its "popular-democratic" ideology. The mining community's mobilizations revealed the contradictions in the Front's ideology of class harmony by pushing its nationalist and "popular-democratic" politics in the direction of working-class militancy.[14] Strikes in the copper mines after 1946 threatened the political and economic stability of the coalition government and led to its demise, as Radical Party president Gabriel González Videla presided over the widespread repression both of labor and of the Communist Party in 1947 and 1948. Despite the dismissal and arrest of hundreds of union activists and Communist Party militants, however, the Popular Front left a legacy of a strengthened labor movement with powerful ties to the Left. The copper miners emerged in 1951 from the repression of the late 1940s to form a national labor confederation that led the fight for the nationalization of the copper industry and whose general strikes played a major role in the movements of the 1960s that led to the victory of Allende's UP coalition in 1970.

To investigate the relation between politics, ideology, and the way these are lived and practiced in the everyday worlds of work, family, and leisure poses difficulties in terms of sources. I have relied on a series of "indirect" or "elite" sources to provide a window on the dialectical relationships between elite ideologies, working-class politics, and what Antonio Gramsci calls "the world of common sense" through which ordinary people order their everyday lives.[15] The personnel records of the Braden Copper Company, now the state-run Sociedad Minera El Teniente of the Chilean National Copper Corporation (CODELCO), were especially helpful in terms of documenting workers' patterns of mobility and issues of work habits and discipline. The writings of the subaltern studies group have demonstrated that a careful "reading against the grain" of official government and elite sources can shed light on the ways in which subalterns imposed their own will on the documents and thus left traces of their consciousness and praxis.[16] In the case of Kennecott's Braden Copper Company, the new style of management that combined rigorous control of everyday life with an extensive social welfare apparatus produced an important body of knowledge about working-class conditions.[17] In essence, the company's interest in reorganizing and regulating workers' lives in the spheres of sexuality and leisure, as well as in the workplace, provided new institutions dedicated to the project of discipline and surveillance that also produced detailed information about workers' lives and activities. The company sources I use in this book themselves reflect the development of new management practices in the form of corporate welfare.

The Braden Copper Company's North American administration left no archive when it abandoned Chile following the nationalization of the mine in 1971. Instead, in what appears to be an act of sabotage, it destroyed documents and threw what remained together in a disorganized heap, thus revealing the ways in which social and political relations of power, in this case North American imperialism, shape the documentary evidence available to the historian. These documents are now housed in plastic garbage bags covered with dirt and animal excrement in a warehouse high up in the Andes in the mine's Coya camp. They provide, however, a wealth of useful information about workers' lives, company policy, and labor politics between 1904 and 1951. The records of the U.S. Department of State, located in the United States National Archives in Washington, D.C., contain detailed documentation of labor relations, politics, and strikes in the Chilean copper industry.

The miners' largest union, the Sindicato Industrial Sewell y Mina, has a small archive with excellent documentation of the first strikes in the mine and a complete collection of the union newspaper *Despertar Minero* (1938–1947). In the Chilean National Archives, I used the archive of the provincial government, the O'Higgins intendancy, for documentation of early strikes, working conditions, and accidents in the mine through the early 1920s. Some of the most valuable sources were the cases of the local court in the mining camps, located in the Conservador de Bienes y Raíces in the city of Rancagua. These were particularly useful in finding information about relations between men and women in the camps. Although criminal cases may not represent a generalizable view of the patterns of local society or an unmediated view of men's and women's subjectivities, I read these sources as texts that reveal the moral and ideological codes and languages, both hegemonic and counterhegemonic, that structured social relations in the mining camps. Courts are arenas in which the hegemony of the state, as well as of class and gender relations, is played out. In this sense, court cases proved an important lens on the contested processes that structured men's and women's everyday lives, including shifting state policy, management practices, and working-class responses.

Finally, oral history interviews with retired miners and male and female former residents of the mining camps provided an important resource, both for documenting aspects of the informal patterns of social and cultural practice in the camps and for providing a window onto the formation of subjective identity. As a number of writers have pointed out, oral histories are complicated; they provide neither a direct account of "what really happened" nor an unmediated and transparent vision of subjective consciousness.[18] Oral histories, like any other document, are shaped by subjective agendas and presentist concerns, are fragmentary, and contain gaps and silences. Like any source they must be read with care, taking into account the arrangement of social power and cultural forces that produced "the document."

Although oral accounts were useful in providing information on social realities omitted in traditional documentary sources—women's work in the household, family life, relations within work crews—they were particularly important to understanding the "structures of feeling" of the mining camps. Oral histories are narratives that, when read critically, may be interpreted in terms of the codes, conventions, values, and traditions that shape the cultural world of historical subjects. Thus, oral histories provide a view, albeit not an unmediated one, of how men and women build their own subjectivity and consciousness with the cultural and ideological resources at their disposal. Oral histories not only bring us the voice of working people who otherwise leave little historical trace but also help us to understand how people build narratives, traditions, and collective identities which explain and make sense of social realities and which thus provide the basis for their active intervention in history itself.

Part I

Gender and the Process of

Proletarianization, 1904–1938

1   The Formation of a Modern Mining Enterprise

Capital, Labor Migration, and Early Forms of

Worker Resistance

In 1920, at the age of forty-eight, Carmen Aceituno began work in the El Teniente copper mine as a day laborer. The mining company was experiencing an explosive period of growth as a result of expanding international markets for copper and had sent agents (*enganchadores*) into the countryside to recruit workers with promises of high wages and pay advances. Aceituno came to the mine from the nearby agricultural town of Coinco and labored in El Teniente off and on for the next eighteen years. After working a short stint in 1920, he left El Teniente, only returning in 1923 to work for seven months. Aceituno went back to work in the mine in 1924, 1925, 1926, and 1928 for short stretches and then worked four straight years between 1934 and 1938. His work in the mine was punctuated by periodic absences and dismissals. Aceituno was fired on three occasions during his intermittent career for absenteeism, lack of productivity, and drunkenness.[1]

Aceituno's experience of work in the mine is characteristic of El Teniente's early labor force. Most workers who migrated to the mine had participated in a transient labor force that traveled the Chilean countryside working on rural estates according to seasonal demand for labor, in the many small, labor-intensive copper mines that dotted Chile's Andean mountain range, in ports and cities, and in the nitrate mines of the northern Atacama Desert since the middle of the nineteenth century. These workers resisted pressures to settle in El Teniente and frequently abandoned their jobs in search of better opportunities elsewhere. Miners also refused to accommodate to the company's demands for work discipline. Drinking on the job, low productivity, and absenteeism posed an endemic problem for company supervisors.

The development of the El Teniente mine represented a shift in the Chilean mining industry from the small, undercapitalized, rudimentary, domestically owned mines of the nineteenth century to large, capital-intensive, vertically integrated, foreign-owned industrial enterprises employing sophisticated technology for the extraction, smelting, and processing of copper ore. By the end of the First World War, El Teniente employed over five thousand workers, and its demand for trained labor grew as it expanded production during the 1920s. The itinerant mining labor force of workers like Aceituno presented a major obstacle to the company's growth. Throughout the 1920s, the company found its efforts to increase production hampered by a population of workers that displayed little conformity to the new rhythms of work and discipline in the modern mining enterprise. These male workers were joined by an equally transient group of single women workers who migrated to the mine's camps, informal settlements on El Teniente's outskirts, and the nearby city of Rancagua in search of work as domestic servants and in petty commerce. Women participated with men in a turbulent popular culture of drinking and fluid romantic and sexual relationships that undermined the North American copper company's efforts to discipline and settle its labor force.

Constructing a Foreign Enclave: The El Teniente Mine and the Braden Copper Company

Beginning in 1873, Chile confronted a series of economic crises. The expansive growth of the previous four decades based on the export of mineral and agricultural primary commodities to world markets had begun to slow. In the mining sector, Chilean producers had exhausted the high-grade copper ore in their small, labor-intensive mines. At the same time, large bodies of copper ore were found in the United States, and by the 1880s North American mines began to supply a large portion of the world's copper, eliminating markets for Chilean exports. Whereas in 1876 Chile produced 62 percent of the total world copper supply, by 1900 its share of international copper production had dropped to 5 percent.[2] The agricultural export economy encountered a similar decline as demand for Chilean wheat diminished as a result of the loss of markets in the United States and Australia and the limits to production on large estates. Further expansion in both the agricultural and mining sectors required reform of antiquated systems of labor relations and investment in new methods of production.

Chilean mining entrepreneurs, however, failed to develop high levels of productive capital in the mining sector or to invest in the modernization of mining and processing techniques. Nineteenth-century copper mines were small enterprises, often discovered and developed by independent prospectors who lacked capital, struggled with chronic debt, and depended on financing from merchants to run their operations and market their ore. Mine owners and producers continued, as during the colonial period, to be subordinated financially to large—and often foreign-owned—commercial houses. Chilean mine owners turned to cheap labor and subcontracting to independent miners rather than mechanization to increase production. Throughout the nineteenth century various foreign writers commented favorably on the ways in which Chilean mine owners combined colonial methods of production with cheap labor. One British writer noted, for example, that mining in Chile was a bad business that was made viable only through the use of "the least expensive labor force imaginable."[3] Similarly, Charles Darwin wrote that "it is now well known that the Chilean method of mining is the cheapest."[4] Most foreign critics were quick to observe that the only profitable mining business lay in financing and commerce, rather than production.[5]

Confronted with continuing cycles of debt to commercial houses, mining producers intensified their exploitation of mine workers (peones and apires). Labor in the copper mines of the nineteenth century was harshly disciplined, intense, and brutal. Mine workers who stole rocks of ore were legally beaten by mine owners and police, mining camps were rigidly controlled by armed guards, and miners were forced to carry identification cards. Work itself was performed almost entirely through physical labor. Miners used hammers and chisels to break off pieces of rock and dig tunnels, while other workers carried leather sacks of rock, weighing as much as two hundred pounds, on their backs as they climbed up ladders on the sides of tunnel walls to the surface above. Charles Darwin was struck by the devastating labor performed by workers in the small copper mines near the port of Coquimbo:

> Captain Head has described the wonderful load which the "Apires" [mine workers], truly beasts of burden, carry up from the deepest mines. I confess I thought the account exaggerated, so that I was glad to take an opportunity of weighing one of the loads. . . . The load was considered under weight when found to be 190 pounds.

The apire had carried this up eighty perpendicular yards—part of the way by a steep passage, but the greater part up notched poles, placed in a zigzag line up the shaft. According to the general regulation, the apire is not allowed to halt for breath, except the mine is six hundred feet deep. The average load is considered as rather more than 200 pounds. . . . At this time the apires were bringing up the usual load twelve times in the day; that is, 2400 pounds from eighty yards deep; and they were employed in the intervals in breaking and picking ore. . . .

. . . it was quite revolting to see the state in which they reached the mouth of the mine; their bodies bent forward, leaning with their arms on the steps, their legs bowed, their muscles quivering, the perspiration streaming from their faces over their breasts, their nostrils distended, the corners of their mouth forcibly drawn back, and the expulsion of their breath most laborious.[6]

In the copper mines of Jajuel, Darwin noted that "the labouring men work very hard. They have little time allowed for their meals, and during the summer and winter they begin when it is light, and leave off at dark."[7]

By the end of the nineteenth century, Chilean copper mining consisted of a number of small mines employing antiquated methods of production that had changed little since colonial times. Only the richest veins with ores of over 10 percent content were mined, and tailings and sulfide ores were discarded because Chilean miners lacked the technology for extracting, concentrating, and smelting low-grade ores.[8] In 1900, of 748 small copper mines in Chile, only 50 employed any kind of mechanization.[9] In addition, while the Chilean mining industry employed the modern reverberatory furnace beginning in the 1830s, two-thirds of Chile's fifty foundries for processing ore in 1878 were still of "colonial design" and were fueled by wood.[10] In 1889, a North American observer noted that most Chilean mines were operated without machinery, that water and ore were still removed from the mines on the backs of peones, and that "in many Chilean mines copper is milled with hammers and washed by hand."[11]

The history of El Teniente followed the general trajectory of Chilean copper mining. Before the arrival of the Spanish, the mine had been worked by native Andean communities, which produced copper tools and jewelry. Following the conquest, the mine was granted to Andrés de

Torquemada for his role in the Spanish conquest of Chile. Torquemada left the mine, with many of his lands, to the Jesuit order. The Jesuits worked the mine as part of their Compañía hacienda in the rich agricultural valleys that surrounded the town of Rancagua, a center of regional commerce. The religious order contracted the extraction of copper ore and the manufacture of copper utensils and tools to private miners.

When the Jesuits were expelled from Chile in 1767, the mine was auctioned off along with the rest of their property and was purchased with the entire hacienda by Don Mateo Toro y Zambrano, a merchant, count of the conquest, and first president of Chile's governing junta when independence was declared on 18 September 1810.[12] Toro y Zambrano's vast lands stretched from the Chilean coast to the *cordillera de los Andes* that separates Chile and Argentina. The mine was passed down to Toro y Zambrano's grandaughter, Doña Nicolasa Correa y Toro, who married a fellow aristocrat, Carlos Yrarrázaval Correa. These families extracted high-grade copper ore (of 5 percent or more copper content) from the mine during the nineteenth century in small amounts, using hand sorting of rocks and the "chicken ladder method." Rocks containing copper ore were removed with hammer and chisel from rich veins, hauled up ladders scaling the sides of mine tunnels, and carried down the side of the mountain by mule. The copper was processed according to techniques that had changed little since colonial days.

The aristocratic families mining El Teniente did not consider the development of ore of smaller copper content to be commercially practicable. Instead, they concentrated their economic activities in agricultural production and commerce. Access to the mine was difficult. Located fifty miles southeast of Santiago in the province of O'Higgins on the western slope of the Andes, the mine lay at an altitude of nearly ten thousand feet above sea level in barren, uninhabited, mountainous terrain. The slopes of the mountain surrounding the mine entrance were steep (most grades were at least 30 percent) and free of vegetation because the mine was located around the sides of a former volcanic crater. Volcanic boulders, rocks, and ash covered the mountainsides. Rancagua, the nearest town, lay roughly thirty miles away at the foot of the mountains and served as a commercial center for agricultural production in the surrounding valleys. Transportation to the mine from Rancagua by mule took three or four days. In addition, work could be carried out only from the beginning of spring at the end of September to the beginning of autumn in early April because of heavy snowfalls during winter months. But the most important limitation on copper production in the El Teniente mine, as in copper mines around the world throughout the nineteenth century, was the lack of techniques and methods for mining and processing low-grade copper ore. During a century of mining, owners of El Teniente extracted only fifty thousand tons of high-grade copper ore and succeeded in sinking a mine shaft only 500 feet deep.

Meanwhile, in the United States during the 1870s, the copper industry experienced high rates of growth. As domestic and international demand for copper grew with the development of the electrical industry, miners, mining engineers, and financiers became interested in the recovery of exhausted silver and gold mines and the exploration of new territories rich in copper ore. They were aided by the expansion of railroad systems throughout the western United States, which provided the essential transportation infrastructure. The expansion of copper markets spawned new techniques of mining low-grade, nonvein ore in huge open-pit mines and through block-caving techniques in underground mines.[13] The most momentous developments in North American copper mining occurred with the development of porphyry copper mines, mines with low-grade copper content (2 percent or less of the ore body), that had been previously thought to be uneconomical. During the 1890s, mining engineers introduced techniques employed in gold mining in order to mine copper porphyries on a mass scale.

The new technologies and large scales of production required for mining low-grade ore required considerable amounts of capital investment and long periods of time before profits could be realized. Companies that could afford extensive investments in mines and that could wait years for their investments to pay off were large and vertically integrated; they combined the mining of the ore with refining, processing, transportation, and marketing of copper. By linking these different, often geographically separated activities, companies could provide large amounts of capital for themselves, control all phases of the production process, dominate the copper market, and thus reduce overall risks. By 1900, the U.S. copper industry had been transformed from a small-scale industry based on the production of a number of labor-intensive mines extracting only high-grade copper ore into a large-scale, capital-intensive industry controlled by a limited number of corporations that maintained an oligopolistic hold on the production, processing, and marketing of low-grade copper ore.[14]

In Chile, the revitalization of copper mining at the turn of the century required similar scales of investment in new techniques for mining, concentrating, and smelting low-grade copper ore. In addition, significant investment in transportation was a necessary prerequisite for producing copper in the geographically isolated and topographically rugged mining regions of the Andes and the northern Atacama Desert where Chile's major copper deposits lay. Chilean miners did not, however, make the move to the extraction and fabrication of low-grade ore and were unable to overcome the bottlenecks presented by a chronic lack of capital, mechanization, railroads, and a dependable labor supply. As North American companies began to explore the possibilities for acquiring Chilean mines, they were welcomed both by the Chilean state and mine owners willing to rid themselves of defunct mines that had fallen out of production during the late 1870s and 1880s.[15]

Chilean copper producers confronted a number of unfavorable conditions that hampered their capacity to compete with their North American counterparts. In the United States, mining entrepreneurs could count on support from the state, whereas in Chile, the state, dominated by traditional agricultural and commercial interests, displayed little interest in protecting or promoting investment in the copper industry.[16] Chilean copper producers encountered the protectionist economic policies of the United States, just as North American markets for Chilean copper were expanding after the 1870s. In addition, Chilean mine owners faced competition for the U.S. copper market with North American companies which possessed an oligopolistic hold on both copper production and fabrication and which dominated the North American copper market. Finally, the constant indebtedness of small copper producers led to the undercapitalization of the industry and restricted the possibilities for investment in new production techniques.

The War of the Pacific (1879–1884) and Chile's acquisition of the nitrate fields of the Atacama Desert provided an easy way out of the economic crisis of the late 1870s. Nitrates quickly became the new engine of the Chilean export economy, providing revenues for the state and the possibility for Chilean elites to reconsolidate their social and economic position without implementing political, social, or economic reforms, in either the agricultural or the mining sector. For Chilean capitalists, short-term investments in nitrates, agriculture, commerce, and finance were more secure and immediately profitable than was investment in the rejuvenation of the copper industry.

By the beginning of the twentieth century, the El Teniente mine was jointly owned by a group whose members came from some of Chile's wealthiest families. The mine had fallen out of production when it filled with water during the winter of 1889 and had been abandoned by its caretakers. The mine's owners claimed that they lacked the money to pump the water out of the mine shaft or to invest in sophisticated forms of copper production and processing of the mine's low-grade porphyry copper and therefore entrusted an Italian engineer, Marco Chiapponi, to search for buyers for the mine in Europe and the United States.

At this time, Chiapponi met a North American engineer, William Braden, who was traveling in South America looking for copper deposits. Braden, a mining engineer who had lived in Butte, Montana, working in the great copper mine there, had been sent by the American Smelting and Refining Company (ASRCO), controlled by William Rockefeller and Henry Rogers of Standard Oil and the largest copper fabricator in the United States, to make a survey of Corocoro, a Bolivian copper mine. Braden wrote to Chiapponi for information and received an inaccurate and unfavorable report about the Bolivian mine. Chiapponi did, however, sing the praises of the Chilean El Teniente mine. Braden returned to New York after surveying the mine and urged his employer, E. W. Nash, president of ASRCO, to buy and develop the mine. They formed the Braden Copper Company in 1904. Original construction and production were financed by the Guggenheim brothers, who saved the company from financial ruin in 1906. And in 1908 the Guggenheims purchased the entire company.[17]

During the 1880s, Meyer Guggenheim had made a modest fortune in commercial trade, which he invested in gold, silver, lead, and copper mining ventures.[18] Observing the rapid growth in world demand for copper, Guggenheim quickly moved to expand his copper mining holdings. During the 1890s, the Guggenheim family, under an agreement with the government of Porfirio Díaz, began large-scale copper mining and smelting in northern Mexico. By 1915, the Guggenheims had purchased a major chunk of ASRCO shares; had acquired copper mines in Alaska, Utah,

Nevada, Arizona, and New Mexico; and had become the largest North American copper producer. Their dominant position in the U.S. copper market was reinforced by their purchase of the two major Chilean copper mines, El Teniente and Chuquicamata in the northern Atacama Desert. In 1915, the Guggenheims merged their U.S. and Chilean copper mines and formed the Kennecott Copper Company, which became the largest copper producer in the United States. Kennecott sold the northern open-pit Chuquicamata mine to the Anaconda Copper Company in 1923 to finance the Guggenheims' ill-fated ventures in the Chilean nitrate industry. Anaconda also purchased the smaller underground copper mine, Potrerillos, in 1916. Together, El Teniente, Chuquicamata, and Potrerillos composed the basis of Chile's copper industry, the Gran Minería del Cobre.

Kennecott's control of a large portion of world copper production and copper reserves in the United States and Chile, as well as the Guggenheims' control of ASRCO, ensured long-term profitability and growth. The major impetus for the company's development came, however, during the First World War when it became a major supplier of copper to the United States and Britain. During the war, the value of Chilean copper production increased fourfold.[19] The Federal Trade Commission, investigating wartime profiteering, found that U.S. copper companies doubled their earnings during the war.[20] Kennecott's net earnings between 1915 and 1918 totaled $140 million dollars, and the U.S. copper industry as a whole was attributed with earning over $350 million in wartime profits.[21]

The First World War stimulated the development of the Braden Copper Company in Chile, along with the growth of Kennecott's other mines in Utah and Alaska. Before the war, the expansion of production in El Teniente was restricted by the mine's harsh, mountainous topography. The mine remained isolated and inaccessible, a four-day journey by mule-drawn cart from Rancagua. In addition, the Braden Copper Company had to close down the mine's operations during the winter months, when the mountains were buffeted by heavy snowfalls. The company faced the daunting task of building new concentrating plants and foundries on the side of the mountain, constructing roads and rail transport between the mine's different production sections and to Rancagua, and engineering new systems for extracting low-grade ore. By 1911, the mine's production of copper was still limited, although exploration of the mine's veins and extension of tunnels over one thousand feet into the sides of the former volcano crater promised great possibilities. Until 1911, Braden's El Teniente project was frequently derided as the "Braden fizzle."[22]

With the demand for copper created by the First World War, however, the company began to increase its output. New technology was brought in to accelerate the concentrating process and to make it more efficient. Modern mills and crushers and new flotation units to separate the copper concentrate from impurities were added in El Teniente's concentrating plant. In addition, the company built an aerial tramway that carried the concentrated mineral from the mine's crushing mills to a newly built smelter that lay further down the side of the mountain at sixty-five hundred feet in the Caletones camp. The increase in production was facilitated by the completion of an electric railroad that connected the mine to the Sewell camp, located at about seven thousand feet above sea level, where the concentrator and most company and administrative offices were located and where most workers lived in company-built barracks. In 1914, the company also constructed a railroad to connect the mining complex to Rancagua and to the Chilean rail network that would transport El Teniente's copper to the port of San Antonio for shipment abroad.

During these years the North American company introduced a number of new and innovative production techniques that made extraction of ore from the mine inexpensive and efficient.[23] El Teniente's major shaft, rather than leading downward, was tunneled upward into the mountain so that the mine was entered from below, emerging sixteen hundred feet above at the main working level. The ore was extracted at various levels above this main level by a "block undercutting" or "block caving and stoping" process that greatly reduced the need for drilling and blasting. Tunnels were run all the way around a carefully selected body of ore. Stopes sixteen feet in diameter were then raised perpendicularly above the tunnels by blasting with dynamite, and 40 percent of the ore was carted away, while the rest was left to support the tunnels' pillars and to allow miners to place the next round of charges, mounting the stopes higher and higher into the mountain of ore. As the stopes and tunnels extended upward, the weight of the mountain itself pressed down and caused the ore to cave, as the base of the stopes was undermined by new tunnels. The broken ore was then taken along the tunnels in carts. The inside of the mountain was thus drained away using the force of gravity section by section. This proved to be less expensive than building traditional tunnels and stopes throughout the mine. As one 1932 report noted, 90 percent of El Teniente's ore was extracted through caving, and "no other mine in the world, including open cut mines . . . uses so small an amount of explosives per ton of ore as Teniente."[24]

Using gravity once again, miners transported the fallen ore in carts to chutes, where it fell two thousand feet to a final main tunnel even further down the mountain and was carted to the mill and concentrating plant. Different types of crushers pulverized the ore into smaller and smaller rocks. In the concentrator the rocks were ground down to a fine dust, and copper was extracted through a "flotation process" in which the ore was mixed with different forms of acid, primarily sulfuric acid, to draw out the copper, which rose to the top of the mixture. Finally, the copper paste extracted through crushing and concentrating the ore was transported by electric train further down the mountainside to the new smelter in the Caletones camp. There the paste was baked in enormous roasters and reverberatory furnaces and poured into molds. The Caletones furnaces produced copper ingots, bars, wedges, and cakes of an extremely high level of purity. Power for the mining, concentrating, and smelting operations came from imported oil and coal (although the company did purchase some coal from Chilean mines), as well as a powerful hydro-electric plant built by the company that channeled three mountain rivers into a giant reservoir.

The Braden Copper Company expanded production just in time to take advantage of a rapid increase in world demand for copper during the 1920s. In response to growing international markets, Kennecott increased its production and extended its operations, and El Teniente came to supply almost half the company's copper. In 1919, Kennecott's Chilean mine shipped 1,175,650 tons of copper ore. By 1923, Braden had more than tripled its production to 3,857,062 tons, mining and processing 10,000 tons per day. The following year the company mined and processed 4,219,000 tons of ore, with a smelter production of 156,758,171 pounds of refined blister copper.[25] In 1926, another new smelter was installed in Caletones and produced 90,522 tons of refined copper from 338,856 tons of concentrate, and Braden's yearly exportation of copper escalated greatly.

By the late 1920s, despite its history of slow growth, the Kennecott-owned Braden Copper Company was the largest underground copper mine in the world and one of the most productive mining enterprises. One writer noted that from 1916 to 1920 the company realized an operating profit of $20 million and continued to do "remarkably well" through the 1920s.[26] A United States consulate report noted that "in 1926 after years of experiments, disappointments, and delays and the expenditure of $50,000,000 the mine and plant achieved their designated capacity of 17,000 to 18,000 tons of ore a day and an average production of 9,000 tons of refined copper a month."[27] The cost of production was as low as anywhere in the world, despite the expense of transporting the copper by rail to the port of San Antonio and then shipping it to foreign markets. Braden was able to pay wages that, although comparatively high in Chile, were a fraction of labor costs in the United States, and its system of production remained one of the least expensive in the world. In addition, during the 1920s, the advantages of large-scale production became clear as costs declined steadily. Between 1925 and 1934, the El Teniente mine supplied 46 percent of the Kennecott Copper Company's total output. In 1932, the United States consulate report concluded that "construction work in building the railroad, which was literally carved out of the canyon wall for much of the way, and in providing housing for 9,000 people in a spot like Sewell on the steep slopes of a mountain was no easy undertaking, and the success finally achieved marks a feat in engineering. Today after all these years of trial and error the Braden mine is one of the lowest cost producing copper mines in the world."[28] A 1933 study of the copper industry echoed the embassy report, noting that "if the Braden enterprise was slow in reaching industrial maturity, its present position makes it the envy of copper producers the world over."[29]

Although labor remained cheap, demand for copper expanded, and the Braden Copper Company's profitability increased during the First World War and the 1920s, the North American company returned only a small fraction of its earnings to the Chilean government. From 1913 to 1922, Kennecott paid taxes in Chile of only 0.8 percent on its gross sales. In 1922, the Chilean government applied an income tax of 12 percent to El Teniente, which lasted until 1932, when it was raised to 18 percent.[30] During the late 1920s, Kennecott earned between 20 and 40 percent a year on its investment in the El Teniente mine.[31] El Teniente in the 1920s was a classic example of a foreign-owned enclave exporting raw materials to "core" industrial countries and returning only a small portion of its earnings to the "peripheral," less-developed home country.[32] After the initial investments and long period required to develop the mine, accessible copper ore, inexpensive labor, and low taxes made copper mining in Chile a profitable business.

Worker Mobility and Resistance to Company Authority

While El Teniente's North American managers experienced remarkable success in overcoming the obstacles presented by the mine's geographic isolation and rugged conditions and in implementing innovative methods of production, they found it more difficult to control Chile's social landscape. As the Braden Copper Company introduced new technologies and expanded production in El Teniente, it increasingly required a settled and trained population of workers. During the first three decades of production, however, the company encountered significant difficulty in attracting and maintaining a dependable and productive labor force.

El Teniente's workers had a long tradition of mobility stretching back to the transience of nineteenth-century agricultural laborers and miners. In response to the boom in Chile's agricultural export economy during the 1840s, large landowners expanded their holdings and evicted many resident tenant farmers (inquilinos) from their estates or increased their labor demands and restricted their access to land and water. Landowners exploited their monopoly of arable land and the easy availability of cheap, landless laborers to keep production costs low. The concentration of landholding in Chile's central agricultural valleys and expulsion of inquilino families led to the creation of a permanent male, rural workforce of seasonal laborers, or peones, who migrated from valley to valley and hacienda to hacienda in search of work.[33] Rural male workers also migrated to cities, ports, mining areas, and even outside Chile in search of work. As historian Gabriel Salazar argues, these peones, because of pressures from landowners and economic necessity, often remained single and unsettled. With the decline of the agricultural export economy during the 1850s and the subsequent boom in Chile's nitrate export economy during the 1870s and following the War of the Pacific, agricultural workers headed north to work in the nitrate mines, often returning to the south and then back to the north again, following the boom-and-bust cycles of the nitrate economy. The labor force of the northern mining districts of the late nineteenth century consisted almost entirely of a landless, male, rural labor force expelled from the countryside.[34]

Until 1914, the El Teniente mine itself relied on seasonal labor, because the company closed down its operations during winter months, when blizzards and cold temperatures made work in the mine virtually impossible.[35] The company required a mobile labor force that could leave the mine during the winter to return to the city, the countryside, or mining districts in the north. Thus, when the Braden Copper Company increased production in response to widening world demand for copper during the First World War and began to need a larger and more stable workforce, it had to deal with workers who were already accustomed to a great deal of mobility as a fundamental strategy of survival. Workers moved throughout the Chilean economy, engaging a series of economic strategies that included labor as agricultural peones during harvest seasons and work on railroads and roads, in ports and cities, and even in the southern coal and northern nitrate mines.

The lack of a reliable labor force constituted the company's most formidable obstacle to expansion and development during and after World War I. The migrant Chilean laborers who traveled to the mine, either contracted by company agents or drawn by rumors of high wages, tended to leave after short stints to return to the countryside or to look for work in other sectors of the economy. Workers from rural areas often hoped to accumulate savings and return to the countryside to purchase a small plot of land. Other workers rejected the harsh living and working conditions high up in the Andes and left in search of safer and easier forms of labor. In addition, the transient early workforce in El Teniente defied the copper company's efforts to impose new forms of labor discipline and efficiency.

Conditions in the El Teniente mine and camps were harsh during its first two decades of operation, despite the relatively high wages paid by the company. A 1923 study found that in 1920 the copper industry paid wages superior to those in all other industries and that among copper producers, El Teniente offered the highest wages, second only to the northern Chuquicamata mine, then also owned by Kennecott.[36] According to the same study, however, the high cost of living in the mining camps eroded the real value of miners' salaries: "The miners earn what they want, people tend to say; but it is important to point out that the businesses also charge in their stores what they want."[37] In addition, work inside the mine was hard and dangerous. It required considerable strength and skill to negotiate the difficult terrain of the mine's tunnels, to drill the rock, and to cart away pieces of broken ore. The mine tunnels were alternately infernally hot from underground gases and cold and wet from mountain rain and snow and filled with copper dust that rendered the air suffocating and produced silicosis and other respiratory diseases.

Accidents from cave-ins, falls down chutes, asphyxiation, and dynamite explosions were frequent in the mine. In the short space of two weeks between 25 June and 8 July 1912, for example, a snowstorm destroyed a small house inhabited by eight workers, and twenty miners were killed in a dynamite explosion. The following week a sixteen-year-old miner was killed when a railcar carrying copper ore spilled on him, and another miner was killed when a piece of rock fell on him from the roof of a mine tunnel.[38] For the entire year of 1920, the company reported an average of twenty-seven severe mining accidents each month.[39] A congressional committee investigating the copper industry in 1920 reported that "the El Teniente mine has cost the country thousands of men. There have been explosions, cave-ins, every kind of catastrophe, which indicates that there is no safety for the workers."[40]

While living conditions in El Teniente in 1920 were better than in the domestically owned, small copper mines where workers were lodged in tents, as El Teniente workers had been during the company's first decade of operation, housing for single male workers was provisional at best, and housing for workers with families was limited and miserable. Thus a deputy on the congressional committee investigating the copper industry noted that "in the camps of the El Teniente mine there exist a series of lodgings that don't deserve that name because their state is more than deplorable, the lodgings that are occupied by families can't even offer close to the minimal comfort, they don't have electricity, light, or ventilation, and in a word, are completely inappropriate to live in. I say nothing of the barracks for the single workers that are so awful as to be irrational."[41] Similarly, in 1919, José Pezoa Varas described his experiences of housing in the mining camps where he worked as a teacher. Many workers lived in cramped barracks where up to twenty men crowded into a small room, three workers sharing a bed and working the three different shifts in the mine on a rotational basis.[42]

Miners with families inhabited two-room apartments in the barracks.

Often two families shared an apartment, one in each room. According to Pezoa Varas, "The two narrow rooms had leaves of galvanized iron for walls and ceiling and the floors were the naked soil." A local Radical Party paper denounced the "yanqui fiefdom" in El Teniente and described the harsh mountain cold "that has frozen to death many people way up in the mountains with miserable hovels made of wood and aluminum boards."[43] Given these conditions, the company found it difficult to convince workers to stay on in the mine.

El Teniente's mine workers came from a variety of backgrounds. Many migrated from agricultural regions in Chile's fertile central and southern valleys. Others traveled from Santiago; such ports as Valparaíso, Talcahuano, Antofagasta, and Iquique; and the northern nitrate mines. A sample of 179 employment records of workers hired between 1917 and 1939 provides a useful picture of El Teniente miners' geographical origins.[44] Slightly over a third of workers came from south-central rural towns and villages, surrounding and including the commercial agricultural centers of Talca and Chillán. Slightly under a third arrived from agricultural towns in the valleys surrounding Rancagua and from Rancagua itself. Just over 5 percent of the workers came from the agricultural valleys north of Santiago around the Aconcagua valley, and approximately the same number came from areas in the south, near the agricultural and commercial center of Temuco. Only 12 percent of workers were from the capital city of Santiago and 8 percent from major port cities along the coast of Chile.[45]

Other company records tend to confirm this picture of workers' origins. In one representative sample of workers, the company reported to the regional government, the Intendencia de O'Higgins, on a group of recently recruited workers. The report disclosed that eight came from the southern agricultural towns of Chillán, Talca, Constitución, and Temuco; three from Santiago; and four from the port cities of Valparaíso and Puerto Montt.[46] In 1912, a company report also documented that an *enganche* (labor recruiter) had been sent to rural areas north of Santiago in the Coquimbo and the Ovalle districts.[47] Ten years later, in 1922, the company Welfare Department informed Braden's director that it had on eighteen occasions during the year sent "agents" to "the main centers for recruiting, . . . Talca, San Javier, Parral, and Chillán," all major agricultural towns in the south.[48]

The records of El Teniente's civil registry corroborate this picture of a labor force drawn mostly from Chile's south and central agricultural valleys. Of 158 miners who married in El Teniente in 1917, 111 had rural origins, listing as their birthplace towns, villages, and landed estates in the countryside. The majority of these workers came from the valleys surrounding Rancagua. Twelve came from Rengo, fifteen kilometers from Rancagua. Seven came from Curicó, another nearby rural town, and another 7 from the neighboring villages of Machalí, Doñihue, and Bulnes. Finally, 10 workers listed the large agricultural town of Rancagua as their place of origin. Slightly less than a third of the workers (47) had roots in large towns, cities, ports, and mining areas. Seventeen workers came from Santiago, and 9 from Valparaíso. Nine workers also came from the southern coal mining towns of Lota, Coronel, and Concepción. Two workers listed their place of origin as the northern port of Iquique.[49]

Thus, while the majority of El Teniente workers came from agricultural regions around the country, a significant proportion listed origins in cities, ports, and mining districts. In fact, the company looked for workers from these areas for skilled jobs in the mine because they had had previous industrial experience.[50] In 1922, for example, the company Welfare Department reported that it had brought in two large groups of men from the government-sponsored hostels in Santiago that housed unemployed nitrate workers from the north.[51] In another, similar case, the enganche recruited a group of coal miners from the southern Coronel mine who had walked out on strike and had then been fired.

The experiment with workers of non-*campesino* (nonrural) origins did not always succeed. Although these individuals had work skills and experience of industrial labor, they often had experience with labor conflicts as well and refused to accept the company's strict regime of labor discipline and the mine's harsh conditions. This was the case of the unemployed nitrate workers brought from Santiago, who stayed only a week in El Teniente. Similarly, the southern coal miners, like the nitrate workers, never entered the El Teniente workforce. Having been "deceitfully" promised a daily wage of eight pesos by the enganchador, the miners were unhappy to discover that the company was offering only six pesos. They refused to work and were sent down to Rancagua where "they remained in a very distressing situation," according to one newspaper.[52]

The company's difficulties with workers from other mining areas and cities led it to look primarily to the countryside for its labor. The mine's managers believed that rural workers, accustomed to hard physical labor and the authority of landowners, would make more productive and obedient laborers.[53] Describing the early workforce in El Teniente, a former North American supervisor and later Braden executive remembered that during times when the company needed to increase production and hire more workers, it would send enganchadores to southern Chile to recruit "*huasos* [a derogatory term for campesino] off the farms." These company agents traveled to southern cities such as Puerto Montt, Valdivia, Chillán, and Temuco, where they would frequent bars and town squares looking for rural workers to "hook." "They would buy rural workers drinks when they came to town, get them drunk, have them sign contracts, which most of them couldn't read, and when they woke up the next morning, they were on the train, and they couldn't get off because the enganchadores would threaten to have them arrested if they failed to fulfill those contracts they had signed." Enganchadores would advance wages to prospective workers and then require them to work in the mine to pay off the loan.[54] A local El Teniente history, written by miner and poet Walter Pineda, describes how the company sent enganchadores to rural areas, armed with the promise of high wages, to recruit its labor force:

> The men arrived in Rancagua from all points of the country attracted by the prospective of good jobs. The "enganchador" did a good job, hypnotizing with his words those who dreamed of a future to embark on the adventure of copper. This singular personage provided the nitrate mines and the growing copper mines the human material for their labors. It was common to see these "manhunters" in the bars and cantinas of various cities of the south and the centers of the country, taking out a stack of bills to show how much money could be made.[55]

The company recruited campesinos in the belief that they were more accustomed to the onerous physical labor required in the mine and more willing to work hard. Former miners recall that as late as the 1940s and 1950s, the Braden jefes in charge of hiring looked for agricultural workers because they were thought to make better miners. One North American supervisor would examine the hands of the workers, rejecting those whose hands didn't show signs of hard physical labor. Some of those he disqualified as miners would be put to work on a piece of land he owned and contracted in El Teniente when they had proven their capacity for work and obedience.[56] The company also weeded out workers brought through the enganche, rejecting many as unfit because they were sick, had lice, or were physically not up to the job. In 1915, for example, the company rejected a number of enganche workers because "they were found to be physically unfit. . . . [W]e were unable to give them work because they were either in the last stages of syphilis, weak heart, bad eyes, or something of the sort."[57] Onetime miners remember the rigorous physical examinations they had to undergo to be accepted by the company and recall bitterly that they were inspected like cattle or horses.

Many agricultural workers would go to work in the mine for a season or a year, tempted by the high wages, and then return to the south to pay debts, buy land, or increase their investments in their small plots of land. Frequently, rural workers from large estates in the agricultural valleys surrounding Rancagua would migrate to the mine during off seasons in the hope of accumulating enough savings to buy their own parcels of land. The case of Manuel Abaitúa Acevedo is representative of workers' mobility. In 1924, Abaitúa Acevedo went to El Teniente from the agricultural town of Doñihue, outside Rancagua. That year he worked in the mine nine months. He returned the next year and worked for only four months before leaving. In 1926, Abaitúa Acevedo returned, but worked only one month, as he did in 1927. In 1928, he did not work, but the following year, his last as an El Teniente worker, he stayed in the mine for five months. In a similar case, in 1924 José Hernández traveled from the nearby town of Rengo to El Teniente. He worked for one month and returned the next year, when he worked for four months. For each of the next two years, Hernández spent three months working in El Teniente before ending his tenure as a copper miner altogether.[58]

Thus, despite the enganche and the recruitment of large numbers of rural workers, the Braden Copper Company found it difficult to secure a stable labor force in the El Teniente mine. Until the 1930s, the company was plagued by high levels of labor turnover. Many workers, like Abaitúa Acevedo and Hernández, left after short stints of a month or two. Others, like the former coal and nitrate miners who arrived through the enganche, left almost immediately because of dissatisfaction with either the wages or working conditions in El Teniente. The company complained to the local court that many workers, after taking a look at the mine or after a sample of the camps' primitive living conditions and harsh climate, simply refused to work.[59]

A 1912 report by the Ministerio de Industria i Obras Públicas noted the high turnover in El Teniente and the miners' propensity to stay in the mine the minimum time required to put together some savings. The ministry, like the company, was concerned about the effects of this mobile labor force on labor peace and discipline. Its report argued that labor transience "could not but help have lamentable consequences because it is easy to understand that relations between patrones [bosses] and obreros [workers] cannot be intimate and stable."[60] Similarly, in 1913 the company reported that "the average man can be depended upon for 18 to 20 days. . . . [O]ne month the men will work the required time and earn the bonus [for attendance] and the next month the call of the 'green fields and pastures new' seems to get them and away they go, in spite of the rewards or consequences."[61]

Despite significantly increased levels of production during the First World War, in 1917, only 22.4 percent of the El Teniente workforce was "permanent," and in 1918, 23.8 percent, according to a 1919 study.[62] The company reported that in 1917, "6,000 individuals went up [to the mine] and descended. . . . [A]lready in the first ten months of 1918 this record of movement has been beaten, since the mobilization reached the figure of 7,000 persons."[63] In 1922, close to 490 workers hired by El Teniente stayed only two to four weeks, and 476 workers stayed four to six weeks. Out of a labor force of 4,638, 2,256 workers labored between two and twelve weeks before leaving.[64] The following year, El Teniente's general manager was informed that of the two thousand workers hired by an enganche in 1922, only 9 percent, fewer than two hundred, stayed on to work.[65] One El Teniente supervisor commented that "he who lasts months is a veteran."[66] As the company Welfare Department saw it, "The enormous Mine turnover should be seriously taken into account as something requiring a remedy."[67]

Forging a stable workforce out of the thousands of workers accustomed to mobility and the rhythms of seasonal labor was a difficult task. Workers would often leave without notice, demanding their pay, which the company often refused to give them. As the mine superintendent argued to the judge in Sewell, who had received complaints from these workers that they hadn't been paid: "There are numerous occasions that arise where a man will come at nine o'clock in the morning, demand his pay to date, and a pass, and it is on these occasions that we must simply decline. If we were to allow every demand that is made here at the Mine, we would have great difficulty in carrying on the work."[68] The problems North American supervisors faced in creating a permanent and obedient labor force reinforced their racially condescending perception that the Chilean workers lacked the discipline, training, and skill necessary for work in the mine. As the same supervisor stated, "The majority of the lower class labor that we employ at the Mine is absolutely uneducated and ignorant, and are [sic] absolutely without responsibility."[69]

Workers found it difficult to adjust to the demands of the job. The company reported that rampant absenteeism and quitting were caused by inexperienced workers from the countryside unprepared for the harsh working conditions and high-paced labor in the mine. For example, company management objected that the *carrero* (carman) "unaccustomed to the mine complains after one or two days of muscular pain and to recuperate misses a day of work." Many workers also became sick because of the extreme temperatures and onerous labor in the mine and remained in bed or refused to work for any number of days.[70] The work discipline demanded by the company and the constant pressures to produce put on workers by foremen and supervisors provoked many to leave the mine altogether. In one typical case, José Arevelano Pérez, hired in 1928, left his job after six days, stating "that he did not like the mine." According to Arevelano Pérez's North American supervisor, he was "too puny for heavy work."[71] In 1923, Santiago Macchiavello Varas noted in his study of Chilean copper mining for the University of Chile that "one of the characteristics of the spirit of our worker is his devotion to adventure: as soon as our miner is in the north he is just as quickly found in the south." But, unlike the mine's North American managers, Macchiavello Varas also argued that workers' mobility came not from their irresponsibility but from the harsh conditions of the mine: "The veritable mobility, this life of vagabondage, of the Chilean miner comes not from love of the new, but the intense suffering that he finds in all the mines."[72]

North American supervisors reported that workers would quit when transferred from one section of the mine to another, particularly to the more dangerous spots. The mine's general manager noted that workers used their leverage in the labor market to play one department of the mine off against the other, searching for the best work conditions and wages.[73] This was facilitated by competition among supervisors for workers. At times, conflicts between the North American jefes erupted over accusations of "stolen" workers.[74] One supervisor warned that competition between work sections for labor contributed to a lack of discipline among the workers.[75]

Workers' unwillingness to conform to the system of labor in El Teniente was reflected in their frequent migration to other sectors of the economy and willingness to risk unemployment rather than remain in the mine. Miners took advantage of opportunities in dynamic sectors of the economy to leave in search of more attractive job opportunities offered by public works projects, the nitrate mines, budding urban industries, and agriculture. During times of economic recession and high unemployment, the mine could rely on a steady supply of labor, but during the First World War and following the postwar recessions of the 1919–1921 period until 1930, the Chilean economy experienced steady growth as a result of a resurgence of international demand for nitrates and the development of the copper industry. In 1917, for example, the company's general manager described the labor shortage due "to the great extension of work at Braden, other large new mining companies in Central and Northern Chile, and the extraordinary production of nitrate with a small and practically fixed native labor supply."[76]

The problem of labor in the mines became even more serious when the government began to use revenues from the healthy export economy to invest in public works programs during the 1920s. In 1924, the company had a hard time finding workers because "the electrification of the State Railroad between Santiago and Valparaíso, extensive construction programs in Santiago, and the execution of several schemes of Public Works, together with the continuous demand from the nitrate fields," had drawn workers away from El Teniente.[77] That same year, the mine's manager noted that workers' favorable position in the labor market was contributing to "the unsettled labor conditions in Chile," a number of wildcat strikes, and the workers' sense "that they have the upper hand."[78]

In his annual report for 1925, Braden's general manager described the company's difficulty in attracting and keeping workers, complaining that "owing to the general acceleration of industry in Chile during the past year there was a greater demand for labor throughout the country" as a whole. Under these conditions it has become increasingly difficult to maintain sufficient forces for the operation of the Plant up to maximum capacity." Job opportunities elsewhere had led, the general manager wrote, to "an exodus of a large number of our most efficient workmen." The company had tried to replace these workers but had been forced to depend on "unskilled labor recruited from agricultural districts." And, he noted, "even this source of supply has proved inadequate." These unfavorable labor market conditions, the general manager concluded pessimistically, would continue for a long time and were contributing to the low productivity of the mines. He noted that "the efficiency of the Chilean workman must be improved."[79] High levels of labor turnover impeded production because the company was continually forced to recruit "inexperienced" workers. Thus, one company report noted that production in the mine was slow because of "the necessity of employing large numbers of new and unexperienced men to build up the organization."[80]

The ebb and flow of male workers to the mine was accompanied by a parallel movement of women who migrated to the camps in search of work as domestic servants and to the informal settlements, or callampas, that sprang up on the margins of the mine's property, where they sought work in petty commerce. These women moved to El Teniente independently and, like male workers, planned to save some money and then move on. In addition, they were an integral part of miners' informal cultural activities. Miners drank at women's bars, ate their food, and engaged in illicit, and often commercial, sexual relationships with them. Initially, most women who went to the mine were single; few accompanied male partners or husbands. They intended to work in or start bars, brothels, and small businesses on their own. Women also looked for jobs as domestic servants in workers' cantinas, in the homes of white-collar workers and North American administrators, or in laundries and shops in the camps. Like many men who went to the mine, women hoped to return to agricultural towns or cities to start their own businesses.

Women had participated in independent patterns of labor migration since the second half of the nineteenth century. Following the agricultural crisis of the 1850s, women, as well as men, left the countryside to migrate to mining areas, ports, and cities. While many men left the countryside during seasonal swings in employment, women often resettled in ranchos, small settlements on the outskirts of rural towns. There, they cultivated vegetables, pastured animals on small plots of land, and engaged in small-scale commercial activities, producing and selling food and beverages such as bread, meat pastries, fruit, and alcohol and entertaining itinerant peones.[81] Women frequently set up household as single mothers, entered into "consensual unions" with men who continued to move around the country in search of work, and labored in a series of informal economic activities.[82] In addition, women who migrated to Chile's cities and rural towns often engaged in prostitution to supplement their otherwise insufficient incomes. Many women set up or managed their own houses of prostitution as a form of small commercial enterprise.[83]

During the nineteenth century, women migrated to mining camps as well, where they engaged in petty commerce and established small businesses. While prostitution was common, women also maintained independent romantic relationships with men in the camps. As Salazar writes, in the mining camps of the late eighteenth and nineteenth centuries, "contact with women was converted into a distant, commercialized, relationship. Matrimony and the family became improbable alternatives."[84] Workers in mining camps developed transitory and informal relationships with women that were usually characterized more by "public scandal" and socializing in the camps' *pulperías* (taverns) than by stable domestic life.[85] In these relationships, both men and women maintained their economic and social-sexual independence.

Judicial records and the records of El Teniente's civil registry provide some sense of the social origins of the women who migrated to the El Teniente mining enclave and reflect the continuity into the twentieth century of the patterns of gender relations described by Salazar. In 1917, 170 women married El Teniente workers. The vast majority of these women had not accompanied male workers to the mine and did not come from the same towns as the men they married. Out of 155 women who listed their origins, only 14 married men from their hometowns. It is probable that these women either accompanied their prospective spouses to El Teniente or followed them later on. The rest apparently either met their partners in El Teniente or in other regions of the country before coming to the mine. Only 13 had parents in the mining camps and had moved with their families to the mine.

A number of marriages between men and women who had come to the mine together reveal the transient nature of the lives of both the men and the women who wound up in El Teniente. In one case, for example, a woman from the rural town of San Vicente married a miner from the town of Curicó. The two legitimized children who had been born in Santiago and Valparaíso. Thus, although both listed rural origins, they had clearly lived and worked together for a number of years in Chile's central port and capital city without getting married. In another case, a woman from the south-central agricultural town of Talca married a man from Valparaíso. The couple legitimized their child born in Santiago, where it is likely that they had met. In a similar case, a woman from Valparaíso married a man from the central agricultural town of San Felipe. The two had had children in Valparaíso, where it would seem that they had met, and in Santiago. One final situation reveals the extraordinary geographic mobility of the men and women who journeyed to El Teniente. A woman from Santiago married a man from the northern port of Iquique. The two had had children in two other port cities, Valparaíso and Talcahuano on Chile's southern and central coast.

Thus, although many women and men listed birthplaces or origins in the countryside, many had lived and labored previously in Chile's ports and cities. Many of the women who came with their male partners to the mine had met them not in their hometowns but in major urban centers or ports and had traveled with them to the mine. Seventeen cases like this are included in the list of marriages for 1917. Added to the 14 women who married men from their hometown and the 13 who had come to the mine with their families, this number indicates that of the 155 women who listed their origins, less than a third (44) had come to El Teniente with their families or male companions. Over 100 women, two-thirds of all women who married in 1917, had migrated to the mine alone, without family or male partners.

Of these 155 women, slightly fewer than a third (40) came from cities and ports—not including those women from rural areas who had lived in cities and towns. This is almost identical to the percentage of men who listed similar urban origins. In addition, twenty-five women came from Rancagua, which confirms the popular wisdom that many single miners married "local" women who lived and worked in Rancagua, a booming agricultural/mining town. Twenty-two women came from Santiago and eight from the city of Concepción, while ten women came from the ports Coquimbo, Valparaíso, Antofagasta, and Talcahuano. Many single women with no children who came from rural areas probably also came through Santiago, Valparaíso, or smaller towns and cities. Women, like men, listed rural origins from Chile's southern and central valleys, primarily major agricultural towns and commercial centers such as Chillán, Talca, Linares, and Bulnes, as well as the smaller and more local towns of Graneros, Rengo, Machalí, and Curicó.

Reflecting their economic independence and previous work experience before migrating to the mine, a number of women listed some form of employment, ranging from tailor (*modista*) and seamstress (*costurera*) to informal commerce (*comerciante*) and domestic service (*empleada*). But a large proportion of the women who migrated to El Teniente never made it to the mine's camps or into formal employment by the company. These women found work in the bars and brothels that lined the railroad to the camp, in Rancagua, or in the callampas near the mine's camps. Many started their own small businesses selling food and clandestine bootleg liquor and providing accommodations for prostitutes and their clients, thus reproducing the economic activities that women had pursued in rural ranchos during the nineteenth century. Court records describe many of these women as prostitutes. Their clients were miners who, on days off and weekends, flooded their bars in search of entertainment.

Local newspapers frequently decried the proliferation of small bars and brothels that were either run by or employed women in Rancagua and the small settlements surrounding the mining camps. Thus, in 1916 the anarchist paper *La Voz del Obrero* denounced "the less than respectable group of taverns, clubs and brothels . . . that in Rancagua are out of proportion to the number of inhabitants and have grown such as to be a public shame." The paper also noted that workers from the mine "lacking honest distractions spend their money in the bars, clubs, and the immense majority, in the houses of tolerance."[86] Similarly, in discussing his 1919 trip up the mountain to the El Teniente camps on the company railroad, José Pezoa Varas described how prostitutes stood at the windows and doors of taverns and brothels in the city and in settlements along the railway up the mountain waving and shouting "flirtatious phrases and burlesque jokes" to the men who were going to work.[87]

Inside the El Teniente camps, women were denied access to employment in the mine because of their sex. The company hired only men and denied wage-paying jobs in the mine to women. Women found work as domestic servants in the camps' cantinas, hotels, and laundries. Empleadas worked up to sixteen hours a day serving meals, cleaning, and washing clothes for hundreds of miners for low wages that represented a fraction of the minimum wage paid to a Braden Copper Company male worker. Empleadas often sought to add to their wages through establishing sexual relationships with miners in exchange for money or other material goods. The writer and former Braden Copper Company employee Baltazar Castro, for example, describes in his stories of life in the camps how single girls "went up to work in the cantinas of Teniente C, the camp next to the mine, where they hoped to earn more money from the passions of the workers than from their work in the pensions."[88]

For the Braden Copper Company, the presence of this autonomous, transient, and unruly population of women workers in and outside the camps contributed to the instability and lack of discipline of its male workers. In the mining camps, men and women established informal relationships that reflected their mutual mobility. Often these relationships were commercial and part of a broader everyday culture of drinking, gambling, and informal sexual liaisons. Workers frequently extended the monthly weekends off granted by the company through Monday, in a Chilean San Lunes (Saint Monday), taking advantage of the opportunity so as to leave their jobs or return to their work anywhere from a day to two weeks late.[89] Miners, according to the company, frequently worked long stretches, accumulated some savings, and then left their jobs to go down to Rancagua, where they spent their money in bars and brothels. For the company, most miners' single status gave them an independence that led to disruptive forms of social behavior. In 1915, for example, the company paper noted how "rarely does the miner have a family. He arrives from who knows where and disappears any day." The miner was, the paper stated, "a gambler, a drinker, a fighter who, for the slightest reason, takes out his knife." The paper quoted a North American supervisor who described how a miner had recently come up to him to ask for his dismissal "because he had $100 pesos and wanted to go down to Rancagua." When the supervisor counseled him to save some of his money, he responded that "I don't have a family, tomorrow I could meet my end and the company would get all my money, it's better that I go down and spend it on the girls."[90] In one typical case, Efraín Acevedo Jara, a miner from the local agricultural town of Graneros, began work in El Teniente in 1923 but was eventually fired because he had received permission to leave the camps for four days' rest and then did not return for over a week. His supervisor in the mine noted that "his work is very poor, mostly because he is a drinking man."[91]

Despite the company's efforts to keep workers in the mine, high levels of turnover were exacerbated by frequent dismissals and suspensions of workers who violated the company's demands for labor discipline. Every month the company fired or suspended large numbers of workers for a variety of reasons ranging from poor work performance and drunkenness on the job to laziness and abandoning their work. In May 1922, for example, foremen in the mine suspended or fired close to one hundred different workers for disobedience, laziness, fighting, insolence, "stealing copper muck," leaving the job, carelessness, sleeping on the job, gambling, thieving, and incompetence. The most common reason for a dismissal, accounting for thirty workers, was the simple "refusal to work" or "abandoning work." During the four-month period from December 1921 to March 1922, the company fired 220 workers for a variety of infractions. The most commonly cited transgressions were laziness and abandoning the job.[92] A review of company personnel records provides a similar accounting of the lack of discipline in the mine. In a sample of sixty-one workers hired between 1916 and 1929, twenty-eight had been suspended or fired, often more than once, for a variety of offenses. Drinking and gambling led the list of causes for punishment. But, workers were also suspended for lack of production, sleeping on the job, abandoning work, and stealing materials belonging to the company.[93]

The everyday culture of the El Teniente copper workers represented an extension of the patterns of sociability of nitrate miners and nineteenth-century copper workers, who were notorious for their mobility, lack of work discipline, and habits such as drinking and gambling.[94] Like the migrant peones who labored in the northern mines during the late nineteenth century, the El Teniente workers held secular, antichurch world views while maintaining folk religious practices.[95] Workers nurtured beliefs in spirits (animitas) that haunted the mine's tunnels, and they celebrated "popular" religious festivals in honor of specific saints, particularly the Virgin Mary. Often these celebrations were occasions for drinking and absenteeism.[96] Until the early 1920s, El Teniente's camps had neither a priest nor a Catholic church owing to the opposition of both workers and Braden's managers.

Only in 1922 did a Catholic priest, Oscar Larson, first travel to El Teniente with the Braden Copper Company's authorization. When Larson arrived, men and women who had congregated at the train station shouted "now it's going to rain" and "now it's going to snow." As Larson noted, El Teniente's inhabitants were not very pious; in fact, they believed that a priest brought bad luck. In addition, Braden administrators were Masons and Protestants who expressed little interest in having a priest in the camps. Company schools had no religion classes, and worker organizations tended to meet on Saturdays and Sundays, days when religious services might be held. However, after being convinced by Larson's arguments that the presence of the church would contribute to the discipline of the labor force, in 1923 the company allowed the establishment of a small chapel in one of the company buildings.[97] Yet miners continued to sustain secularist attitudes. In oral history interviews, members of the mining community frequently noted the minimal importance of the church in the life of the camps with the well-known phrase, "the mine is the miner's god."

Mine workers on the copperbelt of southern Rhodesia and South Africa, in the Belgian Congo, and in the Bolivian and Peruvian Andes sustained peasant economies and communities that allowed them to counter efforts by mining companies and, in Africa, colonial states to transform them into a dependable industrial workforce. In Chile, both single male and single female workers located their independence in their capacity to move from one sector of the economy to another in deeply rooted patterns of labor transience, rather than in the traditions and structures of peasant communities. Male workers demonstrated their resistance to the demands of the modern copper industry in social practices that, in the company's eyes, impeded productivity, including absenteeism, drinking, gambling, and frequenting brothels. Women participated in this everyday culture and informal economy of recreation and entertainment independent of men and often with the same goal of accumulating savings and then moving on. Thus, the mobility of single men and women workers structured the early working-class culture and forms of opposition of El

Teniente miners to the authority of North American capital. To build a steady supply of trained labor and a permanent community in the mining camps, from the perspective of the Braden Copper Company's managers, would require the reformation of both men's and women's forms of sociability and the inculcation of new habits and values.

2 Labor Strife, Social Welfare, and the Regulation of

Working-Class Sexuality

The Braden Copper Company's difficulties attracting and maintaining a disciplined labor force in the El Teniente mine were exacerbated by frequent labor conflicts. As the North American company became one of the world's most valuable copper mining enterprises and a vital engine of Chile's export economy following the First World War, it faced an intransigent labor force that persistently worked to organize an independent union affiliated with the national labor federation, the Federación Obrera de Chile (Chilean Workers Federation, FOCh). While miners maintained high levels of mobility, they also engaged in a number of illegal strikes to protest conditions in the camps and the mine and to demand union recognition. Three strikes in 1911, 1916, and 1919 took the form of full-scale rebellions of miners against the authority of both the company and the state.

In response to workers' labor actions and their patterns of mobility, the North American mining company established a rigorous regime of social control in the mining camps, one enforced by its own private police force and backed by the Chilean police and military, transforming the mining camps into an autocratically ruled company town. The Braden Copper Company complemented these traditional tactics of labor control with a corporate welfare system following the First World War and during the 1920s. The company located the source of miners' lack of discipline, transience, and labor activism in the mining community's fluid world of gender relations and sought to reorganize relations between male and female migrants into stable, male-headed nuclear families. The virtues of the responsible male head of household and female housewife, based on a middle-class ideal of family and domesticity, would supplant disruptive forms of male and female working-class social life. As Chilean politicians looked for answers to Chile's "social question" during the economic and social upheavals that followed World War I, the North American com-

pany's gendered corporate welfare program became a model for enlight-
ened employer practice and state intervention to regulate and reform the
conditions of working-class life and resolve labor conflicts.

Workers' Strikes, Social Control, and State Repression

The first strike to paralyze the El Teniente mine took the form of an
uprising. According to company reports to state officials, the strike was
organized by a group of mine workers who then extended the conflict
to the smelting and concentrating plants. During the summer of 1911, a
period of increased production in El Teniente as a result of the instal-
lation of new machinery for processing copper ore in the concentrating and smelting sections, workers surrounded the building housing the
mine's North American administrators, hurling stones, shouting "subversive slogans," and breaking windows. The workers then proceeded to set
fire to the building, as well as to the company store and the principal
warehouse. Workers who tried to keep working during the strike were
stoned and beaten up. The striking miners cut a number of the company's
telephone lines, destroyed part of the railroad that connected the mine to
the city below, and threatened to blow up the mine with dynamite.[1]

The workers' list of demands reflected the transient nature of the labor
force. Their petition was directed at company policies that restricted their
independence and capacity to leave their jobs. They asked for the effective
payment of salary on demand instead of a monthly wage in order to have
the freedom to quit when they wanted, a 20 percent raise, the dismissal
of abusive foremen, lower prices in the company store, and an end to the
system of payment in tokens redeemable at the company store. The use of
tokens, rather than cash payments, had been employed by the company
as a means of increasing workers' dependence on their jobs. At the end of
each month workers received their wages minus their debts at the company's stores. By forcing workers to wait a month, the company hoped to
limit desertion. The company's control of the camps' stores often meant
that wages would be diminished by debt and that miners would have to
continue working to pay off their accounts.

When the company offered a compromise solution to the workers'
petition, the miners voted it down and headed to the mine with explosives. They also fired some shots at a group of North American supervisors

who had taken refuge in the company administration offices. The conflict came to a violent end when the miners, armed with dynamite, confronted a troop of forty soldiers sent to the mine by the provincial government, supplemented by thirty soldiers on horseback from Santiago. The strike was broken, and the miners' demands were rejected. At the company's request, a permanent troop was stationed in the camps to control the "dangerous and disruptive elements" until production came to a halt in the winter and the company could dismiss its entire workforce until the following spring.[2]

In 1916, again during a period of increased production in the mine, a large group of "recently hired workers" organized another strike to protest payment by tokens and the high cost of living in the mining camps and to demand wage increases. The workers also requested an additional half hour to the twenty minutes allowed by the company for lunch, better treatment by foremen, credit in company stores for all workers, and prompt payment of salaries.[3] The workers' petitions were once again rejected and the strike crushed with the aid of the military and police, although the company did put an end to the token system. Unlike the earlier strike, organizers from the national labor federation, the FOCh, played a role in the strike and in efforts to organize a miners' union. The newspaper of the Rancagua section of the FOCh reported that the company had impeded a miners' union drive organized by the FOCh in El Teniente by prohibiting union meetings in the camps and firing "fathers of families and honest workers without any consideration and with threats and insults."[4]

Until 1919, conditions remained calm in the mine, but when the postwar recession led the company to reduce production, cut wages, and decrease its labor force, the miners once again went on strike. They were joined by nitrate and coal miners, port workers, and urban factory workers, who responded to growing unemployment and the high cost of living with strikes and protests throughout Chile. In El Teniente, workers organized the mine's third major strike to demand an end to dismissals, spaces for union meetings, better treatment from foremen, improved food quality, wage increases, the eight-hour day, and recognition of their union, the Consejo Numero 5 of the FOCh. By 1919, the national union had moved from its Conservative Party and mutualist origins in 1909 to a radical, anticapitalist organization with ties to Luis Emilio Recabarren's Partido Obrero Socialista (Socialist Workers Party, POS) and the artisan- and worker-based Partido Demócrata (Democratic Party, PD). The FOCH represented a variety of militant labor tendencies, including anarchists, syndicalists, and socialists. While the Braden Copper Company was willing to meet some of the mine workers' demands, it refused to limit dismissals and adamantly declared its opposition to recognition of the FOCH.

The wave of labor unrest in Chile in 1919 was brought to a harsh end through the use of military force to repress strikes. The government declared zones of emergency and military rule in the nitrate mines, troops fired on striking workers, and labor activists were arrested and deported. In El Teniente, the 1919 strike ended unfavorably for the workers when government troops headed by Coronel Mario Annabalán forced the miners back to work, kicked the strike leaders and FOCH activists out of the camps, and took control of the union, turning it into an ally of the company. Coronel Annabalán became the first president of the reconstituted company union, the Consejo Federal de los Operarios del Teniente.[5] After the 1919 conflict, as world demand for copper dropped precipitously, the North American company shut down the mine, fired the entire workforce, and only later hired back those workers who had not been active in the strike. The company received full support from the Chilean government for its efforts to destroy the union. Company officials reported that "the Minister of Interior as well as other Government Officials . . . appreciate and are satisfied with the Company's Attitude."[6]

Following the 1919 miners' strike, the Braden Copper Company countered labor unrest, the lack of work discipline, and high levels of turnover with a rigorous regime of social control, backed by the military and judicial apparatuses of the Chilean state. The physical isolation and inaccessibility of the mine and the company's control over space in the camps served its interests in controlling the mobility of the labor force. To restrict movement in and out of the camps, Braden employed its own private police force, *los serenos,* to patrol the camps and their outskirts. Workers were required to carry identification cards and could not leave or enter El Teniente without a pass granted by the company Welfare Department. Because the only way out of the mining camps was by company train or by foot, workers either had to risk the long hike down the mountain or attain a company permit to descend by train. If they left without a pass, they had no hope of returning to work in the mine. When they were granted permission to take the company train from Rancagua to the mine, company police searched workers and their luggage. The company also kept a file on each worker, which included fingerprints. According to one study, these identification cards "lent a great service since in many occasions they have prevented the hiring of criminals and disruptive elements" and had been an "excellent method for combating communism."[7]

The Braden Copper Company's internal regulations mandated the close control of workers' everyday activities and private spaces in the camps. These regulations stated that "workers are obliged to clean the rooms and houses that they occupy and the company reserves the right to inspect them at whatever moment to see if this obligation is being fulfilled."[8] The company's internal laws also established a "dry zone" in El Teniente that prohibited the selling and consumption of alcohol. Braden touted the dry law as the solution to all social problems, from venereal disease and criminality to labor agitation. The dry law, it believed, cut down on absenteeism, desertion, and the infamous San Lunes, contributing to a healthy and stable family life. In addition, the company prohibited gambling, a frequent pastime for workers in their barracks during off hours. The serenos used these regulations as a pretext to enter miners' homes to search for alcohol and stolen goods or simply to maintain their vigilance over the labor force. The company's private police were stationed inside workers' barracks, as well as in the camps' passageways and in the mine.

Periodic mass dismissals threatened the miners' job security and helped keep the workforce under control. During downswings in the international copper economy, following orders from Kennecott headquarters in the United States, Braden would reduce production and fire a significant number of workers. While the workers were assured that they would be rehired as soon as demand for copper increased once again, they were left to fend for themselves for long periods of time. In addition, there was no guarantee that the company would rehire fired workers. Older workers, workers sick with silicosis, or workers known to be "troublesome" were replaced with fresh recruits when the company began hiring. The company thus took advantage of reductions in production to purge its labor force of disruptive workers. In 1920, for example, Braden dismissed two thousand workers out of a workforce of over six thousand in response to a decline in markets for copper and renewed efforts by the mine workers to organize an independent union. These workers were given two weeks' pay and transported to Rancagua. The dismissal allowed the company to remove labor activists following a rekindling of labor effervescence after the 1919 strike.[9]

Braden maintained a blacklist of activist workers that it shared with the Anaconda Copper Company's northern Chuquicamata mine to make sure that workers expelled from one mine could not find employment in another. On 3 August 1925, for example, the general manager of Anaconda's Chile Exploration Company, Chuquicamata, sent a list and photographs of workers fired as "undesirables."[10] Similarly, in 1934, Braden sent a letter to the Chuquicamata mine listing thirty-one "disruptive" workers, the majority from the northern port of Antofagasta.[11] The blacklist contained the names of workers who suffered from silicosis or elderly workers who were not to be rehired, as well as "agitators." One former Braden company clerk described his experiences with the blacklist in the Communist Party paper *El Siglo:* "In the time I worked for the company I realized that of every 100 workers who were on the company's blacklist 70% are 'not to be rehired for silicosis,' 20% are 'not to be rehired for agitator' and 10% 'not to be rehired for age.' (The yanquis are real aficionados of statistics.)"[12]

In addition, the company employed a network of spies to keep tabs on workers' efforts to organize an independent union. Paid informants regularly reported on union activities to the company Welfare Department, and during strikes or important union assemblies, the company received detailed accounts of the workers' discussions and debates.[13] In 1938, for example, the local paper *La Tribuna* denounced the fact that the Braden Copper Company's Welfare Department maintained a number of company spies on its payroll. It noted that informants lined up outside the company personnel office "to give information to Tanascovich [a company administrator] on everything that happens in the union and in the camp."[14]

Until the 1940s, the North American company prohibited public gatherings and meetings in the camps and required the miners' social clubs and unions to obtain company permission to hold meetings. Militant union or "revolutionary" publications were forbidden in the camps. In 1920, the company-established miners' union, the Consejo de Operarios del Mineral El Teniente, petitioned the company for the freedom to sell FOCh newspapers and received a reluctant assent from the company, which replied: "The demand to permit a member of the Federation to sell workers' publications will be conceded as long as said member is a worker of the Company and that this privilege is not abused by bringing in revolutionary publications or publications subversive of order and discipline." Braden reserved the right to ban papers that attacked the company "through calumny and lies."[15]

For the miners, the close ties between the North American company and the Chilean police force in the camps were quite evident. The carabineros served as an extension of the company's private police force. In fact, the company paid the carabineros' wages and provided them with housing and food. Many policemen later found full-time employment with the company as serenos.[16] When police detained workers for drinking or fighting, they sent reports to the Welfare Department, which would then either suspend or fire the worker in question. The company also depended on the carabineros to help remove fired workers from the mine, to evict them from company housing and the camps, and to squash efforts at political or union organizing.[17] In cooperation with the police, the company included copies of workers' criminal records and police files in its own personnel files.[18] During wildcat work stoppages and strikes, police came to the company's aid, arresting picketers and strike organizers for "violating the freedom to work."[19]

The company also maintained public officials on its payroll and exercised its influence in the provincial government and the courts, as well as in the police station. In 1912, the Radical Party paper La Igualdad denounced the fact that the Braden Copper Company maintained "a large body of lawyers and paid bureaucrats" on its payroll and that "the governor and local judge are invited to spend their vacations on company property in the mountains and driven to scenic locations in the company car and treated like kings." "Thus neutralized," the paper commented, "those men entrusted to watch out for the workers completely abandon them." The company had constructed, the paper argued, a feudal kingdom (un feudo) in Chile's Andes.[20] In 1919, in his book on his experiences teaching school in the El Teniente camps, José Pezoa Varas noted that since the judge in Sewell was "well paid by the company, which provides his board and a comfortable house for his family, it is unlikely that he can work with impartiality."[21] During the early 1920s, the local judge was a former Braden employee whose salary and lodgings were furnished by the company.

At the national level, until 1920 a series of Chilean governments maintained a benign distance from activities in the copper mines, content to extract what minimal taxes they could from the U.S. companies. In addition, the Chilean state refused to intervene in relations between the company and its workers. Chile's landholding, mining, and commercial elites, organized in the Liberal and Conservative Parties, supported the North American copper companies during debates in congress over working conditions in the mines, taxes, and national control of copper production and marketing. Employing classic laissez-faire arguments, they maintained that Kennecott and Anaconda had brought Chile millions in new investments, developed the copper industry, and provided jobs. Any regulation of the industry or of labor relations in the mines would reduce the companies' international competitiveness and provoke them to look outside Chile for new investments. In 1916, for example, the conservative national paper *El Mercurio* praised the jobs and import duties provided by Kennecott as "a blessing" to the Chilean economy.[22] Anaconda and Kennecott paid low taxes on their revenues and could count on the government not to intervene in the management of the mine and labor relations except for the periodic dispatch of troops to quell strikes.

Locally, the company enjoyed ties of mutual support with politicians from the Liberal and Conservative Parties. In 1922, for example, Conservative Party senator Juan Enrique Concha of O'Higgins province, a major landowner in the region, expressed his concern that miners from El Teniente might go down to Rancagua to vote and agitate against him in upcoming congressional elections. The Braden Copper Company's general manager assured Concha that the company would let very few men leave the camps to vote. The company rejected a request by workers that it provide "special facilities so that a number of men might go down for this election." Company representatives also assured the senator that they "had done away with the Federation [the FOCH] and that at the same time all the undesirable characters had been expelled from camp."[23]

Corporate Welfare, Social Reform, and the
Regulation of Sexuality

The El Teniente miners' persistent efforts to build a union and high levels of labor turnover moved the Braden Copper Company to complement its repressive regime of social control with a series of paternalist management practices designed to build a reliable and productive workforce in the mine. Inspired by examples in the United States and Europe, Braden established Chile's first corporate social welfare program in 1916. The North American company sought to make life as livable as possible in the hostile and isolated climate of the Chilean Andes and to attract workers with comparatively high wages and other benefits. It offered prizes and bonuses for consistent work attendance and production incentives to keep workers from leaving the mine. Braden also instituted a network of social and cultural organizations with which it intended to counter the harshness of life and work in the mine and to reduce miners' tendency to abandon their jobs.[24] The North American company's corporate welfare system aimed to reform the social practices of its workforce. Social and economic benefits would tie workers to their jobs and induce them to form families. Schools, cultural activities, and social clubs would convince them of a set of values linked to the ideal of middle-class respectability and self-improvement.

During the 1920s, Braden established several material incentives for workers to remain in the camps. The company implemented a system of work incentives and production bonuses to complement mine workers' base wages and began to pay wages that were significantly higher than in other industries. In its 1922 annual report, the Welfare Department, in a discussion of the high level of labor turnover in the mine, wrote that "aside from increasing the number of married workers living with their families in the camps another part of the remedy . . . is an increase of wages to offset the real or imaginary harder work and dangers of the Mine."[25] In 1923, faced with the possibility of losing its workers to other sectors of the economy, Braden also began to provide workers an additional "service bonus." The bonus, the head of the Welfare Department believed, would be "a stimulus for constant attention to work and long service" and would help retain "the old and trained employees, who are almost invariably our most efficient men." This financial incentive would reduce turnover and "prevent future labor troubles almost entirely as it fills the mens' desires to have something they can look forward to when either tired out by life or too old to work." The company also believed that the bonus would help buffer the effects of unionization campaigns initiated by the FOCh.[26] The following year, Braden gave its workers a significant raise and began to pay a 10 percent monthly attendance bonus.

The company Welfare Department supplemented these wage increases and bonuses with awards, certificates, medals, and cash prizes to workers who reached the lofty goal of ten or more years of labor in the mine. In 1944, for example, mine worker G. Albarca received a diploma and cash prize from the company for accomplishing twenty-five years of uninterrupted work.[27] The company paper published weekly articles on workers who received certificates, cash prizes, and such gifts as watches for ten, fifteen, twenty, and twenty-five years of service.[28] During its early years of production Braden also ran a lottery for all miners who worked from May to September to induce workers to remain in the mine during the harsh winter months. Equivalent to about one hundred days of pay, the three prizes were drawn in September, the beginning of spring. In addition, Braden held "security contests" for the most accident-free work section and gave prizes to *cuadrillas* (work crews) for high production levels.[29]

To encourage workers to settle in the camps, the company also embarked on the improvement and expansion of housing for married workers. In 1922, the Welfare Department proposed building more housing for married men because workers who had left families behind usually left the mine after a short time.[30] With better housing, the company believed, "our workmen would thus become more or less permanent, which is, in the main, what we are trying to arrive at."[31] In 1924, the Welfare Department reported that "additional housing and recreational facilities have been provided at the various camps."[32] The company began to build new barracks to house workers with families and continued construction of new housing for married workers throughout the 1920s.[33]

With material incentives, Braden also offered workers a variety of social and cultural activities that would make life and work in the mine more attractive, reform the miners' everyday habits, and serve as an antidote to labor activism. The company provided workers with schools, social clubs, and sports clubs to replace their disruptive leisure activities, such as drinking and gambling, to induce workers to remain in the mine, and to provide training for the labor force. As part of this new system of labor relations, the company created a Center for Education and Social Work; a newspaper; vocational schools; and a network of social organizations, which included a bowling alley, movie theater, workers' social club, and sports clubs, particularly for soccer, basketball, and boxing.[34] Sports, cinema, dances, schools, libraries, and theater would help to structure miners' time away from work and provide an alternative to other illicit forms of recreation. Social clubs and mutual aid societies would teach workers the virtues of self-organization and self-help and instill the value of savings and responsible behavior in their members.

The North American company intended social clubs to provide an alternative to the union and an institutional channel through which workers' demands could be heard and company policies could be communicated and imposed. Company representatives met monthly with workers' representatives from these clubs to discuss problems in the camps and in the workplace. These meetings covered issues ranging from lack of water fountains in the barracks to company policy on transfers and stores in the camps. Braden hoped that these "friendly" meetings between managers and workers in the social clubs would improve communication and divert the workers' efforts to organize an autonomous union.[35] In one meeting, for example, the head of the company Welfare Department met with representatives from a number of the workers' social clubs in the camps, including those from the mill's recreation center, the Club Social Obrero, the school and library of the single workers' Teniente C camp, the Teniente C sports club, and the Club Social Cordillera. Workers from these groups and the company representative discussed the organization of consumers cooperatives in the camps, the company's new policy of giving dismissed workers two weeks' pay, and the maintenance of workers' quarters.[36] In 1925, the Welfare Department reported that "relations between the Company and its Chilean personnel have been bettered through regular meetings between representatives of both parties for discussion and action on matters relating to their mutual welfare."[37]

The linchpin of the North American company's strategies to reform the cultural life of its workforce, however, was its campaign to restructure gender relations and regulate both women's and men's sexual behavior. The company believed that male workers would tend to remain in the mine if they married and formed families there. It sought to tie workers more securely to their jobs by rendering women and children dependent on miners' wages. In addition, Braden's Welfare Department located the sources of conflicts between workers and bosses—and ultimately of social unrest—in workers' homes and private forms of sociability. It identified alcoholism, "promiscuous" living conditions, unclean houses, and unstable families as the sources of miners' lack of discipline. The solution to the problems caused by workers' social habits was the inculcation of values drawn from an idealized vision of middle-class family life and morality. The company welfare program attempted to forge responsible, wage-earning fathers and husbands out of the transient population of workers and to mold the many single women who migrated to the mining camps into housewives. Housewives trained in domestic science and clean and efficiently managed households would exercise a positive moral influence on workers and ultimately contribute to the permanence and productivity of the labor force. Miners would spend their leisure time in the private world of the home, rather than the public worlds of the bar, brothel, and union.

Braden promoted the formation of nuclear families and a companionate marriage defined by mutual obligation, reciprocity, and responsibility in which women devoted themselves to the domestic sphere and the care of their husband and children, while men occupied the central role of wage earner and head of household.[38] The company offered El Teniente's men and women the ideal of middle-class domesticity as a form of social improvement that centered on the individual family and household. Improvement within this sphere through education, cultural advancement, and disciplined work and job training would provide workers and their families access to the world of middle-class lifestyles. Domesticity promised men the possibility of acquiring the status, security, and authority of a middle-class head of household who enjoyed the rights of citizenship and patriarchical authority over his family. For women, domesticity would provide economic security for themselves and their children, social respectability, and an alternative to low-paying and grueling work as domestic servants, cooks, laundresses, and prostitutes.

The North American company viewed the single women who migrated to mining camps and the surrounding callampas as contributing to the disorderly habits of its workers. According to one study of the mine by Alejandro Fuenzalida Grandon, many "disorders of diverse kinds" were manifest in the camps, particularly because "the feminine element is not the best." Because of the presence of a large population of single women, he argued, "workers frequently mock the prohibitions on alcohol and the game of dice is rampant."[39] Outside the formal structures of matrimony, living or sexual arrangements between men and women contributed to the encouragement of other supposed vices. Workers were late or missed their shifts, the company believed, because of the bad influence of these women.[40] Single workers, who composed the bulk of the workforce, tended to drink, gamble, fight, and, the company posited, eventually proved more willing to go out on strike. According to the company, single workers could abandon their jobs and move on in search of new opportunities or engage in strikes because they lacked the responsibilities of married heads of household. As Fuenzalida Grandon observed in his 1919 study, "Especially the population of bachelors is notably floating."[41] Married miners, dependent on their wages and jobs, were perceived to be more constant and reliable workers. Workers who married in El Teniente or who brought wives and children with them would stay on for years, dependent on the job in the mine to support family members.

The company's preoccupation with stabilizing relations between men and women was revealed in regulations it implemented as early as 1912 that required workers who cohabited with women to present papers that proved that they had been married either legally or through the church. A Rancagua paper reported that the company had been forced to take this measure "in order to avoid the successive and continuous scandals that have taken place, the presence of women of *mala vida* that in order not to be bothered and to get lodging pass themselves off as the wives of some workers." The regulation would protect women by preventing the spread of illegitimacy and abandonment by men: "This measure . . . is a guarantee for the women who are truly married, avoiding the abuses that the miners commit, taking up any woman and leaving her abandoned and without resources or legitimacy."[42]

Five years later, the company established an additional regulation that required workers who lived with women to have legal civil marriage certificates. According to Fuenzalida Grandon, after studying "the advantages for order and discipline in the mine, the company ordered in the most resolute and determined manner the legitimization of the civil state of all its employees." The regulation prohibited couples that didn't have a civil marriage license from occupying company housing.[43] The company believed that the creation of a civil registry in the camps and the imposition of legal marriages would "put an end to the shameful percentage of badly constituted marriages. . . . [M]orally, we will have taken a great step toward culture."[44] According to the company, "90 percent of workers' homes are represented by couples whose union is illicit," and thus civil marriage is "a moral and social necessity."[45] The establishment of legally constituted families in the camps would produce "the general moral improvement of the entire population and thus the selection of the best elements of workers."[46]

The company pursued a policy, enforced by the serenos, of forcing workers found alone with a woman either to marry or to leave the camps and their jobs. Women who worked as empleadas also risked losing their jobs. One former miner recalls that "in those days they used serenos, and those poor guys who were caught making out on the stairway or making out in some half-hidden, badly lit corner, simply either he married the girl or they kicked the guy out of his work, they fired him, or they kicked the girl out as well; many of them were domestic servants."[47]

This regulation was accompanied by another rule, which prohibited miners from living with extended family members and relatives in the camps' housing because to do so would "allow in the company's doors innumerable persons who would upset normal life in the camps, who would come to suppress the conditions of hygiene and comfort that the workers enjoy, who would surely alter the morality in the camps, and who, in general, would create difficulties and inconveniences of a diverse nature."[48] One former miner remembers, for example, that "there were inspectors who went through the workers' barracks every day . . . to control those that lived in the lodgings. No one could go up to live in Sewell by themselves, even if they were a brother, mother, father, grandmother; no, everybody that lived in Sewell outside of the family group [did so] because they had been authorized by the company . . . and too bad for the poor guy who was found to have an outsider in his home. First, they sent the person who was living there illegally out of the camps, and second, they gave the worker a very serious admonition." At times, he remembers, workers who had "unauthorized" friends or relatives in their lodgings were fired.[49] Thus, the company sought to replace the patterns of family and sexual life that most men and women had brought to the mine with the "modern," bourgeois nuclear family.

The company lodged serenos in the barracks to increase its control over workers' leisure hours and family life. Periodic searches were an effective way for the company and its police force to display control over the most intimate details of miners' personal lives in the attempt to stamp out gambling, drinking, and sex in the camps. As late as 1938, the miners' union paper complained that "every sereno believes himself to be all-powerful, absolute master and owner. . . . [T]hey enter rooms late at night, strip the bedclothes from the beds to make sure of the state in which the worker is sleeping."[50] Workers' lodgings became contested terrain on which the company attempted to exercise total control. "The serenos interfered too much in workers' personal lives," remembers one worker. "They would harass workers who they found with a girl in the camp and take them to the Welfare Department."[51] In 1946, the company rejected the union's demand for the sanctity of households and lodgings, claiming that "the company makes use in a discretional and prudent way" of its right to search and inspect workers' homes.[52]

The regulation of gender relations in the camps focused on disciplining the single women who migrated to El Teniente and transforming them from itinerant workers into housewives. The company paper, along with the Welfare Department's social workers, led the campaign to reconfigure women's femininity in the mining camps. The paper published numerous articles that instructed women on how to manage the domestic space efficiently. In the "modern" family, it was argued, men brought home their wages, and in exchange, women administered the household and family budget, stretching these wages to provide for the family's sustenance. In one article, *El Teniente* described how social workers and extension classes for women sought "to educate and form good housewives so that they will not be like those who have no preparation for directing a home, a burden first on their fathers and then on their husbands."[53] The presence of an able wife, educated in domestic science and "modern" methods of housekeeping, would contribute to a stable household. Most important, on such a wife fell the burden of making the most of her husband's wages and keeping the family together. The company paper counseled women that their responsibility was to "administer the sums used for everyday expenses."[54]

The company was concerned that poverty would break workers' families apart. It noted that "the high cost of living tends to weaken the ties that unite the family." It was women's responsibility to learn "how to manage in the best way possible the money that she receives from the husband. . . . The finances of the home depend exclusively on the criteria with which the housewife arranges her expenses."[55] Articles in the company paper's "Página Feminina" ("Women's Page"), including one called "Economy in the Home," provided women recipes, tips on economizing in the kitchen, and suggestions for cleaning and maintaining a healthy household. *El Teniente* published the regular column "For the Housewife: There Are Many Home Recipes That You Must Know."[56]

The Welfare Department's promotion of female domesticity reflected the perception that women were susceptible targets for an ideology of social mobility based on a middle-class image of consumerism. The establishment of an ideal domestic space implied the consumption of basic consumer goods such as furniture, clothing, and appliances. Women were urged to aspire to new styles of dress and fashion, furnished living rooms and kitchens, and modern forms of recreation. Social workers and the company paper introduced women to up-to-date ideas about appropriate forms of clothing and household furnishings and decor.

In the spirit of training women to administer efficient households modeled on the middle-class home, the paper sponsored regular "cleaning contests" among housewives, with prizes for those married women who best demonstrated the principles of domestic science and hygiene.[57] In the words of the company paper, the social assistance program sought "to inculcate in the inhabitants [of the camps] the habit of cleanliness, the maintenance of hygienic and cheap housing, keeping track of the quality of food."[58] A clean and attractively decorated and furnished home was important for improving the general moral and physical atmosphere in which workers' families lived. In addition, it would be an incentive for men to stay at home rather than go out into the streets. A well-run home would be the magnet that pulled men away from the temptations of drink, gambling, and brothels and back toward their wives. It would, in the words of the company paper, "make their husbands and sons stay at home with greater frequency."[59] The paper provided women tips for furnishing their houses and making them attractive on a tight budget. Vases of flowers; nice, if humble, furniture; cleanliness; and order: such elements would make the home "an agreeable place," and a husband would "distance himself from it less during his hours of rest." Thus, the housewife had to produce a "cleaned, furnished home . . . where everything is in order, no matter how modest it is, and where everything has the touch of the wife's affection."[60]

The sexual contract that underlay the nuclear family and companionate marriage also demanded that women work to maintain their marriages and to build harmonious households. This required that women adhere to new norms of physical appearance. The "Página Feminina," in concert with the Welfare Department's social workers, instructed women in current ideas about feminine style. The columns of the "Women's Page" suggested that a proper wife and mother devoted herself to her appearance. Thus, one article told women that they "must try to make themselves agreeable, not only by their amiability, but also by their manner of dressing."[61] A social worker reported with disappointment in the company paper that she had seen in the camps "single and married women alike all disorderly with dirty faces, so that it was repugnant to pass by them."[62]

According to the women's page, feminine attractiveness was necessary for maintaining a healthy marital relationship. Thus *El Teniente* published numerous articles with health and beauty tips for women, including articles on "health, beauty, and happiness," "personal hygiene," "dieting," "healthy teeth," "the smile," "firm thighs," and "the importance of gloves." The Welfare Department also sponsored beauty contests for the camps' women. Articles on female beauty reflected middle-class images of femininity that consisted of attributes to which only women devoted to domestic activity and with sufficient resources could aspire. For the company Welfare Department, women needed to work to make themselves attractive in order to keep their husbands interested in them sexually and thus inside the home, rather than in the streets. The company paper counseled women that they "must please their husbands in all the ways that are at their disposal. They must make an effort to please them physically and, principally, with their moral, intellectual, and aesthetic qualities." This would "consolidate the adhesion of the husband to the interior of the home."[63] Articles in the "Women's Page" discussed how important providing husbands sexual pleasure was if marriages were to last and warned women that, especially following pregnancy, they would have to work to make themselves attractive to their spouses once again.[64]

The elaboration of a new ideal of feminine beauty also involved a redefinition of the uses of the body. The "Página Feminina" provided instruction in "healthy" forms of exercise and recreation for women. As with the sports clubs for men, the paper sought to provide women with "hygienic" forms of physical activity and to substitute recreation for "unhealthy vices." And, as with organized sports for men, articles on exercise for women provided messages about the control of the body and physical activity. The paper promoted new feminine attributes by urging women to pursue sports that would cultivate grace and elegance. Articles on "women and exercise," "tennis," "skiing," "the necessity of exercise for women," "the appropriate exercises for women," and "women and sports" emphasized new forms of feminine and middle-class forms of activity for women, the hygienic benefits of exercise, and the importance of physical control. One article advised women on "abstinence and sports." The paper counseled women that to govern their bodies they should take cold showers and exercise regularly. Exercise and cosmetic care would promote modesty, restraint, and grace in women's behavior.

The redefinition of norms of the female body and beauty was accompanied by new emotional responsibilities for women in the nuclear family. Articles in the company paper revealed another element of the exchanges implicit in the nuclear family's sexual contract: because a man labored outside the household and contributed wages to his family's survival, a woman should work hard to maintain the marriage by moderating her behavior. Thus the paper published articles on "the art of marriage" and "women's emotional hygiene," counseling women on desirable feminine qualities, including columns on "simplicity," "goodness," "timidity," "controlling your passions," "the pleasure of serving," "courtesy in the family," and "good manners." A columnist for the "Women's Page" reported, disillusioned, that she had heard both "children and adult women in the camps using vulgar and offensive phrases."[65]

According to the company Welfare Department, the proper mother and wife was modest and restrained and did her best to harmonize relations with her husband. It counseled that "in the home, women must be a moderating element, a regulating element."[66] The paper instructed a woman not to argue with her husband and to look for ways to accommodate and please him. El Teniente advised a woman not to dispute politics with her husband and to be humble and timid. It also suggested that a woman search for ways to make her husband's household life more pleasant, such as preparing his favorite dinner dish. One article asked El Teniente's women, "Are you a good wife?" The article posed a number of questions, including: "Do you make your husband wait while serving dinner? Do you smoke cigarettes? . . . Do you argue over politics? Do you serve him his favorite desert sometimes? Do you think your husband is the best man in the world?"[67] A "Página Feminina" article entitled, with the patriarchical resonances of the Bible, "The Ten Commandments of the Father of the Family" instructed a woman to follow the authority of her husband.[68] Thus, both the economic and the emotional burdens of maintaining workers' families were placed on the shoulders of women.

Women's role in the nuclear family was also to produce and socialize the next generation of miners. In this arrangement of family life, motherhood became a defining feature of working-class women's lives. Social workers and extension classes provided women in the camps instruction in caring for their children with information on children's diets, dress, and health needs. Articles in *El Teniente* frequently focused on such subjects as "the child and the home" and "knowing how to be a mother." The paper devoted one series of articles to the subject of "caring for your baby." In addition to the cleaning contests, the Welfare Department offered prizes to women who "distinguished themselves for their dedication to the care of their children."

Training women to be mothers was especially important because the physical health of children and the "moral environment" in which they grew up would determine the productivity of the next generation of workers. Thus, one column on children and mothering commented on how it was common to see children in the camps "with a crust of many days' dirt, their little hands covered with earth, where they played, abandoned during the day, their little bodies thin and badly dressed." For the company paper the presence of these unsupervised and untidy children signaled the necessity of "training the mothers so they give a more caring attention to their children . . . to teach the mothers how to care for their babies, cure them when they are sick, how to prepare their food." Ultimately, the education of women to be attentive mothers was important because mothers "initiated and prepared children to arrive, as they are supposed to, at the jobs that workers occupy today and that they will occupy tomorrow."[69]

Braden created "industrial schools for boys and girls" that had a curriculum developed by the cultural department of the U.S. embassy. The schools taught boys mechanics and elements of electrical and civil engineering, while girls learned sewing, weaving, secretarial work, domestic science, and home economics. The goal of these educational programs was explicitly stated in a company report: "If we can train and educate our own people and if we can satisfy the Braden workman and employee, there is a large labor element in Chile which would be contented here and would not be continually after the politicians for the instigation of new laws prejudicial to our interests." "One of the most desirable features," the report continued, "would be . . . the education of children throughout the entire property, taking the line of the Catholic Church, Mussolini, and Hitler who always worked on the young people, feeling that if the youth had a proper training there was no need to worry about their later years."[70]

Education was a fundamental aspect of the company's attempts to train its workforce. It established a primary school in the mine to teach reading and writing to the many illiterate miners, vocational schools for adults and children, and elementary schools.[71] Whereas the industrial schools for men offered courses in drawing, carpentry, mechanics, and electronics, the vocational schools offered women from mining families classes in household cleanliness, clothes making, cooking, and household budgeting in order "to contribute to the formation of the perfect housewife."[72] For male workers and their sons, the schools provided instruction in "necessary basic knowledge and practical courses in the different workshops."[73]

Social workers in El Teniente were the foot soldiers in the battles fought against working-class "vice" and in the campaigns to build stable families in the mining camps. Social workers entered workers' homes, embarked on hygiene campaigns, and offered workers' wives education in domestic economy, child rearing, and nutrition. During home visits, miners' wives were interrogated about diet, cleanliness, and the family budget and were "exhorted" to attend classes in domestic economy in the camps' vocational schools.[74] In addition, social workers intervened to solve conflicts and fights between neighbors and to resolve marital problems.[75]

Social workers also organized clubs for housewives so as to teach women, as one recalled in an oral history, "how to organize their homes."[76] Women learned domestic science, hygiene, child care, "morality and culture," and how to maintain their marriages.[77] Married women came together with social workers to read women's magazines, knit and sew, and converse. The magazines and activities in the clubs introduced women to new ideas about clothing and appearance, diet, child care, and marriage. Social workers sought to train women how to dress, speak properly, and keep their homes. As the company paper put it, most important was advice on how to make their marriages work in order to eliminate "the immoral acts that develop in them, . . . and the continuous fights, that are an example of the indecency, lack of decorum of the family and home, that we see among many women in these camps."[78] Vocational schools and the women's groups became an important tool in the company's attempt to reconstruct El Teniente women's femininity. There they were taught not only to accept the burden for the entire family's welfare and to restrict their activities to homemaking but also new definitions of womanhood.

Despite the company's identification of women with the domestic sphere, its social welfare policies also implied new domestic responsibilities and duties for men. By promoting marriage and the role of head of household for men, the company sought to replace public social activities such as drinking, gambling, and union activity with the private functions of family life. The benefits of this new arrangement for men would be both the economic security provided by relatively high wages and bonuses and the status and patriarchal authority enjoyed by wage-earning heads of households. While the company paper described how "the woman is of the house and the man of the street," it also argued that "in his home a man is king."[79] For men, according to the paper, the rights of citizenship were reflected in the "inviolability of the home," where they exercised their authority. The worker who understands that "in his home every man is a king," the paper advised, "will know how to respect the home and make it a fortress where order, morality, happiness, and peace reign." "It can't be denied," the paper concluded, "that a worker's sobriety depends on the comforts he has at home."[80] Thus, the company sought to push men, as well as women, into the world of the household, offering them the patriarchical power of a king over his subjects—his wife and children—in exchange for their domestication.

The company attempted to instill in men, as with women, a sense of their household duties. Raising the next generation of workers was not women's responsibility alone. Men had to assume their roles as fathers and providers as well. The company paper counseled workers on the importance of inculcating in their sons the habits of discipline and morality. Fathers should send their sons to school and participate in their education. The paper frequently lamented the absence of workers' children from the schools in the camps, holding workers responsible. Describing fathers' duty to bring their children up correctly, the paper noted that "the father of the family has this responsibility above all: the preparation of his children. . . . [I]ndustrial schools will provide the educational means and the preparation that his children need."[81] The paper deplored the fact that a large number of children in the camps attended school only sporadically and that their parents did little to combat this truancy.

Fathers, as heads of households, had to assimilate a new set of responsibilities. They could no longer spend their wages and free time as they wished outside the home. Now, as an article on "fatherhood" put it, "every father of a family has the obligation of being the provider and of thinking of his family's future." Workers had to begin to think about dedicating their wages to their families and beginning to save so as "to protect their sons and wives from the blows of misfortune." A worker's savings would provide his family insurance against work accidents and loss of life.[82] One had to plan not only for his own future but also for that of his wife and children.

As part of its campaign to build a new sense of masculine responsibility among the mine workers, the company also instructed workers on how to organize social institutions that would provide them economic security. Schools and the company paper provided information on forming consumer and savings cooperatives and mutual aid societies. In a column on "civic education," the company paper offered histories of mutual aid societies, credit unions, and consumer cooperatives and described how workers should form their own institutions to protect themselves against the insecurities of their economic situations. These forms of social organization would establish a new sense of the importance of savings, serve as a safety net, and supplant union activity and labor conflict as the route to economic improvement. In 1923, for example, *El Teniente* heralded the formation of the Cooperative of Consumption, Saving, and Social Welfare for workers in the camps as a panacea to workers' economic woes.[83]

Consistent with the Chilean state's new role in intervening to administer labor relations and engage in limited social reform during the early 1920s, the company also argued for the need for legislation to regulate and "harmonize" relations between labor and capital and to solve labor conflicts and eliminate strikes. Rather than preach a liberal message of government nonintervention, the company called on the Chilean state to regulate labor relations to ensure labor peace and to implement social programs that, like the programs of its own Welfare Department, would contribute to the social and cultural "improvement" of the work-force. State-sponsored education, hygiene programs, and housing would better workers' material conditions and impede the development of a militant labor movement.[84]

The North American company identified the cultural training and social reform of its working-class population with the need to impart to workers and their families a sense of the rights and duties of citizenship. As company managers argued to Chilean politicians who visited the mine, social welfare work produced both disciplined workers and "better citizens." The company sought to teach its migrant workforce a sense of civic responsibility. Workers' identification with a nation and their sense of belonging to a people and a state, their sense of themselves as citizens, would help them adapt to the new requirements and obligations of labor in a modern enterprise.

Company vocational and night schools offered classes in Chilean history and social studies, and every issue of the company paper carried articles on national historical figures, battles, the Chilean constitution, and social and labor legislation. Workers could open the paper and read biographies of such national heroes as Bernardo O'Higgins and Manuel Rodríguez and detailed accounts of important battles in Chilean history, including the 1879 Battle of Iquique and the various battles fought during the wars of independence.[85] The company paper also sought to educate workers about social institutions and laws, carrying weekly articles on mutual aid societies, savings and credit institutions for workers, consumer cooperatives, and work-related accident and social security legislation.[86] In 1920, the company initiated a series in its paper on "civic education," positing that such "will be profitable for the citizens and the fathers of families, who will extend it to their sons who are the fathers and citizens of tomorrow."[87] *Tópicos del Teniente* thus conflated the duties of citizenship with the obligations of male heads of households. Citizenship, with its rights and responsibilities, was a male domain. The company linked the education of men toward assumption of their role as citizens with their training as workers and household heads. Publishing frequent articles on "civil law," "the articles of the constitution," "the civil marriage law," "the electoral law," and "military service," the paper lamented that "the majority of Chileans" were ignorant of the constitutional foundations and history of the republic, which were ultimately the pillars of "society and the home." Thus, *Tópicos del Teniente* editorialized, "Chileans must study and educate themselves about their duties and their rights."[88] For this purpose, the company's night extension school offered male workers instruction in "the economic, industrial, commercial, political, and intellectual development of Chile."[89]

For the company, the home and the nation constituted the two spheres in which men should carry out the duties of citizenship. Workers should ground their lives in their families and their country. Citizenship thus denoted the legal rights enjoyed by men under the nation-state and their social and sexual rights as heads of homes. The language used to describe the *patria* and the family often overlapped. Thus, in an editorial on "La Patria," the company advised workers that "to remember the glories of the patria is to remember the virtues of the mother." The editorial explicitly conflated identification with the patria with the construction of nuclear families. It counseled that "to remember the glory of the patria is to desire a home, and a home that is tranquil, orderly, governed by love."[90] Similarly, in "Concept of the Patria," the paper told workers that "in this great home everyone has duties and rights . . . and the first of them is to love, respect, and defend the ideals of the patria that are based on a historical and moral tradition, of which we are part." The worker who failed to respect the patria and its history, the paper wrote, "is a degenerate. He is as immoral as a bad son . . . because the patria is another mother that has given us our intellectual and moral being."[91] In another article again evoking the great history and traditions of the Chilean family, the "Madre Patria," *Tópicos del Teniente* described the many military victories of Chilean soldiers and the "marriage" of the "noble Araucanian race" and the Spanish race. In language that evoked images of marriage and the family, the paper looked forward to the day when "there is one sole nation, spiritually speaking, whose union will consist of all the Chilean souls."[92]

Ironically, then, the North American company sought to introduce in its workforce a sense of belonging not just to nuclear families but to the larger family of the nation as well. It hoped that patriotism and citizenship, with the values of family life, would contribute to the domesticization of its labor force. It offered male workers the privileges of citizenship in the nation and the authority of the patriarch in the household. While imposing its own private regime of discipline in the camps, Braden Copper Company attempted to make workers aware of their legal rights and the positive aspects of social legislation and organization. While constructing its own North American fiefdom in the mine, it instructed workers to identify with the Chilean patria and to integrate themselves into the nation-state by assuming the gendered rights and responsibilities of citizenship.

The Braden Copper Company's promotion of national social and labor legislation and the ideals of citizenship and civic virtue resonated to the impulses of Chilean social reformers; politicians from the middle class– and working class–based Radical and Democratic Parties; and representatives of Chile's major industries. Reformers looked to the company's corporate welfare programs as a model for active state intervention to respond to the "social question" during the early 1920s. In 1921, for example, congressional deputy Carlos Briones Luco of the Radical Party wrote to request information about the North American company's dry law and new industrial policies. Briones Luco, an engineer and former military officer, had participated in various national movements for social reform, including as a delegate to the national association of nitrate producers, where he worked on "the welfare conditions of the working class" in the nitrate fields.[93] Briones Luco received a lengthy report from the Welfare Department that elaborated the many advantages for workers of welfare programs: increased savings, involvement in social works and patriotic activities, better appearance, the elimination of criminality, participation in social clubs and sports teams, and attendance at vocational schools. In addition, the company informed Briones Luco that the system of corporate welfare helped to instill the values of citizenship and to build "robust" families based on the foundation of civil marriage. This transformation of workers' social and cultural lives, according to the company, resulted in increased work attendance ("the worker stops celebrating Saint Monday") and efficiency. And, most important, "the social question" in the mine was absent "except for and owing to the influence of foreign organizations and professional agitators."[94]

The following year, Pedro Aguirre Cerda, then a leader of the Radical Party and representative of the Chilean coal industry, wrote Braden to inquire about its welfare policies. Like other politicians, Aguirre Cerda was particularly interested in the copper company's claims that "welfare work tends materially to reduce strikes."[95] Braden supplied Aguirre Cerda with a description of its welfare program and its supposed benefits. Because of the Welfare Department's activities, company representatives argued, "the worker lives better, his family is well constituted, he earns more, he is better educated and more cultured. He and his family are more healthy, understand better and develop the spirit of saving, and he is a better citizen." And, most significant, the company's social welfare system reduced "absenteeism or social crimes."[96]

That same year, the company commented favorably on the visit of deputy Emilio Tizzani of a reformist "social Christian" wing of the Conservative Party to the mine's vocational schools as an important step in winning politicians' support for state welfare programs and for state intervention in labor-capital relations.[97] In response to the deputy's visit, *El Teniente* argued for legislation to regulate and harmonize labor relations: "State intervention is absolutely indispensable to solve [strikes]. The absence of special laws about these matters means that in our country strikes are an endemic and national evil." State intervention in labor-capital relations and social legislation were the solution to worker conflicts. Thus the company proposed that the state establish and bear the financial burden of new programs to "inculcate in the citizens the habit of cleanliness, provide hygienic and cheap housing, control the quality of food, combat alcoholism . . . , legislate and regulate prostitution and prevent syphilis."[98] Similarly, the company noted that Chile was "backward by many years in its social legislation and on the road to progress and social welfare." As a result, the company maintained, it had fallen to "private initiative to remedy the lack of state welfare."[99] The paper applauded the interest of Chilean politicians such as Tizzani in implementing welfare policies at the state level.

Reformers interested in promoting industrial progress and economic modernization in Chile also lauded the North American copper company's social programs. In 1923, in a study written for the University of Chile's seminar in economic and social sciences, Santiago Macchiavello Varas wrote a detailed study of Chile's copper industry in which he echoed the Braden Copper Company's call for national social legislation. Macchiavello Varas concluded that one of the obstacles to Chilean national development, in both the mining industry and industry in general, was the lack of government regulation of workers' labor and living conditions. He argued for the establishment of state-run vocational schools to instruct workers in mining and industrial arts and for the implementation of work security regulations, medical care, improved housing, and better wages as a means of increasing worker productivity and eliminating the social question. Social legislation would prevent "alcoholism, unhealthy living and working quarters, excessive labor, venereal diseases, and moral decadence."[100] He maintained that providing workers legal protections and securities would promote, rather than impede, industrial progress, because "the United States . . . is the country with the most strict regulations and is, however, the most advanced in industrial progress. . . . [T]he state now has the obligation to serve as the harmonizer between the forces of production, represented by workers and entrepreneurs."[101] Macchiavello Varas particularly lauded the social welfare policies of the Braden Copper Company as a national example of how the regulation of family life and social conditions had built a stable and productive labor force: "In El Teniente, to national applause, they have done everything possible to organize the family according to the law, and this has not only contributed to the improvement of the country, but has also made the company more productive and prosperous, making the worker permanent and facilitating relations between capital and labor."[102] Echoing the company itself, he argued that the Chilean state should build on the Braden Copper Company's model of welfare capitalism.

In fact, this national interest in an active role for the state in administering labor relations and regulating social conditions bore fruit in the 1920 election of Arturo Alessandri Palma to the presidency at the head of a "Liberal Alliance" coalition with the support of the Democratic and Radical Parties and many working-class votes. During a turbulent and often conflictive campaign against the right-wing parties of the Chilean aristocracy that included troop mobilizations, assaults on unions, and pitched battles between workers and the police, Alessandri pledged to implement social and labor reforms and bring an end to the exclusionary system of oligarchic rule by the Liberal and Conservative Parties organized in the National Alliance. Alessandri brought many prominent politicians from the middle class–based parties into his cabinet—including Carlos Briones Luco, Briones Luco's brother Ramón, and Pedro Aguirre Cerda—during his five years in office, which marked the first entrance of Democrats and Radicals into the government. Despite the populist promise of the 1920 campaign, however, Alessandri's government found its efforts to pass social legislation stymied by an uncooperative congress controlled by traditional elite interests. Locked in a stalemate with congress, the first three years of Alessandri's presidency were largely ineffective.

In 1924, a military intervention led by senior officers broke the standoff between Alessandri and congress. Alessandri resigned the presidency and went into voluntary exile, while the military junta, with the support of Radicals such as Briones Luco, pushed some of his government's legislative projects through congress, including new social security and welfare laws and laws regulating unionization and labor contracts. As the junta expressed its support for a return to traditional rule by the parties of the National Alliance, however, a second military movement, led by reformist junior officers, including Carlos Ibáñez and future Socialist Party leader Marmaduke Grove, assailed the junta's identification with the oligarchy and called for Alessandri's return. Alessandri came back from exile and, backed by the military, called a constitutional convention that authored a new presidentialist political system that redistributed power from the congress to the executive branch.

Despite Alessandri's victory in 1920 and the implementation of social legislation and the new constitution in 1924–1925, however, state policies toward organized labor changed little. Most social and labor legislation remained unenforced, and Alessandri's military backers, especially Carlos Ibáñez, who remained as minister of war in 1925, pursued traditional tactics of social control in both the nitrate fields and the copper mines. Throughout the early 1920s, the El Teniente miners organized in the company-controlled union attempted periodic rebellions against the copper company's authority, presenting petitions and organizing strikes in an effort to affiliate the union with the FOCh. But, while the Alessandri government turned a blind eye, these workers' movements were routinely crushed and their organizers dismissed.

In 1921, when the leaders of the company-controlled Consejo Federal de los Operarios del Teniente attempted to reaffiliate their union with the FOCh, Braden responded with another wave of dismissals that effectively ended the independent union drive.[103] The national federation had affiliated with the Red International of Labor Unions that year, signaling the completion of its turn to the left and Recabarren's POS, and the company was more determined than ever to eliminate its influence from the mining camps. The workers' strike to protest the firings was quickly crushed by carabineros and soldiers sent from Rancagua.[104] Later that year, after miners' renewed effort to hold a public union meeting, the company dissolved the union and confiscated its locals in the camps with the help of the police.[105] The following year the Communist Party held its founding congress in Rancagua, as did the FOCH, as part of larger efforts to organize the El Teniente copper miners and to incorporate them into the FOCH and the party. A retired foundry worker whose father worked in the foundry throughout the 1920s, remembers that "the second of January 1922 they organized this congress of the Partido Obrero Socialista, and it changed its name to the Partido Comunista de Chile, and the influence of that brought as a consequence that it gave an orientation to the workers who arrived at the mine to give them motivation to keep trying to organize a union, which the Braden Copper Company opposed terribly with all its force."[106]

Two years later, in 1924, the El Teniente workers and organizers from the FOCH and the PC attempted once again to organize an independent union, the Sindicato Industrial de El Teniente, hopeful that the military intervention and new social legislation would open space for labor organizing and social reform. The company Welfare Department reported that "labor agitation" had been extremely active in the mine "on the part of some Chilean organizations which hoped to take advantage of the sudden change of government . . . and the workmen of this and other companies have been subjected to extensive propaganda inciting them to strike."[107] As before, the company refused to acknowledge the law and fired 659 workers, bringing a rapid end to the new organization.[108] Although the company claimed that the number of workers fired was lower, Braden admitted that it had arrested and evicted over 150 workers and 10 union leaders from the El Teniente camps with the approval of a "delegate of the government" and the aid of carabineros. Braden stated openly that while it supported workers' recreational organizations and mutual aid societies, it "would not permit other types of associations and even less so those that are founded to foment class hatred and to pursue activities against discipline and work."[109]

Finally, in 1925 the Braden Copper Company submitted to pressures from the military junta headed by Marmaduke Grove and Carlos Ibáñez and allowed the formation of a miners' union in El Teniente. Until 1938, however, it maintained control of this union by carefully overseeing public and private space in the camps. Nationally, following Alessandri's return in 1925, the government proved no more sympathetic to organized labor. Under Ibáñez's orders the military continued to quell strikes in the nitrate fields and copper mines with bloody force. After Alessandri's resignation in 1925 because of conflicts with Ibáñez, Ibáñez ruled behind the scenes until he was officially voted into the office of the presidency in controlled elections in 1927, placing an emphatic end to the brief period of social reform.

During Ibáñez's government, between 1927 and 1931, the social reforms and labor legislation passed in 1924 and 1925 remained unenforced, and the state continued its traditional coercive response to labor unrest.[110] Ibáñez launched a campaign of repression against the FOCH, the Communist Party, and anarchist groups. The Braden Copper Company welcomed the end of the experiment with social reform and the return to traditional forms of rule. In 1927, President Ibáñez met with William Braden, who was representing the U.S. copper companies in Chile. Braden informed the Chilean president that while the companies and U.S. investors had had harmonious and satisfactory relationships with the governments of previous presidents, they had been troubled by the social and labor legislation and new tax laws passed during the years of the Alessandri administration. He criticized a 12 percent tax on the companies' earnings imposed by Alessandri's government as unfair and discriminatory. In response, Ibáñez assured Braden of his opposition to the "discriminatory" taxation of U.S. companies, promised tax deductions, and pledged the state's support for the North American copper companies. Ibáñez also stated his commitment to maintaining "labor peace" in the copper mines. Ibáñez's pledge was made concrete by his government's failure to enforce the 1924–1925 labor legislation in El Teniente and its support of the North American company's efforts to thwart the organization of an independent union.[111]

Through the 1920s, then, the Braden Copper Company relied on traditional repressive responses, backed by the state, to suppress workers' movements in the El Teniente mine. Although the North American company implemented a social welfare system and engaged in projects of cultural reform based on the regulation of gender relations and sexuality, ultimately only its strict regime of social control guaranteed labor peace in the copper mine. At the state level, the social programs implemented under Alessandri remained unenforced, and organized labor and the Left met with repression from the Ibáñez regime. Migration to other sectors of the economy during upswings in nitrate production and national economic growth after 1927 proved to be mine workers' most reliable strategy of resistance to company authority. Hundreds of El Teniente workers moved to the northern nitrate fields during the nitrate economy's final surge between 1927 and 1929. A U.S. consulate report written in 1932 noted that the Braden Copper Company continued to suffer from high levels of labor turnover. Noting that Chilean miners' work and social habits had not changed, the report described the conflict between "the easy-going temperament of the Chilean working man" and "the relentless driving policy of Braden." El Teniente obreros, the report argued in the same racially condescending tones employed by company management, "like most Latin American laborers . . . will work long enough to keep the wolf from the door but when the immediate future is provided for they much prefer to loaf." According to the report, instead of resigning their jobs, mine workers would "hang on as long as they can without doing any work, until finally they are discovered and fired." Then, the report noted, "after the lazy streak has worn itself off they come back looking for jobs again like truant schoolboys."[112]

Thus, until 1930, the company's corporate welfare program had failed to transform miners' work habits and patterns of sociability. That year, following the world economic crisis and the collapse of Chile's export economy, workers engaged in a wildcat strike led by transient single workers and FOCH activists. The company reported that the strike had been provoked by "pressure from an organized and threatening group composed of bachelor workmen who do not so much need the daily wage and do not share the responsibilities of a man with a wife and children to support." These men, allegedly in concert with "professional agitators," "gave impulse to the strike movement, deceiving the ignorant and credulous mob with wild promises of impossible wage increases, dismissal of unpopular managers, reduction in cost of living, etc."[113] The 1930 strike, like strikes the previous decade, turned into an uprising in which the "mob" of workers revolted against declining real wages and harsh work conditions and was put down by the military and police.

Despite the Braden Copper Company's social welfare policies, the end of oligarchic political rule under the parliamentary republic, and new national projects of social and labor reform, relations between labor, capital, and the state in the copper industry remained much the same at the end of the decade of the 1920s as they had been at the beginning of the century. Mine workers continued to locate their resistance to the demands of the modern industry and authority of the North American company in traditional forms of transience and labor upheavals. The company had been unable to eradicate the disruptive forms of sociability of its "bachelor workmen." As the Great Depression dealt the nitrate industry its final blow and copper became the sole engine of Chile's export economy after 1930, the North American copper company confronted a working-class population unwilling to accommodate to the reorganization and regulation of its social life and labor.

3   Community, Politics, and the Invention

of a Labor Tradition

The 1929–1932 world economic crisis initiated profound transformations in the life of El Teniente's mining community. The international economic collapse threw Chile into a deep recession and led to the final decline of the nitrate export economy that had fueled growth since the late nineteenth century. While the world recession provoked reductions and cutbacks in the copper mines, the nitrate industry experienced a more serious collapse. International prices for nitrates dropped by 50 percent and production fell by over 80 percent between 1929 and 1933.[1] The disruption of nitrate production led to huge budget deficits and major cutbacks in government-sponsored public works projects and railroads, as well as in urban industries and the southern coal mines. As thousands of unemployed nitrate miners moved south to the countryside, copper mining regions, and urban centers, unemployment skyrocketed and real wages stagnated.

The demise of the nitrate industry and growing conflicts between rural workers and large landowners in the countryside during the 1930s limited the opportunities for El Teniente workers to migrate to other sectors of the economy. With their mobility restricted, many men and women began to settle in the mine, attracted by the North American company's corporate welfare system, high wages, and social benefits. As men and women began to make their lives in El Teniente, they found in the labor traditions of the nitrate fields and the ideology of the Left a coherent narrative of the past that undergirded their emergent sense of community and class. Many former nitrate miners moved to the copper mine and brought with them experiences of labor conflict and leftist political activism. In addition, when the copper industry returned to a period of growth after 1933, activists from the Communist and Socialist Parties worked to organize an independent union and working-class base in El Teniente.

Community and Politics

The collapse of the nitrate industry and the usurpation by landlords of common lands and inquilinos' plots on large estates during the 1930s restricted mine workers' mobility and led workers who had migrated to the north or who had continued to work in agriculture to look to a career in El Teniente as the most secure future. Company policy reinforced the tendency of workers to turn to mine labor. During downswings in international demand for copper and cutbacks in production after 1929, the company dismissed workers from the more transient and less skilled population of single workers, allowing the development of a stable core of trained married workers. As early as 1930, the company reported that its "constant concern had been to demand the legal constitution of the workers' families and only after an intense campaign and the dismissal of he who didn't want to submit has it been able to give legal character to all the children and recognized marriage ties to many couples who lived in disorder."[2]

In 1932, the company added an additional bonus to workers' salaries in response to radically declining real wages and increases in the cost of living following the 1929 crisis. The Welfare Department decided to give workers with families a monthly bonus and a "family allowance" that would enable married workers to maintain their families as their real wages stagnated as well as the company to retain its married workforce in the camps. By granting workers with wives and children special bonuses (a standard fee for a wife and then different bonuses for children below sixteen), the company encouraged workers and women in the camps to formalize their unions in civil marriage and to legitimize their children. It thus provided economic incentive for women and men to form households in which women and children depended on men's wages and benefits. In addition, as the cost of living soared nationally during the early 1930s, the company created a new automatic wage increase that would help to keep workers' earnings commensurate with inflation. The *escala móvil* (cost-of-living raise) provided automatic salary increases with every 5 percent increase in the cost of living, although in practice it is unclear how consistently the company actually implemented the periodic wage hikes. Thus, during the 1930s, the company backed its gendered social welfare policies with the establishment of a "family wage" designed to bolster the pillars of the emergent male-headed nuclear family in the mining camps.

Men and women in El Teniente frequently married so that they could qualify for these benefits. The Sewell court heard a number of cases of men and women who wanted to endow their children with legitimate legal status. In 1946, for example, Pedro Antonio Pinto petitioned the court in Sewell to grant his son legitimacy. He and the child's mother were finally marrying according to company regulations and wanted "to legitimize our son because it is necessary so that he can receive the family allowance and so that the conceded benefit be granted and our son's legitimacy be legally accepted."[3] In a similar case, the *capataz* (foreman) Raúl Penvoz Pantay married the mother of his illegitimate son, Alicia Amadadana Buanas Paz, "since it is necessary so that he can receive, among other things, the family allowance."[4] Thus, the North American company's system of social benefits and "the family wage" encouraged men and women to enter into legal civil marriages.

By the 1940s, roughly half of the El Teniente workforce of six to seven thousand was married. The company's restrictions on women's work and sexual relationships in the camps, the institutionalization of the corporate welfare system, and miners' relatively high wages and bonuses had induced many male and female workers to marry and settle permanently in El Teniente. The changes in relations between men and women in El Teniente are reflected in the records of the civil registry. The camps' registry was established in 1917 when the company implemented its regulation requiring that all sexual alliances be formalized in marriage. In that year, 170 couples married. Of these, many were *convivientes* (couples who lived together in consensual unions) who sought to follow the new company rules and also to legitimize their children in order to receive company benefits. Seventy-two of these couples asked that the registry bestow legal status on their children.[5] Five years later, seventy-one couples married, ten requesting that their children be legitimized.[6] And, in 1935, revealing the efficacy of the company's welfare policies and the drop in informal consensual unions between men and women in the camps, of sixty-four registered marriages in the camps, only six couples requested that their children receive legitimate status.[7] By the late 1930s, informal consensual unions between men and women had declined, and the population of married workers and of women in the camps had risen significantly. In 1935, the company Welfare Department reported that "the continuity of operation has built up a fairly permanent personnel whose life is centered in the Plant. They were hired as married men, or married in Sewell and have begotten children here—the family increases year by year."[8] Whereas in 1915 slightly less than 18 percent of the 5,879 adult residents in the camps were women, in 1937 almost half of El Teniente's 7,440 workers were married (3,503), and 3,000 women lived in the camps, triple the number of women from 1915. This trend continued throughout the 1940s; by the end of the decade, although the number of men in the camps had dropped to 6,055 from 7,440 owing to the postwar recession, the number of women had increased to 3,649.[9] The reduction of production had fallen most heavily on the shoulders of the mine's single workers.

The establishment of a permanent workforce during the late 1930s and 1940s did not, however, lead to the industrial peace planned on by the North American company. Although the company was able to consolidate a stable community of workers in the camps, its paternalist policies could not make workers easily forget their material hardships or the lessons of an informal, militant, political culture inherited from the nitrate mines and actively disseminated by former nitrate workers and militants of left-wing political parties. Despite the paternalist veneer produced by social welfare programs, life and labor in the El Teniente mine were still hard, and workers were subject to the constraints of a rigorous regime of discipline in both their work and their personal lives. As unemployed nitrate workers left the north in search of work after 1930, many arrived in El Teniente, where they transmitted the political culture of the northern labor movement. Leftist political parties also played an important role in communicating this militant political culture to El Teniente's workers. They supplied a language, series of myths, and a general historical narrative of the past that found resonance in the miners' concrete experiences of life and work in the copper mine. The El Teniente workers had no common experience of community, no mutual, unified vision of the past, and no labor tradition on which they could draw on to confront changes in their lives and work in the copper industry. To define a shared identity, the miners reinvented a political and labor tradition inherited from the northern nitrate pampas.[10]

Many workers who migrated to El Teniente had worked in northern ports and nitrate fields and had experienced labor and leftist political activism there. Although nitrate production declined steadily following the First World War, periodic upswings in production drew workers away from the copper mine. In 1923, for example, El Teniente's general manager described the "acute scarcity of labor" that had been created because "thousands of workmen have gone to the nitrate fields in the north, and there is a demand for several thousand more, even though only approximately 55% of the 'oficinas' are operating."[11] Similarly, in 1927 the general manager noted that a boom in nitrate production had drawn large numbers of El Teniente workers to the north, thus precipitating another labor shortage in the copper mine.[12] A former Braden Copper Company foreman, supervisor, and general manager also recalls that a significant segment of the El Teniente workforce was composed of often rowdy and unruly unemployed workers from the nitrate fields who found their way to El Teniente following the collapse of the nitrate industry.[13]

Oral histories with men and women who grew up in the mining camps underline that although a majority of miners came from small towns and had worked as agricultural laborers, they also migrated to different sectors of the economy, following seasonal patterns in the countryside and the fluctuations of the nitrate export economy. In a number of cases, El Teniente workers who traveled to the north returned to the copper mine and settled there permanently after 1930. One retired El Teniente employee whose father came from a rural town outside Rancagua and worked in El Teniente beginning in the mid-1920s recalls that most miners came from agricultural areas around Talca, Chillán, and Rancagua. But he also notes that they were not settled and that many moved to the north in search of work: "The miner was a searcher. He went wherever he could in search of the best job and the best pay." His father began work in El Teniente around 1926 or 1927 but then left for the nitrate oficinas. When the nitrate industry went bust in 1929, his father returned to work in the copper mine, married, and brought up his family in the El Teniente camps.[14] Similarly, a woman who grew up in the camps and married the son of a miner remembers that her father-in-law, who came from an agricultural town near the mine, had also left El Teniente in the late 1920s to work in the nitrate oficinas but had returned to the copper mine following the 1929 crisis. He worked for the rest of his life as a miner, as did his son.[15] Stories like these are common in El Teniente. Thus, while company records that document workers' birthplaces depict a workforce with origins in the countryside, it is likely that a significant number of rural workers had journeyed at one time during the 1920s to work in the nitrate fields.

Workers who had been in the north came to El Teniente with the experience both of mine labor and union activism. Popular memory in El Teniente holds that these workers transmitted the traditions of the unions of the militant nitrate miners to the El Teniente workforce. The experiences and culture of the labor movement in the north became part of the El Teniente copper miners' collective memory, constituting a coherent narrative of the past that lent meaning to their present. This narrative began with nitrate workers' struggles against foreign capital; the organization of workers' resistance societies (*mancomunales*) as the seed of future labor organization; the role of Emilio Recabarren and Elías Lafertte in founding the POS and Communist Party and in working with the FOCH; the first general strike in Chilean history; and the repeated massacres of nitrate workers and their families that marked the map of Chilean labor relations during the first decades of the century. The history of the nitrate miners paralleled the experience of the copper miners: brutal and onerous working conditions, geographical isolation in an enclave economy, state repression, authoritarian labor regimes run by foreign companies, constant labor strife, and momentous strikes. In addition, the copper miners shared with the nitrate miners the fact that they labored in industries that drove the Chilean economy.

The sense of continuity between the histories of the nitrate and copper miners was expressed well by a retired miner who remembers that "the miners of El Teniente have an incredible history of struggle because a lot of people came from the north when they closed the nitrate oficinas to work in the mine, and those people were combative [*gente de lucha*] and those people began to teach other people. . . . [T]hey brought their knowledge and experience and practiced it here in the mine."[16] Similarly, a former foundry worker recalls that the Communist Party enjoyed support among copper miners during the 1930s because of its history in the nitrate mines:

> In the country there was a consciousness of what had developed historically, for what had been done in the north, because the first unions were those of the north in the epoch of nitrates, the Federa-

ción Obrera de Chile created the mancomunales, . . . that had a lot of repercussions, together with having brought together thousands of workers that spread all over the country. It had repercussions from Magallanes to the north of the country. The Federación began to facilitate union organizations, including in El Teniente. . . . With the fall of nitrates a lot of people who were organized in the north spread throughout the country because there was a crisis in the year '32. There was a great decrease in the production of nitrates, so a lot of people had to go south during those years. Those people, wherever they went, organized because they brought with them the incipient orientation that had been given them by the unionists in the north, headed by Recabarren, Lafertte was also a great agitator, a unionist also in that epoch . . . and many of them came to Sewell, to the [El Teniente] mine.[17]

Copper miners located the origins of their own history in nitrate workers' heroicized labor traditions. This shared historical past was communicated through the presence of former workers from the north and organizers from the FOCH and Communist Party in the mine. Thus the former foundry worker remembers that one of the leaders of the campaigns to organize an independent miners' union in El Teniente during the 1930s was Oscar Astudillo, a Communist Party militant who "had been in the north," and that "besides him there were a number of other compañeros from the north." Astudillo was "a very valuable compañero and very developed in terms of his condition of a worker-autodidact." He had "developed himself politically being in the [Communist] party and having been for many years a union activist and organized worker also in the north" before he came to El Teniente. He concludes that the "spreading out of the nitrate workers had repercussions in the unions in Chile and in the 'new wave' [of labor militancy] in the copper mines" during the 1930s.[18] Although former nitrate miners may not have composed a majority of El Teniente workers, their presence in the workforce helped to disseminate the traditions and ideology of the labor movement in the north, as these miners remember. At the same time, the narrative structure and teleology of the memories of these miners, in which the El Teniente workers' class militancy is traced to origins in the nitrate fields, the FOCH, and the POS, reflects the ways in which anecdotes and stories of the northern labor movement transmitted by former nitrate miners and militants of the leftist parties became naturalized for the El Teniente workers and part of their own symbolic, collective past.

In his stories and memoirs of life in El Teniente, writer Baltazar Castro, who was raised in Rancagua and worked as an employee of the Braden Copper Company, also describes the role played by former nitrate miners in developing a labor tradition in the mining camps. Castro published stories, letters, and articles in the miners' union paper during the late 1930s and 1940s before becoming a deputy for the Socialist Party in 1949. In addition, he spoke at union meetings and public gatherings. As a deputy from a left-wing faction of the PS, the Popular Socialist Party (PSP), Castro was, for example, arrested in 1951 in the El Teniente miners' union hall for transmitting radio broadcasts in support of an illegal strike.[19] As a writer, he became the pride of the miners' community, known by all and heralded as their own spokesman. To this day almost every miner can talk about Castro and his writings. In addition to providing detailed descriptions of his life experiences in the camps, his texts offer a glimpse of the ways in which an "official" union and leftist narrative was constructed and disseminated in the camps.

In one of Castro's stories of life in El Teniente, the narrator, a mine worker, recounts how he learned of the nitrate miners' militant labor activism from a friend of his father, who "spoke of the time when he worked in the nitrate oficinas where he met Luis Emilio Recabarren." From these stories, Castro writes, "the epic struggles of the northern miners came alive. We entertained ourselves for hours and hours."[20] In another story, Castro recounts how a former nitrate worker "brought that marvelous material with which we delighted ourselves during the long nights in Sewell after dinner. . . . He knew the northern sea, the desert, the nitrate fields, and extraordinary men like Luis Emilio Recabarren." This work comrade described his first experiences with labor actions, strikes, and conflicts with the police and thus imparted to his listeners the world of the nitrate fields.[21] In yet another story, a miner shares his experiences of labor activism in the north, describing how he arrived with Recabarren at a nitrate oficina "preaching the necessity of organization to the working class of the nitrate fields. The police persecuted us like dogs." In addition, the miner tells stories of the mobilizations of the northern workers in support of the populist presidential candidate Arturo Alessandri in 1920: "We went out into the streets: Alessandri! Alessandri! To speak of 'the Lion' [Alessandri] then was like heresy. We received beatings from the police and stonings from the supporters of Barros Borgoño [the traditional rightist candidate]."[22]

Gonzalo Drago, like Castro a writer of national acclaim who had worked in El Teniente and wrote short stories based on his memories of life and work there during the 1930s and 1940s, also contributed to the folklore surrounding nitrate miners. In one story in his book about El Teniente, *Cobre: Cuentos mineros,* he describes how following the Great Depression "the nitrate fields, paralyzed, continued to vomit workers to the four points of the globe. The most fortunate had been able to get work as miners in El Teniente, and there they piled up, noisy, violent or aggressive, attracted by the deceptive lure of the mine."[23] In another story, a former nitrate miner instructs a young El Teniente worker about life in the nitrate pampa: "That's for men, compañero. You have to know life. I went all over the pampa when I was a kid."[24] Like Castro, Drago romanticizes the strength, experience, and essential manliness of the former nitrate miners, whose hardiness, force, and experience he contrasts in various stories with the innocence of young men who go to the mine without prior work experience. Many of Drago's stories, like Castro's, employ a basic narrative structure in which an inexperienced young man from the countryside goes to work in El Teniente, encounters the hard-working and hard-fighting former nitrate miners, and then, after months or years of labor, is himself converted into a man in the mine and wins the respect of the older miners and his work comrades.

The memoirs and stories of Castro and Drago represent the elaboration of a popular mythology and collective historical memory that traced the origins of labor militancy in El Teniente to the northern pampas. As "organic intellectuals," to use Antonio Gramsci's famous phrase, these writers converted popular folklore and anecdotes in the mine into organized narratives. Their stories and memoirs *described* the role of former nitrate workers in the mines. But they also reflected, as well as contributed to, the invention of a labor tradition in El Teniente that located the history of miners in the nitrate fields and the FOCh. The romantic portraits painted of former nitrate workers and union activists in El Teniente helped cement the mythic figures of Recabarren and Lafertte, leaders of both the FOCh and the PC, in the popular iconography of the mine. Writers such as Castro and Drago who rose to national prominence after working in El Teniente joined workers who had labored in the north, along with Communist and Socialist Party activists, in making the history of the nitrate miners' struggles part of the imagined collective past of the El Teniente copper miners.

The cutoff of migration from El Teniente to the north, arrival of former nitrate workers in the mining camps, and dissemination of the labor traditions of the nitrate mines coincided with increasing conflicts between large landowners and peasants in the countryside. Following the 1930 economic crisis, confrontations between campesinos and hacendados in Chile's countryside escalated. In his study of peasant movements in Chile, Brian Loveman notes that during the 1930s "campesinos challenged the extensive political meaning of property in rural land individually and through ad hoc strike committees organized to defend their interests."[25] Peasants and rural laborers engaged in informal acts of resistance and more organized forms of protest to demand the reestablishment of traditional prerogatives such as rights to land that had been rescinded by landowners or higher wages and improved working conditions. In addition, after 1935 Emilio Zapata's Trotskyist Liga Nacional de Defensa de Campesinos Pobres (National League for the Defense of Poor Peasants) embarked on a campaign both in congress and in the countryside to improve the conditions of rural workers and peasants. By the late 1930s, the Communist Party had also begun a campaign to establish rural unions, at times competing with Zapata's Liga. These rural labor conflicts both impelled agricultural laborers from the towns surrounding El Teniente to look for permanent work in the mine during the 1930s and 1940s and contributed to their politicization.

One El Teniente miner, who grew up in the mining camps during the 1940s and then became a miner himself, has discussed the origins of his father's entry into the Communist Party and the El Teniente miners' union after participating in a campesino movement during the 1930s.[26] His father had been a small landholder who resided in the agricultural town of Machalí, only a dozen miles from El Teniente, and worked on the large farms in the area to supplement the family's income. During the 1930s, landowners began to fence off the land in the hills surrounding the town on which peasants grew crops and grazed livestock. This "common" land had been used by the campesinos and their families for generations and provided a significant supplement to the wages they earned as workers on the neighboring estates. As the local landowners began to reclaim this land, the Machalí campesinos formed their own movement to assert their claim to the hills outside town. They called themselves *comuneros* (commoners), referring to the common land they had used and shared for years and their membership in the local community.

Ultimately, the movement was defeated, and the miner's father, like many other Machalí campesinos strapped for cash and work, entered El Teniente, where he settled and worked until his death. As an obrero he participated actively in union struggles and eventually joined the Communist Party. His experiences as a comunero led him to identify with the union struggle and with the PC. In 1948 he was arrested for his role in an El Teniente strike and for his activities in the PC and sent to a concentration camp in Pisagua in Chile's north with hundreds of other miners. When interrogated by military officers about his membership in the PC, he responded proudly, "Señores, I am a comunero," indicating the ideological links that connected the peasant movement with his political identity as a Communist.

El Teniente drew on the population of large, landless agricultural workers and small holders who worked part-time as peones in the neighboring valleys. Many workers actually came from Machalí or from nearby towns, where they may have had contact with the comuneros. More important, as Loveman shows, it is likely that many workers in the south, as well as in Chile's central valleys, had suffered similar conflicts with landowners over access to land, wages, and work. The case of one miner, the son of an agricultural laborer, who, like many El Teniente workers, periodically left the countryside to work in the mine, illustrates the prior experiences of many of the landless campesinos who migrated to El Teniente from nearby agricultural estates.[27] When the miner's father had saved a sum of money after a short stint in the mine, he would return to the Santa Carolina estate, seven kilometers north of Rancagua, where he and his family worked as tenant farmers. In return for their labor on the estate, they were provided with a house and a small parcel of land, on which they relied for their subsistence. The miner's family lived and worked on Santa Carolina until the late 1940s when the landowner changed the terms of their arrangement by taking over the plot of land they had traditionally cultivated. He offered them instead another plot of land near a dried-up riverbed. The land was barren and impossible to cultivate because of the lack of irrigation, so the miner's family complained to the landowner. Their protest fell on deaf ears. Carabineros kicked them off the land after they had organized a collective protest with six other families that had also been displaced.

The inquilinos of Santa Carolina did not give up their fight with the *patrón*. They petitioned the Inspección General del Trabajo and went to Santiago, where they were aided by union leaders, the miner's first contact with political parties and unions. As the struggle with the Santa Carolina patrón continued, the miner entered El Teniente to earn money to help his family survive. He stayed until 1973, saving money, which the family used to purchase a small plot of land outside Rancagua. He was active in the miners' union and became a militant of the Communist Party.

During the 1930s and 1940s, then, some rural migrants who arrived in El Teniente, both peasants with access to small plots of land and landless, estate-resident laborers, had already experienced some form of conflict, if not collective movement, with landowners or employers. Rather than an obedient workforce accustomed to the paternalist authority of landowners, these workers came to the mine with a sense of class antagonism. If rural migrants to El Teniente had not had contact with unions before, after arriving in El Teniente they encountered workers from other sectors of the economy—the coal and nitrate mines, ports, public works projects, and urban industries—with experience in the labor movement and leftist political parties.

World Recession and the Reorganization of Labor and the Left

The establishment of a permanent community of married workers and the reinvention of a labor tradition inherited from the north during the 1930s in El Teniente coincided with the reorganization of a unified national labor movement and the rebuilding of the political Left following the years of repression under Ibáñez. Militants of the leftist parties, particularly the Communist Party, and labor organizers worked clandestinely to organize an independent union in El Teniente. In addition, following the world recession a new labor code was passed, and unions were integrated into a state-administered system of labor relations. In El Teniente, the state made its presence felt for the first time when it investigated work conditions and labor relations in the mine. Unlike the traditional enclave economies described in the historical and sociological literature on Latin American mines and plantations, after 1930 the Chilean copper mines remained well integrated into national political life because of the role of the state in regulating labor relations. The significance attached to copper production as copper became Chile's major export gave labor relations in the mines added importance in the world of national politics, and leftist political parties actively sought a working-class base among miners during the 1930s.

The spread of social unrest throughout Chile provoked by the recession, including the 1930 wildcat strike in El Teniente, led the regime of Carlos Ibáñez to implement the hitherto unenforced 1924 labor legislation in a new labor code in 1931. The labor code established a state-directed system of labor relations with which Ibáñez hoped to control labor effervescence and organize working-class support for his regime. Despite these reforms and a declared state of emergency, however, Ibáñez was forced to step down in 1931 because of discontent across the political spectrum with his government's handling of the economic crisis. After a series of military and civilian governments, including the short-lived "Socialist Republic" led by Marmaduke Grove, Arturo Alessandri returned to the presidency in 1932 with the support of the traditional right-wing parties and without the populist political rhetoric and programs of social reform of his first presidential campaign.

Alessandri sought to confront Chile's economic collapse with a series of orthodox austerity measures and conservative fiscal policies. Despite appeals to a new economic nationalism, Alessandri was dedicated to the maintenance of past laissez-faire policies. The Alessandri administration rejected proposals to implement significant tax increases on the foreign-owned nitrate and copper companies, which produced over 90 percent of Chile's exports and provided the bulk of its foreign earnings. Although the government did increase the tax on the nitrate companies to 25 percent, the mostly U.S.-owned organizations continued to control both the production and marketing of nitrates.[28] Alessandri's second administration raised the tax on the North American copper companies to a minimal 18 percent.[29] As copper production expanded between 1933 and 1938, the tax burdens of the North American copper companies remained low. In addition, the government used nitrate and copper revenues to service Chile's foreign debt rather than to promote internal economic growth or industrialization.

Despite its conservative economic policies, the Alessandri government presided over the implementation of the 1931 labor code passed under Ibáñez. The labor code established a corporatist system of labor relations that integrated unions into a network of labor courts, inspectorates, and arbitration boards.[30] It imposed obligatory unionism, compulsory arbitration of labor conflicts, and state direction of union elections and financing. In addition, the code regulated a series of bureaucratic procedures before labor inspectors, labor courts, and arbitration boards that unions had to go through to go on strike. Strikes and union petitions were limited to individual companies, and industry-wide federations were given no legal standing on which to bargain collectively. Workers' unions were divided between obreros (blue-collar workers) and empleados (white-collar workers), each having different legal status and rights within individual firms. In spite of its more restrictive features, however, the labor code established the legal basis for collective bargaining, unionization, and strikes and put in place a state apparatus that might enforce new laws on social security deductions and working conditions. Under Alessandri, hundreds of new unions were organized and legally recognized by the state.

The implementation of the new system of labor relations after 1931 was accompanied by a period of significant political change in Chile. In 1933, following the demise of the Socialist Republic, the Socialist Party was founded, grouping together a diversity of political tendencies under the umbrella of a Marxist commitment to socialism, including former members of the Radical, Democratic, and Communist Parties, as well as anarcho-syndicalist groups. Unlike the Communist Party, which drew on a largely working-class constituency, the Socialist Party located its base in a variety of social sectors: middle-class professionals and intellectuals, white-collar workers, students, urban industrial workers, and former military men such as Grove.[31] Although the Socialist Party became an important force on the Left and in the labor movement, the Communist Party also expanded its base among miners and industrial workers. In 1936, the Socialist, Communist, and Radical Parties forged a Popular

Front political coalition in opposition to Alessandri and the Liberal and Conservative Parties.

The left-center coalition owed its genesis to many factors. Most important was the Communist Party's shift from the isolationist and revolutionary strategy dictated by the Third International to a policy of parliamentary participation based on cooperation with the reformist political parties of the middle class.[32] In 1936, the Communist Party made gestures to both the Radical and Socialist Parties and joined the PS to found a unified national union federation, the Confederación de Trabajadores de Chile (CTCh), which had as its president a Socialist, and as its secretary-general, a Communist. The CTCh combined the remnants of the Communist-led FOCh, with its base among nitrate, coal, and copper miners, and the newer Socialist-dominated Confederación Nacional de Sindicatos de Chile (CNS), which had its base of support among urban industrial workers and white-collar employees.[33]

The temptation of increased electoral power determined the decision of the Radical and Socialist Parties to enter the coalition. A number of Radical Party leaders saw alliances with the leftist parties as the only alternative if they wished to gain national power. Without the working-class votes guaranteed by the Socialist and Communist Parties, the Radicals, who drew on the support of the urban middle class, professionals, and white-collar employees, had little chance of winning the presidency. As Gabriel González Videla, a Radical leader from the left of the party, argued, without an alliance with the PS and the PC, the Radicals would lose the support of the "great workers' unions."[34] Similarly, many leaders of the recently formed Socialist Party were convinced that the experiences of coalition governments based on alliances between the Left and middle-class parties or sectors in Peru, Mexico, and Europe indicated that they should follow a reformist rather than a revolutionary path to socialism. Ultimately, the Socialists understood that they could gain significant electoral support through participation in the coalition.[35]

In El Teniente, the unification of the Left and labor at the national level and the establishment of the new system of labor relations had an important impact on local politics. The FOCh and the Communist Party had played a role in organizing the first miners' union in El Teniente following the First World War but had suffered from company and state repression throughout the 1920s. After 1930, Communist Party militants and union organizers entered the mine's camps once again and, as during the period between 1919 and 1924, sought to wrest the miners' union from company control. Although miners could look to the national labor movement and the Popular Front for support, they received little help from the Alessandri government, which proved to be no more friendly to labor and the Left than Ibáñez had been. Under Alessandri the number of legally recognized unions doubled with the implementation of the labor code, yet the government actively supported employers in labor conflicts and intervened to put an end to strikes. As several writers have noted, the disproportionate number of illegal strikes during the 1930s indicated a high level of working-class mobilization, the restrictive nature of the labor code, and the Alessandri government's antagonistic stance toward organized labor.[36] The Alessandri regime sought to integrate workers into the new system of labor relations through sponsoring unionization, at the same time quelling labor unrest by declaring strikes illegal and turning the state labor apparatus against unions.

In the copper mine, officials appointed by the government supported the copper company's efforts to control union activity, repress left-wing political militants, and suppress strikes, while they moved to enforce certain of the code's provisions in the camps. In 1934, the PC militant Carlos Gaete was elected to the head of the miners' union, which remained under company control. As Gaete went about organizing a petition of workers' demands to present to the company administration following the protocol dictated by the labor code, he was dismissed by the company and evicted from the camps. Moreover, he was arrested by the police for "offenses" (injurias) and then declared an "unhealthy element" in workers' activities and unfit for his post as union leader by the Alessandri-appointed governor of O'Higgins Province. The company rejected a union petition that Gaete be rehired, arguing that it was impossible given his "well-known inclinations for sowing discord."[37] Over the next two years Gaete worked to organize a regional labor federation, the Federación de Sindicatos de O'Higgins, out of local unions and chapters of the FOCH. The federation, with Gaete as its president, lent support to efforts to organize independent unions in El Teniente and became the basis for the formation of a regional branch of the CTCH in 1936.[38]

In 1935, as workers within the union continued to try to establish their independence from the company and protested Gaete's dismissal, Braden fired a number of other union leaders. The local Radical Party paper, *La Tribuna*, accused the Braden Copper Company of consistently violating the 1931 labor code, noting that "since the very beginning of the union, the Braden Copper Company has systematically persecuted all obreros and empleados who have accepted leadership of this organization."[39] The paper denounced the firing of a union leader who, like Gaete, had been evicted from the camps and taken to Rancagua by police, who treated him like "a vulgar criminal." *La Tribuna* also charged provincial officials, labor inspectors, and "representatives of the executive" with supporting Braden and colluding in its efforts to strip union leaders of their legal positions. The paper listed nine other union leaders who had been fired since the early 1930s.[40]

In 1936, after the formation of the Popular Front, CTCh organizers began to enter the El Teniente camps to help build an underground union movement. Organizers from the PC and CTCh scaled the mountain by foot and entered the mining camps clandestinely to hold union meetings at night.[41] In response, according to *La Tribuna*, a North American mine superintendent named Stanley began to demand that workers in the mine withdraw from the union; those who refused, he fired.[42] *La Tribuna* also denounced the joint actions of the company and the provincial governor in trying to break the union and close down the local organizations of the Popular Front in El Teniente. Company officials and the state governor accused the miners' union and Popular Front groups of plotting a "revolutionary strike" and of stealing boxes of dynamite. Despite the energetic denials of the workers and local Popular Front militants, the North American company used these accusations to fire workers and union activists with the support of the governor, who sent special police to detain union leaders and Popular Front activists in the El Teniente camps.[43] In spite of hostility from the company and government, however, two former El Teniente union activists and Communist Party militants, Carlos Riquelme and Carlos Gaete, were elected to the Machalí city council and to congress in 1935 and 1937, respectively, on the Popular Front ticket with the votes of mine workers. This represented the first flexing of the miners' electoral muscle in local elections and demonstrated that their votes and political organization could have an impact at the national level.

The ambiguous nature of state labor policy during the 1930s was reflected in the Alessandri regime's alternately repressive and corporatist stance toward the union movement in El Teniente. While the state continued to back the company's repression of workers' strikes and organizing campaigns, the Ministry of Labor attempted to implement the labor code in the mine and extend the rights to unionize and bargain collectively to the El Teniente workers. In 1937, for example, the minister of labor, Bernardo Leighton of the Catholic social reformist Falange Nacional reported that the unions in El Teniente did not correspond to the rules laid out by the labor code. He noted that there were no union halls in the camps because the company owned and controlled all the buildings in El Teniente. He also complained to Braden Copper Company management that union leaders were frequently fired and harassed, "giving one the sensation that exercising the job of union leader is badly looked upon by the company."[44]

A similar 1938 Ministry of Labor report denounced the "anomalous" situation of the El Teniente unions, the company's failure to adhere to the labor code, and the obstacles it placed in the way of unionization. The report noted that workers were continually pressured to withdraw from the union by their bosses and that it was the workers' widespread belief that the company employed a system of spies to infiltrate the union; thus they mistrusted the organization. According to the labor minister, workers in El Teniente had never been given the opportunity to vote for or against the union: it had simply been handed down by the company. He suggested an immediate union election and then the obligatory unionization of all El Teniente workers. In line with the Alessandri regime's labor policy, the minister was less interested in guaranteeing the miners' rights than in preserving social peace and copper production in the mines. Obligatory unionization, he argued, would establish "the social harmony that should exist between the company and its workers and to which the unions should concur as institutions of mutual collaboration between the factors that contribute to production."[45]

Despite the Ministry of Labor's intervention in labor relations in the mine, during the 1938 presidential elections the company, with the support of the Alessandri government, impeded efforts by mine workers to campaign for the Popular Front and participate in the elections. Three workers were arrested by the local police and fired for passing out flyers for the Popular Front's presidential candidate, Radical Party leader Pedro

Aguirre Cerda. The flyers, which included a song called "The Worker's Creed," were confiscated, and the workers were arrested and jailed.[46] The day of the elections, Braden allowed workers to mount a train and then delayed their arrival until after polls had already closed. While the company attempted to prevent workers' participation in the elections, *La Tribuna* reported that it allowed a "campaigner and vote buyer" for the right-wing candidate, Gustavo Ross, Alessandri's minister of finance, to set up shop in the camps.[47]

The company also attempted to thwart the wave of union organizing in the mine in two mass dismissals in which it fired over one thousand workers. According to a report given in the House of Deputies, the fired workers were mostly union members who were registered to vote. Their dismissal, according to opposition deputies, constituted both an attack on the newly independent union and on the Front's 1938 electoral campaign.[48] In response to the dismissals, the miners walked out for eleven days on an illegal wildcat strike. The Alessandri government reinforced troops already stationed in the El Teniente camps with an officer and twenty-five soldiers at the request of the company, while the regional police headquarters pledged that it was ready to send even more reinforcements to "guard the public order and the freedom to work." The miners' strike was brought to a quick end with the militarization of the camps. Once again, the North American company rejected the miners' demands, closed the union hall, and dismissed union leaders with ties to the Popular Front who had directed the strike.[49]

Nonetheless, the decade of the 1930s had brought significant changes to El Teniente. As a settled community took shape in the mining camps, it found in the labor traditions spread by former nitrate workers a language for articulating a shared sense of class. The activities of Communist Party, Popular Front, and CTCH activists helped to cement this invented labor tradition in the mining community's popular consciousness and strengthened ties between the miners and the Left. In addition, the new system of labor relations and the growing power of the Left nationally seemed to hold the promise that the state might be put to work on the side of the miners. The attempts by Alessandri's ministers of labor to intervene in the administration of labor relations in the mine, while offset by the more general antilabor attitude and policies of the government, signaled that the configuration of relations between the miners, the North American company, and the state was slowly changing. When the Popular Front won the 1938 presidential election, the possibilities of active state intervention on behalf of the miners became material reality and consolidated both the mining community's ties to the Left and integration into a new, state-administered system of labor relations and social welfare.

Part II

Gender, Culture, and the Politics

of Everyday Life

4 Miners and Citizens

The State, the Popular Front, and Labor Politics

In 1939, President Pedro Aguirre Cerda traveled to Rancagua to meet with the workers of the El Teniente copper mine following his electoral victory at the head of a Popular Front coalition of parties that included his own Radical Party, as well as the Socialist and Communist Parties. Aguirre Cerda was not the first Chilean president to make the journey. In the early years of the mine's operation, Chilean presidents and their ministers had enjoyed the comforts and pleasures of tours of the mine and its camps at the invitation and expense of the Braden Copper Company. Aguirre Cerda was, however, the first president to be invited by the mine's unions. During the 1938 electoral campaign, the North American company had refused to allow Aguirre Cerda to speak to the El Teniente workers and had helped to fund his right-wing opponent, Gustavo Ross. Now, he was about to enter El Teniente's camps, despite the company's opposition, to speak directly to the workers and their families.

On his arrival in El Teniente, Aguirre Cerda was met at the train station by a demonstration of miners eager to express their support for a president who had been elected with the backing of workers and whose program met many of their aspirations and demands.[1] The 1938 victory of the Popular Front coalition, which also included as a pillar of support the CTCh, marked an important moment in the trajectory of the labor movement in the copper mines and in the Chilean labor movement nationally. The El Teniente miners, like workers throughout Chile, had voted for the Popular Front and believed that the Chilean state would now assist them in their struggles with their foreign adversary.[2]

The Popular Front government established a new relationship of mobilization and incorporation between organized labor, the state, and the left-wing parties and thus contributed to the transformation of the political culture of the El Teniente miners.[3] After the 1938 election, the government began to intervene in the administration of the copper industry and in labor relations in the mine. By protecting and enforcing workers' constitutional rights and the rights to unionize and bargain collectively inscribed in the 1931 labor code, the government opened the camps up for the first time, and workers built independent union structures with strong ties to the Socialist and Communist Parties. Left-wing political parties sent activists and organizers to the camps, and their representatives in the Popular Front government frequently took action on behalf of the copper miners. After 1938, the first independent and democratic union elections were held in El Teniente, and militants of the PC took control of the miners' union, the largest and most important in the mine, and the small Rancagua union of warehouse workers, while militants of the Socialist Party were elected to lead the foundry and electrical plant workers' unions.

Following the Popular Front victory, the miners began to look to the state for the first time to adjudicate labor conflicts and intervene on their behalf. The El Teniente workers now defined their struggles in nationalist terms and identified their interests with those of the Chilean state. The copper miners understood their relationship to the state in terms of a series of perceived rights and guarantees and drew on new languages of citizenship promoted by the modernizing project of the Popular Front and the Left to build their "imagined community" of class.[4] Rather than isolated and autonomous, like many of the mining communities described in the literature on economic enclaves, the miners developed both their class and community identities in terms of their integration into the corporatist system of labor relations and their political alliances with the Socialist and Communist Parties. The formation of a stable working-class community in the mining camps was shaped through the active intervention of the state and the Left in regulating labor and living conditions in the mine.

The election of the Popular Front coalition in 1938 initiated a profound transformation in Chile's processes of economic development and state formation. In Chile, as in other countries in Latin America, a populist government articulated a democratic-nationalist ideology; promoted the rights of citizenship; oversaw a new strategy of economic growth based on import substitution industrialization; and established a proto-welfare state rooted in active state intervention in the economy, labor relations, and social welfare. The state sought to protect and stimulate domestic industrial growth and to integrate the urban industrial working and middle classes into the national political community. The mobilization of workers and the expansion of unionization provided political support for the programs of middle- and upper-class reformers who sought to wrest control of the economy and the state from traditional oligarchic, landed interests. The Popular Front governments viewed a disciplined and educated working class imbued with the responsibilities and duties of citizenship as both an important source of political support and an integral part of Chile's economic progress.

Workers—and particularly copper miners—played a central role in the democratic-nationalist project of the Radical Party–led coalition governments between 1938 and 1948. Along with promoting domestic industrial growth, Chile's Popular Front governments sought to redefine the role of foreign capital in the economy and the relationship between foreign companies and the state. As copper came to dominate the Chilean economy, miners' movements helped to shape the new relationship between foreign capital and the Chilean state. Mine workers built their own national project and elaborated their own ideologies of democracy and citizenship. In doing so they often appropriated the language of nationalism, citizenship, and democracy of the populist governments and rearticulated it with their own class-specific intonations.

Joining the Popular Front meant that the Communist and Socialist Parties and the CTCh had to temper their revolutionary rhetoric and stifle their more radical demands in order to win support from middle-class sectors and to secure their alliance with the Radicals. For members of the Popular Front coalition, nationalism, democracy, and social reform supplanted socialism and class struggle in their platforms and programs.[5] The Popular Front elaborated a strategy of state-sponsored industrial development and public works programs that would provide employment for workers and prosperity for the middle classes and entrepreneurs. During the 1938 campaign, Pedro Aguirre Cerda promised to promote domestic industrialization, expand public spending, and rein in inflation, measures which would benefit workers as well as sectors of the middle and entrepreneurial classes and which would maintain intact the privileges of the traditional landed elite. In large part, this program of economic recovery and industrial expansion was to be funded by revenues from copper exports and credits from the U.S. Export-Import Bank, rather than by any increased taxation on either landed or industrial elites. The Popular Front program called neither for increased Chilean control of basic resources such as copper and nitrates nor for reform of the archaic agrarian structure in the countryside.

Aguirre Cerda was explicit in his reassurances to landed elites and determined in his rejection of the leftist parties' efforts to mobilize and organize agricultural workers. In a campaign speech at a major demonstration in Santiago, he reassured landowners and industrialists that the Popular Front did not represent a return to the turbulent populist electoral campaign run by Arturo Alessandri in 1920, which he characterized as "disorderly and chaotic with the secret hope of overturning the existing order." Rather, he stated, the Front included "responsible parties that want not a revolution, but an ordered social and economic reconstruction."[6]

Aguirre Cerda made a specific effort to reassure the United States government and U.S. investors that he did not intend to nationalize the large North American companies operating in Chile. In an interview with a North American reporter, he stated that "Chile is not ready to nationalize or socialize its great copper and nitrate industries. It lacks the capital for that. We do not intend to use foreign capital as football." In addition, he pledged to continue Chile's servicing of the external debt, an issue of central importance to the U.S. Department of State. He did, however, vaguely qualify this promise, telling the reporter that "we propose to respect existing obligations, attempting at the same time to assure that they cause the least possible damage to our economic development."[7]

Yet while Aguirre Cerda and his supporters made efforts to assuage the fears of traditional elite and foreign economic interests during the 1938 presidential campaign, the Popular Front's leftist parties and labor cells engaged a populist rhetoric and campaign strategy at odds with their candidate's more moderate posture. The coalition, dependent on the CTCH and the leftist parties to mobilize the working-class vote, articulated a militant rhetoric that went far beyond the scope of its official program.[8] Even Aguirre Cerda, who assumed a campaign style fashioned to win middle-class support, riddled his speeches with attacks on the Chilean social structure, which "left 40% of all fertile lands uncultivated" and "the copper, nitrates, iron, and electrical power in the hands of foreign companies."[9] The U.S. Department of State commented nervously on "the radical and anti-capitalist utterances of Aguirre" but passed them off as campaign rhetoric "designed to stiffen the resolution of his proletarian partisans."[10]

The Popular Front program also employed a radical rhetoric, attacking the "uncontrolled exploitation by imperialistic capital" and the "oligarchic dictatorship" that was responsible for the "desperate situation of misery of all kinds in which our people find themselves." It proposed the suppression of monopolies, a state-planned economy to increase production, government regulation for a more equitable and just distribution of wealth, agrarian reform, and a reassessment of foreign debt payments to provide funds for housing and health care for workers and white-collar employees. Most important for the El Teniente miners, the program pledged to regulate "imperialistic enterprises with the fundamental purpose of defending the national patrimony and the interests of the state, of office employees and of laborers."[11]

Concretely, the populist rhetoric employed in the 1938 campaign by the Popular Front parties was backed by a platform that addressed many of the basic demands of Chilean workers. Program pledges to enforce the rights and freedoms granted to workers in the constitution and labor code; to provide cost-of-living raises, housing, and health care for working-class families; and to do away with unemployment: these were significant for workers who had suffered either the benign negligence or the open antagonism of the state during previous decades and who had felt the brunt of the world recession during the early 1930s.[12] Thus the El Teniente copper miners joined workers in Chile's ports, coal mines, nitrate oficinas, and small industries in their expectation that the new government would, for the first time in Chilean history, put the state to work on the side of labor.

A week before Aguirre Cerda arrived in El Teniente, leaders from the mine's four blue-collar unions had met with him in Santiago, along with representatives from the Unión Industrial del Cobre (UIC), a federation of unions from different copper mines; the Federación Nacional Minera (FNM), which represented coal miners; and the CTCH. The miners presented the new president with a list of demands, approved in union assemblies, and asked that he do something immediately to prevent a mass dismissal threatened by the Braden Copper Company. Aguirre Cerda promised that he would call the head of the company to demand explanations for the firings and act to ensure that all workers could return to their jobs. Those who remained unemployed, he said, would find jobs in the recently created public works projects in the province.[13] He ended the meeting by assuring the miners that, unlike his predecessors, he intended to govern "for all Chileans."[14]

The El Teniente workers were, then, optimistic that the president meant to do something to defend their rights and support their most fundamental demands. In his speech to the assembled workers after arriving in the mine, Aguirre Cerda promised that he would implement the program of the Popular Front and little by little solve the difficulties of the workers, asking only that union leaders go to him with their problems in order to meet, "in harmony and with justice, the aspirations of the workers."[15] Aguirre Cerda then embarked on a tour of the mine and its camps, accompanied by union leaders. The significance of the president's discourse was not lost on the miners. For the first time, they were the subjects being addressed by a president who seemed to understand their problems and support their demands. Aguirre Cerda's very presence in the mine, his use of nationalistic language, and his meeting with union leaders held deep, symbolic importance. Before 1938, as the union newspaper pointed out, public demonstrations had been banned by the mining company, and workers had been prohibited from holding political meetings, giving talks, or distributing political literature.[16]

Union leaders met the president after the speech and presented him a list of demands that included wage increases, bonuses for night work, compensation for the hours spent in transportation to and from the mine, and special vacations for miners to remedy the "nature of the work which is the most exhausting, arduous, and inhuman and that always ends by rendering the worker sick and incapacitated at a prematurely young age." The miners' petition also asked the new government to bring the regime that governed everyday life in and outside the mine to an end. It denounced the constant abuse of workers by foremen and the company blacklist. The miners demanded the elimination of the internal rules that governed the camps and the work sites, freedom of transportation in and out of the mine's camps, and protection of workers' homes from arbitrary search by the camps' carabineros and los serenos.[17]

The workers' new sense of possibility was reflected in a description in *Despertar Minero,* the union paper, of a conflict between the concessionaires in the camps and the miners. When the miners complained to the owners of pensions and cantinas about high prices, they had been answered, "Go talk to Don Pedro." "They must realize," the newspaper editorialized, "that the name of His Excellency Señor Aguirre is not made for the mouths of robbers in order to slander him; he is the citizen who occupies the highest position in the Republic in order to implement the laws, make justice, and castigate speculators."[18]

The hopes inspired by a "citizen" president were reinforced when the new Popular Front minister of labor, Antonio Paupin, visited El Teniente to meet with union officials and inspect the mine and the camps. The labor minister's entourage in El Teniente included former El Teniente worker and Communist Party deputy Carlos Gaete. Paupin reviewed all the mine's sections, taking assiduous notes on working conditions and on the "many irregularities" he found. As he toured the mine he commented to the head of the company's Welfare Department on the "inhuman and bestial" work in the mine and exclaimed, "How is it possible that the workers can support so much brutality!" The day following the inspection, Paupin spoke to more than three thousand assembled miners about the new government's commitment to the workers and the obligation he had to "leave his office to go to the sites where workers of this company labored and suffered." He ratified the miners' demands by condemning the attitude of the bosses, the low wages, and the work conditions. "I'm going to let the workers return to their jobs," he promised, "with the conviction that the company will recognize a just wage increase in the next round of collective bargaining. . . . I am aware of the inhuman form in which the workers labor, and to solve these irregularities I will call the director of the company."[19]

Not long afterward, Paupin reiterated his support for the miners in a meeting held in his office in Santiago with El Teniente's union leaders; a representative of the CTCh; and a representative of the Braden Copper Company, H. Mackenzie Walker, head of the Welfare Department. The labor minister began the meeting by assuring the El Teniente unionists that the full cabinet had reviewed the workers' petitions and that the government "would bring all the pressure possible, within the present legislation, to make the Company comply or give in to the various requests." Paupin and Walker quickly clashed over seventy-seven workers fired on 29 October 1939. Although the company claimed that these men represented less than 1 percent of the workforce, Paupin replied that "to the government, which had so many unemployed on its hands, it was a large number, and [Braden] could and must find work of a similar nature for all of them in other departments or camps of the Company." When Walker offered to transfer the fired workers to other occupations, Paupin "immediately jumped up and, smacking his fist on the table, said that the Government could not tolerate a solution of that kind; that this was rebating the specialized workman's dignity, reducing his income, and probably placing him on the plane of a common peon." The labor minister additionally infuriated the company representative by demanding that the company pay these men for the workdays they had missed.[20]

Paupin also dealt with the workers' other petitions, including the demands that workers be suspended, rather than fired, as punishment for minor transgressions; that union leaders be given a pass to use the company-controlled railway for travel; that workers be paid the expense of transportation between Rancagua and the camps when hired and fired; and that the company fire abusive foremen. This last request sparked an hour-long argument over the bad treatment of workers by a number of North American foremen. The workers again had the support of Paupin, who told Walker that "not only from his own experience, but also from that of a previous colleague of his, not a Popular Front man, he knew that there were a number of bosses . . . who were little better than slave drivers and 'nigger' whippers [Walker's words]." Walker replied by denouncing the fact that since the Popular Front had come to power, "the men themselves had changed their attitude to their bosses completely and discipline and efficiency had seriously decreased over the past year." [21]

The Braden representative was alarmed by the militancy of the minister of labor, who responded to the company's arguments "with aggressiveness and threats." At one point Paupin told him that the government "had ways and means of compelling acceptance of its point of view." During an argument he also burst out in anger, shouting that "here, you see, is the attitude always taken by these imperialistic companies. . . . [Y]ou may tell your principals, if they do not already clearly understand it, that Chile is for Chileans, and we absolutely refuse to countenance any foreign outlook or opinion in regard to the manner in which our legislation is applied." [22]

It is not difficult to imagine the effect this meeting had on the miners. *Despertar Minero* had commented earlier that "the resolute attitude assumed by the minister of labor, having interceded with justice and rectitude in favor of the workers, deserves praise."[23] For the first time, they had a minister of state on their side, threatening to bring the full weight of the state to bear on Braden. Minister Paupin's nationalist rhetoric of "Chile for Chileans" and his defense of the dignity of the worker must have resonated deeply with miners. Practically, the minister succeeded in getting the company to agree to rehire the seventy-seven fired workers. Most important, Paupin had spoken for the president and identified the government with the workers' cause by addressing the foreign company as an enemy of the workers, the Popular Front government, and all Chileans.

The hope that speeches and meetings of this kind instilled in the miners was made clear following a coup attempt in August 1939, only months after Aguirre Cerda's visit to El Teniente. The evening of the attempted coup, thousands of workers congregated in the union hall to begin a protest and formed "an enormous crowd that for the first time in the history of the camp" marched through the streets of Sewell. At the head of the march walked the union leaders carrying the Chilean flag and the union standard, followed by thousands of workers shouting their support for Aguirre Cerda: "The workers of El Teniente with Aguirre until death!" The workers were joined by their wives and children, as the entire community filled the streets of the camp. In the mass meeting that followed, the assembled workers and their families sang the communist international, the socialist *marseillaise,* and then the Chilean national anthem. After listening to speeches by union leaders, the miners agreed to send telegrams of support to the government, and asked the government to distribute arms so that they could fight the "traitors of the people" and "defend Chilean democracy." Before the miners dispersed they broke into another rendition of the international, again followed by the marseillaise and the national anthem, which revealed the particular ideological blend that the Popular Front signified to them: democracy, nationalism, socialism, and communism.[24]

This event, like the demonstrations of support for Aguirre Cerda, signified important changes for the miners. Miners' public demonstrations represented a reconquest of the camps, an assertion of control over the community and the space in which they lived and worked. As the union newspaper put it; "The latest mobilizations prove that . . . the barriers that made this camp a true penal colony are beginning to give way and be defeated by a people that loves liberty. The demonstration . . . in which the parties and the organizations of the people have made their voice heard is only a minimum conquest of the rights acquired by the citizens of this country. . . . The company has to understand that times have changed." [25] The Popular Front's emphasis on the rights of citizenship, individual freedoms, and national sovereignty offered miners the promise that the company's system of social control in the camps would be ended. The union paper pointed out that "the memory of the disgraceful regimes of the previous governments that made tabula rasa of the most fundamental principles of the Constitution and the law is still fresh." [26] But, it affirmed, the miners were beginning to win "the rights of citizens of this country." [27]

One year later, union leaders informed Aguirre Cerda that the company had continued to fire hundreds of workers during a lull in production. Aguirre Cerda told the El Teniente miners that he had called the representatives of the copper companies to his office and that "he had told the Managers of the Companies that his Government could not permit this crime against the national workmen and the national interests." He concluded by stating that the copper companies had to maintain a stable labor force and that as long as he was president, "he would not allow them to disrupt the labor market as had been their custom in the past." [28] According to company reports, the president also intimated that, if necessary, the government would take over the copper mines, perhaps the first threat of nationalization the company had ever heard. [29]

Building a Nation: Citizenship and Class Consciousness

The Popular Front supplied, with measured state support for the miners' union, a nationalist language of citizenship. Popular Front ideology proposed an inclusive national community and promised to expand and enforce the rights guaranteed workers in the constitution. Aguirre Cerda and the Popular Front emphasized the rights of all Chileans and claimed to rule for the common citizen, including workers and peasants who had been traditionally disenfranchised. The Front's promise to workers of the full benefits of citizenship implied an understanding of the legal equality of workers and capitalists, peasants and landowners. While workers and peasants may not have enjoyed the economic power of factory or land-owners, they were now endowed with the universal dignity of citizenship and recognized as members of a new national category: Chileans.

Aguirre Cerda's Popular Front government embarked on a campaign to redefine the nation or, in Benedict Anderson's words, to imagine a new national community. The Front attempted to refigure the nation as a community of the middle and working classes, the true "people." Aguirre Cerda riddled his rhetoric with appeals to the "collective welfare of Chileans" and to the family of Chileans in which "the land is a loving mother who supports all her children equally and not a stepmother who gives privileges to the least needy."[30] While the Front spoke for "all Chileans," it explicitly defined two sectors—the landowning oligarchy and foreign capital—as its antagonists. Its nationalist language defined a community composed of workers, peasants, middle-class sectors, and "national" capitalists.

The national community proposed by the Popular Front could, however, be imagined in different ways. The partners of the coalition placed emphasis on different aspects of this community. Workers appropriated the nationalist-populist ideology of the Popular Front and gave it a more radical content. For the miners, the subject of the nation was workers, and for "Chileans" and "people," they read the working class. Similarly, they understood the rights of citizenship to confer economic power and social equality, unlike the urban, middle-class supporters of the Radical Party, who tended to read "citizenship" to imply legal rights and the democratization of state power.

The miners combined the rhetoric of rights with the nationalist language of Popular Front politics to press their demands against the copper company. The Braden Copper Company, the workers argued, not only trampled on their rights in the workplace and in the camps, it also trampled on the Chilean constitution, violated Chilean law, and threatened Chilean sovereignty. "We want," *Despertar Minero* editorialized, "to show to Chilean workers that we live in a free country where the Constitution of the State is followed to the letter and where we have broad freedoms. . . . [T]he company must understand that we are in Chile and that they should not treat us badly, that they should respect us as free citizens and not as slaves."[31] The Popular Front's promises of the rights of citizenship implied for the El Teniente miners the dismantling of the repressive regime of social control exercised by the Braden Copper Company in the North American fiefdom.

For the miners, "citizenship" signified important restrictions on the company's capacity to control their lives in the camps and their work in the mine and guaranteed them fundamental rights that went far beyond formal political participation. In 1940, for example, *Despertar Minero* denounced a growing campaign against the union. The company had prohibited both union meetings and meetings of the Communist Party. The union protested that "in Sewell they are violating the Constitution" and asserted that "all citizens of Chile, according to law, have the right to organize themselves in any political party; the authorities that represent the actual government must implement the laws of our country."[32] The miners' union also invoked the constitution to protest against the constant searches of workers' homes and cited the articles that protected their right to privacy, ending with the inflammatory declaration, "Chile for Chileans!"[33]

The appeal of miners to their constitutional rights fit the nationalist rhetoric of the Popular Front. A violation of their rights as citizens signified both a violation of Chilean sovereignty and disrespect for and defiance of the Popular Front government. Thus in 1940, as the El Teniente workers confronted the dismissal of more than 25 percent of the mine's labor force, the union paper noted with outrage that the company proceeded "with an absolute contempt that signifies a bloody mocking of the organized workers and especially of our government and our laws."[34] The many firings and the shifting of workers from job to job represented "a trampling of our labor code." With a government that promised to implement the constitution, social legislation, and the labor code, the El Teniente workers began to see the potential of these formerly useless arms in their battles with Braden. They could also employ these to expand their struggle to include the government and ultimately all Chileans. The inclusive "we" used in their declarations signified that the miners hoped to confront the company not just as workers but also as Chilean citizens and as members of a newly constructed nation. In this sense, the miners transformed the language of patriotism and the responsibilities and virtues of citizenship promoted by both the company and the state into an ardent and militant nationalism.

Before his death, in July 1941, Aguirre Cerda initiated a campaign dedicated to *Chilenidad,* or Chileanity. The Chilenidad movement sought to eduate Chileans about the rights and duties of citizenship and to mobilize them behind the economic nationalism and new discourses of democracy, freedom, and equality central to Popular Front ideology. The miners strove to convert this new nationalism to serve their own interests. The rhetoric of Chilenidad allowed them to draw on the themes of anti-imperialism and opposition to foreign companies and the rights of workers as Chilean citizens in foreign enclaves. Thus, for example, the union paper read into Aguirre Cerda's patriotic rhetoric about Chilenidad concrete social meanings having to do with their rights as workers and citizens. "It is Chilenidad," the union paper declared, "to go to union meetings, to help in the resolution of our problems for the good of our class, to elevate our social, cultural, and economic level, and in order that indirectly and as a true support for Chilenidad, we should contribute to make Chile a country of freedom and respect, welfare, regrowth, . . . a full and serene democracy." [35]

Following Aguirre Cerda's death, the miners' union accused the government of betraying its own Chilenidad campaign by raising the price of wheat and thus the cost of living for the "popular" classes: "They have agreed to raise the price of wheat. . . . [I]t can't be possible that they allow attacks on the very existence of the popular classes, that isn't to create Chilenidad, that is to offend the memory of the illustrious citizen and statesman don Pedro Aguirre Cerda." [36] The miners thus converted "the people" into "popular classes" and "citizens" into "workers," inscribing the popular-democratic rhetoric of nationalism and citizenship with their own language of class. Citizenship meant more than formal political rights or membership in a new national community for the El Teniente workers. The miners constructed a notion of Chilenidad that included the right to job security, a controlled cost of living, a living wage, social benefits, and unionization. They collapsed the Popular Front's vague promises of political equality with its promises of social reform and justice and defined political rights in economic and social terms.

The North American company, however, like the workers, extracted the strands of Popular Front rhetoric that suited its purposes. The Aguirre Cerda government's ideology of industrial development based on cooperation between labor and capital and its vision of active state intervention in the economy and in labor relations fit the copper company's corporate welfare approach to labor relations and could be drawn on to condemn strikes as harmful to industrial progress and to the interests of the nation. In addition, Braden had viewed the process of inculcating the virtues and responsibilities of citizenship among its workers as integral to securing a stable and productive labor force since the 1920s. Thus, following Aguirre Cerda's 1939 visit to El Teniente, the company newspaper reminded the workers of the president's plea for understanding and cooperation between labor and capital and his request that workers avoid strikes. On May Day in 1939 the paper recalled Aguirre Cerda's words: "El Señor Aguirre Cerda has clearly expressed his opinion in the sense that the unions must remain distant from politics. . . . [Aguirre Cerda] expressed that he considered that the workers had to place their trust in the government and not foment strikes or conflicts that can lead to nothing constructive."[37]

In his speech at El Teniente, Aguirre Cerda had spoken about the need for harmony between labor and capital on which to base "progress" and "economic development." He asked the miners to give him time to realize the program of the Popular Front and to meet the demands of the most needy classes. In addition, he exhorted them "to work without rest without violating the law, and try by all means to avoid conflicts with their superiors."[38] The following day he conveyed the same message to workers in the Caletones foundry, asking them to look for solutions to labor conflicts peacefully and within the parameters of the existing legislation.[39]

These speeches, which the union paper neglected to print, were highlighted by the company paper, *El Teniente,* which came to be an avid advocate of the Popular Front ideology of harmony between labor and capital. Thus, on May Day the paper published a lengthy editorial devoted to the theme of labor relations:

> On this sacred Labor Day, we salute the manual laborers, and the workers of intellect, worthy both of their collective welfare, and on this date we cast a vote for harmony with the capitalist forces, a not too far off reality, for the good of all the social sectors, understanding each other's legitimate interests, that signifies true cooperation for the world that new generations are forging. . . . Señor Aguirre Cerda has clearly expressed his opinion that the unions must main-

tain themselves apart from politics. . . . Aguirre Cerda manifested
that he considered that the workers must confirm their confidence
in the government and had pledged not to foment strikes or conflicts that can lead to nothing constructive, as long as they had been
able to converse with the company about all their problems and received the cooperation that exists on the company's part to study
and resolve them.[40]

Braden accused the miners' union of violating the spirit of cooperation
and conciliation championed by Aguirre Cerda and of letting the workers
be led astray by agents and agitators from leftist political parties. The
company argued that the workers were not following the prescriptions of
the current social legislation, which "can't and doesn't recognize the existence of a 'working class,' but recognizes patrones and trabajadores, and
the labor law determines clearly that the patrones and trabajadores of each
workplace, workshop or factory constitute a separate entity."[41] According to Braden, by letting political organizations subject the union to their
will, "the workers only manage to disturb the 'progress of industry' and
make remote any possibility of comprehension between patrones and trabajadores, establishing finally social struggle . . . that signifies disturbance,
backwardness and poverty for the country." Referring to a recent spate of
conflicts in the mine and the workers' antagonistic and confrontational
posture toward the company, the paper asked, "Is this loyalty toward the
government and cooperation with the president?"[42] Employing definitions of citizenship taught in the camps' schools and cultural centers, the
company paper invoked the duties and responsibilities of patriotic citizenship, rather than the rights encoded in the constitution and labor code.

The Braden Copper Company attempted to use the ideology of the
Popular Front to its own advantage, extracting meanings and intentions
from Aguirre Cerda's rhetoric which served its own purposes and which
coincided with its own ideology of labor relations. For the miners, Aguirre
Cerda's presence in the mine and meetings with union leaders signified an
important blow to the control exercised by the company in the mine and
a ratification of their most fundamental demands and aspirations, yet the
company was able to draw on and emphasize Aguirre Cerda's comments
about cooperation and conciliation to depict the workers' conflictive behavior as a betrayal of their government and president and as contributing

to the underdevelopment and poverty of the entire country. This constituted an effective use of the Popular Front's language against the very subjects it purported to serve and represent.

That the workers and the company could construct contradictory and opposing interpretations of Aguirre Cerda's visit to the mine and speeches reflected the protean nature of Popular Front ideology and its imagined national community. While the workers, the government, and the company shared a common commitment to economic growth and development, they understood the direction and goals of this development differently. The flexible nature of Popular Front rhetoric made possible conflicting readings by all three parties. At the same time, the malleability of this political discourse allowed the El Teniente workers to appropriate it for their own ends and to give radical class content to a nationalist language that emphasized class harmony.

Citizenship, Responsible Manhood, and Female Domesticity

The Popular Front government, organized labor, and the North American company shared common understandings of gender, social welfare, and cultural reform. The harmony between labor and capital that would be the basis for industrial progress, these different parties agreed, would be founded on an extensive state-sponsored system of social welfare that would establish a trained and culturally reformed working class. The rights of citizenship for the Popular Front's working-class constituency entailed new duties. Workers had to be disciplined, educated, and responsible to fulfill the demands of citizenship in the new national community. Unions, the Left, and the Popular Front concurred with the Braden Copper Company's recipe for cultural reform and the reorganization of workers' social lifestyles to conform to the gender ideology of domesticity. The Left and organized labor promoted the ideal of a respectable male worker and head of household who acted at the "vanguard" of the union movement, whereas the Popular Front and the state after 1938 imagined a new national community of citizens composed of male wage earners and female housewives.[43] The nationalist and popular-democratic ideology of the Popular Front guaranteed men's monopoly of the labor market and political spaces, as well as authority within the home. Thus, the construction of a working-class community according to the North American company's ideology of welfare capitalism in El Teniente was articulated after 1938 with the gendered construction of an activist state.[44]

The North American company's emphasis on reorganizing family life, cultural uplift, the social reform of living conditions in working-class neighborhoods, and the virtues of citizenship accorded with the social reformist orientation of the Radical Party politicians who took power after 1938 and the new industrial employers who emerged during the process of import substitution industrialization during the 1930s and 1940s and who confronted the daunting challenge of forming a stable workforce out of the large population of rural migrants who inhabited Chile's urban working-class neighborhoods. As we have seen, since the early 1920s, Radical Party leaders such as Carlos Briones Luco and Pedro Aguirre Cerda had expressed their interest in the Braden Copper Company's corporate welfare programs as a blueprint for social reform. The company's campaign to transform working-class life and its introduction of social welfare as a substitute for labor conflict neatly fit the ideology of the Radical Party and the coalition Popular Front governments. Popular Front ideology obscured class conflict with the promises of a modernizing project of domestic industrial growth from which all social classes would benefit. The lives of workers would be improved not through a redistribution of property or income but through a series of reforms that offered them the benefits of citizenship in an improved standard of living, access to education, decent housing and health care, and better working conditions. The modern industrial economy imagined by Radical Party leaders and by the leaders of the leftist parties, who largely shared their vision, required a modern, semiskilled workforce. New state-run social programs and agencies and employers' welfare systems were designed to meet this need.

Recent literature on state formation has underlined that state-building or state-making projects involve the establishment of hegemony through cultural transformation and revolution. In this sense, the Popular Front sought to build, with its languages of nationalism and citizenship, a new national culture. This entailed a project of moral and cultural reorganization, as the state sought to regulate and reform what Phillip Corrigan and Derek Sayer refer to as the "social forms of life." The Popular Front, much like the North American company, strove to instill new values associated with patriotism and a set of moral codes in workers, peasants, and a growing population of urban poor. As historian Karin Rosemblatt argues, after 1938 the Chilean state embarked on a close regulation of men's and women's everyday lives through the establishment and extension of social welfare apparatuses. Education and literacy campaigns, public health and hygiene programs, and housing projects aimed to build a population of disciplined and responsible citizens. The consonances between the Braden Copper Company's corporate welfare programs and the ideology of the Popular Front were made clear in Aguirre Cerda's emphasis on the need for education and training to make workers and peasants responsible citizens. In an interview with a North American reporter, Aguirre Cerda repeated his famous slogan "to govern is to educate" and continued: "I mean education in the widest sense. I do not limit the term to formal instruction in the school room, . . . I mean fitting adults as well as children for a better life, giving them healthy bodies and trained capacities for the world in which they earn their bread." Like the Braden Copper Company, Aguirre Cerda intended cultural uplift to create the conditions for self-improvement "to help the Chilean people help themselves." Making clear women's role in the Popular Front's program of social reform, Aguirre Cerda argued that the state's new educational programs would "teach the mother how to care for herself, so that her children may be strong and healthy."[45]

Like the Braden Copper Company's corporate welfare system, the Popular Front's project of social and cultural reform was gendered. As Rosemblatt contends, the Popular Front governments viewed their efforts to sponsor economic modernization as inseparable from the establishment of new forms of citizenship based on the nuclear family. Stable families composed of male wage earners and female housewives would be the foundation of the new industrial economy and modern state.[46] The Popular Front government, like the North American copper company, sought to eradicate transient and unstable forms of family life and to establish civil marriage in which responsible fathers and husbands earned a family wage and women cared for and raised new generations of disciplined workers and responsible citizens. After 1938, Rosemblatt shows, a new social security administration provided workers health care and social security benefits, and the Ministry of Health, Social Security, and Welfare, directed by Socialist Party leader Salvador Allende, embarked on campaigns to improve the living conditions of urban working-class families.[47]

Organized labor and the Left, integral members of the Popular Front coalition, participated in the campaigns of social and cultural reform carried out by the state after 1938. The CTCh and the Socialist and Communist Parties often coincided with the copper company and the government on recipes for social betterment. Unions, like the Popular Front, defined their cultural activities in terms of Aguirre Cerda's slogan, "To govern is to educate." Thus, for example, the 1939 platform of the CTCh made central demands for accessible free public schooling for all working-class youth and adults, a literacy campaign, and the formation of "libraries, popular theaters, radio, movies, conferences, and concerts" to promote the cultural development of the working classes.[48] Similarly, in El Teniente, the miners' union identified the education and cultural improvement of workers as one of its most important activities. In a column entitled "Struggle and Study, Study and Struggle," the union paper equated education and study with the "proletarian morality" necessary to pursue class struggle effectively.[49] As the paper editorialized on the inauguration of the union's first primary school for adults, "All the workers of Sewell should go to the school to receive the necessary preparation that will place them at the same level of those workers who thanks to tenacity and constancy today are in the vanguard of the Chilean union movement." For the union, culture and education, the virtues of middle-class respectability promoted by the company, meant "more class consciousness" and provided the means by which workers could "become the teachers and guides of the laboring masses of our country."[50] Similarly, in its comments on Aguirre Cerda's Chilenidad campaign, the union invoked the moral discipline dictated by responsibility to the nation through its encouragement of workers to exercise their patriotic duties by "going to union meetings" and "elevating" their "social, cultural, and economic level."[51]

Like the North American company, the miners' union frequently complained of workers' dismal attendance record at night schools and schools for adults and their failure to use the union library. *Despertar Minero* noted, for example, that "looking around us we note that rarely do compañeros interest themselves in world events, and especially in local and national events. There is a lack of interest in reading the newspapers that defend the people and in discussing social problems. The workers frequent the libraries very little, not knowing that healthy reading orients us and instructs us in the duties that we have and the obligations to our class."[52] Like the state and the copper company, the union saw education as fundamental to inculcating in workers a new sense of duty and responsibility. And, like the copper company, the union encountered great difficulty in its efforts to "raise" the cultural level of the miners.

The miners' union was also concerned with the "unhealthy" lifestyles and disruptive forms of sexuality of workers. The union frequently couched its demands for improved housing in the camps in terms of the need for reformed family life and working-class morality. In 1941, for example, the union newspaper employed language that evoked the rhetoric of the company Welfare Department when it editorialized that the lack of housing and the cramped conditions in the barracks were responsible for family problems "improper to a civilized country, since the workers live in absolute promiscuity, a pernicious moral problem."[53] The paper called on the state and the company to provide workers hygienic housing that would improve the "moral" conditions of the miners. Similarly, like the state's new social service agencies, the miners' union was concerned with prostitution and the spread of venereal disease among workers. When the governor of O'Higgins came to El Teniente to meet with the miners in 1939 following the election of the Popular Front, one of the union's major demands was that he and the mayor of Rancagua do something to combat prostitution because the miners who went down to the city on their off days "were constantly infected."[54]

The miners' union also regularly condemned excessive alcohol consumption and gambling and called for discipline from its members based on solidarity and sacrifice in the name of a common struggle. Both the CTCh and FNM made crusades against alcoholism and gambling central to their programs and advocated the education and cultural uplift of workers. In 1938, the CTCh initiated a campaign against gambling, and in a national miners' congress held in Rancagua, the FNM made alcoholism a central theme.[55] The miners' union participated vigorously in the proselytization against games of chance. In 1941, for example, *Despertar Minero* editorialized that the union's efforts to educate and raise the cultural level of the workers were failing. One of the principal reasons was the prevalence of gambling, which "destroys our consciousness and morality."[56] The paper assailed the "clandestine gambling tables that exist in abundance in this camp" and suggested that workers leave this "unlucky vice" aside and spend their time instead working on "social problems that confront us, adding their grain of sand to solve them, rather than becoming pitilessly brutish." Similarly, in a column entitled "A Shame That We Must Avoid," *Despertar Minero* railed against the commonness of gambling among the camp's youth and young people's "shameful laziness." The paper, echoing the company's own rhetoric, suggested that "once and for all we put an end to this evil so that our youth dedicate themselves to study or work, dignifying their modest homes with strict proletarian morality."[57]

The proletarian novels of the Left also conveyed messages about morality and discipline and condemned popular working-class "vices." Baltazar Castro's stories and novels, for example, reflected the union's notions of morality, respectability, and manhood. His memoirs and stories of life in the camps produced critiques of gambling and drinking and an insistence on the emancipatory discipline of the union. In a number of stories, young mine workers follow a rocky road to salvation in the union through the slough of working-class vices. Often, they foolishly lose their money through drinking, gambling, and frequenting brothels and wind up indebted or jobless. Only later do they learn their lesson and join the union, in which they find redemption, moral discipline, and a new sense of their own manhood.[58] As one miner testifies, describing his personal experiences and articulating the moral message of the Left and the union: "I then joined the union. . . . Compañero Corales put me in the social assistance commission. There I do what I can and we all help one another. It's good work and I enjoy it a lot. Before, I spent my time in the barracks playing cards. Now I go to the union hall. I'm happy."[59]

Castro's stories offered the experiences of solidarity and community within the union and the party as an alternative to the informal forms of solidarity constructed in illicit recreational activities. Castro emphasized the dignity and discipline of union activity. The miners who were active in the union won respect from their fellow workers. This respect was also given to miners who performed their jobs well and fulfilled the ideals of manhood within the mine. Strong and skilled miners who stood up to foremen were "natural" leaders. As a union activist tells one of Castro's heroes, "You are respected by the people of the mine. It's true that you've never joined the union, but you've been strong in going face-to-face with the gringos. There's a silent admiration for you among the miners. They know that you are a man in every sense of the word."[60] The union narrative thus constructed an ideal of masculinity drawn from the work culture of the mine and combined with its own insistence on discipline and respectability. Castro describes one union leader who combined the masculine characteristics of the mine: "He was the product of a hard, suffering, heroic existence tamed through the force of . . . internal discipline, courage and a tremendous capacity to mold destiny to conform to ideals which in the end came to be the spinal column of his life."[61] Thus, Castro's language echoed the company's definition of true manhood as based on moral strength and discipline.

The miners' union also rearticulated the company's gender ideology of female domesticity and the nuclear family. Thus, the union advocated education for workers' wives so that they could more effectively care for and exercise a positive moral influence over their husbands and children. The union reproduced the ideas of the company's Welfare Department about companionate marriage and women's place in the domestic sphere, indicating a shared discourse revolving around gender. Both the miners' union and leftist parties asserted the importance of an educated wife and mother to improving the morality of male workers and their children, just as the company and state focused on women in their own campaigns of social reform and moral uplift. Labor and the Left shared the company's concern with the household, women, and family as the central arenas in which workers' culture and consciousness were to be developed. *Despertar Minero* editorialized, for example, that "the authorities must take care of the problem of women, particularly in this mine, instruct the housewives so that they know how to guide their children from the first days, feed them, take care of their lives and the lives of their families."[62] A well-ordered household was as important for improving "proletarian morality" as it was for promoting labor discipline.

At the same time, however, the union's vision of gender relations expanded the possibilities for miners' wives in the context of class-based forms of collective action, albeit within the circumscribed space of the domestic sphere. From the middle-class model of a companionate marriage between male wage earner and female housewife, the union constructed an ideal of marriage between compañeros, or comrades. The union advocated education, literacy campaigns, and new forms of cultural activity for women in order to develop their political and cultural level. The union thus departed from the strict version of the company's ideology of female domesticity to describe a range of new political possibilities for working-class women in struggles around class issues:

There was an epoch when it was thought that the compañera of a worker must be a machine to manufacture children; the truth is very different: women must prepare themselves to struggle and confront life. . . . But for this we need a literacy campaign among the women. We demand that there be night schools for them. . . . [T]he company must construct special centers so that the women have adequate entertainment, where they can hear conferences, obtain knowledge and necessary skills. . . . [T]here must be all that the culture brings: theater, recreation, libraries.[63]

The union urged women to develop their responsibilities as mothers and wives to include political struggle. Union editorials, for example, spoke of the examples of women who were unforgettable "as fighters and as mothers." Similarly, it assailed the "bourgeois prejudice" that consigned women as a "serf in the household and also from the sexual point of view" and argued that it was time to recognize the "revolutionary role of women" so that they could "participate in the social struggles in defense of the interests of their children and their compañeros."[64] According to the union, women should be educated so as to participate in working-class struggles as mothers in defense of their families. It thus advocated its own version of what has been called "revolutionary motherhood."[65]

The miners' union was concerned to offer possibilities beyond housework for women and to draw on women's potential political power. Education, the union emphasized, was important so that women could take their place at the side of the workers in their struggles with the company and in the larger political battles of the country. Despertar Minero critiqued the "prejudices" that defined women as "nothing more than good housewives" and stated forthrightly that "no women should dedicate themselves only to knitting socks and washing plates."[66] Thus, while the union emphasized the importance of educating women to be good mothers and wives, it also advocated the widespread political organization of women and broadened the definition of appropriate female activities. The very notion that women had an important role to play in social, cultural, and political activities contradicted the general tenor of the company's ideology of domesticity and opened up potential public spaces for women's organizations. Although the union's vision of a politicized working-class household still imagined women's mobilization in terms of their position within the household, the meaning of female domesticity was extended to include labor politics. A compañera had possibilities that a mother or wife—in the company's definition, at least—lacked. Thus, while the company and union both focused on the training of women as central to the establishment of a disciplined worker morality, the union's moral code inflected the company's paternalist discourse with the ideals of class discipline, mobilization, and organization.

The instillation of a labor tradition, leftist political identity, and ideology of citizenship among El Teniente's men and women was not a direct or unmediated process. Although a militant core of miners belonged to leftist parties and the majority of miners threw their weight behind Communist and Socialist leaders in union elections and behind the Popular Front in national elections, the ideology of labor and the Left conflicted with the everyday forms of sociability of the mining camps. The insistence of the state, organized labor, and the Left on education and cultural improvement and their condemnation of drinking, gambling, and illicit sex revealed both the similarities between the North American company's system of welfare capitalism and the modernizing state welfare project of the Left and the Popular Front, and the contradictions between the informal working-class culture of the mining camps and the formal ideology of organized labor and the Left. The path that led from the disruptive culture of insubordination within the mine and the camps to more organized collective action under the auspices of the union and the leftist parties was not always direct. While the election of the Popular Front intensified the identification of workers with the Left and integrated their unions into the national labor movement and the state-directed system of labor relations, at times the crevices between the program of the union and the informal forms of working-class sociability and militancy in the mine and the camps undermined the bases of cooperation between workers, organized labor, and the parties of the Popular Front. Miners' everyday, informal forms of opposition to company authority often conflicted with the discipline demanded by the union and leftist parties, and miners pushed union leaders to take militant stands that threatened the Popular Front's fragile social and political coalition.

Masculinity and the Labor Process inside the Mine

The formation of a permanent labor force in El Teniente during the 1930s and 1940s depended on what Michael Burawoy calls the willingness of workers to play by the "rules of the game" and accept the organization of the labor process.[1] Both men and women traveled to the mine in search of wage labor and remained there to reap the economic benefits and promise of social mobility that life in the mine offered. The North American copper company paid its workers high wages relative to other sectors of the Chilean economy, bonuses, and a number of social benefits. Miners came to define their work and demands in terms of the wage system created by the company and strove to fulfill their appointed tasks so as to win work incentives.

Although historians of Latin American labor have recently drawn attention to the importance of the workplace as a central arena in which working-class labor politics are elaborated, in El Teniente, the ties between the labor process and life outside the workplace were especially tight because of the structure of the mining camps.[2] Beyond the extreme physical proximity of the mine to the camps, every aspect of day-to-day life depended on the company and was linked to workers' jobs inside the mine. Because the inhabitants of the camps were somehow related to work in the mine through a father, brother, or son, the labor process was a constant presence in the everyday lives of even those El Teniente residents who did not work in the mine. As oral histories with former residents of the camps point out, every El Teniente citizen had close knowledge of the life and workings of the mine. Conversations among women, for example, frequently dealt with subjects relating to their male relatives' work. Thus, while an analysis of the culture and politics of the workplace is essential to any understanding of the hegemony of social relations in the modern copper industry, the labor process must be understood as tied to the social and cultural worlds outside the mine. The labor process in the mine constituted a site where gender, as well as class and politics, was constructed.

Inside the mine, workers built an intensely masculinized work culture by sexualizing their labor, locating manly pride in their physical capacity for work and figuring the mine as a feminized object on which they exercised their will. Miners strove to overcome alienation at work by asserting a sense of masculine dignity in their labor. By signifying labor in the language of sexuality, miners transformed dehumanizing mine work into a source of masculine affirmation, implicitly predicated on the metaphorical control of female sexuality embodied in the mine. Thus, the construction of work as a source of pride led workers to participate in meeting production goals and to accommodate to the organization of labor. In addition, miners' workplace codes of manhood reinforced the company's gender ideology of female domesticity by naturalizing wage labor as masculine and defining masculinity in terms of men's control of women's sexuality.

But miners' work culture also located masculine dignity in independence and self-assertion. A challenging attitude toward company authority and an irreverent and insubordinate style defined the codes of behavior of mine workers. Miners built a strong sense of solidarity within work crews based on mutual dependence for survival inside the mine. They articulated a specific *manera de ser* (way of being) in their own language, set of anecdotes, jokes, myths, ways of holding their bodies, and codes of manhood that became the basis for a shared work culture of opposition. Thus, the tensions between accommodation and resistance in the workplace were mediated through a culture of masculinity in which miners defined manliness in their capacity to dominate the mine physically, earn high wages, stand up to supervisors, and defend their honor and autonomy in fights and loyalty to work comrades.

Despite the Braden Copper Company's efforts to improve work security and prevent accidents through training for workers, security contests, and bonuses for accident-free production, working conditions in El Teniente during the 1940s were still, as a Popular Front minister of labor noted, both "inhuman and brutish."[3] The minister and a labor inspector who later came to examine El Teniente noted how workers in the mine labored, sometimes crouched over in tiny spaces, for eight hours at a time in mud, freezing water, and snow. The El Teniente workers were entitled to only twenty minutes a day for lunch and no other breaks. They had no bathrooms and no place to rest, to change their clothes, or to eat their lunch; the air they breathed was filled with smoke and dust from the dynamite explosions. Along with water from snow and rain, the miners were also soaked by the water from hoses used to spray the rock to keep dust from filling the air. Whereas some sections were freezing cold, others were inhumanly hot. From shifting between these extremes, workers frequently suffered bronchial infections, asthma, tuberculosis, and silicosis.

In 1942, the Communist Party paper *El Siglo* offered a vivid description of the miners' working conditions: "Weeks and weeks pass sometimes with terrible storms of wind, water, and snow. To get to the mine, the miner has to walk, climbing the hill, for at least an hour. He works more than ten hours in the depths of the mine performing labors where there is no ventilation, with an insupportable heat sometimes, and other times with an intense cold that freezes even the tea and coffee."[4] The paper also published detailed descriptions of the miners' work and the risk of accidents: "The miners work breathing in the mineral dust, the origin of the terrible silicosis, and dynamite smoke, in an infernal temperature when not under a rain of corrosive waters in freezing temperatures. One bad calculation can produce a catastrophic erosion that crushes a group of workers."[5]

The miner's day began early in the morning, around four or five, when he went to have breakfast at a cantina or at the house of a family that offered pensions.[6] By six, the miner had begun the walk through the Sewell camp and up the mountain to the train that would take him into the mine. The train was like a cattle car, made of steel, without windows, and completely enclosed to prevent accidents. On arrival in the principal tunnel at the very bottom of the mine, the miner gave his work card to one of the North American supervisors, who jotted his name on a time card, and then took the giant elevator—the *jaula* (cage)—and with six hundred or more other workers went up to one of the different levels in the mine. He then joined a *cuadrilla* (work team), composed of around fifteen people, at work in one of the many tunnels within the mine. A second shift began work at three in the afternoon, and a night shift took over at eleven in the evening.

Baltazar Castro describes a miner's first work experience in the mine in his stories of life in El Teniente:

> I had been transferred to the mine where I worked as an assistant to the *buitrero* [unloader], . . . and of the *muestrero* [tester], taking portions from the different tunnels to send them to the sample section so the technicians could determine the quality of the mineral that came from these places. . . . At first everything was hard and complicated. To learn to move in the interior of the mine is an intricate task. The mine is like a city placed inside of the mountain; kilometers and kilometers of tunnels, levels, detours, cliffs, drops. . . . Seen from outside the mine appeared to me like a huge tangle of narrow, dark, wet streets.[7]

Once the crew began work, the *canero* (lead miner) advanced first, laying down the pipes and tubes that provided compressed air and water for the drills. As the miners drilled, the machine threw water against the rock to keep the lethal dust from filling the air. Despite the ventilation and water, however, the air was often saturated with dust so thick that the miner could see no further than two meters. The caneros were followed by a miner, who drilled holes to place dynamite, and a lookout, whose job was to alert other workers in the area before an explosion.

After the dynamite exploded, the other members of the team began work. The *enrieladores* (railmen) rushed to put down the rails for the cars that would cart the ore away to a chute, and the *enmaderadores* (timbermen) began to construct supports in the new part of the tunnel with wooden beams. While the miners kept drilling new perforations for dynamite, the *carreros* (carmen) began loading the ore and carting it, using brute physical force, to the chutes (*buzones*), where it was unloaded and sent to the concentrating plant by *buzoneros*.

Most of this work required great strength. Mechanization in the mine was relatively rudimentary. Aside from the miners' drills and the rail system, machinery was less important than the actual labor of the workers. These jobs required a significant level of skill and knowledge. Miners had to know how to handle a drill, where to place the holes for dynamite, how to place explosions strategically, and how to avoid blowing up everyone in the tunnel. The enmaderadores required similar types of knowledge about where and how to place beams and supports. And buzoneros and carreros used similar types of self-taught skills in their jobs. If, for example, a carrero didn't know how to manage the cart or was careless, he could easily wind up crushed underneath the cart or decapitated by the roof of the tunnel.

In general, workers in the mine learned their jobs through experience. They began work as assistants (peones or *jornaleros*) at the bottom of the crew hierarchy for low pay, performing different tasks and aiding the other members of the crew in their jobs. After they had demonstrated both discipline and capacity for work, they could then hope for a promotion to the more lucrative and stable positions within the crew. Jornaleros and peones were often single and younger men who, because they lacked skill, experience, and seniority, were frequently the first miners fired during cutbacks. After a worker had labored at a particular job in the crew for a number of years and had shown his knowledge and reliability, he could hope to be promoted to crew chief (*cabo*) or foreman (*capataz*) and win the highest salary within the cuadrilla. Almost all crew chiefs and foremen had worked as miners at different jobs in the team. Promotion from peón or jornalero to a well-paying and more secure job as a miner or possible ascent to a position as work crew chief or even skilled technician (*empleado*) provided workers the possibility of social mobility in both earnings and status.

In the concentrating plant, workers operated the mills that ground down the rock, added the reactive chemicals that were used in the flotation process, lubricated machinery, and operated the filters used to lower the temperature of the copper substance until it became solid. As inside the mine, work in the mill required skill and knowledge and involved great danger. Workers had to learn to manage the mill's sophisticated machinery. They, more than other workers, labored as machine operators with specialized knowledge. For example, workers adjusted the levels of chemicals added during the flotation process and took samples of the mineral to determine copper ore content. At the same time, the mechanized and skilled nature of the work did not render labor in the mills free of danger. Workers frequently suffered burns from spilled liquid or from the toxic fumes emitted during the milling process. In addition, these fumes provoked fainting and respiratory problems among most workers. Along with these more minor day-to-day work hazards, the most serious and dramatic accidents in the mill occurred when workers fell into the mills or into the gigantic cauldrons for processing copper ore.

In the Caletones smelting plant, workers operated the reverberatory ovens, maintaining a constant flame and watching the distribution of copper in the ovens. Converting blister copper into refined copper involved operating giant ovens, placing molding clay, introducing sticks into the oven, taking samples, heating huge spoons for the molds of refined copper, molding refined copper into diverse forms, and controlling the pouring and cooling of the copper. As in the mill, these jobs required workers to operate sophisticated machinery but were not free from risk. Fumes from the smelter's chimney covered the mining camps and produced silicosis in the lungs, and workers frequently experienced terrible burns and fractures during the smelting process.

Workers in all sections labored without sufficient protective gear. According to the Inspección General del Trabajo, the workers in the mine and the Sewell workshops lacked basic protective clothing, gloves, masks, and boots. The mine and workshops lacked fans and ventilation systems for expelling gas and dust. Dust from both the blasting and the processing in the mills thickened the air that workers breathed. The labor was physically exhausting, and workers suffered an almost certain future of early retirement and death from silicosis. And, if silicosis didn't kill them, constant accidents in the mine's tunnels brought many careers to an abrupt end. Miners were killed and injured by falling rocks, by dynamite explosions, and in long falls down mine shafts. In addition, they frequently suffered illnesses or death caused by the accumulation of gases in the mine's tunnels.

Workers in the processing plants in the mill and the foundry suffered different forms of hardships: excessive heat from the ovens, toxic fumes from the chemicals used to purify the copper, and air heavy with dust and soot. Like those in the mine, they worked without such basic security equipment as smocks, gloves, or overalls. In 1937, a labor inspector noted that a large number of workers in the Caletones foundry labored without protective clothing, "exposing themselves permanently to serious accidents." In the mill, the report noted the need for adequate ventilators to expel the poisonous sulfurous gases that the workers breathed in daily.[8] Records of accidents reveal that workers every day lost arms, hands, or eyes or suffered more minor injuries, such as fractures or burns, that prevented them from working for short periods of time.[9]

The company's indemnification policies provided little help. Workers received half-pay and hospital fees when injured. An accident had dreadful consequences. If it resulted in death, the miner's family was left destitute with a small pension and no home and dependent on the company's goodwill to provide some kind of indemnification.[10] When an accident did not lead to immediate demise, the company provided small levels of short-term compensation for work-related injuries. However, workers lost wages for the days they couldn't work, were frequently dismissed for carelessness and violating security codes, and, if unable to work, lost both their incomes and their lodgings in the camps.

In 1939, a miner's widow wrote a letter to the president begging for aid for her family. Her husband, she wrote, had lost his life in the mine, leaving her and her four children without any resources apart from a small monthly pension from the company, which "barely is enough to feed the little ones." Emilia Rivas asked Aguirre Cerda to intervene and request that the company administration increase this monthly pension so that she could buy a house, "because currently I have nowhere to live." Her tenure in the mine's barracks was about to come to an end, and with widowhood she now also confronted homelessness.[11] The desperate situation of El Teniente widows received national attention in 1945 when, because of a fire in the mine's tunnels, 355 workers were killed in the worst accident in the mine's history, known nationally as the tragedy of "*el humo.*" The families of the deceased miners, who had lost their rights to housing in the mining camps, moved into makeshift tents in the central plaza in Rancagua.[12]

Silicosis combined with accidents to bring miners' careers to an early end. Almost every miner suffered from the disease and eventually had to retire with a small company pension after a number of years underground. In July 1943, for example, the company paid each of seven workers pensions of between $15,206.40 pesos and $31,687.20 pesos for silicosis disabilities. Most of these men, although young, were totally incapacitated and unable to work. One was twenty-eight years old and had worked in the mine since he was sixteen. The others were thirty-five, thirty-eight, thirty-nine, forty-one, forty-eight, and sixty-eight years old. They had labored in El Teniente from twelve to twenty-seven years, usually their entire adult lives.[13]

The small number of miners given pensions because of silicosis indicates, however, the company's unwillingness to diagnose or recognize the illness. Miners became sick or died not from silicosis, according to the company, but from tuberculosis, influenza, or any other number of diseases for which it bore no responsibility and refused to compensate workers. In addition, Chilean law did not include silicosis as a work-related disease requiring employer indemnification.

A particularly revealing 1935 company memorandum detailed Braden's policy on silicosis. The memorandum argued that the company should recognize only five cases of men incapacitated by silicosis. These men were to receive pensions and small plots of land on company property. The memorandum also, however, described "quite a number of other laborers who are known to be suffering from tuberculosis . . . who, due to a tubercular condition, are physically unfit and unable to render services sufficient to justify the comparatively high wage they are now being paid." The memo recommended that "as rapidly as possible men in such physical condition should be gotten rid of."[14] Personnel records reveal that a number of workers were dismissed or, after their contract had ended, not rehired by the company "for medical reasons" or because they were physically unfit. A 1942 company medical report listing all cases and illnesses treated during the year mentioned not one case of diagnosed or treated silicosis.[15]

The case of the obrero Leopoldo Riquelme Garrido was representative of the lot of silicosis-stricken workers. Riquelme Garrido, after retiring, sued Braden for a disability pension because he suffered from silicosis. He had entered the mine in 1930, fallen sick in 1936, and repeatedly visited the company clinic, where he was diagnosed with bronchial asthma and emphysema that was attributed to his "weak constitution" rather than to his work in the mine. Despite the testimony of doctors for the Dirección General del Trabajo about the debilitated state of Riquelme's lungs, he failed to win his case and had to survive without any kind of workers' compensation or pension.[16]

While work sections outside the mine employed significant numbers of workers, the mine and its cuadrillas composed the bulk of the El Teniente labor force. The sections devoted to the copper refining process, the mill and the foundry, along with such other support sections as the hydroelectric plant, the workshops, and the warehouses, employed relatively few workers. These were the sections where workers labored primarily as machine operators or mechanics and where the level of technology was extremely high.[17] In general, wages in the mine were highest, and most

El Teniente workers hoped eventually to work their way into the mine from other sections.

Workers often sought work in the mine because base wages and work incentives were higher there. Workers earned a salary for the completion of a specific job assigned by supervisors at the beginning of the workday. For work completed beyond the assigned task, they could earn bonuses. Most bonuses, as incentives for production, were available to workers in the mines because all areas of production—the concentrating plant, the mills, and the foundry—depended on a steady flow of mineral from the mine and because production in the mine, unlike in the processing plants, was relatively undermechanized and highly labor-intensive. One former miner remembers that work in the mine before the 1970s was "extremely hard, extremely hard, it was very hard, since it wasn't at all mechanized, everything was done with physical force, by hand." But, he recalls, workers also toiled hard to meet production goals and earn bonuses: "It was rare that you got out of work on time because you worked to earn more, there were times that in eight hours you could earn forty hours [worth of wages] and it didn't matter to the gringo to pay that, what mattered was to advance."[18] Another worker recalled that under the North American administration, material conditions were better than after nationalization in 1971 because "the gringo had a way of giving bonuses that made it in the interest of the workers to work overtime; if you worked four hours they paid you five or six according to how much you got done in the four hours, so they gave you incentives."[19] Workers in the more highly mechanized processing plants could earn relatively high wages as machine operators but didn't have the same work incentives as were available to those in the mine.

The company offered salaries well above what an agricultural worker could earn as a peón or inquilino. Wages of El Teniente workers were also significantly higher than those earned by workers in other industrial sectors. In comparison with workers in the two other mining sectors, nitrates and coal, copper miners also earned more. In 1937, for example, the average daily wage for an obrero in nitrates was $19.80 pesos; for a coal miner, $14.18 pesos; and for a copper miner, $20.88 pesos. A textile worker made only $11.61 pesos daily in 1937; a leather worker, $13.70 pesos; and a shoe worker, $10.32 pesos. In 1941, nitrate obreros earned an average daily wage of $26.48 pesos; coal miners, $24.84 pesos; and copper miners, $38.82 pesos. In this same year textile workers earned $21.77 pesos daily, and shoe workers, $23.05 pesos. By 1946 these wage differentials had grown even greater: nitrate workers earned an average daily salary of $59.47 pesos; coal miners, $55.50 pesos; and copper miners, $83.68 pesos. In El Teniente, obreros received an average daily wage of $117.18 pesos, twice the average wages of nitrate and coal miners.[20]

Inside the mine, workers also received bonuses both for individual production levels and for the production of the crew. In addition, crew chiefs and foremen received similar bonuses for increasing output. This system of incentives, rather than fostering divisions and competition among the workers of a crew, established the basis for unity and solidarity as workers labored for the shared goal of increasing the crew's production level. Also, the incentive system meant that workers, crew chiefs, and foremen often shared a common interest in increasing production in competition with other teams and in terms of their relation to the company's North American supervisors who oversaw production in the mine, established jobs, and awarded bonuses.

Bonuses thus served a disciplinary function by providing incentive for workers to increase production and by bringing crew chiefs, foremen, and cuadrillas together. Crew chiefs and foremen were almost always Chilean and were frequently former cuadrilla members. They thus shared with team members experiences of work and ethnic identity. This frequently placed them in united opposition to North American supervisors inside the mine, while cementing the authority of the crew chief. Crew chiefs and foremen also represented to miners the possibility of social mobility and promotion out of the ranks of the "laboring" classes (obreros) and into world of "professionals" (empleados). As empleados, foremen were paid on monthly contracts, received higher wages, and gained access to better housing for their families in the camps. In addition, their status granted them a series of legal rights and benefits not available to obreros. Thus they embodied for miners the promises of social mobility implicit in the company's paternalist program of social control.

The common interests of crew chiefs, foremen, and workers were revealed in the illicit practice of "altering the marks." Both workers and foremen describe the systems they devised to increase the numbers of cars of copper emptied into the chute and registered by the card checker.

Usually this was done with a stick to prompt the lever that triggered the marking mechanism. This false marking allowed the workers to take it easy in their work and still meet production goals.[21] At times crew chiefs and foremen participated in this subterfuge so that they could beat other team bosses in the monthly production competitions and win cash prizes and promotions. While workers were frequently punished for changing the mark, sometimes their capataces joined them in what was clearly a common means of gaining space, given the rigid demands for production made by the company and the North American supervisors. In this way, the company's incentive system and the organization of work in the crew established solidarities between all members of the mining crew, including crew chiefs and foremen.

The solidarity of the work crew was expressed and reconstituted in the shared slang and forms of speech of miners. The world of the mine had its own lexicon. Each miner had a special nickname, and within their own crew miners called themselves "*gancho*" (hook) or "*ganchito*," signifying the close links that bound them together. Each job or part of the mine also had its own name: the "*carcheque*," for instance, got his name from the English "carchecker." Specific jobs assigned by supervisors were called the "*nombrada*" or "*nombra'*." The miners maintained a close relation with the figure of the Virgin Mary, whom they called "*viejita linda*" (pretty old woman), supplicating her for protection or cursing her when she proved deaf to their requests.[22] Miners developed an idiom impenetrable even by other Chileans, a set of common terms and references that expressed the bonds that tied them together in the mine. As one former miner remembers: "If we began to talk in front of you [the interviewer] here, you wouldn't understand a thing. . . . The system hasn't changed for forty years, words that only we know, for example . . . [for] '*tu estai enfermo de la columna*' [you have a bad back] we say that '*tu estai enfermo de la vigah*' [you have a bad beam]. . . . [T]hat's why I say that if we talked between us in miners' terms, nobody would understand us, only another miner. I always told my wife, we live in a world apart, and we have a vocabulary apart." Miners' shared language reflected the close ties of workers in work teams who depended on one another to meet production goals and to ensure their mutual safety in the dangerous conditions of the mine. The same miner recalls that "the comradeship [*compañerismo*] was great, very united, . . . compañerismo and respect . . . because the circumstances obligated one to be more than a compañero, obligated you to be a gancho because you needed all kinds of things from one another."[23] Miners depended on one another both inside and outside the mine for their survival. Inside the mine, teamwork and mutual solidarity were necessary to the work crew's safety and its capacity to earn bonuses. Outside the mine, work comrades helped one another out with small loans, shared illegal alcohol, and other forms of support.

Miners defined their labor as a source of masculine affirmation and pride. They celebrated the pure physicality of their work and the risk and danger of their struggle in an environment that constantly threatened their lives. Within the mine, workers competed among themselves to prove their strength as miners. Competition was extended to contests between work groups, fostered by the company, which offered prizes and bonuses to the groups with the highest production. Symbolic of this competition was a board placed at the entrance of the mine and divided into sections, with a little wooden horse representing each cuadrilla. The horses advanced (or failed to advance) in a simulated race to the finish, with progress measured in terms of accident-free production. Similarly, the company conducted a lottery within the mine, with cash prizes. Only workers who had worked a minimum of twenty days a month could participate.[24]

Miners also competed within the cuadrilla to demonstrate who was the strongest, who had the most force, or who could perform a difficult job more ably. A worker won a large measure of respect from his fellow workers and from foremen for his capacity to work hard. The company helped to foster this cult of physical strength and to reinforce it by implementing a system of competitions among workers for prizes for high levels of production. These contests included drilling competitions, in which workers would compete to see who could drill most skillfully. The miners also participated in a series of other competitions, according to one observer, "of perfectly useful works, competitions stimulated and awarded by the company."[25] In fact, the miners took great pride in their capacity to work hard and their skills in negotiating and managing the difficult terrain of production in the mine. As one oral source remembers, "Among the workers there was a certain competitiveness that made them, well, 'I'm agallado [strong, brave, enterprising] because I can carry so much, I worked this much, I advanced that much.' . . . [T]here are workers who were truly animals for work."[26]

To work inside the mine implied a certain stature and status in El Teniente's internal hierarchy. As Castro writes in one of his stories about work in El Teniente, "I never looked down upon my compañeros in the mills and the workshop, nor at the others who worked above ground, but I can't deny that my aspiration was always to be transferred to the mine, to feel that I was a miner in every sense of the word." True manhood and respect from one's comrades could be won only by working in the mine and proving one's strength. For Castro's narrator, the prospect of working in the mine inspired the desire to dominate the mine itself and prove one's self. He writes that "the incentive to penetrate and remove what was inside grew every day, especially when I heard the conversations of my father, Floro Alcántara, Corrales, and Manquelpe to whom they had given a drill to begin preparing the path of the dynamite."[27] The miner who operated the drills that pushed the tunnels into the mountain had one of the most physically demanding jobs, but also one of the higher-paid jobs among the work team and one of the most respected.

Miners developed a sense of self based on their capacity for hard and dangerous physical labor. Thus one remembers that the true miner "was the man who liked the mine, who came into himself in the mine and who stayed in the mine; there were workers when I entered in 1948 who had been working twenty years. But for those who didn't like the mine, who were incapable of doing the work because they lacked skill, because they lacked strength . . . they disappeared rapidly from the mine; the true miners 'made in the mine' were the hard guys, those who had stature, had force [ñeque], had strength, and endured and supported all the pressures."[28]

The physical strength of miners became an essential element of their masculinity. Castro's stories, for example, repeatedly celebrate miners' physical virility and construct an iconography of miners' bodies with constant references to their "wide hands," "wide shoulders," "firm arms like two hammers," and "impressive moustaches."[29] Castro describes one miner as a "mountain of tight muscles . . . massive, robust."[30] The miners found pride in the physical skills required by their jobs in the mine. As Castro writes, they "knew that sensation of triumph, that action as victors, when the miner thunders the twenty-five explosions and the enmaderadores hurry to extend the tunnel."[31] Castro writes appreciatively of a skilled miner "who knows the effects of the explosion in all its details, who had located the perforations in such a way that . . . the explosion blew the rock away in an extensive stretch, each explosion supporting the other successively until all twenty or twenty-five had thundered."[32] Similarly, he describes a miner "who enjoyed fame as a true enmadera-dor, capable of stepping on the heels of the explosions as he advanced into the mountain."[33] The miners expressed their overcoming of alien-ation and danger inside the mine in the language of masculine pride and sexualized conquest. In myths and lore, they figured the mine as feminine and sexualized their labor, transforming work into a source of masculine affirmation. They defined the exercise of strength and skill at their jobs as the domination of the female mine. One popular song described, for ex-ample, how "el pico del minero es el mas duro que hay / parte a pedazos la roca y le saca el mineral" [the miner's pick is the hardest that there is / it breaks the rock to pieces and extracts the ore].[34]

Yet labor in the mine provided an uneasy basis for self-assertion and dignity. The constant danger of accidents and the more gradual but equally devastating effects of silicosis rendered a life of work in El Teniente fragile and took their toll on the bodies of mine workers. The company's regime of discipline in the mines and the camps and the permanent proletarian-ization of the labor force exacerbated the erosion of workers' command over their daily lives, their labor, and their bodies. As they settled in El Teniente and committed themselves to a future in the mine, workers ex-pressed their sense of loss of control by depicting the mine as a threat-ening, consuming, and vengeful female presence. Although they might assert masculine pride and dignity in mastery of their work and domina-tion of the mine's treacherous topography, ultimately the mine governed workers' lives. As a miner in one of Castro's stories declares: "The mine is that way, you enter her and you can't leave no matter how hard you work. She's a very vexing and chastizing woman."[35] Thus miners both sought to overcome alienation at work by constructing labor in terms of sexual conquest and expressed their sense of loss of power in terms of sexual anxiety. By figuring the mine as a feminine object of conquest and a feminine source of danger, miners articulated their understanding of class relations in the modern mining enterprise in the language of sexuality.

Anxieties about women and sexuality permeated the language and cul-ture of El Teniente miners and revealed the ways in which they under-stood their own lives and labor to be consumed by the mine. Miners believed that a woman entering the mine provoked accidents and spoke of the mine as a jealous and punishing woman. In addition, they attributed accidents to female spirits (*animitas*) or to the ghost of a woman, "*la llorona*" (the crier), who haunted the mine's tunnels; they also described the activities of the ghost of a woman who was executed for killing her miner husband and chopping him to pieces. Similarly, miners believed in a spirit called *la lola* (the girl), who dwelled in the mine and did away with workers. One miner characterizes la lola as "a horrible and disheveled woman whose cries drive the listener insane" or as "a strange monster, mixture of monkey and woman, who guards a secret treasure in the mine." Other versions describe an "invisible and intangible being that only announces its presence with its cold breath in the back of the neck of the victim." [36] El Teniente's female spirits represented both danger and protection. They punished with accidents but could be supplicated for protection. Because these spirits guarded the copper that the miners sought to discover and extract, they had to be treated delicately. Death in the mine could result from crossing the female spirits, who jealously protected a hidden treasure. Labor in the mine could be dangerous because it involved sexual conquest, domination, and betrayal. Thus one story tells how "the mountain, alive, wounded, bloody, revenged itself against those miserable men for the desecration of its millenary bowels." [37]

The miners' definition of the mine as a threatening female presence was also expressed in a prevalent fear of adultery. Many workers attributed the distinctiveness of their identity as miners to turbulent marital lives. Miners had their own terms to describe unfaithful wives, using the phrase "hacer las diez ultima," or "to do the last ten," to mean to be unfaithful to a husband, as in "do the last ten to the husband." [38] The miners also had a name for the man who slept with the wives of miners: "Jorge." This name came from a miner who was notorious and legendary for sleeping with other miners' wives. It was a custom to call an unfaithful miner "Jorge" or to tell a miner that his wife had been seen with "Jorge." [39] Similarly, miners sang a little refrain about adultery to taunt and torment the many miners who had left their wives behind and gone up to the mine alone: "El minero en las minas 'ta trabajando / y la mujer abajo lo esta gorreando" [the miner in the mines is working / and the woman below is deceiving him]. [40]

During the 1960s, social workers employed by El Teniente ascribed the miners' extraordinary combativeness to a general dissatisfaction with their lives in the camps based mainly on the problems of working as a miner and the difficulties in maintaining healthy marriages. According to company social workers, because more men than women lived in the camps and because they enjoyed little privacy and little entertainment and often worked night shifts, there were constant problems between neighbors with respect to possible adultery. Also, the many workers who lived in the camps away from their families experienced "tensions and anxieties" because of their constant fear of infidelity.[41]

In oral history interviews, many miners emphasize adultery as prevalent and as a fundamental way to explain their distinctive "manera de ser." For one miner and union leader, work hours, the dehumanizing and consuming quality of the labor, exhaustion, sickness, and the little time spent at home led to constant family problems, adultery, and alcoholism. This fact, he believed, helped shape miners' particular identity based on their sense of hardship and sacrifice, as well as machismo, and ultimately explained their discontent and combativeness. "You see, the worker arrives tired . . . from work and sleeps, gets up, drinks, arrives home drunk . . . he doesn't have a good relationship with his family, he doesn't have a good relationship with his wife. . . . [L]ife in the camps is harder because there you noticed more those women that cheated on their husbands, and everyone knew that the woman cheated on her husband."[42] Thus, miners built a work culture that was defined by the tension between a sense of affirmation and pride in work and a sense of loss of power and manhood owing to the nature of mine labor.

This masculinized work culture fit the North American company's scheme of gender relations in which women were relegated to a subordinate and dependent role within miners' households. Miners defined the meaning of social power, both its loss and its conquest, in terms of a cult of manhood based on a sense of opposition and antagonism to women. By sexualizing labor, the miners excluded women from their world of work and thus implicitly reaffirmed an ideology that restricted women to the household and the domestic sphere. The cult of masculinity in the mine was not necessarily tied to this ideology, but it helped to reinforce and reproduce it within miners' families. The myths and images produced by the miners to lend meaning to their work helped to naturalize mine work as men's work, to render the exclusion of women from the mine common sense and obvious, thus obscuring a concrete process within which women were increasingly relegated to the household and feminized sec-

tors of the labor market. The signification by miners of work as a
of masculine pride and power predicated on the conquest of the fem.
nized object, the mine, also served the company's interests in increasing
production. As miners built a sense of dignity based on their strength
and skill, they became productive workers. Thus, for example, competitions between and within cuadrillas led workers to intensify their labor
in order to prove their manliness.

This same sense of manhood contributed, however, to a culture and
identity that fueled a deeply rooted combativeness and solidarity among
miners in opposition to foremen and supervisors. The pride that workers
found in their labor was also expressed in what David Montgomery has
called "a manly bearing toward the boss."[43] Miners' codes defined manhood in terms of independence, strength, and solidarity with one's workmates. The true miner stood up to foremen and supervisors and stood by
the workers in his cuadrilla. While miners worked hard to dominate the
mine and show off their courage, strength, and skill, they also resisted the
power exercised by their foremen. Work was a source of self-affirmation,
and miners sought to exert their control over it. Fights between workers
and bosses and between workers occurred with enormous frequency in
the mine. In these conflicts, workers upheld workplace codes of honor
based on loyalty to fellow workers and an independent and challenging
attitude toward supervisors and foremen.

Mine supervisors and foremen exercised absolute control over the organization of work in and outside the mine and over the workers, whom
they constantly harassed, swore at, made fun of, and often forced to engage in extra, unpaid tasks. Despite the bonds of friendship, camaraderie,
and shared economic incentive that united crew chiefs and their cuadrillas, many Chilean foremen responded to their position in the mine's hierarchy and to incentives to increase production and meet the demands of
North American supervisors by driving their work teams hard. Workers
were constantly threatened with dismissal, suspension, or punishment if
they failed to meet the demands of their foreman or to fulfill their assigned tasks. In 1939, *Despertar Minero* noted that "for many years we have
had to support insults, abuse, mockery and taunting from the jefes. . . .
In the mine there are supervisors and foremen who despise the worker,
who treat him like a dog and not a human being. . . . There are supervisors who confiscate the wages workers have earned through their labor,

they punish them, they suspend them, they antagonize them."[44] When workers complained to the company administration about these abuses, the union newspaper continued, they were threatened with dismissal. For every foreman who acted as a comrade to his crew, there were many more who exercised an "iron fist," as the miners' union frequently put it, over their workers.

For the miners, the system of internal rules that governed work in the mine resembled "more a dictatorship than a system of work."[45] One former mine supervisor describes this as a time when "supervisors had a very wide command of technical knowledge and also of discipline. . . . [A]ccording to this system, the supervisor never made a mistake, even when the mistakes were obvious, because the mistakes were always the workers'."[46] Workers suffered the constant vigilance of a hierarchy of shift leaders, foremen, and supervisors who oversaw work in the mine. Workers could not answer back or protest the commands or abusive treatment of the cabos and capataces. Nor could they provide any input or advice on labor and production. Any sign of resistance was summarily punished. Chilean foremen jotted down workers' names in the infamous "La Peñeca," the book of punishments, and later reported back to North American shift bosses and supervisors, who then handed out punishments. Usually, workers were suspended for one or two weeks and lost their wages. Many workers, however, lost their jobs for lack of work discipline. Jefes fired or suspended hundreds of workers every month, enlisting the support of carabineros in kicking workers out of the mine and at times out of the camps.

When a worker refused to carry out an unremunerated job not included in his contract, the infamous "nombrada" in El Teniente, a boss would apply the internal rules for "lack of fulfillment of production goals," note down the worker's name in "La Peñeca," suspend the worker, or simply fire him.[47] For example, miners were forced to do extra jobs cleaning the boxes that transported the copper, work that was unpaid. Foremen would oblige a worker whose job was to attend the pumps in the mine to abandon his machines to do some other small job and would then punish the worker for failing to do his job, either suspending him, firing him, or taking away his wages.[48] The assignment of extra tasks was a common method of extracting more labor from workers and a frequent subject of complaint by the union.[49]

To undermine workers' efforts to exert some control within the mine through union representatives or workplace delegates, jefes forced disruptive workers or workers involved in union activities to perform the most onerous tasks in the mine, to work unpaid overtime hours, and to do jobs not included in their contracts. They also provided a constant stream of harassment and abuse in an effort to drive rebellious workers to quit or to provoke an incident that could provide an excuse for a quick firing. A report by a delegate of the governor of O'Higgins noted how, following the major strike in 1919, "the majority of foremen treat their workers abusively, with much rancor because of the strike, hatreds that become intrigues with their high superiors to fire them."[50]

Foremen directed their most violent treatment at workers who challenged their authority either by complaining to the company or through union activity. Supervisors employed a strategy of assigning known union activists extra work and onerous jobs that, combined with a torrent of abuse, aimed to provoke the miner either to slip up on the job or to quit altogether. In one case, a foreman would not let a union leader use the bathroom and warned his fellow workers that if they were found talking with him they would be fired.[51] In another case, a worker who participated in a strike committee was detained by carabineros on the orders of a supervisor. After a few days in jail, this worker returned to the mine, where his foreman warned him he would last only another few days and then suspended him for fifteen days. When the worker again returned, he was accused of not doing his job properly and escorted out of the mine and then kicked out of the camps by carabineros.[52]

Supervisors and foremen routinely called on the carabineros to arrest or to remove from the mine the workers who were "unionists," "revolutionaries," or "bad elements" or those who simply challenged their authority by not succumbing to demands for extra labor or to abuse. At times workers were detained or fired under the pretext of "lack of production" or "lack of security" because they refused to invite foremen to share their contraband liquor or to "grease their foreman's palm" with a share of their wages.[53] In one case, a foreman constantly harassed and abused a worker because that worker's daughter had rejected his amorous advances.[54]

The severe discipline within the mine did not produce quiescence among the El Teniente miners. Reports from the mine during the 1930s and 1940s record hundreds of workers dismissed or suspended every month for abandoning work, failing to fulfill the required production levels, altering the marks on the buzones to increase their production figures, insolence, violating the camps' dry law, fighting, missing entire workdays, immorality, disobedience, and dishonesty. Absenteeism was rampant. Workers tended not to show up to work a number of days every month, particularly for "San Lunes."[55]

Frequently, miners responded to jefes with "insolence and vulgarity." In one of many cases in 1943, a boss transferred a worker to a new job. The worker refused to do the work and "answered the Jefe Sr. I. Contreras with insolence and insults."[56] That same year the enmaderador Luis Miranda García was ordered by his foreman to clean up the area in which he was working. Miranda García, like many workers, answered what he believed to be an unreasonable demand with insults. At the end of the shift the foreman returned to find the area completely dirty and a number of cars overturned, and he yelled at the worker, who again responded with "insolence and threats not only for Valenzuela [the foreman] but also for the other capataces and jefes, inciting the other workers to attack the jefes and capataces."[57]

Miners expressed an independent and oppositional work culture in their own particular idiom, ways of speaking, jokes, pranks, anecdotes, and myths. The cultural and linguistic differences between the Chilean workers and the North American bosses underscored the broad social inequalities that separated them and exacerbated conflicts in the mine, subverting Braden's attempt to inculcate a set of paternalist values in its workforce. In 1919, for example, a study noted that "the ties and union [between North Americans and Chileans] that the use of a common language establishes leaves a lot to be desired here."[58] The workers' sense of national and ethnic antagonism toward their North American bosses reinforced the concrete conflicts that were structured by the struggles over power within the mine.

The miners often made fun of and mocked the way of speaking of the North Americans. Thus the hotel for supervisors, called the Staff House, was referred to by the miners as the *casa de estafa* (the swindle house). The Welfare Department, or *Departamento de Bienestar,* received the name *Departamento de Bienfregar* (the Harass Well Department), thus revealing its unpopularity among the miners. The miners had various Spanish nicknames for their bosses, which the Americans could not understand. Workers also used a code language to communicate among themselves. When they were slacking off in the mine, for example, and a jefe arrived unexpectedly, they shouted *loro* (parrot) or *fuego* (fire) as warning signals.[59] In one example, the miners named one jefe who severely punished workers who slacked off "El Gringo Malo." One day, when this jefe was descending the tunnel in the mine, a miner took a laxative and dumped it on him, while the miners, in mockery, claimed that it was raining. Not one of the miners in the work gang denounced the perpetrator, revealing the solidarity of the miners and the vast social and cultural spaces that separated the North American bosses from the Chilean workers.[60]

This work culture of disrespect for authority and irreverence was expressed in a mocking humor that united the miners in opposition to company authorities. Castro describes one incident in which a group of miners taking "the cage" up to a mine shaft began to make fun of the serenos who accompanied them and who were present to impose company authority. "Lowering their voices, the most daring spoke: 'Wow, what a terrible smell there is here.' 'It's because there are some serenos here that's why, we're going to have a bad day of it. There's nothing worse than going up to the mine in the same car with fags [*maricones*].'"[61] These forms of expressing disrespect and antagonism toward foremen and supervisors are also depicted by Gonzalo Drago, who describes how after a blast in the mine, "some lamps were extinguished because of the vibrations from the explosion, giving the workers the opportunity to mumble lewd and vulgar insults [against their bosses]."[62]

Stealing from the company was another way in which workers flouted the authority of foremen and supervisors and helped bring in a little extra income. Miners frequently stole materials, tools, coal, and even copper from their workplaces. They used materials or tools to make improvements in their own living quarters or at other times sold their booty in Rancagua.[63] Workers also often stole dynamite from the storerooms. This was doubly threatening for the company because dynamite could be used by workers in labor conflicts. As one North American supervisor testified, "Even though the company gives the buzoneros dynamite under strict control and observation and even though they are watched by the supervisors, there are plenty of clever ways to avoid this vigilance and collect the sticks that haven't exploded and to have the supervisors note them down as having exploded."[64] A package of thirty sticks of dynamite could be worth two days of wages to an obrero.

Constant altercations with foremen frequently escalated into individual acts of physical violence. Many workers were fired for fighting with jefes. In 1940, for example, a mechanic in the mine workshop, Juan Fernández Videl, was arrested by police for injuring the face of the second jefe of the workshop. That same month, an enmaderador in the mine was fired for arguing with and then punching a capataz, and a jornalero "vulgarly insulted" and struck with a wood board a capataz who had reported him for laziness.[65] In a similar case, Carlos Castillo Arce, a forty-two-year-old enmaderador punched his foreman, Rafael Manríquez Medel, because he consistently noted down Castillo Arce's name in "the book." According to Castillo Arce, "Without any motive at all, only out of ill will, he put me in the book again." The next day, the same foreman refused to note down the work completed by Castillo Arce, and when Castillo Arce complained, he was insulted and challenged to a fight. Castillo Arce declined to fight, afraid of losing his job, but Manríquez Medel attacked him the next morning on Castillo Arce's way to work. According to the foreman, it was Castillo Arce who provoked the fight and challenged him.[66] In another typical case, the electrician Alejo Bustamente San Martín charged his capataz with abusing and beating him. He told the Sewell court that when he had complained to the foreman Grogg about being transferred to a different shift, Grogg told him that the change had been made by the supervisors higher up and that if he didn't like it, he could "go fuck himself." Bustamente San Martín replied sharply, Grogg began to push him, and "in defense" he punched the foreman in the eye.[67] Similarly, Ernesto Bernal Orellano punched his boss, Eliseo Naranjo Rojas, because "I was up to here with him hurrying me on the job, a job I couldn't have done faster, and threatening to fire me."[68]

Conflicts in the mine were so frequent that in 1947 the Sewell court noted a plethora of cases having to do with fights between foremen and workers and stated that "there exist continual conflicts and tyrannies in the relations between obreros and capataces."[69] At times, conflicts between workers and supervisors became deadly, as in the 1940 case of one enmaderador who murdered P. M. Kinney, a mine foreman, "in revenge for a mild reprimand for failure to do his work."[70] In oral testimonies, workers recall that a number of unpopular North American supervisors suffered deadly "accidents" in the mine tunnels by the miners' hands. In one case, the miner Carlos Cavieres was fired and arrested in 1936 after showing up to work drunk with his workmate and then taking out a pistol when the North American supervisor informed them that they couldn't work. Cavieres pulled the trigger, but the gun misfired and the supervisor escaped unharmed.[71]

Fights, like irreverent humor, practical jokes, stealing, and altering the marks, constituted important interventions by workers in the process of production. They represented a resistance to and resentment toward the authority of foremen and the power of the company. Fights also revealed workers' efforts to impose their own will on the process of production and the ways in which workers within the mine maintained a sense of self and dignity. Such conflicts served as an expression of the workers' will and independence and as a means to winning time and limiting the demands placed on them for production.

Fights between workers were also a constant feature of daily life in the mine.[72] These conflicts reflected the codes of masculinity that governed work in the mine. Workers fought to defend their honor and to assert their independence, physical strength, and capacity to stand up to authority. In addition, workers' fights were structured by the informal norms that defined manhood in terms of loyalty to work comrades and opposition to the company. Scabs, strikebreakers, supervisors, and foremen were figured as unmasculine, homosexual, and even feminine and as violating workers' codes of masculine honor.

An example of the codes that ruled relations within the mine was a fight between the capataz Oscar Jara Osorio and the obrero Neftali Cáceres. Jara Osorio had noted down Cáceres in the book of punishments for failing to meet the minimum production standard. Cáceres avoided a suspension but lost a day's work and wages. He appealed his case to a North American supervisor. The next day Jara and Cáceres bumped into each other in the barracks and the empleado told the obrero, "Well boy, you got out of that one." Cáceres responded that it was "real funny" putting him in "the book," and Jara answered back that he had to put "*huevones*" (assholes) like Cáceres in the book all the time. They exchanged more insults and threats, and Jara challenged Cáceres, saying, "Make no mistake, nobody has put their hands on me yet." They began to fight, and Cáceres won easily, overcoming the foreman. After thoroughly beating him, however, he helped him up, and the two left the barracks together. Jara told Cáceres that he wouldn't complain because "he had been beaten fairly."[73] In another similar case a worker attacked a jefe because, in his words, "He challenged me. I'm no coward and won't let anyone hit me."[74] Challenges and fights were accepted ways of defining and establishing one's manhood and honor.

Fights frequently broke out between striking workers and scabs. Workers who refused to honor a strike were threatened and often beaten by strikers. During a strike in 1946, for example, a group of one hundred workers went to a scab's house and were taking him away with them to the union hall when they ran into police who promptly arrested the leaders.[75] During the same strike, other workers were beaten up by strike committees for scabbing. During wildcat work stoppages, pickets often used force to keep production paralyzed, boarding the train that took workers to the mine to intimidate scabs.[76]

In one instance, a pair of brothers assaulted another worker, Cabezas, who was returning home from a soccer match. During the game, the fans of the opposing team had heckled one of the brothers, Guillermo Morales, calling him a scab. The commotion was so great among the fans, who hurled insults at Morales, that police jumped into the stands and ordered the unruly spectators to quiet down. The fans, however, continued to insult Morales, accused him of working during an illegal wildcat strike, and called him "scab [krumiro], that is a suck up to the company [chupa de la compañía], and traitor." Morales returned the insults, and after the game a fight broke out. While almost the entire stadium heckled Morales for breaking the strike, he singled out Cabezas as an instigator and attacked him in order to defend his honor.[77]

The codes of manhood that miners upheld in their strikes were expressed in one telling incident during a 1942 labor conflict. While the miners were on strike, a picket guarding the mine came upon a scab. The workers abducted the krumiro and took him to the union hall, where he was submitted to an impromptu trial. The workers' court found the man guilty and sentenced him to dress as a woman. The workers' brigade then took the scab, dressed in women's clothes, around the camp as a form of public humiliation.[78] Here, quite clearly, the miners expressed the sense that to break a strike or to be a company loyalist was unmanly. Strikebreakers were attacked as violating not only the workers' solidarity but also the shared culture of manhood that lent this solidarity strength. A strikebreaker was figured as "female" or "unmanly" because scabs not only crossed picket lines but also crossed the carefully defined rules and codes of heterosexual masculinity that soldered work teams together within the mine. Similarly, as we have seen in another case, workers mockingly referred to serenos as "fags," figuring company agents as homosexual and unmanly.

To be called a "krumiro" or "chupa de la compañía" was not a matter to be taken lightly. A miner who had punched one of his workmates because the man had called him "chupa de la compañía" explained: "The imputation of 'chupa' is an insult; because it is a derogatory term that means traitor of the workers, I became indignant and punched him."[79] Similarly, the miner Juan Antonio Fritz punched a fellow worker and called him "chupa de Mister Ross," a North American supervisor.[80] The victim, it appeared from testimony, informed on other workers to the boss. In another case, a worker and his brother-in-law provoked a fight with a third worker on their shift because he had insulted them and "attacked their honor." The worker had called them "chupas de los jefes," words that, as one of the brothers-in-law testified, "injured me deeply."[81] The insult of being a company loyalist was signified in these cases by the sexualized and homoerotic implications of the verb *chupar* (to suck).

The culture of masculinity within the mine revealed the varying tensions between accommodation and resistance, consent and conflict, in the labor process. Miners' codes of manhood fueled a combative spirit of resistance to managerial authority. Informal forms of solidarity that were defined by rules of masculine honor in the mine supplied a basis for a strong militancy when strikes occurred. During labor actions, whether informal wildcat stoppages or legal organized strikes, the codes of the mine bound the workers together in common opposition to the company. At the same time, however, the cult of masculinity drew on respect for hard work and skill and represented an overcoming of the workers' alienation from their labor. Inside the mine, workers found pride and satisfaction in their capacity to work hard, not just objectified labor. In this way, their assertion of dignity and self-will through a masculinization of their work could, at times, serve the interest of supervisors in getting their crews to work hard and the company's interest in increasing production. In addition, miners found in the system of wages, incentives, and bonuses the possibility of achieving economic security and the capacity to attain a position as head of household in a stable family in which they enjoyed social status, respectability, and authority.

The tensions between accommodation and resistance at work can be seen in the system of payment in the mine. The company realized that its real "hook" for keeping workers in the mine was the relatively high wages and the bonuses it paid. In numerous interviews, workers explained that they endured the difficult work conditions of the mine and living conditions in the camps because of the high wages. As a group of retired workers and women who had lived in the camps put it, almost unanimously, in an oral history interview, "It was the money; they paid well."[82] Oral histories reveal workers' identification with the labor process in the mine and accommodation to the system of production. Almost all former miners, while noting the harshness of treatment in the mine, recall positively the valorization of work by the North American supervisors. "*Valorizaron el trabajo*" was a frequently used phrase in interviews. While the North American company demanded work and discipline, it appreciated and paid for a job well done. As one retired miner put it: "As long as you worked, they paid well and the treatment was good. If you didn't work, they fired you."[83] Another worker described how "the gringos had a different mentality—all they cared about was work. If a worker put all his force into his work, that was all that mattered." Thus, he describes how workers who had demonstrated capacity for labor in the mine, when fired for an infraction like drinking, would be rehired after suspension of one week or ten days, while a worker who was "lazy" would not be rehired. Many workers recall with some nostalgia that, despite supervisors' despotism, they rewarded skilled and hard labor.[84]

This same former miner remembers with admiration how even North American supervisors and engineers did the work of the lowest day laborer. The company sent new North American technicians and supervisors to work jobs in the mine in work crews so that they could familiarize themselves with every aspect of the production process before assuming their jobs. In addition, he recalls, if some job needed doing right away, an engineer or a supervisor would, if necessary, do it himself to keep production rolling. Similarly, one former North American supervisor recalls that, along with working in the crews, he also participated in fights, earning the miners' respect for his capacity to stand up for himself.[85] Supervisors' own capacity for work, respect for hard labor, and participation in the mine's codes of manhood lent legitimacy to the system of work and wages in the mine.

The miners' acceptance of wage labor and a career in mining signaled a victory for the company, albeit a victory that the workers had helped to forge through the strategy of using a favorable labor market to their own advantage. Yet while the miners' high wages, benefits, and bonuses served as the glue that cemented the workforce to the mine, they did not produce increased political quiescence, industrial peace, or work discipline. Workers came to regard the high wages and benefits paid by the company not as the result of its paternalist beneficence but as their hard-won rights after onerous labor and the continual sacrifices of arduous lives in the mining camps. In labor conflicts and petitions to the company, they constantly evoked the demanding work in the mine, silicosis, the high risk of accidents, and the difficulty of life high up in the mountains to justify their demands for higher salaries. While they may have earned high wages, they argued, they certainly earned far less than the North American workers in Kennecott's U.S. mines, and they suffered sacrifices and hardships that Chilean workers in other industries did not have to endure.

As the El Teniente workers remained in the mine, they established forms of workplace solidarity and nurtured a combative culture of insubordination and informal opposition to company authority. Miners' masculine identity became a source of militancy expressed not only in frequent fights or occasional murders of North American supervisors and Chilean foremen but also in work stoppages and collective conflicts. During the late 1930s and 1940s, the miners' work culture laid the basis for the first major legal strikes in the mine's history and for the reconfiguration of labor relations in El Teniente. Leftist political activists and union leaders played a crucial role in directing the informal, unorganized militancy of the mine into collective movements and in articulating miners' discontent and dissatisfaction in a formal ideological language and political praxis.

A militant work culture did not, however, translate directly into more formal political and ideological opposition or to collective labor action under the auspices of the union. Elements of the miners' masculine work culture collided with the programs, moral codes, and strategies of union leaders and their allies in political parties. At times, the miners' disrespect of authority and resistance to the organization and ordering of their lives in and outside the mine led them to oppose the direction of the union, as well as the power of the company. The miners' rebellious work culture frequently overflowed the limits imposed by the union leadership in wildcat strikes, and the miners often prodded union leaders and political activists to take more combative stands than allowed for by the labor code or mandated by the leftist parties.

Welfare Department personnel (date unknown)

(above) Worker housing in the mining camps, 1916
(below) Cantina workers, 1919

(left) Buzonero at work
in the mine, 1919
(below) Timbermen at
work in the mine, 1919

(above) Mine workers, 1931
(left) Mine workers, 1919

Drilling in the mine (date unknown)

(above) The mining camps, 1922
(below) Company vocational school, 1921

(above) Mining camp at night (date unknown)
(below) Workers on train during strike (date unknown)

(left) Miners at work, 1919
(below) Miners at work,
1919

"Rotos Macanudos" and Football Stars

Popular Culture, Working-Class Masculinity,

and Opposition in the Mining Camps

The North American administration of the El Teniente mine attempted to exert total control over both the physical and the cultural space of the mine's camps. Company police and the local carabineros surveilled camp passageways and searched workers' houses for illicit sex, alcohol, stolen goods, and clandestine gambling. Public meetings, events, concerts, and celebrations required the company's permission. Even the union hall was company property. Braden regulated the nonwork cultural space of miners by restricting and reorganizing their recreational activities and by establishing a network of social organizations. Company-sponsored cultural activity was intended both to replace workers' preferred recreational pursuits and to replace the union as their central social organization.

Despite the Braden Copper Company's monopoly of social institutions and ideological production in the camps' schools, recreational organizations, newspapers, theater, and cinema, these cultural spaces came to constitute sites of conflict or, in the words of Terry Eagleton, "theatres of confrontation" between the miners and North American supervisors."[1] The North American company's campaigns of cultural and social reform failed to alter the everyday forms of working-class sociability in the camps. Braden confronted a population of workers who were disinclined to accept the company's messages about moral uplift and cultural improvement and who fashioned their own forms of social life outside the workplace. Workers extended their rebellious and intensely masculine work culture into the camps and the city of Rancagua through such everyday forms of recreation as drinking, gambling, and sex and rejected the company's strictures concerning moral behavior. Through these activities miners reproduced their bonds of workplace solidarity and expressed a sense of independence and masculine pride that challenged the control of public spaces and daily life in the camps that was exercised by the company and the state.

While many male workers directly opposed the company's regulation of their everyday behavior, other miners adopted many of the precepts of the Braden administration's paternalist social welfare system. These workers assumed the responsibilities of head of household, participated in the company schools and social clubs, ascended through the hierarchies of job classifications in the mine, and absorbed the company-inspired aspirations to middle-class lifestyles. In doing so, however, they contrasted the grim material realities of their lives with the promises of middle-class domesticity, social mobility, and consumption broadcast by the company. Workers who took the company's paternalist ideology seriously often looked to the union and collective action to fulfill their newly formed desires for a better life. Although social clubs, schools, and sports clubs contributed to the reorganization of workers' activities, habits, and values, they also became places where workers built new senses of community and expressed their antagonism toward the company and commitment to collective action. Those workers who best fit the company's prescriptions for disciplined and responsible behavior also made dedicated union militants and political activists.

"Bad Habits," Resistance, and Working-Class Masculinity

Battles over the control of space and social life in the camps constituted a central element of everyday life in El Teniente and were part of a more general war over the company's efforts to transform the social habits of its workforce. Workers' attempts to make their lives their own and express a sense of affirmation, dignity, and pleasure contributed to an informal, everyday, working-class culture, separate from and frequently antagonistic to the formal politics of the Left and organized labor, that subverted the regime of social control exercised by the company and the state in the mine and its camps. The struggles of workers over alcohol consumption, gambling, clothing styles, sex, and other forms of leisure activity formed part of a private, ongoing effort to express control over their nonwork lives in the camps' barracks and passageways and to create alternative forms of autonomy and community.

From the early 1920s, when the North American copper company began to implement its welfare program, through the 1940s, the miners displayed minimal interest in attending the camps' social centers and vocational schools. In addition, despite company regulations and the constant vigilance of the company police, workers continued to play cards, drink, and engage in unsanctioned sexual activity. Miners also rejected the company's efforts to transform them into responsible husbands and fathers and thus reshape their sexuality. They expressed their acute sense of masculine pride in social practices that contradicted the middle-class ideal of the monogamous and reliable head of household, often at the expense of women.

In 1922, the company paper, *El Teniente*, put forth the complaint that workers failed to show any interest in the educational and cultural opportunities offered by the company: "it is truly incomprehensible the scorn and lack of interest that the majority of the workers show . . . for the cultural centers. . . . With much pain we read yesterday that already some teachers, who had dedicated themselves to the sublime mission of the struggle against ignorance, are disillusioned, seeing the stubborn refusal of those hard heads to go to classes of instruction and of spiritual, moral, and material progress."[2] According to the paper, the "hard heads" preferred to drink, shoot craps, and play cards and billiards. As *El Teniente* lamented, "There is not one [worker] who says, 'tonight I'm going to the library.'"[3] The paper published an interview with a young teacher who declared himself defeated after experiencing the continual emptiness of the camps' schools, libraries, and cultural centers.[4]

In 1922, 2,807 men, women, and children were registered in the public and company-sponsored schools in the camps (out of a total population of 10,216), with an attendance rate of only 50 percent.[5] Six years later, a leader of the company union complained about workers' lack of participation in the camps' vocational schools. He decried the "shameful fact" that only seventy workers attended the classes and stated that "it is hard to admit it, but it is necessary to say it clearly and loudly: our people are ungrateful toward their governors and toward those who work to get them out of their lamentable state of moral and material misery and the ignorance to which they are subject; they are ungrateful to their educators." The independent miners' union also continued to editorialize about workers' lack of interest in education during the 1940s. As late as the 1960s, social workers interviewed by Manuel Barrera noted that "in

Sewell there is practically no cultural life, no literary, theatre, or artistic groups." And, a librarian remarked on a lack of interest in books, stating that "in general people are apathetic when it comes to cultural activity."[6]

Along with their lack of interest in participating in vocational schooling, many miners also continued to flaunt the company's dry law and restrictions on gambling. Violation of the dry law was a frequent cause of arrest and resulted in dismissal, a fine, or suspension. The miners enjoyed a steady supply of smuggled moonshine and alcohol as they engaged in a constant contest with the company over the enforcement of the dry law. In addition, during their days off at the end of every month, many miners descended to Rancagua to drink in brothels and bars, returning to work the next day or even a few days later half-drunk or hungover. Often carabineros and company police threw miners off the train and prohibited them from returning to work because they were inebriated.

Miners were also often apprehended and fined for gambling, a popular pastime in the camps. Groups of workers would get together in the barracks with a bottle of hard liquor and play cards. The Sewell court was flooded with cases during the 1930s and 1940s of workers arrested for gambling. Although gambling did not provoke suspensions or dismissals, workers risked losing their confiscated winnings and had to pay a fine. If they were also found with a bottle, the crime became more serious. The enormous number of arrests for gambling during these years indicates, however, that the threat of punishment did little to stop workers from playing cards and drinking.[7]

The local police in the mine's camps provided the company Welfare Department weekly and, at times, daily reports on workers arrested for violating company regulations. Almost all arrests were for gambling, drinking, and fighting. On 10 October 1934, for example, the police reported to the company that they had arrested thirty-five workers, ten for drinking, nineteen for gambling, and six for smuggling alcohol.[8] In a similar report, on 2 May 1937 the police listed twenty-seven arrests for drinking, moonshining, gambling, and "immorality."[9] On 11 December 1935 the police reported having arrested forty-five workers for gambling, drinking, bootlegging, and public inebriation.[10] During the 1930s, police arrested on average eight workers a day, mostly for drinking, gambling, and smuggling alcohol. In a random sample of eighty-seven workers hired between

1919 and 1939, twenty-seven had been fired, arrested, or suspended at one time for drinking, gambling, and "immoral acts."[11]

Conflicts over alcohol and gambling further reinforced cultural differences and social resentment in the camps and in the mine. Both gambling and drinking were collective activities that brought workers together. Bottles were shared and work comrades invited to partake of a recently scored stash of illegal aguardiente. Similarly, as oral sources point out, gambling, more than an activity aimed at winning money, was a way to pass the long hours between work shifts together, particularly for single workers who did not have families.[12] It was a collective form of recreation and ritual that reproduced miners' workplace codes of masculinity and solidarity. Thus, for the company, drinking and gambling might have appeared to be socially disintegrative, disruptive of disciplined work habits and of the nuclear family, but both activities helped to bond workers and to establish a collective form of identity, especially in resistance to the company's efforts to eradicate them from the camps.

The miners' awareness that the North American supervisors kept well-stocked bars in their lodgings and also gambled added to their sense of a discrimination that was based not just on exploitative work conditions but also on social and ethnic differences. As one observer noted in 1919, the recently implemented dry law "met with enormous resistance. There were protests, bitter complaints. . . . The company was inflexible: either submit or abandon the mine."[13] Workers complained that the dry law existed only for them and that supervisors frequently smuggled fine liquors into the American camp in their automobiles. "Does the dry law apply only to obreros or to everyone in the camp?" asked the union's *Despertar Minero*. "Only workers' domiciles are violated late at night and only workers are obliged to respond to a series of questions and to have their beds and trunks searched."[14] The manifest hypocrisy of the dry law exacerbated workers' sense of injustice. Former miners also remember the double standard of the dry law with a sense of indignation. A onetime servant in the North American camp during the 1940s and 1950s recollected that every North American had a private stash of alcohol in his closet.[15]

The legendary status of moonshiners in the camps' folklore reflected the significance of alcohol as a symbol of the subversion of the company's control of workers' lives. The bootleggers (*guachucheros*) who did battle with the company security forces in order to provide the miners with alcohol enjoyed mythic fame among the miners. The guachuchero and "guachucherismo" occupied a central role in the life of the camps and became an important cultural symbol of workers' discontent with the company. The former El Teniente employee and writer Baltazar Castro described the guachuchero in his stories as "the furtive salesman of liquor that plots to mock the careful vigilance that the serenos exercise at all hours, day and night, in the streets and the pathways, in the lodgings and in the work place, in the train and in the hills [surrounding the camps]."[16] In oral narratives today, the miners endow the guachuchero with the sort of mythic characteristics that Eric Hobsbawm describes for a particular kind of social bandit.[17] Stories about guachucheros represent a celebration of the resistance to the discipline and close control of space in the camps imposed by the company.[18]

The guachucheros earned their reputation among miners through frequent conflicts with carabineros and serenos that often turned into gun battles and shootouts. In the early 1920s, for example, the company reported to the provincial government that three guachucheros had killed a sereno as he patrolled the outskirts of the camps. In another, similar case, the company reported that a carabinero had been killed at the mouth of the mine when he tried to apprehend a group of guachucheros.[19] Spruille Braden, William Braden's son, recalls in his memoirs that "enforcing prohibition in the mine was a bloody business, with actual battles in the surrounding mountains with men wounded and even killed. . . . It was a matter of grim necessity to keep booze away from the mines."[20] In 1917, despite their losses in confrontations with the smugglers, the company's security forces succeeded in capturing sixty-three moonshiners, and in 1918, seventy-three.[21] As late as 1943, the police in the mine continued to do battle with guachucheros. On 3 May 1943 the police reported that they had arrested two workers who were accompanied by two guachucheros carrying bottles of wine on the train to the camps. Despite the gunfire from carabineros and serenos, the two guachucheros, who had recently attacked a sereno and a carabinero according to the report, fled into the hills.[22]

Often the guachucheros were outsiders from neighboring towns who sought to make a quick profit by selling liquor at ten times the price paid outside the company's dry zone. In one case, the company complained to the provincial government that a local hacendado, responding to the new market provided by the miners, had turned to moonshining as a full-time business and was flooding the camps with his particular brew.[23] Castro describes one famous guachuchero in his stories of life in the camps: "He was Domingo Asenjo, the most famous contraband smuggler of all those who introduced alcoholic beverages clandestinely into the mine. His fame began in the tunnels and passageways of the mine, descended to the camps near Rancagua and then marauded under the noses of the police, of which the great majority maintained secret relations with him."[24] This guachuchero, like many others, had begun his career smuggling a dozen bottles of liquor hidden under packages of cigarettes and cologne in the carts that brought goods to the company railroad to be transported to the camps. He also scaled the mountains and snuck into the camps on foot or on horseback to avoid other guachucheros who controlled the area. At times he confronted bands of his rivals and engaged in Wild West–type shootouts. After growing success, he formed his own band that controlled the towns around the mine. He then invested in a number of bars and brothels in Rancagua. Other, more small-time guachucheros, however, were miners or family members of miners who smuggled liquor into the camps in all kinds of inventive ways. Workers were often apprehended on the train to the camps with hidden bottles. Similarly, oral sources describe how some housewives hid bottles under piles of dirty diapers and laundry and then sold the contraband from their homes to supplement their husbands' income.[25]

The guachuchero won his mythic status among the miners because he embodied their own hopes and desires. He was "audacious, an enemy of all established law and order, blasphemizing against the police, the serenos, and the gringos; confronting danger with an open profusion of courage. Thus they loved him and had raised him up on a kind of pedestal."[26] The guachuchero represented the fulfillment of the miners' masculinized code of ethics. He enjoyed independence and stood up, often with arms, to the power of the company. The guachuchero also represented a form of economic mobility and success to which most miners aspired when they came to the mine in search of high-paying work.

The popular mythology surrounding the guachuchero may be read as a "hidden transcript" of resistance to domination and a tacit critique of the company's power.[27] The stories of bootlegging and the actual practice of drinking are far more complex, however, than a direct expression of class antagonism. Like stealing from the company or altering the mark, alcohol smuggling and consumption represented an assertion of the miners' self-will and subversion of the authority of company superintendents, the police, and foremen. On the other hand, the independence, courage, and prosperity of the guachuchero, like the practice of clandestine drinking in the camps, did not have obvious implications for any kind of class solidarity or collective militancy. The admiration the moonshiner inspired among miners was a result not only of his rebelliousness but also of his economic success and social mobility. Like many of the social bandits described by Hobsbawm, the alcohol smugglers represented a route of social mobility and an escape from poverty that did not necessarily coincide with collective action. Moonshining and smuggling constituted acts of individual economic entrepreneurship and disruptive social behavior that implicitly contradicted the efforts of the union and the Left to organize the miners in disciplined collective struggle with the copper company.

The celebration of the guachuchero in miners' folklore and collective memory reflects too the ways in which miners' informal forms of pleasure and assertions of will in their everyday activities were played out on the field of masculinity. The moonshiner was, inevitably, a masculine figure. Although many women sold alcohol clandestinely or smuggled small amounts into the camps as a means of supplementing household incomes, the subjects of miners' anecdotes and tales were invariably men. Women did participate in the alcohol business, but they were excluded from the narrative of the guachuchero. The major guachucheros, those who climbed the mountain to deliver large quantities of alcohol, did battle with the company police, or presided over a band of smugglers were men, and they, not the women who sold small amounts out of their homes, were the heroes of the miners' folklore.

This silence with regard to women's involvement in the illicit alcohol industry indicates the ways in which the mythology surrounding the guachuchero reflected codes of manhood that the miners mobilized in other social arenas and at work in the mine. The guachuchero's independence, strength, and courage constituted the miners' ideal of manhood and masculine behavior. Physical descriptions of guachucheros often resembled the celebrations of the physical strength and virility of mine workers. One El Teniente story by Gonzalo Drago, for example, lauds the guachuchero hero as a "primitive and lustful macho always ready to jump on his female prey." The story romanticizes the moonshiner's adventurous life and the deep solidarities and friendships that the dangerous profession forged among men. Entitled "Camaradas," the story deals with the friendships among guachucheros and describes how "shared danger brought the men together," in a manner similar to the shared danger of the mine.[28]

The absence of women in these tales indicates the extent to which, for the miners, these character traits defined their ideal of the masculine. The guachuchero's dangerous work, male friendships, adventurousness, mobility, and rebellious spirit were badges of manhood. In the guachuchero's risky and independent life and work, miners saw both what they saw in themselves and what they aspired to. In popular lore the moonshiner, like the miner, challenged and dominated the mountain and nature, as well as the authority of the company. Like the miner, the moonshiner in one tale "was full of pride and hardheaded"; "he believed that he dominated the mountain"; he was "young and robust."[29] In another, "His solitude of the free man, free of feminine chains, allowed him to be a rebel and a vagabond." Like the miner he had traveled and labored in the northern nitrate pampa and had "shared his life with the hardened and vigorous men that cities and countryside throw deep into the mine."[30] The guachuchero thus embodied the lifeways of the nineteenth-century peones, and his celebration by the El Teniente miners signified the maintenance of these cultural traditions in opposition to the new forms of discipline demanded by the modern copper industry.

Bootlegging also became one more activity through which men built a shared, collective culture based on friendships and bonds of solidarity forged in work. Gambling, drinking, and alcohol smuggling were constructed as male activities and were male forms of sociability from which women were excluded. Only men came together in groups to play cards and drink. When women were arrested for violating the dry law, they were arrested as individuals and almost always for selling, not consuming, alcohol. Women never took part in the romanticized expeditions to scale the mountains and sneak liquor into the camps. They merely served as go-betweens or petty sellers. Men, however, were the major smugglers and purveyors, as well as consumers, of contraband. And when they drank, they drank not as individuals but collectively in the barracks or in the camps' passageways. Most miners arrested for drinking and gambling were arrested in groups. The informal, underground culture of the camps was, then, highly masculine. The exclusion of women from these forms of social interaction, public space, and the folklore of the guachuchero meant that the private forms of opposition constituted by these activities were an exclusively male domain.

Miners' efforts to express control over their nonwork lives in illicit forms of recreation produced an unruly and rebellious sense of masculinity that conflicted with the mining company's efforts to train them to be responsible heads of households. El Teniente workers consistently sought to subvert the company's efforts to regulate their sexuality and prescribe their family duties. Workers, many of whom lived in a barracks for bachelors, continued to have sexual relationships with empleadas, pay for sex, and frequent brothels in Rancagua. Through the 1940s, workers were often detained and fired for sexual activity with empleadas. In 1927, for example, miner José Castro Cáceres was arrested and fired for "immoral conduct" with an empleada who worked in one of the cantinas in the barracks for single miners. According to the Welfare Department, this was his third offense of this nature.[31] Similarly, in 1946, two workers were fired when discovered alone *en flagrante* with two empleadas in the barracks.[32] In 1943, mine foreman Jorge Emilio Achurra Achurra wrote a letter to the Welfare Department to request that his lover, an empleada, be rehired. She had been discovered in his room by serenos one morning, had lost her job, and had been evicted from the camps. The foreman, probably because of his rank, kept his job, although his request that his lover be rehired was denied.[33]

Miners frequently rejected the company's insistence that they formalize their sexual relationships in civil marriages. In 1919, for example, Alejandro Fuenzalida Grandon noted in his report on El Teniente that many miners rented or purchased counterfeit marriage licenses to circumvent the company's marriage requirements.[34] Twenty years later miners still maintained this practice. In 1939, the head of the company Welfare Department wrote to a department social worker that in the camps "there exist families without legal status and many children, the products of such unions, do not have legal status; there have even arisen cases of the complete falsification of the civil marriage license book, of the union and of the registration of the children." The report also noted that some miners forged marriage licenses "to cover up another illegitimate union."[35] The issue of required civil marriage was so important to miners that in 1946 in negotiations between the miners' union, the company, and the provincial governor, the workers demanded that Braden rescind the internal rule that required dismissal and expulsion from the camps for workers found to be sexually involved with women outside civil marriage.[36] The demand was rejected.

A number of miners had two wives—or at least one wife and a serious lover, one in the mine's camps and one outside the mine—and often purchased bogus marriage licenses to cover up their bigamous practices. Oral sources and company Welfare Department reports comment on the frequency of miners' bigamy. One former worker remembers that "everyone knew of miners who had more than one wife."[37] In addition, at times men abandoned their wives. In a 1936 report, a social worker noted, for example, that "cases of abandoned women with families present themselves with enormous frequency" in the mining camps.[38] Miners' sense of intense masculinity derived from their capacity to assert their own sexual independence and to control women's sexuality. They found pride in their relatively high earnings and their capacity to translate this economic power into sexual conquests and multiple relationships with women.

A 1939 company report provides a glimpse of men's failure to live up to their prescribed responsibilities. The report details the discovery by company social workers that many workers used the family allowance as a form of work bonus, giving limited funds to their wives for the sustenance of their families. The social workers found that "in general the amounts given by the married workmen to their wives for the weekly food bill is far below what they could allow." The report condemned workers for forcing their wives to take in laundry, boarders, and sewing and for spending their wages and family allowance on "wine, women, and song, . . . while their wives and children are underfed and worse clothed."[39] Although there is no indication as to the number of these families, they were numerous enough to provoke the interest and alarm of the Welfare Department. In these cases, the victims of miners' resistance to the norms of social discipline dictated by the company were miners' wives, who depended completely on their husbands' wages for their own survival.

Both married and single miners left the camps to travel with a company pass down to Rancagua every three or four weeks for a weekend off. In the city, they frequented the city's many bars and brothels and expressed an intensely masculine identity that differentiated them from other workers. According to the company Welfare Department and oral histories, they often spent their wages and returned to their families and the camps "with only their pants."[40] Store owners in the camps or in Rancagua could instantly recognize a miner for his bearing and for his *pinta* (look, style). Miners dressed sharply, with suits, hats, and scarves composing the basis for their style. Castro describes one El Teniente miner out on the town in Rancagua for the weekend: "His clothes showed clearly that he had recently come down from the mine: a felt hat, black suit, handkerchief around the neck and loudly colored shoes."[41] Copper miners drew criticism for dressing like urban, middle-class professionals and for their dandyish appearance. Thus the company Welfare Department reported that "it is a well known fact and has been commented on by people who are far from friendly, that the Teniente workmen dress as well as the average employee of the middle class in Santiago."[42] Similarly, one veteran El Teniente miner remembers that "the miner liked to look good . . . he liked to dress well."[43]

The El Teniente workers also usually had a lot of available cash and an arrogant and overbearing attitude that frequently led to fights and brawls, according to those bar or store owners who had to serve them.[44] During their monthly weekend leaves in Rancagua, miners spent their accumulated savings lavishly. As a former miner recalls:

> When the guys went down by train for vacation, . . . there were cases where they ordered beer for everyone in the compartment; they arrived at a business, and they didn't ask for a dozen beers, they asked for a box full, so immediately everyone knew "that's a miner," and everywhere he characterized himself for being a big spender he asked for everything on a large scale, because he spent his time above in the mountain saving money . . . and then went directly from Sewell to Rancagua. . . . That was the way the miner acted; he was a man to whom it didn't matter whom he was with, he paid for everyone: they tell stories about Parque Roseal, a famous dance hall, that was on Gran Avenida in Santiago, and a miner went there and ordered drinks for everyone, even ordered for the band. . . . I would say the miner was notorious for this, he distinguished himself from others for this way of being.[45]

In addition to spending their money on drinking in bars, miners also spent their savings on sex. Thus this same miner recalls that during monthly weekends off, both married and single miners "went to the brothels here in Rancagua, they left the brothels and they returned to Sewell, and then returned [after a month] once again; it was notorious. There were miners who arrived at a brothel and locked themselves in and were there on a 'spree' for a couple of days."[46]

Another former miner recalls that "the workers, to satisfy their appetites for alcohol, went down to the valley, and they were there not only for their seven days [of vacation every four months] drinking, but they spent an entire month and lost their work. . . . [T]hese workers spent themselves until they had lost all their money, had sold their clothes, and the only thing they needed was to once again go to work . . . for that Rancagua was characterized for having many houses of prostitution that the miners closed themselves in and didn't leave until they had nothing left, that was normal in those days." According to this miner, both married and single men engaged in these drinking bouts in brothels because "to have the satisfaction of drinking and being with comrades, the current carried them to Rancagua."[47]

The El Teniente miners' lavish style and swaggering arrogance expressed both a claim to a middle class–based norm of respectability and a challenge to the authority of accepted social hierarchies. As William French has argued for mine workers in Mexico, through fine dress these workers claimed equality and violated "the social hierarchy of appearances."[48] Miners' masculine pride rested on a potentially transgressive claim to be on par with members of the middle class. They backed up their assertions of equality with high wages and pride derived from their physical capacity for dangerous and difficult work.

As one former miner notes, the miners' distinct manera de ser was rooted in their work and relative economic power. The miners' pride had its origins in the culture nurtured within the mine, in the common language, references, myths, and work in teams. The mine's workplace codes of physical strength, independence, and a challenging attitude toward authority found expression in the arrogance of miners once out on the streets of Rancagua. To be a miner was to be something more than an ordinary worker. Miners' overbearing attitude and sense of style constituted both a rejection of the traditional, pejorative elite designation of

miners, peasants, and workers as *rotos* (literally, "broken ones") and a claim
to dignity and equality:

> That's what makes the miners different, you see? For their form of
> being at work, for their system of work and what the atmosphere
> there is like. Traditionally, the miner has always distinguished him-
> self for being a roto chorro [a cool roto], like we say, un roto maca-
> nudo [a first-rate roto] . . . un hombre sobresaliente [a distinctive
> man, a man who stands out] because . . . he earns money, and that
> earning money at work makes him different, makes him be seen in
> a different way.[49]

This passage displays the ways in which the miners' assertion of masculinity involved a claim to dignity. The miners earned respect both through
their capacity for difficult and daring physical labor and for their earnings, which were high compared with those of other members of the
working class. The use of the word "roto" in an affirmative, rather than
pejorative, way in this passage and its coupling with such positive adjec-
tives as "chorro," "macanudo," and "sobresaliente" transform the meaning
of the word. Rather than "broken ones," the miners bore their roto status
with pride and lent it self-esteem and self-respect. The very use of miners'
slang in this passage and the more general celebration of their language
in interviews reflect a sense of cultural distinctiveness and cultural pride.

Miners affirmed their position as rotos and invested it with dignity
by appropriating the badges of middle-class respectability. In addition,
by employing middle-class trappings and staking out their possession of
public space through their arrogant demeanor and swagger, miners challenged accepted norms of behavior and social hierarchy. Rather than submissive rotos, they presented themselves as social equals and expressed a
sense of self that constituted a constant challenge to authority. This transgressive "manera de ser" was continually expressed in the miner's language
of masculine pride. The challenging aspect of miners' claims to equality
lay in their domineering sense of manhood. Their dandyish appearance
laid claim to the domain of masculine privilege and pride usually pre-
served for the middle class, in which they exercised independence through
spending money, drinking, and engaging in sexual conquests in Rancagua's bars and brothels. By spending their wages on clothing, liquor, and
sex, miners exerted control over their own leisure time, style, and sexual

practices and displayed their economic power. In this way sexuality and codes of manhood and masculinity mediated workers' expressions of class antagonism and structured their responses to the authority of capital.

Paternalism, the Promise of Social Mobility, and the
Seeds of Working-Class Discontent

Although many workers who stayed in El Teniente nurtured the rebellious culture of the itinerant peón or roto macanudo, others began to conform to the model of responsible head of household and disciplined worker. These workers labored to earn work bonuses and to ascend the hierarchy of job positions within the mining company. Many attended vocational schools and participated in mutual aid societies, social clubs, and sports teams. They did not, however, become loyal to the North American mining company. Rather, these workers contrasted the difficulties of labor in the mine and the harsh material conditions of life in the camps with the promises of middle-class lifestyles disseminated by the company Welfare Department and embodied in the neighborhoods of North American supervisors, turning to the union and left-wing parties.

Despite the company's efforts to improve and provide housing for married workers and their families, through the 1940s life in the El Teniente camps was much what it had been when the mining enterprise was founded at the turn of the century. Workers lived in crowded and cramped barracks in the camps without adequate heat, water, toilet facilities, or electricity. By 1939, although the company had made efforts to increase the quantity and improve the quality of housing in the camps, the Welfare Department still reported that families lodged in workers' housing lacked sufficient room and even beds for all their members. The company had built new barracks for workers' families, and earth floors had been replaced with wood boards, but the report noted that "crowded and promiscuous bedding conditions appear to be nearer a rule than an exception. . . . [I]t is quite a battle to convince the people that they use two rooms as bedrooms, one for their elder children, the other for themselves and the probable baby." The Welfare Department statistics showed that most beds were shared by at least two and, at times, as many as five people.[50]

A 1937 report by the Inspección General del Trabajo also recommended that the barracks for single or "bachelor" workers be remodeled so that every worker would have his own bed rather than sharing one bed with one or two other workers and rotating by shift. The report noted that the barracks needed new bathrooms because the existing facilities lacked adequate running water and were equipped with "Turkish" rather than regular toilets and were unhygienic.[51]

In 1938, the Falange publication *Lircay* described housing conditions in El Teniente:

> The workers of El Teniente live in constructions that look like cages and in each one of them there are fifteen to eighteen workers. These living quarters have a kerosene stove with which the miners dry their clothes since there is so much dampness and a lot of dripping water . . . and there they sleep in this unhealthy and humid environment. The barracks for married couples are few since the majority of housing is for single men. Their conditions are insufficient from the point of view of sanitation.[52]

Miners' families were typically large, and lodgings were small. One woman recalls that her family, composed of nine children and the parents, lived in a three-room space in the workers' barracks: "Well, we women had the bedroom because there were six girls and three boys, so in the big bedroom were only women, in the other room was my father with the boys, and in the other the kitchen."[53] Another woman remembers that "it was terrible. There were families that had ten children, and the ten lived in one bedroom and the parents in another room; there were only two rooms and a kitchen."[54]

The barracks provided little protection against the harsh climate of the mountains. Tin walls and roofs allowed the cold to penetrate in the winter and turned workers' rooms into ovens during the summer. The company prohibited electric heaters, irons, or stoves. Instead, families used small wood-burning and kerosene stoves, but because wood was scarce and kerosene expensive, lodgings often went unheated and lacked hot water for washing. Miners' families shared common taps for washing and cleaning and common toilets. One woman remembers that "we shared the bathrooms, let's say three toilets for women and girls and in another area a bathroom for men and boys. You had to go out in the night, even though sometimes it snowed and was cold, you had to go outside to the bathroom."[55]

Worker housing was a major area of conflict between the workers and the company. Workers constantly demanded that Braden supply them with more and better housing. Former workers, even now, recall with great bitterness conditions in the barracks and are able to describe in detail the difficulties they had in becoming accustomed to these crowded living conditions after life in the countryside. The company's only solution to the housing problem, according to the union newspaper, was to "paint the outside of some cabins during the summertime." Satirizing the company's propaganda, *Despertar Minero* commented that "in the American Paradise of Sewell there are cabins that have neither bathrooms nor electricity."[56]

A more fundamental and deeper source of conflict with the company during the late 1930s and 1940s was the price of food and the cost of living in the mining camps. Prices in the camps' stores and cantinas sparked confrontations between the miners and the company as frequently as did work and wage-related problems. Despite mine workers' relatively high wages, they paid inflated prices in camp businesses that exacerbated the galloping inflation of the late 1930s and 1940s. Nationally, the cost of living rose steadily between 1936 and 1947, averaging 16 percent annually and eroding gains in wages made by miners and industrial workers. Government spending to promote industrial growth and periodic cost-of-living increases for industrial workers and white-collar employees contributed to endemic inflation. In El Teniente, the cost of living increased by 184 percent between 1936 and 1946.[57] In 1942, *Despertar Minero* editorialized that "in this camp nutrition and food are a terrible problem as a consequence of the high cost of living . . . and a cause of infant mortality and deaths of children from illnesses."[58] Inflated prices ate away at the wages of miners, threatening the very survival of their families. In 1938, *Lircay* noted that despite the high wages in El Teniente, "the cost of living in the mine is very high." The paper pointed to the monopoly over stores in the camps exercised by the concessions, indicating that "in practice every rise in salaries is overcome by unjustified rises in prices in the camps' stores." The paper argued that the workers' wages were insufficient because many workers had to support extended families who either lived in Rancagua or in the countryside.[59]

In a 1939 CTCh congress in Rancagua, El Teniente union leaders made control of the cost of living their central demand. Union leaders called for "free commerce" in the mine's camps, maintaining that "commerce . . .

has been a very worrisome problem for all the union leaders." They also called for "a solution to the high cost of living, particularly with reference to food," and for an end to the speculation with articles of primary necessity. "Today," they said, "more than ever, the government authorities must concern themselves with this subject, because the owners of businesses, stores, and cantinas have again raised the price of food."[60] Cantinas and pensions in El Teniente were run as concessions of the company. According to its contracts with concessionaires, the company exercised control over the prices and even the quality of food. Final authorization for a price hike in the cantinas and pensiones could come only from the Braden Copper Company's Welfare Department. In addition, stores in the camps were run by just a few major monopolies, which also depended on the Welfare Department to fix their prices.

In 1944, the miners' union compiled a daily budget for a family of four, including food, clothing, and basic necessities, according to the prices in the camps. The total came to $91.40 pesos. The average wage for a worker in the mine was $46.95. The family allowance augmented this salary by ten pesos ($4.50 pesos for the wife, $3.25 pesos for the first child, and $2.25 pesos for the second child).[61] The following year, the union did another calculation. The daily cost of living for a single worker came to $49.14 pesos. The average wage, however, amounted to $330 pesos a week, or just over $47 pesos a day. The situation was worse for married workers, who averaged a higher wage of $55 pesos daily and, with two children, received $12 pesos for the family allowance. But the daily budget for a family of four still came to $86 pesos, according to the union's estimates.[62]

With the high cost of living in the mining camps, the other major threat to the survival of the workers and their families came from the international copper markets. When demand for copper decreased and copper prices fell, the Kennecott Company in New York would order radical cuts in production in the El Teniente mine. These partial shutdowns of production resulted in the dismissals of large numbers of workers, who remained unprotected by either Chilean law or the Chilean government. For workers with families, a dip in the curve of the copper economy could mean total disaster.

A former Braden Copper Company executive recalled the mass dismissals and one, particularly devastating, that began following a call from Kennecott's New York headquarters with the order to cut production by

40 percent. After poring over reports and figures from each work section, the Braden administration selected 1,800 workers to be fired. The following week these workers were given two weeks' wages and were shipped out of the camps by train with their families and their meager belongings and dumped onto the streets of Rancagua outside the main offices of the Braden Copper Company. "There wasn't a damn thing anyone could do about it," he remembered, "neither the workers nor the government. It was legal. We paid them their two weeks of indemnification."[63] The miners were thus at the mercy of not only inflation and the high cost of living in the camps but the capriciousness of the international copper economy as well. When world recessions struck, the copper industry, always one of those most affected, shut or slowed down production, and the workers found themselves in the streets.

Dismissals, as well as a means of disciplining the labor force, were also a company strategy for bypassing laws protecting workers. To fire and re-hire a worker often worked to the company's advantage because it could then avoid having to pay indemnifications and pensions for lengthy years of service. A rehired worker could also be paid a lower beginning wage or could be transferred to a different work site. The miners' union constantly complained that the company fired older workers or workers suffering work-related illnesses, mainly silicosis, to avoid paying costly pensions or indemnifications. It also criticized the company's policy of firing and then rehiring workers as a means to cut down workers' entitlements for years of service.

The conditions imposed by the rising cost of living during the 1930s and 1940s and the miserable housing offered by the company limited the capacity of families to fulfill the ideal of domesticity and consumption advertised by the Welfare Department. Although the company told workers, and especially workers' wives, that they should form healthy and harmonious households replete with a wide array of consumer goods and furnishings, many families couldn't afford even an adequate meal. While workers and their wives were urged to pursue a fantasy of middle-class consumption and to build households drawn from a middle-class ideal, material conditions in the camps constrained their aspirations. Women were told that to be feminine required a variety of dresses and fashions and a particular physical appearance defined by thinness, healthy teeth, and makeup, yet the conditions of their lives impeded achievement of this image. For most El Teniente women, wearing gloves, exercising, dieting, skiing, and playing tennis remained a remote fantasy.

In 1940, the miners' union invoked the discrepancy between the ideal of middle-class domesticity and the realities facing an El Teniente family. It pointed out that while such an ideal was within reach of North American copper workers, who had seen their wages rise steadily since the beginning of the century, Chilean workers earned only a tenth of the salaries of their counterparts. Thus while the company disseminated pictures of North American workers in households that had "terrific bookshelves, handsome upholstered sofas and chairs, a radio, and many other comforts," *Despertar Minero* pointed out that El Teniente's Chilean workers often "don't have chairs to sit in." The promise of social mobility, defined as it was by images of domesticity and consumption, remained "a dream of every empleado and obrero."[64]

El Teniente's workers and their wives may have been readily receptive to the Braden Copper Company's paternalist promises of social mobility. But the company was either unable or unwilling to provide its workers the means to attain the ideal of a domestic life defined by a house outfitted with consumer goods. The Chilean copper workers and their wives may have favorably received the messages that a family's social mobility was accessible through cultural improvement, education, "moral" behavior, hard work, and the organization of gender relations to conform to an ideal of domesticity, but conditions in the mine and in the camps prevented workers' families from fulfilling these newly ignited desires. The frustrated aspirations for a better life thus sowed dissatisfaction and discontent among workers and their families, preparing workers and their wives to look to the union for solutions to their material situation and making them receptive to the messages transmitted by leftist political parties.

A useful example of the contradictory results of the company's paternalist policies is the El Teniente worker Carlos Pérez. Pérez was seventeen when he left the village of Machalí to look for work in the neighboring El Teniente copper mine in the 1940s. After five years of working in the mine as an obrero, during which time he followed a correspondence course with a "U.S. university" offered by the company, he moved to a better job in the Department of Construction and finally to a series of skilled jobs as a carpenter, electrician, and mechanic in El Teniente's electrical plant, fulfilling the company's promised ideal of social mobility. During his many years in El Teniente, he participated actively in a mutual aid society and in various social clubs and starred on the Sewell soccer team.

In an oral history, Pérez describes with great pride his good relations with North American jefes and the way in which he even saved the life of one supervisor, Mr. Turner, inside the mine. He praises the system of American administration that allowed him to rise from a mere laborer to a master carpenter, as well as the opportunities for education offered by the Braden Copper Company. This education, he believes, was far better than Chilean education. He proudly displays his old workbooks, "all with the North American system and form," and shows off the furniture in his house, all of which he has made himself, "and all constructed according to North American principles." "The United States has been better, has a better cultural level and a better technological level," he says. He speaks highly of the company administration, which, he remembers warmly, supplied workers with sports and social clubs, as well as schools.[65]

The career of Carlos Pérez was not unusual in El Teniente. In a similar case, a retired miner described how he had begun his career in the mine at the second to the lowest pay scale, working as a jornalero. Over twenty-three years of labor in the mine, during which he attended a vocational school, he gradually climbed the salary scale and through the hierarchy of jobs within work crews. Like Pérez, when he retired he had moved from his position as an obrero to a job as an empleado and foreman within the mine. Also like Pérez, this worker remembers with nostalgia the North American administration, the high wages, the system of work, and the possibility for social mobility.[66] Similarly, he was an active participant in social clubs and a mutual aid society in the camps. This was an experience shared by many workers who began at the lowest levels within the mine's hierarchy and eventually earned promotions to increasingly skilled jobs within the work crew and ultimately to the position of jefe.[67]

The admiration of Pérez for the North American company's system of administration and North American culture was repeated in many interviews in which retired workers described how "the gringos had a different mentality," "the gringos knew how to run things and work hard, not like the Chilean," and "the gringos valued work." In interviews, workers reflected on the tremendous feats of engineering that had gone into building the mine and the camps and spoke in detail, with pride in their knowledge, about the different processes of production in the mine and its plants. Similarly, many workers spoke about how, beginning with nothing as mere day laborers, they had managed to work their way up the ladder of positions in the mine to white-collar status, form families, and educate their children. In these interviews workers define the narratives of their life histories in terms of respectability, hard work, skill, and social mobility, rather than the disorderly culture of the roto macanudo.[68]

In many ways these workers appear to be company loyalists who have internalized the messages disseminated through the company's social welfare program. But, every one of these workers also expressed similar pride in their participation in union activities and stressed the importance of the union in their lives and the lives of their families. Pérez, for example, was a leader of the electrical plant's small union, the Sindicato Industrial Coya y Pangal, and a militant of the Socialist Party. He proudly remembers receiving Salvador Allende in his home during a presidential campaign in 1964. Pérez attended and participated in the founding congress of the Confederación de Trabajadores del Cobre (CTC), the national federation of copper workers, held in his home town of Machalí in 1951.

Admiration for North American accomplishments and methods and his own successful career reinforced this worker's nationalism and support for the Left. Discussing the nationalization of the copper mine in 1971, Pérez argues that nationalization was necessary to allow Chileans to develop their own technology and to give opportunities to Chilean professionals and technicians. In the same way, the union was important because it struggled to get for Chileans what the North Americans already had—that is, to improve their cultural and material level. The union and leftist parties, for Pérez, were only trying to obtain "what the gringos already had."[69]

Workers who had successfully moved up the hierarchy of jobs in the mine and ended their careers as empleados noted the limits on their professional possibilities. They commented with some rancor that the company's vocational schools prepared them only for work as skilled laborers and that they were denied access to training for jobs as engineers, technicians, and supervisors. As one woman commented, "The gringos wanted it that way, they knew what they were doing. They needed them [miners] to do their jobs."[70] Older workers who had ascended the mine's social hierarchy from day laborer to empleado recall that most miners never finished their secondary education and that most viewed work in the mine as their only possible future. Even workers who enjoyed middle-class respectability and the success of their careers in mining remarked on the internal job hierarchies that imposed a barrier on just how far they could go in their lives.[71]

The hardship of labor and life in the camps had an important effect on Pérez. He recollects, for example, that life in the camps and the mine was extremely difficult, and contrasts the poverty of workers' lives with the relative luxury in the neighborhood of the North American supervisors: "In cultural and social life the gringos lived in a form very distinct [from the workers,] which made many people dislike the gringos. . . . If you even looked at the gringo camp they would haul you up to the Welfare Department to be disciplined, and if you went near it or tried to enter, they would fire you."[72]

A similar set of overlapping and contradictory representations of life in the mining camps can be found in the testimony of other retired workers and women who grew up in the mining camps. Most were born during the 1920s to mining families and either went to work in El Teniente or married mine workers. Their memories evoke a powerful nostalgia, and many agree that life in the camps was better than below in the city. One woman, for example, notes that "the camps were very pretty, especially when it snowed, it was a great childhood, children running up and down the stairways, hiding, flirting." She recalls with pleasure how the company distributed toys to all the children in the camps on holidays, held dances for Chilean independence day (September 18), and showed movies, recollecting with fondness the Mexican films and their actors. She also echoes Pérez's admiration for the North American system of work and the way "the gringos valued work." Conditions in the mine were better when it was owned by the North American company, she maintains, because "the gringos appreciated hard work and paid for it."[73]

The nostalgia for the dances and parties held by the company to celebrate both North American and Chilean holidays was a constant refrain in oral history interviews. Former workers and women from the mining community frequently recall with nostalgia the festivities organized by the company for both July 4 and September 18. One retired worker, for example, mentions how "for Christmas they went around distributing presents to the children, because there were jefes of the camps who had all the plans of the workers' homes, how many children each head of household had, how many girls, how many boys and according to this they left toys, they had parties for kids . . . and they also organized dances for the new year with really good bands."[74] In fact, many old-timers emphasize that the bands that came to the camps were "the best" and "first-rate" musical ensembles.[75]

While constructing a romanticized portrait of life in the camps, however, workers and their wives also remember with bitterness the segregated structure of the camps and the discrimination against Chilean workers. The same woman who invoked happy childhood memories also describes how "there was racism. The gringos lived in their own camp with houses, a golf course, and tennis courts, it was called the americana, and the empleados lived in chalets, while the workers lived in barracks. It was a kind of discrimination."[76] Similarly, other interviewees recalled how they were not allowed to step a foot into the North American camp, how the hospital had separate wards for North Americans and Chileans, how North American children attended separate schools, and how participation in the North American social clubs and cultural activities was prohibited to Chileans. In one telling anecdote, former Sewell residents recount how a Chilean empleado married the daughter of a North American engineer but even then had to enter the North American social club through the back door. Similarly, they describe how the camps were divided into three social tiers and how there was a lack of respect for those people who lived in the poorest barracks for obreros, which, fittingly, were situated the farthest down the mountainside in the camps.[77]

Workers and their families were sensitive to the social discriminations and barriers that separated them from access to middle-class lifestyles in the mining camps. In oral histories, members of the mining community frequently recall with resentment the segregated neighborhoods of the camps:

> What was shocking for me was how many differences there were of all kinds. The American jefes lived in a neighborhood that they called American where they lived with the maximum comforts that the common worker didn't have, chalets with all the facilities that the company gave them to live comfortably and all the luxuries. The white-collar workers, they lived at another level of housing that was of lesser quality than the Americans', and then the workers that were

obreros, who lived in other places with fewer comforts, where there lived a family with six or seven children in three rooms. . . . You saw that difference in the social club for the Americans, the social club for the empleados, and the social club of least status for the obreros; the fact that they had different forms of traveling to Rancagua, for example, there was a train that was the train for the Americans . . . and also there was a difference because the empleados and foremen traveled in first class, and the workers in third in cars made of wood. So these were things that made an impact on me, so I began to go to the union and in the union hall we discussed these problems.[78]

Deeply felt inequalities undermined the efficacy of Braden's paternalism. Even a worker as enthusiastic about the North American administration as was Pérez could not but feel the hardship of his material situation and the blatant inequalities that he confronted every day in the mine and in the camps. It was, in part, the desire to eliminate these inequalities—to acquire the social, cultural, and economic superiority of the gringos—that led to Pérez's participation in union activities, his militancy in the Socialist Party, and his support for the nationalization of the mine.

These oral histories offer another way of understanding the failure of Braden's corporate welfare system. The difficult material conditions of work in the mine and life in the camps, particularly when juxtaposed with the relatively luxurious lifestyles of North American administrators, undermined the company's efforts to win the loyalty of its workers. The North American camp provided workers and their families with an image of social mobility. Its playgrounds, houses, gardens, tennis courts, and swimming pools concretely illustrated the company's promises of social and cultural improvement. Every El Teniente resident remembers the wonders of the North American neighborhood. Yet, the camp was strictly guarded, fenced off, and the Chilean workers and their families could only gaze at it from a distance.

One former union leader described a fundamental event in the evolution of his own political consciousness. As a child in the 1930s he was apprehended by serenos in the North American camp's playground. He was delivered to the Welfare Department, where his parents were admonished for their failure to control their child. At home, he was beaten by his father, who feared that another such incident might cause him to lose his job and throw the large family of nine into destitution. He remembered the easy lives of the North Americans and the deep poverty of his own family, as his father struggled with periodic bouts of unemployment during downswings in the international copper economy and the family was forced to leave the camps and make do on the streets of Rancagua. And he recalled the appeal of the North American camp's gardens, pools, and playgrounds.[79] Another former union leader remembers how in the camps "they applied North American ideas, in a Chilean city these were the norms, when a North American passed by, the obrero, the empleado, women, or children had to step to one side so as not to touch him, because if they touched him, he complained with the consequence that they fired the man and made him abandon the camps."[80] Resentment of both class and ethnic discrimination was thus bred into El Teniente's workforce.

The miners frequently pointed out that their wages and standard of living did not come close to the wages paid workers in the United States, often in the same industry. In 1936, for example, *El Cobre* pointed out that copper workers in the United States had seen their real wages rise by as much as 80 percent since 1900 and had had their workday lowered from ten or twelve hours to eight, for which they earned $5.50 (at the time, around 143 pesos a day), at least ten times more than the Chilean miners, who earned an average of 9 pesos and 10 centavos daily.[81] To support this data, the paper quoted an economist from Stanford who had told the *New York Times* that "the devaluation of the [Chilean] currency signifies riches for the exporters of Chilean products that they produce cheaply, but for the poor worker of Chile this signifies ruin and misery."[82]

In 1942, in a speech to the El Teniente miners, the Communist Party deputy and CTCh leader Salvador Ocampo noted that he had sent a message to the president of the Congress of Industrial Organizations (CIO) in the United States "so that the workers of that great country see the difference in treatment, in work conditions, and the astronomical difference in salaries that they pay in Chile compared to what the copper miners in the United States receive for the same work and less hours."[83] Similarly, *Despertar Minero* argued that "while the obrero yanqui does everything mechanized, the worker here performs his job with physical force."[84] Also in 1942, the U.S. ambassador in Chile, Claude Bowers, noted that "the workmen have two things in the backs of their minds: a) that workmen in the mines in the United States receive for substantially the same work wages which are several times greater, and b) that the Company is making enormous profits because of the recent increase in the price of copper and that they should obtain a good share of these." The ambassador argued that the difference in living standards between Chilean and U.S. miners "is constantly used by agitators to promote discontent." He gloomily concluded that the workers wouldn't be convinced by the company's "rational" arguments that their wages were high in comparison with other Chilean workers and would continue to demand a greater share of Braden's profits.[85]

The miners were acutely aware of the growth experienced by their company and the industry in general as a response to increased worldwide demand for copper, as they were also aware of their own strategic role in copper production. Thus, in 1936, the union paper *El Cobre* noted that the North American copper companies had reduced their costs through mechanization and the employment of new production techniques. The profits the companies earned, the paper argued, were far greater than in any other country because the taxes, wages, and expenses were a small fraction of what the companies had to pay elsewhere.[86] The paper backed up its assertion with a series of statistics that had been published in the Santiago daily *La Nación* on the expenditures of these companies in Chile and their net profits. Similarly, during the Second World War, *Despertar Minero* editorialized that "it is unacceptable that in the moments in which the copper industry throughout the entire world has entered a stage of the greatest known industrial development, for the situation created by the war, thus being as a consequence one of the most lucrative industries, they deny a modest increase [to the workers]."[87] The union began to draw on the prosperity of the copper industry and the financial well-being of the Braden Copper Company resulting from the demand for copper generated by the war to underline the justness of its demands. In 1942, a union leader declared to *El Siglo* that "we have made discoveries that leave little doubt that . . . the company has earned in the last years fabulous profits, increased now by the higher price of copper and by the greater production."[88]

The Communist Party's *El Siglo* contrasted the labor of the miners with the easy life of the North American superintendents. The miners worked twelve- or fourteen-hour days in the mine, and the company denied them stoves to heat coffee or their lunches (one of the miners' demands), the paper editorialized. "The high functionaries of Sewell . . . have their houses, their huge salaries, their nice wardrobes, their cigars, their liquors, and their cups of hot coffee. . . . The miners have to keep laboring for hours and hours without a little heater and without hot coffee."[89]

The schools and social and cultural institutions set up by the company created expectations of social mobility among workers. Workers who had access to education began to aspire to a new standard of living that was concretely represented to them by the North American camp and the company newspapers. But the company's promise of social improvement through cultural uplift and education confronted the material limits of the workers' situation in the camps. Work remained onerous; living conditions, arduous; and the possibility of joining a middle class outside the mining camps, remote. The new aspirations of workers schooled in the company's social and educational organizations to the company's "good life" led, ironically, to participation in the union and struggles with the company, rather than to accommodation. Although alcohol, poker, billiards, and going to brothels in Rancagua were the preferred recreation for many workers, others did attend the schools, frequent the social centers, join mutual aid societies, and participate in sports clubs. This participation, however, because of the similarity between the insistence of organized labor and that of the company on moral discipline, education, and "culture," did not preclude political militancy.

The network of recreational and social clubs established by the company provided workers space for organization denied them in the company union before 1938. The company intended social clubs to serve as "a via de comunicación" between the workmen and the company "to discuss in complete liberty . . . their ideas and opinions regarding their welfare in and out of the shops" and as an alternative to the union. Yet clubs often took on a more political cast.[90] In the 1920s, for example, the Welfare Department set up regular meetings with delegates from the social organizations in the camps "to take the pulse of the workers" and maintain better discipline. Much to the Welfare Department's annoyance, however, the meetings with members of social clubs became a forum in which workers could make demands of the company. In a meeting in 1923, for example, one delegate outraged the company by suggesting that it supply the workers tools rather than have the workers supply their own.[91] In addition, the Welfare Department complained that the Club Social Obrero in

Sewell had "a touch of politics and we have told them to keep this branch of their activities indoors."[92]

Often mutual aid societies, social clubs, and the union worked together or supported one another, for their members were the same. In 1938, for example, the mutual aid society, Sociedad de Socorros Mutuos de Obreros de "El Teniente," expelled the capataz Victor Cuadra for denouncing union leaders and opposing a strike. According to the company, the society had caved in to pressure from the union. But, over 85 percent of the members of the mutual aid society had voted against Cuadra and expressed their solidarity with the union leadership and the strike.[93] These social networks often overlapped instead of competing with one another. In this way, mutual aid societies and social clubs, devoted to the satisfaction of the immediate and individual economic demands of their members, could easily become politicized and provide the basis for wider forms of collective action.

Schools in the camps also provided workers spaces to come together and discuss their problems collectively. Rather than institutions that molded workers' consciousness to the precepts of the company's paternalist ideology, schools played a contradictory role in workers' lives. Frequently, Chilean teachers sided with workers in their conflicts with the company and shared an equally antagonistic relationship with the company administration. The company Welfare Department often blamed Chilean teachers for the failure of its educational program. According to the Welfare Department, instructors in the company-sponsored schools shared the bad habits and vices of the workers. In 1922, for example, the Welfare Department reported that "in general the educational facilities afforded by our schools have been at a disadvantage on account of a lack of teachers, and deficient attention on the part of those working . . . the teachers attended 53% of the possible classes."[94]

In fact, some teachers who found employment in the schools soon learned to resent the company's system of social control in the camps. From either working-class or lower-middle-class backgrounds, they commonly identified their interests with those of mine workers and articulated a nationalist opposition to the North American company. In 1919, for example, José Pezoa Varas traveled to El Teniente to work as a schoolteacher. Shocked by the harsh treatment of the workforce and the blatant social inequalities of the camps, he penned a tract describing his experiences and deriding the mine's North American administrators. In *En el feudo* ("Inside the Fiefdom"), he painted a devastating portrait of social conditions in the camps, articulated a nationalist critique of El Teniente's "yanqui" managers, and called for the nationalization of the mine.[95] Like many mine workers, Pezoa Varas left El Teniente after only a few months.

In addition, teachers usually shared workers' antagonism to the company and supported them during labor conflicts. In the middle of a strike in 1946, for example, the company fired and evicted a number of schoolteachers for donating financial support to the union's strike fund. In response, the eighty Chilean teachers in El Teniente began to organize their own strike in protest and petitioned the minister of education for support. A teachers' strike was averted only when the minister of education ordered Braden to withdraw its order to dismiss the teachers.[96] Thus, many of the Chilean mediators of the company's welfare policies, more than simple instruments or agents of company-imposed social control, joined the workers in their opposition to company authority and supported them in their labor struggles.

Union leaders often began their careers through participation in social clubs or mutual aid societies. In these organizations they demonstrated their capacity for leadership, established networks of support among workers, and learned their first lessons about collective action. Within social or sports clubs, workers created important bonds of solidarity, often when spaces for more formal labor organization were not available. Workers who played on soccer teams or who attended vocational schools were often militant unionists and members of leftist parties. In sports and social clubs workers could reconstruct and reaffirm the ties they shared with their fellow workers in the mine or the more informal forms of companionship that were created in the collective activities of drinking and gambling.

A number of union leaders made their careers in the mine's sports leagues. A significant number of union leaders interviewed had played soccer in a serious way at some point in their lives. At least two had played soccer professionally. As soccer players they won fame and respect and extended their reputations among other workers. Thus Carlos Pérez was known for his soccer playing before becoming a union leader. In another case, a former leader of the miners' union described how he came to be elected to the union leadership through his sports activities: "The truth is when I arrived at the mine I was very athletic, I practically spent all my time between my room in the barracks and the football field. . . . [F]irst I was director of the Sports Club where I played, then I became a delegate for a football association that was here, I represented my club to the association, . . . thus I began to get enthusiastic about leading."[97] In the mine his workmates discussed trying to elect someone from their section to the union to represent their section interests and nominated him because of his previous leadership experience in sports clubs. The following year he was elected to the union directorship.

Loyalties to a soccer club frequently reinforced miners' work identity. Workers tended to support the teams that represented their work sections. Castro describes in one story how "I and my father were fans of the 'Abraham Lincoln,' a club formed by workers from the mine. Another sector belonged to the 'Independiente Mina,' organized by empleados, crew chiefs, and foremen. The workers of the workshop above ground formed the 'Democracia,' . . . the empleados of the Time Office came together in 'Deportivo Andes.' "[98] While the soccer clubs reproduced workplace loyalties, these ties did not cross the lines that divided empleados, capataces, and cabos from the obreros. Rather, the separation of clubs for foremen and those for workers reinforced the divisions and antagonisms that prevailed within the mine. As Castro writes, "The workers disrespectfully called the empleados' soccer club the 'the prick of society' and drew a clear distinction between their institutions and the 'Andes.' "[99] Thus, the masculinized forms of sociability within the mine and their implications for informal combativity were sharpened rather than blunted in soccer clubs, as the sexualized language of this passage indicates.

The Braden Copper Company organized sports clubs to offer a form of recreation for workers that would help increase the health, discipline, and productivity of its workforce. As an alternative to drinking and gambling, soccer, boxing, and basketball imposed a form of control over workers and their nonwork lives. Sports were intended to provide a particular definition of the body and the use of the body that was attached to the morality of work and family. At the same time, however, the meaning sports held for the miners was quite different. Sports clubs helped to weld informal social networks and alliances among workers and to reinforce their masculine identity. The competitive machismo celebrated on the soccer field

contributed to the general construction of a combative masculine identity based on a sense of personal strength and resilience. While in some
aspects this aggressive competitiveness may have served the company's
purposes both in the mine and on the playing field in terms of increasing workers' production and fostering divisions among work groups or
different sports groups, it also helped to fuel workers' contentiousness. A
good soccer player could become a successful union leader because, like
the guachuchero, he exemplified the codes of manhood—the physical
strength, courage, independence, and honor—that ruled miners' behavior inside and outside the mine. Workers also elected union leaders who
had demonstrated their capacity for leadership in other social organizations and who thus displayed the qualities of a model worker—discipline,
responsibility, and respectability.

Sports and social clubs in the mining camps, like the masculine worlds
of work, cards, and moonshine, excluded women. Women could go to
soccer games as spectators or to sell drinks and cakes, but sports clubs were
a space reserved for men. In this sense, sports re-created the masculine
culture produced in the mine and in the rituals of drinking and gambling.
Together, work, drink, games of chance, and sports created a collective
masculine identity and a cultural universe into which women could not
enter. As an important source of organization and leadership within the
mine's community, the network of sports and social clubs effectively reproduced male domination and the exclusion of women that occurred in
the workplace, the union, and political parties.

Thus, while workers who maintained the rebellious culture of the roto
macanudo as well as those who conformed to the model of responsibility and respectability fashioned forms of opposition to company authority, both styles of resistance coincided in producing a masculinized
working-class culture. The unruly oppositional culture expressed in gambling, drinking, and carousing and the culture of the "responsible" workers
who participated in company-sanctioned social activities and the union
excluded women. These masculine "languages of class" conflicted in their
notions of discipline and morality but corresponded in placing codes
of manhood at the center of the symbolic universe of the miners. The
working-class politics that emerged from these two languages of class in
the camps relegated women to a subordinate position within the community of class it imagined.

Both styles of working-class masculine behavior corresponded in their claims to a dignity and manhood possessed by the Chilean middle class and North American supervisors. The transgressive social habits of the roto macanudo endowed miners with honor, social power, and the masculine privilege and prerogatives of elites. Similarly, the model disciplined worker located pride in his capacity to fulfill the ideal of social mobility, attain social respectability, and exercise the patriarchical authority of the head of household. In both cases, workers' assertions of dignity were defined in terms of masculine honor. And, in both cases, this claim led workers to oppose the power of the company, the roto macanudo through informal forms of resistance to the everyday regime of social control, and the respectable worker through collective action in the union. These different forms of working-class culture were often contradictory but also, at times, overlapped in producing a militant class politics in the mining camps.

The formation and reproduction of an experienced and permanent labor force in the mine was contingent on the regulation of gender relations in the camps and the transformation into housewives of the single women who traveled to El Teniente in search of wage labor. The Braden Copper Company's efforts to construct nuclear families in which women occupied the role of housewife and men the role of wage earner were tied to the process of class formation in El Teniente, as part of the process of proletarianization, and to a form of gender relations based on the sexual subordination of women within the nuclear family.[1] The definition of wage labor and the wage laborer as male implied the domesticization of women sexually and socially, as well as economically. Thus the nuclear family, made viable in the mining camps through the "family wage," was more than an economic arrangement; it also implied an unequal organization of sexuality. This, as a number of feminist critics have argued, accounts for the support of male workers for the ideology of female domesticity, their acceptance of the exclusion of women from the labor market, and the masculinization of work and class identity.[2]

Women did not simply conform to the new sexual arrangements structured by the nuclear family. Some single women who had migrated to the camp in search of wage labor asserted their sexual and economic autonomy both through their work as domestic servants and by maintaining informal and, at times, multiple, romantic relationships with miners in the camps. The policing of single women's social behavior and the benefits and securities associated with marriage, however, impelled many women toward the domestic sphere. Life as a single woman became increasingly precarious economically and socially, as the company, the state, and male workers aligned to assert a set of gendered moral codes of behavior predicated on women's sexual and economic subordination within the household. The ideals and norms of middle-class respectability and family life promoted in the company's welfare programs replaced the fluid and autonomous culture of single, female migrant workers. Marriage and motherhood came to represent the surest future for women who confronted a shrinking horizon of social and economic possibilities.

Single Women, Work, and Marriage

Through the 1940s a significant population of women continued to work in the economy of bars and brothels in the city of Rancagua and in the informal settlements on the outskirts of the mining camps. Like women who populated semiurban ranchos during the late nineteenth and early twentieth centuries, these women engaged in petty commerce, operated small businesses, sold illegal alcohol, took in boarders, and transformed their own homes into places to drink and socialize. In addition, many women engaged in informal and often commercial romantic relationships with male workers.

Selling alcohol to miners became a major business for women in the underground economy of El Teniente's callampas as a result of the restrictions imposed by the company within the mining camps. In one typical case in a callampa on the outskirts of the mining camps, Juana Zamorano García was arrested for selling alcohol to the miner Angel Sepúlveda and to "the prostitute Carmen Soto Rojas." The pair were found drinking in one of the bedrooms of Zamorano García's house. Zamorano García had transformed her house into a commercial establishment and place of entertainment.[3] In a similar case, Juana Donoso Saaverda was arrested for covertly selling wine to three miners. Donoso Saaverda had converted her house in the callampa into her "place of business."[4] Women frequently worked as prostitutes in these businesses or rented out rooms in their homes to prostitutes. In one case, police apprehended three prostitutes whom they had discovered sitting around a table in a "dance room" in a house in a callampa outside the mine drinking bootleg alcohol.[5]

Some women, who neither owned their own business nor worked in one of the bars or brothels in the callampas or in Rancagua, sold food and alcohol to miners in the train station or hawked their wares in the streets. Peddling illegal alcohol to miners to take with them to the camps became an important source of income to women in Rancagua. For example, Edelmira Sandoval Garrido, who sold produce informally in the train station, was arrested for also selling wine to miners. Admitting her crime, Sandoval Garrido told the court that she had been driven to violate the North American company's prohibition of alcohol on company property by her "state of poverty."[6]

Like these women, the single women who found work as domestic servants in the mining camps did not readily conform to the company's expectations concerning their social behavior. Many maintained their economic and sexual independence by entering into semiformal romantic and economic arrangements with miners. Men would provide their lovers "presents" such as clothes or other goods or pay money directly to the women in exchange for companionship, sex, and, at times, even domestic service. Such was the case of twenty-six-year-old enmaderador Pedro José Muñoz Muñoz, who maintained a sexual relationship with the empleada Rosa Cornejo Martínez, who labored in one of the camps' cantinas. For six months Muñoz Muñoz "gave her clothes and everything she needed" until he discovered that she had also had similar relationships with other men. When Muñoz Muñoz confronted Cornejo Martínez and slapped her in the face, she told him that her other relationships were no one else's business and that she was "the owner of her own body."[7] Cornejo Martínez's attitude toward her relationship revealed the nature of these kinds of sexual relationships and the degree of autonomy that empleadas enjoyed. Cornejo Martínez seemed uninterested in establishing a monogamous relationship and refused to capitulate to Muñoz Muñoz's insistence that he had rights over her body and behavior because of his relationship with her. Her relationships allowed her a degree of sexual independence, as well as a means by which to supplement her wages as a domestic servant.

This case also reveals the different perceptions of rights and obligations implied in the informal sexual contracts between men and women. While men assumed that they could acquire a monopoly over women's bodies and expected complete loyalty in exchange for the money and presents they gave their lovers, women often didn't recognize men's expectations of monogamy. When men found that their expectations were not being met, they often resorted to violence. In one case, for example, Angel Custodio Aguillera Yáñez beat his lover, empleada Pilar Medina Roa, because she had spoken with another man whom he had prohibited her from seeing. According to Aguillera Yáñez, he had had a sexual relationship with

Medina Roa for six months, during which "I gave her money so that she could support herself." Aguillera Yáñez believed that because of this relationship, he could prohibit Medina Roa from having other friendships or relationships, and he justified his abuse by claiming that she had responded "insolently" to his claims of proprietorship.[8] These cases show that some single women could maximize their position of power within relationships with the opposite sex. In a world where women enjoyed little social power and even less control over their relationships with men, empleadas made the best of a bad situation by extracting what they could from the relationship and by asserting their own independence.

Empleadas were exploited both as workers and as women. Their work was defined by a sexual division of labor which relegated them to domestic service and which restricted them from more lucrative, "masculine" forms of wage labor. Limited to feminized spheres of the labor market, their work was devalued, and they earned substantially less than men. In 1939, for example, *Despertar Minero* noted that women workers in the laundry earned only five pesos a day, compared with an average salary of thirty pesos for male obreros. In 1941, the paper noted that empleadas in cantinas often put in longer than twelve-hour days for between sixty and eighty pesos a month.[9] The gendered and sexual nature of the subordination of empleadas was revealed in the close control exercised over their bodies and behavior by their employers and by the company. They often worked sixteen-hour days, were confined to their rooms by curfews, and were vulnerable to sexual abuse by clients and employers. Empleadas experienced harassment from the hundreds of men they served in the cantinas and from male employers. Some pensioners hit empleadas for providing slow service or for talking back or responding to their harassment with insolence. Narciso Riveros, for example, beat an empleada for talking back to him after he had berated her for being slow. According to Riveros, he beat her and swore at her because "she was insolent and fresh."[10] Similarly, José Heriberto Rojas punched the cantina worker Laura Jiménez Ruiz for not serving him faster and for responding to his insults. Like Riveros, he justified the beating by saying that she "was insolent and insulted me and didn't want to serve me."[11] The owners or managers of cantinas or more affluent white-collar workers who could afford to hire maids also tried to take advantage of their female employees. Teresa Palacios de Fuentes, for example, accused her employer, Indalicio Contreras

Vargas, of trying to rape her as she prepared breakfast in the kitchen.[12] In a similar situation, Felicita Palma Bravo accused the owner of the cantina where she worked of entering her bedroom and trying to rape her while his wife was away in Rancagua.[13]

These cases indicate the sexual as well as economic subordination of single women workers. The labor of empleadas was based on forms of exploitation that implied more than the economic forms of alienation and domination inherent in wage labor. They received low pay and worked long days because they were women. In addition, empleadas were under the constant vigilance of male cantina and pension owners. Their social and sexual activity was closely policed, and both the male workers they served and their employers often acted as if their position as domestic servants implied control over their bodies and behavior. When empleadas asserted their independence from the men they served by talking back or through establishing their sexual autonomy in informal relationships with men, they risked physical punishment. In this context, single women's informal romantic relationships with men served as a means of increasing their sexual and economic autonomy.

Not all single women workers, however, asserted their independence as forthrightly as Rosa Cornejo Martínez. Many accepted the implicit strictures against polygamy and independence imposed by their male partners. Either because they feared losing an advantageous economic arrangement or because they shared men's assumptions about the nature of relationships, some empleadas yielded to male assertions of the right to control their bodies and to male abuse without protest. This was the case of Emperatriz Yáñez Yáñez, who dropped charges against her companion who had stabbed her because she had flirted with another man. Yáñez Yáñez told the court that she didn't want to press charges, stating that "if he hit me it was because I was to blame because I wanted to have a friendship with Droguett. . . . I provoked him and I pardon him."[14] Yáñez Yáñez acquiesced to the dominant moral code of the camps that gave men rights over women's bodies out of actual agreement, her own economic self-interest, or affection.[15]

Although an empleada such as Rosa Cornejo Martínez could claim ownership of her own body and pursue relationships with a number of different men, a single woman who followed this course of action risked losing the material support provided by her lover and the violence of any lover who felt betrayed. When empleada Rosa Quintana brought an end to a relationship of many years with miner Eduardo Pérez Ahumada, he sold all the things he had given to her, stripping her room bare. A couple of months later, on discovering his former lover talking with another man, Pérez punched her in the face, knocking her unconscious. Thus Quintana had to pay a price for her independence. Her attitude toward her relationship with Pérez was made clear when she complained to the Sewell court that he had sold all the furniture he had given her and kept the money, "even though I had served him for years."[16] Despite Quintana's argument about her rights based on an informal sexual contract, the court sided with Pérez. Men still maintained the upper hand in terms of social power over women.

The nature of these semistable relationships based on the exchange of sex, companionship, and domestic service for money is revealed in one empleada's testimony to the Sewell court about a miner who had stabbed her in the chest. According to Cristina Ferrera López, José Ortíz Monsalves was a pensioner in the cantina where she worked and had made a number of passes at her, which she had rejected. In her statement, she denied that he had given her money or clothes and stated that she had refused to have relations with him. She was echoed by her attacker, who also made a point of the fact that he hadn't had a relationship with her, stating that "I haven't given her anything, nor has she asked me for money or clothes."[17] This exchange of goods was understood by both the defendant and the victim as the fundamental basis for an amorous relationship. Both implied in their statements that they would have understood the attack better had such a relationship existed, even suggesting that such a relationship might have legitimized the stabbing or, at the very least, made it comprehensible.

Empleadas who entered into semistable sexual relationships based on the exchange of sex for material goods or money frequently fell victim to the terrible jealousy of miners. Men punished their lovers for imagined or real engaños (betrayals). When Rosa Cabañas broke off a relation with miner Gregorio Contreras because of his abusive treatment, Contreras began to follow her around and threatened her with a knife.[18] Similarly, Sara Salas Briones broke up with her lover of four years, Aníbal Gutiérrez Gutiérrez, "because he constantly hit me and I was sick of him and I had intimate relations with [another man]." Gutiérrez Gutiérrez, finding Salas Briones in the company of her new lover, beat her and pushed her down a staircase. The independence of these women—their capacity to cut off abusive relations, to break up with a partner, or to have other relationships—often provoked violent consequences as men read the sexual contract to imply full control of their lovers' bodies and behavior, even after the affair ended.

Empleadas also engaged in direct forms of sex work, sleeping with a wide variety of men to supplement their income. Some empleadas, according to testimony, worked as prostitutes to save money to start their own businesses in their hometowns or in Rancagua. In one case, for example, empleada Mercedes Zapata was described as having gone to work in the camps "to provide the single miners service in order to earn a little more money to start a business in Rancagua."[19] In oral testimony miners also refer to the prosperous prostitution business in Rancagua. One former North American supervisor and administrator remembers that the only socializing between Chileans and North Americans during the 1940s occurred when the North American supervisors frequented Chilean empleadas who worked as prostitutes. The women who worked in the cantinas of the various camps, he recounts, often worked as prostitutes, saving up money to go down to Rancagua to begin their own businesses. For this North American, former cantina workers owned the "best brothels in Rancagua."[20] The supervisor also recollects that in the barracks for single workers, "Sunday was a day of rest with every worker in his bed, and Saturday, the bed was occupied by the 'cantinera' [cantina worker]." The barracks for single workers, he recalls, "were a center of prostitution because there was a person who made money with some cantineras, . . . arranging dates with them."[21]

Women who exchanged sex for money were perceived as inviting male violence. In the eyes of residents of the mining camps, their "improper" forms of behavior legitimated abuse and rape. When Julio Tapia along with Alejandro Valenzuela, saw Mercedes Parra enter the barracks for obreros accompanied by a miner, "I had the impression that this woman was a prostitute, so when my compañero and I saw her enter with a man, we told her that we would also pay to sleep with her." The two friends offered this as their defense when Parra accused them of attempting to rape her. What is striking is that the two men would use as their defense their assumption that their alleged victim was a prostitute. Their statements indicate that prostitution was commonly accepted, so much so, in fact, that the court was convinced by the defendants' statements and found them innocent.[22] The case also indicates that a woman who was defined as a prostitute had little legal protection from male violence.

In a similar case, the above-mentioned Mercedes Zapata accused a large group of men of locking her in a room and raping her. One of the accused gave a different version of the story, claiming that he had paid Zapata for sex on a number of occasions, as had other men in the same barracks. In general, the feeling of the men and women in the cantina was that if she had been raped, it was her own fault. Her attitude toward sex and sexuality and her purported informal activity as a prostitute legitimized the rape in the eyes of the community. Thus the female owner of the cantina cited Zapata's statement that "she was the owner of her actions and that nobody was going to interfere in her business" and her flirtatious behavior as signs that the empleada "had it coming." As the owner put it, "From my point of view this girl's head doesn't work right, and if what she says really happened to her she alone is to blame, since she is very backward and I know that she has had relations with a lot of people."[23]

The case reveals the risks run by empleadas who worked as prostitutes or who maintained more informal but stable arrangements with men based on the exchange of sex for goods. According to the shared, gendered moral codes of the mining community, the company, and the state, the lines were blurry between single women's public, independent social behavior, sex with a prostitute, and rape. In more than one case, men accused of rape countered with the assertion that the woman had been a prostitute and that they, like other men, had merely paid to have sex with her. The consistent use of this argument to defend against charges of rape and sexual abuse in court cases reveals both the broad legitimacy of informal prostitution in the camps and a code of ethics shared by some women and most men that viewed rape and violence as a natural consequence, even an inevitable extension, of women's open and independent sexual activity outside the bounds of marriage.

In his recollections of his activity as a deputy for Rancagua in 1949, Baltazar Castro describes how he dealt with the problems of his constituents on a day-to-day basis, including the example "of the miner from Sewell who was arrested for raping a woman in the barracks." Castro comments that the woman herself "was not very innocent because she spent time in the single workers' barracks despite the [company's] prohibition." Castro implies that the woman was to blame for the rape because of her behavior and possibly even was working informally as a prostitute in the barracks.[24] Like the court cases, Castro's anecdote indicates that the dominant moral codes in the camps, reinforced by the state at different levels, held single women responsible for rape and violence because of their sexual autonomy. In addition, the story reflects the fact that the Socialist Party deputy viewed his constituent to be the male miner rather than the female domestic servant and that the miner himself felt enabled to make his case to his congressman because of the shared understandings of appropriate female behavior and male prerogative.

Thus, despite their relative freedom and independence, single women were also vulnerable to the whims and sporadic violence of men who held legal, social, and economic power over them. Without the protection that a family or a closely knit community network could offer, they were easy prey to male violence. One woman who had worked as an empleada during the 1940s noted that life was hard for single women workers because they were treated "not like the daughters of families, but as empleadas — the treatment was hard." She describes how single women "didn't have the protection of a father or a family" and had to be "very strong" to get ahead.[25] Through their work in the cantinas or as prostitutes, single women could win some measure of economic independence and maybe earn enough to start a business in Rancagua, as Mercedes Zapata planned to, but in the eyes of the community and the state, their transgressions of the codes of appropriate female behavior made them the legitimate targets of male violence.

The legal system offered empleadas little protection from abuse and rape. In most cases, charges against men accused of abusive behavior were dismissed, or at the most, men were warned and threatened that if they came before the court again, they would be punished. In almost all rape cases the male defendants were acquitted for lack of evidence or because the women simply dropped their charges. Empleada María Córdova Trincado de González, for example, after accepting a date to have coffee with a pensioner in her cantina, was abducted and raped by a group of men. During the days following the rape, she reported, the pensioners in the cantina made fun of her with joking references to the rape. Traumatized, María Córdova Trincado left the camps, and charges against the miners were dropped.[26]

Women who engaged in independent sexual activity also risked the censure of the mining company and dismissal from their jobs for their "immoral" behavior. The copper company made a concerted effort to curtail single women's social behavior. The Welfare Department imposed curfews on them, fired them if they were caught with a *pololo* (boyfriend, lover), and forbade them to frequent the social clubs where miners gathered to drink and socialize. If they were caught by the serenos in the men's barracks or engaged in "immoral acts" in the camps' passageways, they could be fired and kicked out of the camps. Single women who became pregnant also lost their jobs. In addition, although the practice of illegal abortion was fairly commonplace, the penalties were severe, including arrest, as well as dismissal. Single women threatened the ideal of appropriate family life and sexual behavior promoted by the company and the state and, in the company's eyes, helped subvert the stability of the labor force.

The regulation of the sexuality of single women workers was embodied in laws and rules prohibiting both pregnancy and abortion. If a single woman became pregnant, she was fired as a bad moral example. In 1943, for example, the company dismissed pregnant empleada Rosa Zúñiga, who had apparently earned extra money through prostitution, "to demonstrate to these girls that they will always be the victims and that they must observe proper morals." Without such a severe lesson, the company argued, "the number of women who give themselves for money would increase and little by little any notion of morality and good habits would be lost." The unfortunate empleada's pregnancy was, according to the report, one of many similar cases that resulted in the birth of numerous illegitimate children. In these cases, "when the single mother actually has the child, neither the presumed father, nor any of those possibly responsible, have sympathized with the situation of misery in which the unhappy woman is left, and since they have nobody to turn to, they go to the company in search of help." [27]

Many pregnant empleadas resorted to clandestine abortions to end an unwanted pregnancy. In *Un hombre por el camino,* Castro describes one empleada who was "frequently asked for by the men amidst such brutal abstinence" and who "had provoked an abortion . . . as she had done other times." [28] Since unmarried women received no support from the male responsible for the pregnancy and frequently lost their jobs, abortion was a logical choice. A number of single women in the camps were actually arrested on the suspicion of provoking illegal abortions after discarded dead fetuses were found, demonstrating the state's interest in regulating female sexuality. Otilia Navarro Gálvez, for example, was arrested for provoking an abortion. According to Navarro Gálvez, she miscarried after falling down the stairs and hid the dead fetus in a box, which she intended to bury later because she knew that the company fired pregnant single empleadas. She had hidden the fact that she was pregnant from everyone, scared that the Welfare Department would discover her condition and have her dismissed.[29] In another case, empleada Piedad de las Mercedes Muñoz Muñoz was hospitalized and arrested after having an abortion. According to her fellow workers, Muñoz Muñoz had had at least one other illegal abortion.[30] Because aborting a fetus was criminal, it is difficult to ascertain the number of women who went to midwives and friends for help or who, alone, practiced abortion. Testimony in these cases, oral sources, and the popular literature seem to indicate, however, that many single and married women resorted to some form of abortion as a means to ending unwanted pregnancies.

The strict legal control and castigation of single women who bore children or who had abortions served to drive them from the camps or into marriages with miners that legitimized both the child and the mother. In such circumstances, marriage provided single women economic security for themselves and for their children. Legal and economic necessity thus helped enforce the company's ideal of domesticity and its efforts to form nuclear families in the camps. Low wages and the lack of job opportunities denied women the economic independence and power enjoyed by the male miners. The company regulations requiring men and women to formalize their sexual arrangements in marriage provided women a certain protection and security. As a company report argued, "families that lived in the mine in a decayed situation owing to the illegality of religious matrimony, matrimony that was in that epoch (1917) common, but whose celebration was legally null," often left women and children without economic support.[31] Single women and single mothers benefited from the company's efforts to impose family responsibilities on their male partners. By obliging miners to marry and to provide economic support for their wives and children, the company furnished an important alternative for women who otherwise faced an insecure future.

As feminist theorists and women's historians have noted, the sexual segregation of the labor force, which entailed the construction of the workplace as a preserve of men and the restriction of women to low-paying occupations (primarily domestic service) meant that marriage became economically beneficial to women during industrialization.[32] In El Teniente, the economic forces that impelled single women workers to enter into marriages were reinforced by social and cultural pressures. Single women workers were stigmatized as immoral, their behavior was policed and regulated by their employers and the state, and they were placed in a socially vulnerable position. Marriage bestowed on single women a legitimate social position and gave them a whole set of rights denied them if they remained unmarried. It may be that single women welcomed marriage to miners. As empleadas their livelihoods were precarious. Not only were they vulnerable to violence, but they also worked long hours for low pay. As one woman recalls, "Women married someone from El Teniente because of their economic situation," and as another added, "It was the security, not that the wages were so high, but the security."[33] The El Teniente worker received relatively high wages; such benefits as credit in stores, health care, and education; and bonuses such as the family allowance.

Marriage to an El Teniente miner represented the extension of the less formal exchange involved in the relationships of single empleadas with men. On a spectrum that began with outright prostitution and extended to more or less informal monogamous relationships based on an exchange of goods and money for sex and company, marriage was the end at the other extreme, often a logical step. In the case of marriage, however, the sexual contract between men and women was ratified and backed by the state and the copper company's Welfare Department. Company policy and the legal system guaranteed married women important benefits and securities denied to single women. They had access to their husbands' wages, the family allowance, and the protection of the company's Welfare Department and the camps' court, which recognized their rights and those of their children to economic support from their husbands.

In exchange for this security, married women sacrificed their economic and social independence. Company policy, their husbands' authority, and the prevalent gender ideology restricted married women's opportunities to work and forced them into a situation of dependence on their wage-earning husbands. Both the company and the cantinas hired only young, single women. In addition, the camps' stores were concessions, leased by the company and run mostly by men. They offered few jobs to women, and only a small number of women actually had their own business. Of 102 concessionaires who ran small businesses in the camps in 1925, only 8 were women.[34] Twenty-seven years later this situation had barely changed; only nine of the eighty-nine concessionaires were women.[35]

Work outside the household or wage labor was widely seen as contributing to the moral corruption of women. Thus one miner recalls that domestic servants "came from outside, they weren't the daughters of workers . . . the mine worker didn't permit his daughter to work in that kind of job."[36] He is echoed by a former empleada who remembers that miners did not let their daughters or wives work and that the company "brought girls from Rancagua; of course, they gave them medical exams to make sure they were healthy."[37] A miner remembers that "the girls who worked in El Teniente were from Rancagua, and logically here they gave them a small medical exam, because the gringos were very careful about venereal disease."[38] To work as an empleada implied dubious character and a lack of respectability. As one woman recalls, "Generally the women who went to work didn't have as good behavior as [those who didn't work]."[39] And another recollects that "the women who came to work came from Rancagua. I don't remember anyone born in Sewell who worked there or who worked in the cantinas."[40]

Miners exercised their patriarchical authority within the household by refusing to let their daughters or wives engage in wage labor that they saw as placing women in a position on the verge of prostitution. Women were brought up by their families not to work outside the household. One woman remembers that women remained in their homes because of their fathers' or husbands' "machista mentality." Another woman recalls that many miners' wives didn't have work outside the home because "the wives of workers stayed in their homes, the miners considered that what they earned was enough to live on, moreover they had another kind of machista mentality that the woman stay in the home."[41] A mine worker who grew up in the camps and married there notes that "the wives of miners never worked during those years, . . . in our world, the wife, . . . my wife, dedicated herself to the home, to bringing up the children, because the worker's salary, it wasn't enough for a maid . . . but imagine I have six children . . . of course that was the work of the housewife."[42]

The company's gender-based policies on work and education were reinforced by the families of miners, who dedicated their small resources to
the education of their sons. A high school education was almost unob-
tainable because few miners could afford to send a son or daughter to high
schools in Rancagua. In addition, a high school education made less sense
as an economic investment than the vocational schools in the camps and in
Rancagua. Miners' families sent their male children to vocational schools
to prepare them for work in the mine. Girls, denied jobs by the company
and access to either secondary or vocational education, held little future
economic weight within families, except for what small sums they might
earn taking in laundry, helping their mothers with boarders, or making
and selling baked goods. One woman recalls that "they practically taught
this to you, through upbringing and life. The father since he had money
to live supported you, and one didn't ask for more, one didn't have other
aspirations. Very few women left to go to Rancagua, Santiago. . . . The
vast majority of women didn't study more [than elementary school]."[43]
Thus families came to see that the only possible secure future for a daughter was marriage to a miner. Miners joined the company in the belief
that women should be confined to the household, denied opportunities
for wage labor, and limited in education and training. As one woman remembers: "Before, men were machista. If I had been with my father, he
wouldn't have let me work. My father had the idea that women should
be in the house and not go out. Many men think the same, even now, but
before they were much more machista."[44]

Thus the daughters of many mining families left the household only
when they married, and many married at young ages. In 1930, the average
age of women who married in El Teniente was eighteen and a half. Of
these women, 39.2 percent were eighteen years old or younger. Many of
these women were daughters of mining families. Older women tended to
be either widows of miners or empleadas, although many empleadas also
belonged to the eighteen-and-under category as well. In 1935, the average
age of women who married was twenty-two. Of these women, 41 percent
were eighteen or under. In 1940, the average age of women who married was twenty-three and a half, with 31 percent eighteen or younger. In
1945, the average age was twenty-three, and 26 percent were eighteen or
younger. Of the women under eighteen who married in 1945, all but one
had grown up in miners' families, largely in the El Teniente camps.[45] One

woman who grew up in the camps and married young herself recalled that the daughters of miners' families almost always married young: "We all married young, above [in the camps], at eighteen, seventeen, fifteen."[46] Women also had large numbers of children. Oral testimonies record the frequency of families with seven or eight children. One former miner recalls, for example, that "generally the families were all very numerous, every year there was another child, so the family that didn't have six, seven, eight children was rare."[47]

Miners' wives and daughters had an ambiguous relationship with the other women who worked in the camps. Single women had a life different from those of women in miners' families. Describing their lives, a miner's wife commented that "they had separate rooms, single women's lodgings, that's where you saw more, they lived a different life, without problems." This woman recalls with a touch of envy the lives of these single women, despite their reputation as "immoral" and "disrespectable." They enjoyed a freedom and independence, a lifestyle, that despite their enormous work burdens, was denied to married women and their daughters. Single women, regardless of the vigilance of the company, could go to dances and clubs to socialize with men and have a good time. Married women could go to dance or go out only when accompanied by their husbands, and miners' daughters were rarely given permission to go out: "It was very rare that parents let their daughters go out alone. . . . It was very hard for a girl to get permission to go to a dance. . . . My father didn't let me go to dances, I didn't even use makeup when I was single. Afterward, when I was married, I began to use makeup."[48] Another woman reflected on the strict patriarchal control exercised by fathers over their daughters, recalling that when she was fourteen her father discovered her with her boyfriend and sent her out of the camps to live in Rancagua.[49] Similarly, another woman who grew up in the mining camps during the 1930s and 1940s remembers that her father was very strict and would not permit her to go to dances or on dates: "I didn't go to a dance until after I was married." To avoid her father's strict control, she lied to him about the date of her birthday and age so that she could marry her lover.[50] Within miners' families, the male head of household exercised almost complete control over the social lives of his wife and any daughters.

In the El Teniente camps, women could no longer engage in the agricultural activities that had been essential to the household economy in the countryside. In the arid and barren mountains, restricted to tiny living quarters in enormous barracks, raising livestock or tending gardens was no longer a viable activity. Married women thus turned to other forms of work to help maintain their families, engaging in numerous informal economic activities in their own homes. To supplement incomes, many sold homemade bread or drinks; took in laundry, ironing, and sewing; or took in boarders—single male mine workers.[51] While this activity was largely informal, in 1952 the company authorized twenty-three women (and twenty-six men) to sell goods or services from their houses, apartments, or rooms. Of these women, the vast majority were married and only a few widowed, whereas none were single. Also, twenty-three of fifty-one traveling vendors who made periodic trips to the camps to sell goods were women. Almost all were widows or wives of former El Teniente workers and received their permits from the company as a form of pension. For the most part, they sold clothes and assorted small goods.[52] Oral sources confirm, however, that the number of miners' wives who engaged in these types of work was far larger than the number of permits given out by the company.

Nonetheless, miners' wives were limited in the kinds of work they could perform. One woman remembers that she had always wanted to open a cantina but that her husband didn't want her to. Instead, she made and sold cakes and bread. Women also engaged in illegal activities. Some, for example, ran underground bars in their homes and smuggled liquor into the camps. This was the case of Zoila Gilberto Marchant, the widow of a miner, who, to survive, sold liquor out of her home. She was finally detained while smuggling alcohol in the Sewell train station.[53] One miner recounts how some women engaged in the bootleg alcohol trade: "On the train you saw women with babies who kept diapers . . . so in their bags they threw dirty diapers and underneath they put the alcohol."[54] Other women rented rooms in their apartments or houses to be used for clandestine assignations. Single women and empleadas often used these casas de citas to meet with their lovers. Married women's work remained, however, supplementary and an extension of the housewife's domestic activities and workday in the household.

While the economic rewards of married women's labor were small compared with the salaries earned by the miners, women's work was just as onerous and exhausting as was that of the men. A woman's domestic workday began at the crack of dawn as she prepared breakfast and lunches to be consumed in the mine by her husband and sons and, possibly, her boarders. During the day she labored washing clothes and sheets by hand and preparing dinner for the men. One woman described her daily work with her mother and her sisters, who gave pensions to a large number of workers:

> We had to get up at four in the morning to go get bread. At night we left the miners' thermoses washed, with sugar and everything ready. We made their sandwiches and the men began to arrive around five to eat breakfast. We gave them breakfast and then got their lunches together. They went to work their shifts and another shift, the night shift, arrived at seven. Then two of us had to take care of those who arrived at seven . . . two others, until one in the morning, worked during the afternoon and evening. The last to eat arrived at eleven. Then we had to wash sheets and have everything clean for the next day. . . . It was all day washing plates, serving, preparing food. We worked a lot.[55]

Women began to work when they were young. Daughters helped their mothers cook and clean. They made candy and drinks and then went into the streets to hawk their goods. Daughters also helped their mothers provide always scarce firewood for cooking and heating. In some families, male workers brought back what wood they could find or steal from their jobs, but in others, collecting wood was women's work. As one woman describes it:

> There was a man who informed us when there would be wood, . . . and we the women went to Romana and we threw the wood down the hill over the fence. And we pushed the wood down the hill toward home and we arrived at the edge of the barracks where we lived at the foot of the hill and there our father waited for us because he didn't like to go look for wood because it shamed him. We the kids went and stole, that's all.[56]

Female family members also added informal economic activities to their already lengthy workdays. One woman remembers selling blankets as a girl through the union. And others recall selling *empanadas* (meat pies) cooked by their mothers on Saturday nights, during Sunday soccer games, or going from door to door selling bread and candy.[57] Still another describes how her mother earned extra money by taking in pensioners and preparing baked goods, which her daughter sold in the camps.[58]

Women's economic activities not only contributed to the family budget but, in some cases, also provided married women with a small amount of economic independence. One woman described why she continued to work washing and ironing clothes at home for money after she was married: "I've always liked to work in order to have my own money, to have my own things, to buy myself perfumes, lipstick, or Christmas presents . . . so that no one can ask me what I did with my money."[59] In general, however, women's labor, more than a source of independence, was necessary for the survival of miners' families.

The company looked on informal forms of women's work benevolently because the work took place within the household. Taking in boarders or laundry constituted an extension of the ideal housewife's everyday activities. Braden allowed, and even encouraged, married women to engage in informal economic activities as a means of alleviating their families' financial problems. These forms of labor both fit the company's gender ideology of domesticity and helped it to place responsibility for a family's well-being on women. The company could blame a family's poverty on housewives' inability to economize or failure to master the skills of "domestic science." The Welfare Department located the source of poverty of many miners' households in women's lack of training in "domestic science," arguing that the difference between prosperous and poor homes was the woman: "Here there has to be another problem and cause of poverty, since in the [first] case the housewife knows how to invest the money more advantageously for the health of her children and for her husband's wallet, while in the other case, the woman never had the opportunity to learn the rudiments of domestic economy."[60] A woman's labor extended her husbands' wages, providing a crucial supplement to the family budget. Both male workers and the company perceived this work to be a woman's duty and assigned the woman the responsibility for the welfare of her family.

Women's informal labor was often necessary, however, because male workers refused to hand over their wages. The Welfare Department reported many cases of families neglected by the husband and father. Some miners used the family allowance as a bonus for themselves, without remitting the money to their wives. This happened more frequently with miners whose wives lived either outside El Teniente, in Rancagua, or in different camps because of the shortage of housing for workers' families. Such was the case of one Miguel Ramírez, fired because "he fraudulently received the family allowance for his wife and children for years and neither gave it to his family nor helped them in any form."[61] In other cases, miners gave only the family allowance to their families, keeping their wages for themselves. In 1943, for example, the company complained that "there has been deception by workers who registered their women and children as dependents to obtain the family allowance and then only contribute this to the family sustenance. . . . The Company doesn't want to have workers who do not fulfill their duties as husbands and fathers and who, while they leave their families with a starvation ration, spend on themselves ten times the sum they concede to their families to maintain themselves."[62] The Welfare Department received frequent complaints from miners' wives about the small sums they received from their husbands.[63]

The vulnerability of married women's position in the household was also revealed in abandonments by their husbands. While some workers neglected to hand over their wages or the family allowance to their wives, others simply left their families. Many women complained to the courts in Rancagua and in Santiago, asking that they be awarded a portion of their spouses' salaries. According to one social worker's study in 1936, "Cases of abandoned women with families present themselves with enormous frequency" in the mining camps.[64] At times, married miners contracted second marriages with other women. This kind of bigamy represented a serious danger to married women, for it could signify a loss of access to husbands' wages and benefits, portions of which husbands might give to other wives. In fact, bigamy was a luxury that only miners could enjoy, because their comparatively high wages allowed them to establish more than one relationship.

Wives' complaints of men's irresponsibility point to the precariousness of their economic situation, despite their marriages to miners. In the camps they were placed in a position of complete dependence on their husbands and their husbands' wages. They could not rely on networks of extended family relations to provide alternative bases of support because the company explicitly prohibited extended family living arrangements in El Teniente. Many women either arrived at the mine alone to work as empleadas or followed their husbands up the mountain, leaving their families behind, either in Rancagua or in the countryside. Others grew up in mining families, with their only viable option being to marry young. And once married, they were subjected to the authority of their husbands.

The economic dependence of women on their husbands and women's subordination within the household contributed to conflicts between husbands and wives. Miners often used their wages and days off to travel to Rancagua, where they went to bars and brothels. As one woman recalls, "Every Saturday the men went down to Rancagua; they had a superlibertine life, the men. I think more married men than single men went down and afterward they came back up Sunday in the night without a penny, hungover."[65] Frequently they returned to the camps and their homes still drunk and penniless, and in some cases they beat their wives. For many women violence against wives was attributable to the nature of miners' work and to alcoholism, both intertwined facets of "the miner's character." Another woman commented: "The miner drinks a lot, is an alcoholic. The violence against women is due to alcohol." But she also connected both alcoholism and domestic violence to the nature of the miners' work: "They say that the miner is more of a brute, because his work is more brute work, and this brutalizes him even in his way of thinking, of acting, of being. . . . The mechanism of work is dehumanizing . . . so it's a hard mentality that the man has up above [in the mine], and what does he do when he leaves work? He goes to drink, to unburden himself."[66] For this woman, at least, violence against women was linked to the nature of work and the work culture of the mine.

Women, like their male counterparts, also link extramarital relationships to the nature of the work of miners. Confined to the home, women sometimes resorted to having an extramarital relationship. One woman testified that "there are problems, great conflicts, because the woman feels bad in her home, she feels bad that this man is there always ordering her, squashing her . . . and there are problems of communication, that's what leads many women to free themselves and to go out in the street and 'make mischief.' "[67] Echoing testimony by miners themselves, another woman identified the source of conflictive marital relations in the camps in miners' work: "Generally women fell in love with another man because of the men's work. I would say that the shifts are very hard [*jodidos*]; the night shift that enters at eleven and left at six or seven, that played a large role in the infidelity."[68] Women thus echoed the explanations given by male workers for the sources of conflictive marital relations in the camps by locating the origins of adultery in the dehumanizing nature of miners' work. On the other hand, other women, as the above sources make clear, explained conflict and infidelity in terms of the inequalities in relationships between men and women within the families of miners and the restrictive patriarchical control miners exercised over their wives.

The masculinized work culture of the mine with its definition of dignity and self-affirmation in terms of the sexual conquest of women and its concomitant expressions of anxiety about male control of female sexuality shaped men's violence against women. As we have seen, pride in one's masculine virility, defined in opposition to the feminized mine, became one way in which miners strove to overcome alienated labor. Although full proletarianization led men to relinquish control of their lives and labor to the mining company, as fathers and husbands they were, in exchange, guaranteed patriarchical power over their wives within the emergent nuclear family. The intensely masculine work culture of the mine accorded with the definition of masculine identity by the company and the state as residing in the worker's role as head of household. Just as married men's infidelity, drinking, and abandonment of their wives derived from a culture of masculinity that emphasized independence, cases of domestic violence were structured by men's sense that manhood rested on the exercise of patriarchical authority through the control of women's labor and social behavior.

Like the relationships maintained by empleadas with miners based on an exchange of sex for monetary remuneration, marriages were also arranged around an exchange: men provided women the economic security of their wages, and women attended to the house and children. And as in the case of relationships with empleadas, men understood the marriage contract to give them rights over women's bodies and behavior, as well as over their labor power. Women cooked, cleaned, and slept with their husbands, fulfilling their part of this reciprocal arrangement, while men worked in the mine and brought home their wages. In some cases, when a woman failed to fulfill the demands of domesticity to her husband's satisfaction, her husband responded with violence.

Working-class domestic violence was also a historical construction of the times, part of the "social question" elaborated by middle-class reform-

ers. Only in the late 1920s and 1930s did domestic violence become a subject for the social workers employed by the company and for the courts,
as the company began to implement its welfare policies and began its
campaign against working-class "vice." Domestic violence took its place
alongside drinking, gambling, and promiscuous sexual behavior in the
Welfare Department's characterization of workers' social and cultural lives
as pathological and in need of reform. Such violence was nothing new
and not restricted to working-class families. During the 1920s and 1930s,
however, middle-class strategies of social reform brought domestic violence out in the open and defined it both as a working-class problem and
as part of the more general "social problem" created by industrialization,
urbanization, and new class tensions. In El Teniente, the new attention
to domestic violence was expressed in the active intervention of social
workers in the family lives of workers and in the new role of the police
and courts in regulating family relations. Domestic violence became a
problem in El Teniente when, like alcoholism, it threatened the company's efforts to establish stable nuclear families and a reliable workforce.
Ironically, it was precisely the changes, tensions, and imbalances created
by the construction of a permanent wage-earning workforce and a community of households that created conflicts between men and women.
The state and company stepped in to protect women. But women needed
to be protected because of their situation of social and economic dependence and subordination within the family.

A large number of domestic violence cases were caused by husbands'
anger at the failure of their wives to perform expected domestic responsibilities. Abusive husbands often drew on the ideology of domesticity
and its prescriptive codes of female behavior to explain why they beat
their wives. To defend themselves as responsible husbands and heads of
household to the court, they marshaled arguments about wives' lack of
submissive respect ("she talked back to me") or refusal to follow orders.
For example, Ramiro del Carmen Herrera Rodríguez beat his wife because
he didn't like the way she was serving his meal and because she answered
back when he scolded her.[69] Miners constantly complained that they were
forced to hit wives who nagged, scolded, refused to accept orders, or were
generally *porfiadas* (stubborn).

Another common cause of domestic violence was husbands' anger at
wives who left the house and engaged in independent social activities.

A wife who went out alone or with friends without obtaining permission risked punishment. When Olga Moya Hall de Marchant went to the cinema with a cousin and a friend without permission, she received a beating when she arrived home. According to her husband, "I hit her in the head because my wife doesn't obey me and leaves the children abandoned so that she can go to the theater alone."[70] Likewise, Ana Mena Vera de Madrid was beaten by her husband because she went to a dance without permission.[71] Men also hit their wives simply for not being in the house. After arriving home late from a dentist's appointment, Sara Figueroa Echeverría encountered an angry husband, who beat her because he had come home to find the house empty.[72] In a similar case, Elsa Saaverda de Beltran went out one night to buy medicine, leaving her children alone for a short while, asleep. Her husband returned from work, went to look for her, and, believing that she had been with another man, beat her and had her arrested for abandoning the home.[73] Men's testimony in these cases suggests that they held to the prescriptive notions about female behavior advertised in the North American company's ideology of domesticity, drawing on such notions to define women's role within nuclear families and their own rights as heads of household.

In one case, Carlos Crespo Davalos beat his wife, Rosa, because her involvement in union activities frequently absented her from the house. Crespo Davalos complained that he couldn't contain himself because his wife had neglected their seven children, didn't prepare dinner, and spent all her time in union meetings. Rosa had ignored his prohibition to leave the house. Importantly, the court supported Crespo Davalos and lectured the wife on her domestic duties: "The court . . . made the wife see that she was neglecting her fundamental duties that are principally to attend to the home."[74] The court thus supported men's efforts to restrict their wives to the household and helped to implement the company's ideology of domesticity. In this case, the court was probably even more condemnatory of the wife's "negligence" because she spent her time away from the house in union meetings.

Quarrels over family finances and control of men's wages or the family allowance were also frequent. As we have seen, women often went to the Welfare Department or to court to object to the refusal of their husbands to hand over their wages or the family allowance. These conflicts frequently escalated into violence and revealed the tensions implicit in the situation of dependence to which many women were reduced. As Irma Luengo Carrasco told the court, "My husband doesn't give me enough money for my necessities and because I ask him for money he gets angry." After a fight about money, she denounced her husband to the police for hitting her. Men, in turn, often defended themselves against charges of abuse by complaining that their wives tried to control the family finances or demanded that they hand over their wages and the family allowance, thus attempting to usurp their husbands' central role of breadwinner.[75] For men, control of wages and economic power was an important source of their sense of manhood.

These cases indicate how conflict-ridden the exchange of money for services as a basis for marriage was. They also reflect the imbalance of power in these relationships and men's expectation of their rights to control women's labor, social behavior, and sexuality. The weaker social and economic position of women within the family rendered them vulnerable to male violence. Thus, while marriage to a miner represented a measure of economic security for women, it placed new burdens on women's shoulders. Married women labored to support their families and to fulfill the responsibilities dictated by the gender ideology of female domesticity. In addition, they experienced a significant loss of autonomy as they became increasingly dependent upon and subordinate to their husbands.

Women's Strategies of Resistance

Women confronted the inequalities of family life and gender relations in the camps in a variety of ways. Within the arena of marriage women resisted their complete subordination. They drew on the ideology of domesticity and its institutional supports to protect themselves from male abuse and exploitation. They thus appropriated the hegemonic ideology of gender relations in the camps in their efforts to limit their subordination to their husbands. In addition, although both single and married women were frequently the victims of physical violence by men, some women resisted abuse with their own violence. Women in the mining camps actively participated in fights and conflicts with husbands and lovers. Not all women accepted male abuse passively; many went to court to prevent further abuse, and many responded literally by hitting back.

Married women employed a number of strategies for coping with abusive husbands. Women viewed the police and the court as sources of protection. Many of the women who complained to the police of wife beating did so because they feared that if they let the abuse go unchallenged, their spouses would get into the habit of beating them. They used legal denunciations as a preventive measure to ensure that abuse did not continue. Women often dropped charges against their husbands after telling the court that they had patched things up with their attackers or that the arrest and trial had served its purpose of a warning against future abuse.

A typical case was that of Margarita Vásquez de Bustamante, who accused her husband of hitting her with a chair. In court, Vásquez de Bustamante dropped the charges against Anselmo Bustamante, explaining that after her husband hit her, "I was upset so I went to the police to denounce him. . . . I did it so that he wouldn't do it again."[76] Another woman told the court that she had charged her husband with abuse "so that he not become accustomed to hitting me for any reason."[77] Many women brought charges against husbands who had beaten them when drunk and then dropped charges, explaining that their spouses were violent only when under the influence of alcohol. Rosa Leiva Briones desisted in the prosecution of her husband because "he has promised me not to do it anymore; it was the first time he hit me and it was because of the aguardiente he had drunk."[78]

Women sometimes dropped charges against their husbands out of economic necessity. An imprisoned husband could not work and could possibly lose his job. The danger of pursuing charges against a spouse was the loss of income to the entire family. The economic dependency of women on their husbands' wages meant that their efforts to restrict and punish domestic violence in the legal arena were limited. Margarita Vásquez de Bustamante, for example, dropped charges against her husband because the initial arrest had served as an effective warning and because, as she explained, "I don't want him to lose work, since he would have to come from Caletones [to court] and would have to lose a day's pay."[79]

For married women, the Welfare Department's close control of family and domestic life in the camps, while certainly repressive, may have served their interests. Braden's attempts to regulate the behavior of husbands who neglected their wives and contributed little to the household budget provided married women important support. Married women frequently turned to the company and the court to complain that their husbands were devoting their wages and the family allowance to the pursuit of their own pleasures rather than to the family budget. The company's policy of warning and then suspending or firing men who "through vice cannot fulfill their family obligations" in order to "obtain decent living conditions for a number of mothers and children who at present suffer conditions worse than those of the unemployed" could help wives through the close supervision of the family life of miners.[80]

This imposition of company and state power in the miners' private lives provoked their anger and rejection. They complained frequently of the Welfare Department's intrusiveness and the company police's "home visits" and attempts to investigate and "reform" their lives in the barracks. The union demanded an end to invasions by serenos of miners' homes and reported complaints by women that serenos would spy on them through windows and doors. For the union, the Welfare Department and local court represented agents of the company's repressive forces and threats to workers' freedom and autonomy.

Some women, however, welcomed the intrusive activities of serenos, social workers, and the police. In the case of domestic violence, the positive role played by the otherwise despised social workers was clear to women: according to oral testimony, women complained to the Welfare Department about abusive or negligent husbands and often received aid from social workers. One woman remembers that "we were always close to a social worker . . . and if the social worker heard that a marriage wasn't functioning well, she went to the house and conversed and tried to solve the problem. . . . They visited with the daughter, the couple. . . . The social workers were around, very close, in order to help."[81] Similarly, police sometimes assisted women who requested their help, although at other times they only talked to abusive husbands. According to the same woman, "One could go to the police without worrying. . . . If they could help you, they helped you."[82] In this way, the company's efforts to regulate the private lives of miners and their families through the activities of serenos and social workers, while an invasion of privacy that irked both men and women, also provided women support in dealing with abusive or negligent husbands. Resort to the courts and the Welfare Department for protection from their husbands was one way in which women could use to their own ends the social institutions responsible for producing and implementing the ideology of domesticity in the camps.

Beyond looking to the legal system or the company Welfare Department for protection, women also responded to verbal and physical abuse with their own violence. Thus when Ramiro del Carmen Herrera Rodríguez lectured his wife, María, because he didn't like the way she was serving dinner, she spoke back sharply "with insults," and when her husband slapped her, she took a cup and threw it at his head and took a stick of firewood to defend herself from further blows. Despite her vigorous self-defense, her husband managed to hit her a number of times. She then denounced him to the police. She explained that "I threw a glass at his head because it was the only way I had to defend myself. And I also took a stick of firewood because he had already hit me on a number of occasions. I'll defend myself if he hits me."[83] In a similar case, Ester Cerna Yáñez denounced her husband to the police for hitting her. As in the previous case, Cerna Yáñez had responded to her husband's pushing her by bashing him in the head with her iron, then suffering the consequences when her husband overpowered her.[84] When her husband was jailed, Cerna Yáñez then left him, taking her son with her. She was denounced to the police by her still incarcerated husband for deserting him. The restrictions on women's independence were made clear when the court ordered Cerna Yáñez to be located and arrested for the crime of "abandonment."[85]

At times, neighbors and relatives came to the defense of abused women. Usually, however, only when a beating became very dangerous or took place in a public space did neighbors interfere in domestic violence. In one case, for example, Delia Soto Guzmán de González had suffered beatings by her husband for years. When her husband tried to stab her with a knife on the staircase of the barracks while she was attempting to flee, three women who lived nearby rescued Soto Guzmán de González and managed to restrain her attacker and then hide her in one of their apartments. This wasn't the first time female neighbors had tried to protect Soto Guzmán de González. Rosa Miranda de Cherrer had gone to her neighbor's house in response to her cries for help several times before.[86] In a similar case, when a former lover began to abuse and tried to rape the married María Moreno, she sent her daughter to her neighbor and friend María Bustos de Valencia to get help. Bustos de Valencia arrived on the scene, preventing any further abuse and giving Moreno time to flee. She took the children to her own house.[87] In other cases neighbors hid abused women or counseled abused women to denounce their husbands and seek protection with the police.[88]

Mothers frequently defended their daughters from abusive husbands and fathers. For example, Clementina Zúñiga Méndez de Villablanca got into a physical fight with her husband after she discovered that he had tried to rape their daughter Aida. She told the court that the reason for the violent fight had been that she had "told him that I would kill him if he raped her [the daughter]."[89] Similarly, Elena Guzmán de Lira hit her husband—and in turn received a number of blows—and then denounced him for beating their seventeen-year-old daughter.[90]

Mothers also defended their daughters from the abuse of their sons-in-law. They tried to stop fights, hit their daughters' husbands, and offered their daughters refuge. Filomena Navarrette pressed charges against her son-in-law, Vidalgo Henríquez, for hitting both her and her daughter. She had intervened in a beating he had been giving her daughter and had "insulted" him.[91] In another typical case, when Zulema Medina de Valdivia went to get water, she ran into her son-in-law, who had been hitting her daughter. As she described the incident: "I asked him why he had hit and treated my daughter María badly. He answered that he was her owner and had the right to hit her and spoke to me in a vulgar way. I threw the water pot I had with me at him because I will not permit anyone to treat me in this way."[92] These forms of female resistance to male violence indicate how women responded to the changes in their lives. The networks of aid and solidarity between neighbors were an essential resource for women living in the barracks, far from the protection of the extended family or local community that they may have enjoyed in the countryside. In these cases, as when they appealed to the police, court, and social workers, women contested men's claims that the sexual contract in marriage gave men the right of "ownership" over their wives' bodies and behavior. These women invoked their own rights, encoded in the ideology of the companionate marriage, to safety and security.

Informal bonds of reciprocity and support among neighbors emerged as women came together to wash clothes and pots and pans at the shared public water taps that each barracks provided workers' families. The public washing place was the only space in the camps that was not dominated by men and where women could enjoy a certain autonomy and gather to discuss events in the camps, the barracks, and the mine. There they talked about quarrels among neighbors; problems in families; issues having to do with their husbands' work and wages; the union; and conflicts with the company. Women, like men, shared very confined private and public spaces with their neighbors. The details of their private lives became public knowledge in the cramped living quarters.

While this forced proximity helped to establish close ties of support among some women, as in the case of neighbors who protected abused women or who shared scant economic resources, helping with the washing, lending food or money, it also contributed to conflictive relations. Close relationships of friendship and solidarity could often turn into violent conflicts based on feelings of jealousy, resentment, or a sense of unreciprocated support. Women, like men, fought among themselves, but their fights were different because of their dependence on men and their subordinate position in the household. Often fights revolved around women's economic and sexual insecurity and competition. Because economic security was tied to the sexual contract women established with their husbands, fights over economic issues were often articulated in the codes that governed sexuality in the camps. Similarly, sexual rivalry involved economic competition as much as sexual jealousy.

The forms of alliance and rivalry women established among themselves can be seen in the fight between two neighbors and former friends in the workers' barracks. The women had helped each other out, sharing wood, food, and small amounts of money. As Elena Echeverría told the court, "We were very close friends, and I gave her and her children whatever I had in the house." But one day, when her neighbor Rosa Palma de Poblete came to ask for firewood, Echeverría refused because she had only a little left, just enough for her own family. Palma de Poblete then swore at her friend and spit at her. The next day, when they met at the public tap, the conflict between the women escalated into a physical fight.[93]

This case reveals the delicate balance of expectations and reciprocity that structured women's friendships with other women. Women relied on and expected help from friends and recognized their own duties to help out neighbors. However, reciprocity could easily become a point of conflict. When women refused to help or when they placed demands that went beyond commonly accepted limits, they could provoke fights

and feuds. For Palma de Poblete, Echeverría was neglecting and rejecting a responsibility implicit in friendship between neighbors, whereas in
Echeverría's eyes, Palma de Poblete exceeded her rights to neighborly aid
by asking for wood that Echeverría needed for her own family. Duties to
family outweighed responsibilities to friends.

The fight between the two women also reveals another tension among
women. When Palma de Poblete attacked and insulted Echeverría, she accused her of being an adulterer. In almost all the cases of fights between
women, regardless of the cause of the conflict, women phrased their condemnation of their enemy in terms of sexual impropriety. Women called
other women "whores" and "sluts" and accused them of sleeping with
many men or of cheating on their husbands. Zulema de la Hoz Acuna,
for example, provoked a fight by calling her neighbor Margarita Fuentes
"shameless, slut, whore." She had allegedly seen Fuentes in the company
of a man (not her husband).[94] Apparently, transgressions not only of an
economic code of reciprocity but also of the camps' dominant moral code
of appropriate sexual behavior provoked tensions between friends and
neighbors.

What does the existence of such a moral code tell us about women's
ideas about sexuality? The use of such insults as "whore" and "slut" and
the accusations of adultery seem to imply that women shared men's ideas
about female sexuality. The language they used in altercations with friends
and neighbors and in court was also used by the men in the camps who
beat their wives out of jealousy and sought to keep them restricted to
the household. In court cases, women defended their conflicts with other
women by invoking labels that implied the "immorality" of their enemies.
By charging another woman with being an unfaithful wife, they appealed
to an accepted code of respectability and social honor and thus legitimized
the conflict. While some women had extramarital relationships, fought
back against their husbands, and formed networks of support with friends
and neighbors, women also spoke the dominant language of female domesticity. Married women's informal and private strategies of opposing
male dominance within the home coexisted uneasily and in tension with
beliefs about appropriate forms of female behavior drawn from the ideal
of the respectable mother and wife. As in the case of Echeverría and
Palma de Poblete, a conflict about economic reciprocity between friends

and neighbors was phrased in the language of the norms that governed social behavior in the camps.

For women, other women's adultery had another meaning, distinct from male views of women's extramarital relationships. Condemnations of other women's sexual behavior may have come out of jealousy. But the source of this jealousy was not necessarily a desire to control their husbands' sexual activity. For men, the possibility of women's extramarital relationships threatened their sense of manhood. For women, on the other hand, sexual jealousy arose from the economic threat that other women could pose. Men were valuable economic resources, and an unfaithful husband could eventually neglect his family's necessities or even abandon it completely. Other women represented competition for economic resources and security. The community codes that governed relations between men and women in the camps, at least for women, thus had an important material underpinning based on married women's economic dependence on their husbands.

The case of Margarita Tagle Peña and Mercedes Ruiz de Núñez illustrates the threat other women could pose to married women. Ruiz de Núñez was married to a worker, Alberto Núñez Montiel, who perished in a mine accident. When she went to claim her husband's pension and indemnification for the accident, she encountered difficulty. Her husband's longtime mistress and common-law wife, Tagle Peña, was also claiming her right to the benefits. Actually, Núñez Montiel had married both women, Ruiz de Núñez in 1918 and Tagle Peña in 1938. The court found that both women enjoyed legal status and should thus split the pension and benefits.[95] For Ruiz de Núñez, the court's decision spelled disaster. As she told the judge, criticizing his decision, "my situation is desperate since I am already elderly, I have been in bad health for many years, and I am not in condition to work like before. Without the kindness of some of my husband's friends, I wouldn't have had the means to survive while I awaited your decision."[96] Ruiz de Núñez had married in 1918 and therefore was probably in her forties, whereas her rival, Tagle Peña who had married in 1938, was younger and worked as an empleada.

The case of these two wives was not uncommon. As we have seen, according to company social workers and oral testimony, many miners had more than one wife or lover because their economic power allowed them to maintain relationships with more than one woman at a time. For the original wife or lover, however, a second or third woman in her husband's life meant a decrease in income both during and after her husband's lifetime. Núñez Montiel had clearly established a second marital relationship with the younger Tagle Peña after years of marriage. For Tagle Peña the relationship was also an investment. Although she had to compete with Ruiz de Núñez for Núñez Montiel's salary and benefits, the relationship signified an important addition to her monthly income. For both women involved, the existence of a rival meant economic insecurity and a tightened budget. Thus women's condemnation of other women as "promiscuous," "adulterers," and "whores"—as disrespectable—had its origins in the competition between women for men's wages and the potential threat posed by other women, as well as in the internalization of hegemonic ideas about appropriate female behavior.

Gendered social codes of "respectable" behavior constrained women's sexual and social activity. Men were rarely exposed to the censure of the courts or the community for their extramarital relationships, which sometimes earned legal recognition. Women, on the other hand, faced severe condemnation not only from their husbands but also from members of the mining community, including their female friends and neighbors, for behavior that transgressed the unwritten codes of gender relations and sexuality in the camps. Single women empleadas and married women who engaged in "inappropriate" forms of social and sexual behavior met with the rejection of women in the camps, as well as that of men. That women both engaged in private forms of resistance to men's authority within their families, including infidelity, and employed the dominant language of respectability and morality signaled the difficulty women faced in building an alternative to the ideology of female domesticity. Economic competition and the reigning moral codes of respectability in the camps served as impediments to the elaboration of an autonomous female sphere of values and beliefs.

A number of forces acted simultaneously to push single women into marriages in which they occupied the role of housewife. Most important were company policies restricting women's work, the low wages earned in domestic service, and the potential economic security women could gain through marriage. In addition, the regulation and policing of single women's sexual and social lives made it increasingly difficult to live and work in the mining camps and remain single. Within the family, women's economic dependence on men and their sexual subordination created severe tensions that often led to domestic violence, abandonment, and adultery. Married women crafted private and informal strategies of resistance to male authority, but their most effective tools in limiting men's violence and acquiring access to men's wages were the legal system and the company Welfare Department.

Ultimately, women's reliance on the institutions that upheld and implemented the dominant codes of gender in the mining community and their own identification with notions of respectability limited the possibility of building an alternative female culture in the camps. Women established networks of reciprocity and support, but their major form of identification was with their husbands and families. The household became the primary world they inhabited, and female friends and neighbors, although important to married women's lives, constituted possible competitors and rivals, as well as potential allies.

A woman who grew up in the camps and married a miner commented on women's lack of participation in social activities outside the household: "I think that the women were of their homes, they were very domestic, they spent their time enclosed in their homes."[97] Similarly, a miner remembered that "women's participation in the life of the mining camps was very small. . . . Women dedicated themselves more to the life of the home."[98] Another miner recalls that in the camps, women lived "closed in their homes" because of a dominant "machista mentality" and that "women didn't have an active participation in social organizations in the camps."[99] Another woman remembers that the social world of women revolved around their families and that women went out or participated in social clubs infrequently: "Everything was the marriage, the family, a life of each one in her home, there was no freedom, as they say."[100] As a woman who grew up in the camps during the 1930s and then married a miner commented, "I didn't go out of the house much. I stayed inside doing my housework and taking care of the children. . . . Most women stayed at home. There were a lot of children to take care of."[101]

The economic dependence of women on men within the nuclear families in the mining camps and the hegemony of gendered languages based on the ideology of female domesticity led married women to identify with their husbands and families. They experienced public space and life outside the household through their contact with their husbands' worlds of work in the mine and politics in the union. Public spaces and social institutions in the camps were dominated by men. Married women thus entered the public sphere and the world of politics at the sides of their husbands, with whom they shared fundamental interests in common.

Part III

Men and Women on Strike:

The Mining Community and the

Demise of Populism, 1942–1948

8

Workers' Movements, Women's Mobilization,

and Labor Politics

In 1942, the El Teniente copper miners launched the first major strike in the copper industry since 1919. The strike revealed contradictions in the ideology and politics of the Popular Front and signaled the reemergence of a powerful labor movement in the copper mines. Despite the support lent by the government and parties of the Popular Front to workers' organizations, an escalating cost of living during the late 1930s and early 1940s eroded gains made by workers in wages and social benefits. By 1942, the cost of living in El Teniente had brought miners' real wages down to their 1930 level. But the miners were now able to confront declines in their standard of living with independent unions that drew strength from the support of the state and from the left-wing members of the Popular Front coalition. Between 1938 and 1942, the mining community organized a series of grassroots movements to demand government intervention to control prices in the stores and pensions of the mining camps. These movements often took place outside the union and were led by women organized in women's committees and cost-of-living committees. The miners combined workplace actions with forms of community mobilization that included their entire families and that tied their work-related demands to issues of consumption and services that affected all members of El Teniente's working-class population.

The consolidation of a permanent population of workers and their families in the El Teniente mining camps, rather than bringing accommodation and discipline to the workforce as the company had expected, established the basis for a unified and militant working-class community. Despite the conflictive nature of domestic life, the construction of the modern nuclear family in the mining camps brought men and women together in shared antagonism to the company around a set of common interests. Conflict between the workers and the company penetrated every crevice of daily life. The miners union came to represent workers not only in work-related struggles but also in movements for better housing, social services, and a controlled cost of living. Strikes in El Teniente became conflicts between the entire community and the company, in which women and children marched, picketed, and participated in protests. Thus, the Braden Copper Company's strategy of settling workers in stable nuclear families backfired. More women stayed in the camps and married workers, and more men began to stay on in the camps with their families. This stable population of married workers and their families satisfied Braden's need for labor, but it also provided the basis for a unified community that lent strength to miners' strike movements.

In addition, the intervention of the state in the mining camps after 1938 and the organizing activities of the Communist Party contributed to the intensification of the mining community's ties to the Left. The efforts of the state to control the cost of living in the camps, to adjudicate labor disputes, to prevent mass dismissals, and to enforce the provisions of the labor code helped sustain the new world view of miners and their families that imagined life in terms of the rights guaranteed by the regimes of corporate and state social welfare and the promises of social mobility and benefits of citizenship. Links to both the Socialist and Communist Parties allowed the mining community to articulate this sense of rights and citizenship in the language of working-class radicalism and nationalism.

The Cost of Living and Community Mobilization in the Mining Camps

In January 1941, shortly after signing an agreement with the miners' union and the Braden Copper Company on the prices of pensions in the camps, hotel and cantina concessionaires raised their price nonetheless. The cost of living had risen steadily in Chile during the late 1930s and early 1940s, increasing 83 percent nationally between 1939 and 1942.[1] While union leaders went to complain to the head of the Welfare Department about the new price increases, workers in the mine began a spontaneous work stoppage.[2] Meanwhile, over a thousand miners convened in the union hall to discuss what to do. Union leaders explained that they had consulted the Welfare Department without success and that according to the labor code they could not lead the illegal strike. The workers then appointed strike leaders from among their own ranks and agreed to continue their stoppage until the company agreed to lower the price of pensions. In addition, they formed picket brigades to enforce the strike and sent telegrams outlining the situation to the president, the minister of labor, the minister of the interior, and the CTCh. Union leaders had their hands tied by restrictions of the labor legislation. Although they may have supported a strike, they had to stand aside and let the workers take control of the movement. As one paper commented, "The present strike movement is outside the activities of the union, because the strike has been declared by the workers' committees, having nothing to do with the union."[3]

The next day more than four thousand miners met with a labor inspector, who told them that their strike was illegal and that there was nothing he could do. Dissatisfied, workers agreed to continue the strike. While union leaders journeyed to Santiago to meet with the minister of labor, miners who lived in the barracks for single workers began a hunger strike. Finally, the miners committee met with the labor inspector and representatives of the company administration, who agreed to rescind the price increase and to form a commission to study the issue of the cost of living.

Following the wildcat strike, workers in their union assemblies decided to form conflict committees (comités de lucha) at every work site. The objective of the committees was "to organize the struggle for all the demands felt by the workers in their actual work so that we can carry out our future struggles better."[4] In the electrical department, for example, the comité de lucha devoted itself to improvement of the workshop, care of the tools, job classification, and enforcement of the slogan "equal salary for equal work."[5] Workers organized the committees in order to channel demands that came from each work site through the union and to strengthen the union by building an organizational base in the workplace. In addition, the committees worked with the local base committees of the Popular Front that workers in Sewell began to form at this time. Delegates from workplace committees participated both in the union and in the Popular Front committees.

By the end of 1941, the level of tension in the mine had reached a breaking point. The camps' cantina and pension owners provided the final blow by raising prices in violation of the union's agreement with the company. In October 1941, Despertar Minero had noted an "alarming increase in the cost of living" owing to "a wild rush of speculation by the monopolies . . . the few firms that control the sale of articles of primary necessity. . . . [T]here are a few businesses that control all the commerce in Sewell y Mina and they are thus easily able to agree to raise the prices of goods, especially goods of primary necessity."[6] One month later, the union paper reported that "the miners, justly indignant and fed up with the abuses and arbitrary dismissals that they suffer, before this new blow to their miserable wages have resolved not to go to work."[7] Between December 1940 and December 1941, the cost of living in the camps had risen 23 percent, according to company estimates.[8]

The union newspaper editorialized that it was the duty of the government to brake price inflation and reminded "the president of his oath to fulfill the program of the Popular Front against the high cost of living." But by 1941, the miners' faith in the Popular Front government had slackened significantly. Thus *Despertar Minero* urged the entire community to initiate a "vigorous movement which would include all consumers, housewives, the youth, the entire working class. . . . Only by mobilizing the entire population of the mine into a great movement for the lowering of the cost of subsistence will we be capable of detaining the unbraked race of the increase in the cost of living." The union exhorted the women of the community particularly to join the Sewell chapter of the Movimiento Pro-Emancipación de la Mujer Chilena (Movement for the Emancipation of Chilean Women, MEMch).[9]

On 6 November, miners once again began a wildcat work stoppage, and the following day thousands of workers and their family members came together in a mass public meeting. At this meeting the governor of the province gave a speech acknowledging the justice of the miners' demands and promised he would help them come to a reasonable agreement with the cantinas. In the presence of the governor, several miners described their situation and the refusal of the Braden Copper Company to receive their petitions. Among the speechmakers were members of the MEMch, who received an enthusiastic ovation as they read a letter to the governor asking for the liberty of three miners who had been arrested during the work stoppage. At this meeting, miners also complained about abusive supervisors and demanded raises. As in January, the company settled the conflict over the cost of living by appointing a commission to oversee the prices and quality of the food served in the camp cantinas. This commission, however, was more favorably balanced toward the workers, including representatives from the union and from the provincial Inspección del Trabajo, and soon released a report that condemned the quality and quantity of the food supplied to the miners. The commission found "that the quality of the food provided to the workers, like the quantity, is deficient and cannot satisfy the quantity of calories that a worker consumes doing hard physical labor like the miner."[10] In a meeting with the governor, the miners and the cantina owners hammered out a precise agreement on the exact quantity of food to be served and the cost of each meal.[11]

Although the governor's support had been helpful in the conflict, the miners realized that only the mobilization of the entire community in the camps could force the company to control prices in the cantinas and the pensions. Thus, in January 1942, workers and their wives began to organize cost-of-living committees (*comités pro baja de las subsistencias*) and women's committees (*comités de mujeres*) to keep a vigilant eye on prices in the camps' stores.[12] The new organizational drive in El Teniente signified the miners' attempt to reintroduce themselves as the protagonists of the Popular Front government. The responsibility, the miners perceived, fell on them to make the Popular Front's "Program for National Salvation" a concrete social reality. *Despertar Minero* expressed this attitude toward the Popular Front government when it editorialized in January 1941 that "it is necessary to organize hundreds of Popular Front base committees throughout the country in order to impel from the base the accomplishment of the program promised and sworn to by the actual President of the Republic in various opportunities."[13] The Popular Front program, the union stated, would not be implemented from above through government action but from below by the organized working class: "It is not with memorandums from ministers that you satisfy the needs of the people, it is not in this way that you are loyal to the people. . . . [A]ll the workers of Chile united in the only federation, the CTCh, must force the accomplishment of this program."[14] The Popular Front program, the union claimed, was not a creation of the government, of the president and his ministers, but "has been inspired from within proletariat culture."[15] And it proposed to return the Popular Front to its working-class origins and reconstruct it through the mobilization of working-class parties and organizations.

Just before his death in 1941, Aguirre Cerda spoke to his cabinet of the failure of his government to implement the basic program of the Popular Front: "We promised the people to pull them out of misery, to raise their social, economic, and moral level. Apart from the intelligent and constructive action of some of my ministers, we have wasted time here with long debates and discussions, without ever arriving at practical and effective solutions for the great problems. It burdens my soul with profound sorrow, because I imagine that the people, whom I love so much, could think that I have deceived them."[16] A U.S. State Department delegate echoed Aguirre Cerda's sentiments in his own, far-from-sympathetic evaluation of the first Popular Front administration.

> I think it may fairly be said that the Aguirre Cerda regime has failed rather more signally than is normal in these cases either to justify the hopes of its supporters or the fears of its opponents. The masses in Chile continue to live in the greatest poverty; social legislation and wage increases are barely keeping pace with the rising tendency of the cost of living. On the other hand, the rightists retain to a very large extent those economic rights and privileges which they feared would be taken away from them.[17]

Under the Popular Front, industrial interests, middle-class professionals, and white-collar employees received important gains in terms of state subsidies for private investment and state jobs, housing, health care, social security, and increases in real wages, whereas urban workers, miners, and campesinos saw little change in their material situation, as a steadily rising cost of living eroded their real wages.[18] For the El Teniente miners, job instability and inflation continued to exacerbate the insecurity of their lives.[19]

At the national level, by 1941 the Popular Front coalition had fallen apart with the withdrawal of the Socialist Party.[20] Already in 1940 a group of leftist Socialists, the "Nonconformists" (*inconformistas*), had withdrawn from the PS and the Popular Front to form the Socialist Workers Party (Partido Socialista de Trabajadores) and a radical alternative to the Popular Front, a "Workers Front" based on the support of "truly" working-class organizations. While the Nonconformists failed to win any significant following among workers and unions, their withdrawal from the PS revealed the internal conflicts that rent the Popular Front coalition.

In 1941 the Socialist Party followed the example of the inconformistas and left the Popular Front. The official withdrawal of the PS had less to do with dissatisfaction with the government's moderation and cautious reformism, however, than with the Socialists' growing feud with the Communist Party. The Socialists competed with the PC for working-class and union support and had seen the PC gain labor adherents at a rapid rate since the late 1930s. In El Teniente, this schism was represented in political divisions between El Teniente's four obreros unions. Although the Communist Party controlled El Teniente's largest and most important union of mine workers, with between three and four thousand members, the Socialist Party held leadership posts in the smaller unions from the Coya electrical plant, the Rancagua warehouse, and the Caletones foundry. In terms of international politics, the PS rejected the PC's support for the Hitler-Stalin nonaggression pact between Germany and the Soviet Union and advocated the construction of firm economic and political ties with the United States, a position repudiated by PC leaders.

Socialist Party leader Oscar Schnake, the Popular Front minister of development, led the campaign for a strategy of United States–financed national industrial development and denounced the detrimental effects of Communist-sponsored strikes and stoppages on economic growth. According to Schnake and other anti-Communist, Socialist leaders, the presence of the PC in the Popular Front jeopardized Chile's possibilities for obtaining credits and loans from the United States. After the rightwing opposition and the Socialists failed in their efforts to dislodge the PC from the coalition government and to make the PC illegal, owing to Aguirre Cerda's veto, the PS withdrew from the coalition, although it left its ministers in the government.

Despite these internal conflicts, the parties of the Popular Front, with the PS running alone, managed to increase their overall votes in the 1941 congressional elections. Including the Socialists, the Popular Front parties won 59 percent of the vote, with the Radicals taking 20.7 percent; the Socialists, 17.9 percent; and the Communists, 12 percent.[21] The Front's success in the elections had coincided with a crackdown on union organizing in the countryside. Faced with a threat from the rightist parties to boycott the elections and from attacks by the Socialist Party, Aguirre Cerda began to clamp down on the wave of organizing that had swept rural Chile since the 1930s.[22] As Paul Drake notes, "The Front quashed strikes, restrained the Leftist press, restricted union political activities, and banned remaining paramilitary organizations."[23] The price of electoral success for the Popular Front in 1941 was, then, a turn to the right and repression of workers and the Left.

Rather than reject the Popular Front, however, the miners reasserted their faith in the coalition's possibilities. They continued to express their confidence that the Front was their only hope for significant change. The union paper argued that the response to the government's failure to support the workers in their struggle with the company had to be "the base committees of the Popular Front, strengthened and supported by the comités de lucha and the impulsion of struggles based on workers' demands." "This is the only way," the paper continued, "that we will be capable of demanding that señor Aguirre Cerda fulfill the program of the Popular Front."[24] The miners' union proposed the organization of a mass movement, established in the base committees of the Popular Front and the workplace committees and supported by the union, the CTCh, the Socialist Party, and the Communist Party, to win what the government had failed to grant them and to "break the American empire in Sewell, obtaining absolute liberty and making use of all of our rights consecrated in the Constitution of Chile."[25] In early 1942, the miners lent their electoral support to Aguirre Cerda's successor, Radical Juan Antonio Ríos, and a reconfigured political coalition, the Democratic Alliance, of the Radical, Socialist, Democratic, and Communist Parties.

The Miners on Strike

In January 1942, the miners' union presented a petition, approved unanimously in a massive union assembly, to the company. The Braden Copper Company rejected the union's demands and maintained an unbending posture in front of the labor inspectorate's arbitration board. In the mine, conflict between workers and jefes had come to the point where the company paper, *El Teniente,* was forced to recognize that "it is possible that in some cases there have been methods [of treatment] considered by the miners as too rigorous." But, the paper continued, citing workers' decreased lack of respect for foremen in the mine, "the discipline in the mine has been falling so much as to warrant these measures."[26]

Tensions within the mine were exacerbated by the intensification of the pace of labor. As markets for copper expanded owing to the wartime demand of the 1940s, the company sought to increase production. Instead of hiring more workers, however, the Braden Copper Company made every effort to squeeze increased production from the existing workforce. The demands on workers in the mine grew, and foremen became correspondingly dictatorial. A U.S. embassy official explained that labor difficulties in El Teniente were due to the fact that "although production has been vastly expanded, the number of employees has increased very slightly; in other words, there has been a speed-up of production without any corresponding increase in the number of people employed." [27] The company was reluctant to hire new workers because of the added expense but also because it feared that it would later be unable to cut its labor force when demand for copper fell, given pressures by the Chilean government to limit dismissals. In addition, the company believed that an expansion of the workforce would place the miners' union in a more favorable position during collective bargaining.

The speedup of the pace of work in the mine led a U.S. embassy adviser to report that "there are many signs of exhaustion among the workers." [28] The embassy also attributed the conflict in the mine to the fact that real wages in the copper mines were at their 1930 level, one dollar per day, and to "the high-hat attitude of American employees [the supervisors] towards Chilean employees." [29] The U.S. ambassador in Chile, Claude Bowers, telegraphed the secretary of state that "in my opinion the strike cannot be attributed solely to 'politics.' . . . [T]he workmen feel that they are entitled to a larger direct share in the profits which higher prices and volume production are supposed to have brought." [30]

After a month of frustrated negotiations between the company and the union, the government arbitration board authorized a strike in El Teniente, and the union began to organize its bases. The strike lasted twenty-two days. During these three weeks, the miners organized picket brigades to impede strikebreakers from working and to guard the mine from "sabotage." In addition, they organized committees for administering the strike, sanitary committees, and committees for distributing provisions. By the end of the three weeks, the workers had won not only an unprecedented wage increase and other benefits but also, as *Despertar Minero* wrote, "experience and the consciousness of our own force." The mobilization of miners in workplace and strike committees also included women, the youth, and the "progressive sectors" of the empleados, who supported the strike in different ways. In addition, the striking miners received economic aid from unions across the country—most important, from the coal miners' unions, to whom the El Teniente miners had sent economic aid during their strike the previous year.[31]

The miners' demands included a 30 percent wage increase, an end to the high cost of living in the camps, and the dismissal of abusive jefes. Workers interviewed by *El Siglo* emphasized the rise in cost of living, "which is being felt enormously, especially in Sewell, where the concessionaires who sell articles of basic necessity . . . fix speculative prices. For this reason the workers demand that the company establish stores in which they sell merchandise at a price consistent with the workers' salaries."[32] In a widely attended union assembly, miners assailed the company's refusal to offer a significant wage increase and denounced a recent threat by the owners of pensions and cantinas to raise the price of food, ignoring the prices fixed by the commission appointed by the minister of labor.[33]

Braden Copper Company managers attributed the strike to the political maneuvering of the Communist Party and predicted that if they gave in to the union, the North American copper companies in Chile would be forced to give significant wage and benefit increases to all workers. One Braden administrator told the U.S. State Department that "it would be better to shut down for a month than to surrender to the 'reds' whose victory now might ruin efficiency for years."[34] For the company, the strike represented a struggle over control of production and the union's growing independence and power, as much as a conflict over economic demands. A union victory would serve to consolidate the independent Communist leadership of the miners' union and increase the power and popularity of the party in the mine. More fundamental, it would erode the company's control of labor relations and the organization of production in El Teniente. A month-long shutdown was far preferable, in its eyes, to the possibilities of a fortified union and strengthened leftist leadership.

Although the company clearly felt little fear at the prospect of a strike, the Chilean government wanted to avoid a paralyzation of production at all costs. Following the failed negotiations, the minister of labor called a meeting with the head of the labor inspectorate and the local labor inspector and telephoned New York to discuss the strike with the heads of Kennecott in the United States.[35] The government's preoccupation with the strike reflected the new importance of the revenue from taxes on copper exports, as well as the more interventionist role of the Popular Front government in labor conflicts. The government's import substitution industrialization policies, public works programs, and mildly populist efforts at income redistribution required increased foreign exchange, particularly if inflation was to be held in check. By the 1940s, copper exports were providing the bulk of Chile's foreign currency earnings, and the government hoped to reap the benefits of increased wartime production.[36]

The governments of Aguirre Cerda and his successor, Juan Antonio Ríos, depended heavily on copper production and revenues to finance their economic development program and social reforms. In 1941, the Aguirre Cerda government imposed a new tax on the copper companies and a series of indirect taxes, including discriminatory exchange rates, that raised the proportion of the copper companies' contributions to the Chilean state from 18 percent to over 33 percent. The Corporación de Fomento (CORFO), the agency created by the government to promote industrial growth by providing credits to private entrepreneurs in the manufacturing and construction sectors, depended on copper revenues for a significant portion of its funding. Other funds for CORFO came from credits from the U.S. Export-Import Bank, which influenced the direction of CORFO investment to aid both U.S. companies in Chile and Chilean enterprises and ensured Aguirre Cerda's commitment to service Chile's foreign debt. A large portion of Chile's debt service payments to its U.S. creditors was derived from the increased taxes on the U.S. copper companies.[37] The health of the Chilean economy and the success of the government's economic program had come to depend on revenues from the North American companies' copper production and exports to U.S. copper markets.

The new national interest in copper production had already emerged in 1938 when the first efforts were being made in congress to increase the tax on the North American companies. The 1938 wildcat strike in El Teniente and Braden Copper Company's opposition to new taxes had provided leftist congressmen the opportunity to attack the company's labor policies and unlimited exploitation of Chilean labor and resources. Popular Front minister of labor Juan Pradenas, then a Democratic Party senator, had argued for increased state intervention in the copper mines since "the production of copper . . . is the most important productive sector in the country. . . . [U]nfortunately it is not Chilean wealth since its value leaves the country or stays in foreign countries: what stays here are the salaries and wages, which constitute an insignificant percentage." Pradenas pointed out that

U.S. copper companies had benefited enormously from the devaluation of Chilean currency during the 1930s, which decreased workers' real wages, arguing that "unfortunately our governments, overseeing and producing the devaluation of our currency, have committed the error of not supporting the thousands of obreros and empleados who work in the mines."[38] Employing nationalist logic he proposed that the Chilean government protect both its workers and its national resources through increased state intervention in the affairs of the mines. Pradenas was supported in the House of Deputies by the Communist congressmen Carlos Contreras Labarca, Carlos Gaete, and Angel Vega, who, after a detailed history of labor strife in the mine and a discussion of Braden's earnings, declared that "when this company earned millions and millions, Chilean workers remained with low salaries, kept working brual workdays, with a high cost of living and with houses fit for animals. Today, when the company gives orders to reduce production the workers have misery, and worse than losing their wages, they have sicknesses that they acquire in this fiefdom because of excessive work, inadequate food, and terrible housing."[39]

Thus, when the El Teniente miners walked out on strike in 1942, they did so within a political context markedly different from years past. Now their strike constituted a national political event. Not only could they count on a government more sympathetic to labor and the support of the leftist parties, but they could also play on their strategic role in the Chilean economy and the development of new nationalist languages. The government had already proven its willingness to intervene in the company's affairs with the new copper tax and with the support of the state governor and labor inspector for miners' petitions. In addition, the governor had informed the company that the provincial authorities would enforce compulsory arbitration in the case of a strike.[40] It seemed clear that the government, whether because of its concern with copper production or because of its rhetorical pro-labor stance, would intervene to solve the strike.

The new role of the state in labor conflicts was made clear to the miners when left-wing members of congress and the minister of labor intervened to prevent the company from hiring scabs and to keep the police from threatening the strike committees and pickets of miners. In Santiago, two deputies from the Communist Party, José Díaz and Reinaldo Núñez, the subsecretary of the CTCH national council, and representatives from the FNM met with the president to denounce the company's infractions of the labor code and to ask for his direct intervention in the conflict.[41] After a similar meeting, this time in the Ministry of Labor, Pradenas immediately telephoned the head of the labor bureau, the governor of O'Higgins, and the provincial labor inspector to order that they enforce the workers' right to strike and prevent the company from hiring scabs or replacing striking workers with white-collar workers from other sections of the mine.[42]

The support that miners received from unions across the country, the CTCh, and the FNM also played an important role in sustaining the strike. The 1942 strike represented the new national importance of copper not just to the national economy and to the government but also to the national labor movement, which lent the miners material assistance and advisers and lawyers to help them in their negotiations with the company and the government. The miners themselves linked their struggle to the strikes of coal miners and nitrate workers and to a broader social movement sweeping the country which also included campesinos and industrial workers and which was closely identified with the Popular Front. They saw their strike as having national significance beyond their concrete demands: they were striking to defend their government, to protect democracy in Chile, and to reaffirm the rights of industrial workers, peasants, and miners.

For the labor movement in general, the strike in the copper mines held as much importance as the strikes in the nitrate fields during the first decades of the century. Even before the miners voted to strike, the CTCh, the FNM, and the Communist Party had begun to orchestrate a national campaign to collect economic aid for the El Teniente workers.[43] In addition, leaders from the CTCh and the FNM attempted, through their members in congress, to pressure the government to intervene in the Braden conflict and served as intermediaries between the various ministers, the president, and the miners. Most important, the shipments of supplies that these labor federations and local unions delivered to El Teniente allowed the miners, isolated in the Andes, to sustain their strike movement.

The striking miners received food, clothing, and economic assistance from unions across the country. As *El Siglo* commented, "The first important shipment of provisions caused a profound impression among the high employees of Braden Copper. Maybe they understood that it would be useless to oppose the strike when they saw the strikers unloading sacks of potatoes, beans and numerous sacks and boxes of vegetables, sugar, noodles, tea, coffee, onions, etc."[44] *El Rancagüino* noted that "large quantities of food and money collected by workers' organizations from all over the country are arriving in Sewell" and that the port workers of San Antonio, where Braden's copper was shipped out, were also threatening a solidarity strike.[45] Working-class families in Santiago and Rancagua took in the children of the striking miners of Sewell in a campaign organized by the CTCh, the MEMCh, and the FNM when food supplies began to grow scarce.[46]

The national importance of the copper strike was also reflected in the presence of a number of Communist and Socialist Party congressmen in El Teniente during the conflict. The Communist deputies Salvador Ocampo, Angel Vega, and Carlos Rosende lent important support to the miners, representing their demands in congress and placing pressure on the government to intervene on the miners' behalf. In an article originally published in *Despertar Minero* and later in *El Siglo,* a miner discussed the role of Angel Vega, who arrived in Sewell at the miners' request following the outbreak of the strike.[47] The article granted Vega the title of "honorary El Teniente worker" and credited him with helping to organize the workers in a disciplined strike movement composed of strike brigades, women's committees, sanitary committees, supplies committees, first aid committees, and committees to organize cultural and recreational activities.

Salvador Ocampo (Communist deputy for O'Higgins Province and subsecretary-general of the CTCh) also journeyed to El Teniente, where he was received with rousing ovations.[48] The congressmen met with the head of the carabineros in El Teniente and tried to make it clear to him that the workers were striking against the company, not against the police.[49] The secretary-general of the CTCh and Socialist Party deputy Bernardo Ibáñez also traveled to the mine to meet with the miners and discuss strategy.[50] Ibáñez and Ocampo both met frequently with government ministers on behalf of the workers, made speeches supporting the strike movement, and helped organize economic aid. Ocampo served as the miners' representative to the government arbitration board. The conservative daily *El Rancagüino,* lamenting the workers' decision to go on strike, accused these members of parliament of influencing the workers in order "to play the strike as one of their first electoral cards." The paper was also scandalized by the Communist aldermen of Rancagua and Machalí (elected with El Teniente votes) who proposed to donate municipal funds to the strikers.[51]

While neither the government nor Radical Party politicians lent the strikers active support, papers affiliated with the PR or sharing Radical Party orientation did side with the workers. Striking the chord of economic nationalism, they supported the workers' claims as part of Chile's more general right to participate in the profits of the copper industry. *La Opinión,* partially owned by Minister of Foreign Affairs Rossetti, noted recent increases in copper prices, "the fabulous profits of the company," and the pressure on workers to produce more to meet expanding markets, arguing that "the companies are incorrect to refuse [workers' demands], . . . when they resist disbursing the little that the exploitation of this immense Chilean wealth leaves in the country: some few pesos more in wages for Chilean workers." The editorial maintained that the greater salaries paid to Chilean workers would affect the national economy and signify the return to Chile of a few million dollars that would be incorporated "in the process of our native commerce." The copper miners would be better consumers and thus strengthen "our internal market that needs this now more than ever."[52]

The U.S. embassy in Chile, following the strike closely, felt that the logic of *La Opinión*'s nationalist position would find "considerable support in this country." According to the ambassador, "Most Chileans feel that they are entitled to a greater share in the exploitation of an irreplaceable natural resource."[53] The embassy also echoed the charges of company officials that the strike would have ended early on "had not the government newspapers [*La Hora, La Nación,* and *La Opinión*] encouraged the strikers."[54] Ambassador Bowers, underlining the nationalist basis for consensus between the workers and the government, argued that "Chilean politicians desire to obtain from the copper companies 'all that the traffic will bear' and are quite ready to abet the workmen in getting their share. . . . They attempt to justify this attitude by the fact that copper is an irreplaceable natural resource."[55] Both the U.S. government and the U.S. copper companies feared the alliance of the Chilean government, middle-class parties, and workers in their demands for greater shares of copper profits.

The support of the political parties and the national labor federations revealed the importance of the changed political climate. Although the government itself may have lent only lukewarm backing to the miners, the leftist parties and unions that belonged to the coalition were able to operate with a new freedom and strength in an opened political space. Unlike previous strikes in El Teniente, the state did not intervene to repress the union and the striking workers or turn a blind eye to the company's efforts to break the strike by firing workers, hiring scabs, and cutting off the camps from communication with the outside world. The miners had the protection of a labor minister more attuned to their demands and a number of newly elected congressmen and party leaders who placed themselves at their side.

Gender, Community, and Politics in El Teniente

When the miners strike broke out in February 1942, the members of the MEMCh in the camps held a mass meeting at which they agreed to lend complete support to the strike movement and to plan a demonstration to demand lower prices in the camps.[56] This was particularly important because, according to El Siglo, the company had pressured the camps' pension and cantina owners not to feed the strikers. Women from workers' families began to form ollas comunes (communal kitchens) funded by the economic aid they received from around the country.[57] Women also picketed with their husbands, organized material support for the strikers, and participated on cost-of-living committees that kept a vigilant eye on the prices in the camps' concessions and supported movements to control prices.

Women from miners' families held a series of meetings to plan actions to strengthen the strike movement.[58] In a massive assembly of striking miners "and their women," one of the speakers was a miner's wife who "received a long ovation, calling on all the women of the community to lend unlimited aid to the strikers."[59] In a similar demonstration of the entire mining community in Rancagua's major plaza, Elena Prieto de Carrasco gave a speech as a representative of the Committee of Wives, Mothers, and Daughters, along with Carlos Riquelme (PC); the subsecretary of the CTCh; the secretary of the union; and representatives from the union of railway workers and the CTCh.[60] The MEMCh organized the feeding and later the evacuation of the workers' children.[61] Interviewed by El Siglo, the daughter of one miner described women's role in the strike: "Since the strike began the women of this mine without distinction of political or religious creed immediately demanded a place of honor in the combat, and they collaborated in effective forms in the organization of the population."[62]

During the strike, committees of women organized recreational activities for miners' families. *El Siglo* reported that "during the eleven days of the strike the youth, as well as the women and the workers, competed in camaraderie and mutual assistance. They have organized various literary-musical acts that allow them to pass more happily the struggle for the workers' demands. For today [Sunday, 1 March] they have programmed a large matinee for children at 3 P.M. and at 8 P.M. a large family party and dance in Sewell."[63] Every social organization in the camps was involved in supporting the strike. The camps' Boy Scouts participated in cultural events and parades to support the strikers, and Catholic miners and their families met and organized in the Sewell church to form support groups. Thus miners and their families continued to participate in community organizations that had been constructed by the company during the 1920s. These social organizations, originally the pillars of the company's paternalist labor regime, contributed to the formation of social solidarities and the El Teniente workers' sense of a cohesive community.

The organization of women during the 1942 strike did not end with the signing of the new contract. The strike had taught the Sewell community an important lesson: to beat the company, they had to mobilize the entire community. When the strike was over, women in the camps began to organize committees in support of the union's next set of petitions to the company. These committees worked to collect money for a strike fund and to organize community support for their compañeros.[64] The miners realized that a successful strike movement could not depend "exclusively on the workers." As *Despertar Minero* put it, "This mobilization must embrace all the women and families."[65]

The union and leftist parties had displayed a clear understanding of women's organizational potential since 1938. In one editorial, *Despertar Minero* called on women to assume their appropriate revolutionary role in social struggles and organize in groups of "housewives, domestic servants . . . under the following slogans: equality of political and social rights for women and men; immediate concession of the right to vote for women. . . ; unionization of domestic servants who work in homes, cantinas, and hotels; the lowering of the cost of living; for an increase in salaries; and adequate housing that will guarantee their health and that of their children."[66] The miners' union tried to reinitiate the organization of the Sociedad Aurora de Chile, a progressive women's group, and called a meeting of "the housewives and ladies" of the camps in the union hall "to exchange ideas and name a new leadership and to renew definitively the diverse necessary activities."[67]

The union's call for the organization of women in the camps was made "especially to the empleadas who work in the pensions, hotels, and work for the company." The union condemned the working conditions in the Sewell laundry, "where various obreras labor for a not very flattering salary, the work is very hard and exhausting with the constant vigilance of the person who is in charge of female personnel who they exploit cowardly. . . . The washing women only earn 5 pesos a day and the ironers, 7 pesos [as opposed to an average salary for male obreros of around 30 pesos]."[68] The union lamented that the "vast sector of proletarian women" in the camps was completely unorganized and without ties to political movements. *Despertar Minero* denounced the fact that female and hospital employees earned "a wage that is almost half of what an obrero earns with the lowest salary that the company pays," positing that "the same thing occurs with all the other activities where women work. In the cantinas . . . our compañeras receive miserable treatment for an insignificant salary that varies between 60 and 80 pesos monthly, for 10- to 12-hour days."[69] In some pensions, the union wrote, only two empleadas had to wait on over one hundred miner *pensionistas.*

Mensaje Obrero, the CTCh's regional newspaper, also condemned the exploitation of the empleadas "who aren't treated like human beings."[70] The paper denounced the fact that empleadas were forbidden by concessionaires to go out at night to social clubs or to the camps' educational centers and schools. In addition, after Braden had been informed by the provincial labor inspectorate that empleadas' workdays had to be limited to eight hours, the concessionaires began a campaign of reprisals, forcing their female workers to pay for all the cleaning equipment they used, thus "creating a justifiable discontent."[71] The miners' union and the national labor movement thus viewed the camps' empleadas as valuable allies in struggles with the company based on work and class-related issues.

Responding to the union's call for the organization of women workers in the camps, the empleadas of Hotel Sewell went on strike in January 1941 and won a small wage increase.[72] This began a wave of organizing among domestic servants and maids, and in 1943 the empleadas formed their first union, the Sindicato Feminino de Empleadas de Pensiones.[73] In 1944 in one case, the empleadas' union complained to the company that cantina owners had failed to adjust their wages or to pay them the 10 percent tips required by law. It was the custom of the owners to hold on to these tips and then refuse to pay empleadas when they left work. The company responded by ordering the cantina owners to give workers their tips and to raise their wages.[74]

Occasionally, the miners' union attempted to support and represent empleadas in their conflicts with cantina and pension owners. In 1943, for example, a union leader went to the company to demand that several fired women workers be rehired by their cantinas. The company, however, refused to recognize the union's intervention in matters concerning empleadas.[75] In the case of one empleada who was fired for being pregnant, the company rejected the union's petition that she be rehired after giving birth.[76] Braden asserted that the union had no legal right to represent domestic servants. Nonetheless, the organization of the union for domestic servants provided additional support to the efforts of the union and leftist parties to mobilize the entire El Teniente community and demonstrated the strength of alliances between the single workingwomen in the camps and the miners' union during conflicts with the North American company. The support of miners for a domestic workers' union also indicated the willingness of the miners' union and the Communist Party to organize women in labor and political struggles around class-based issues. The union addressed both single workingwomen and housewives in the camp in terms of their importance to a broader, working-class movement in the camps.

The union urged both workingwomen and housewives to join the local branch of the MEMch. The program of the MEMch set out a wide range of demands relevant to the well-being of miners' families. The Sewell MEMch stated that "we struggle for better living conditions in the mine, demanding from the company improvements in the barracks, against the high cost of living and the monopolies of concessionaires, to obtain real facilities for the education of our daughters in the camps, and playgrounds."[77] The Sewell MEMch, with the union, also endorsed the MEMch's national program, which included equal working conditions and wages for women, social legislation to protect women workers, protections for pregnant workingwomen, paid maternity leave, the establishment of an adequate health infrastructure, and health insurance for workingwomen and for workingmen.[78] The MEMch held meetings in the union hall, provided support for the workers during stoppages, and organized cost-of-living committees to monitor prices in the camps' stores.

Commenting on the 1942 strike, *Despertar Minero* articulated the basis for solidarity between men and women in the mining camp: "This mobilization must embrace all the women and families. This is why the women's committees are so important, more than to us, to our wives, our daughters, our mothers who share with the worker their daily bread. These family members, directly affected by the daily devaluation caused by the growing cost of basic necessities, have a stake in the head of the household getting a better salary in order to keep the specter of hunger away from their table."[79]

Married women's participation in the strike movements of the male miners and their organization in committees, cost-of-living committees, and the MEMch drew on their role in the household and the ideology of domesticity. Braden placed the responsibility for the sustenance of their families on the shoulders of miners' wives. Their work washing clothes, collecting firewood, cooking, taking care of children, taking on boarders, sewing, and selling bread and pastries and the networks of solidarity and reciprocity they established with other women were oriented toward maintaining their families. Informal types of both unremunerated and paid labor were part of women's domestic duties, but as the company Welfare Department and social workers insisted, they were essential to the survival of miners' families.

At the same time, marriage implied certain rights for women. The gender regime in El Teniente and the ideology of domesticity purported to guarantee women economic security for themselves and for their families. When company policy and the cost of living seemed to threaten women's ability to maintain their households and fulfill the demands placed on them through the sexual division of labor, their acceptance of domesticity could be transformed into radical collective action. Women's desire to ensure the security and rights promised by the company's ideology of domesticity—to keep their households going—often led to their involvement in collective movements. Thus, the participation of women in cost-of-living committees and women's committees focused on demands that were part of the female sphere of responsibility within the dominant sexual division of labor in El Teniente: consumption of such goods as clothing and food and of services, such as education and health care. The central demands of the Sewell MEMCh concerned the cost of living, housing conditions, and education for miners' children.

Political solidarities between married men and women in the El Teniente camps had their origin in the dependence of all family members on the wages of the husband and father. Such reliance created the basis for the cohesiveness of the nuclear family and its unity in struggles with the company. These relations of dependence meant, however, that women's participation in labor or community struggles was limited to the specific social role defined by their subordination to men within the family. Women's political, community, and labor activities reflected the gendered division of labor and the unequal balance of power in miners' families. The solidarities created by the structure of the mining enclave and the composition of a community of nuclear families were based on gender relations that were far from balanced or harmonious. As one woman put it in trying to explain the apparent contradiction between conflictive marital relations in El Teniente and the history of solidarity between men and women in strikes: "For me it's very simple: I explain it because whenever there was a strike it was for economic things, so, there, the married couple united because . . . [the company] was attacking their interests."[80]

While the company Welfare Department and its team of social workers may have identified workers' family lives as pathological—distorted by adultery, alcoholism, and neglect—in fact, despite new tensions and conflicts between the sexes, the organization of sexual relations in the nuclear family and women's dependence on men's wages created the conditions for a form of class solidarity that extended beyond the divisions established by gender. Pushed into full economic dependence on their husbands and, by extension, the company, married women came to identify their interests with those of their husbands and to regard the company as a common antagonist. Thus as miners formed families and as single women increasingly turned to marriage, a community took shape in El Teniente's camps. This community was fractured along gender lines and ultimately based on a terrible imbalance of social power between men and women. Yet the miners' families confronted the company with a unity that lent them great strength in their strikes and collective struggles.

Although the miners' union reproduced elements of the company's conservative ideology of female domesticity by focusing on the role of married women in political struggles as mothers and wives and by locating the development of a "proletarian morality" within the household, the efforts of the union to organize empleadas and married women behind a broader program of class-based demands illustrated the progressive possibilities of its gender politics. By helping to organize a union of empleadas, the miners' union recognized domestic servants as workers, supported their rights, and sought to draw on their potential as a political force.

The union also lent its support to women workers in conflicts over nonwork issues, demanding that the restrictions on empleadas' social lives be lifted and supporting the case of pregnant single women who had been fired. By standing up for the rights of women workers and by endorsing the platform of the MEMCh with its explicitly feminist program, including demands for the vote and equal wages for women, the miners' union demonstrated that the working-class movement it envisioned would also address inequalities between men and women.

At the same time, organized labor's understanding of the role of women in the labor movement and support for the feminist program of the MEMCh conflicted with informal norms of masculine behavior and the everyday conduct of gender relations in the mining camps. The union's efforts to empower domestic servants, for example, contradicted many men's assumptions that cantina employees owed them their obedience and service. Similarly, the union's attempts to get married women to attend union meetings and meetings of the MEMCh collided with a general code of gendered expectations that restricted women to a subordinate role within the home. As we have seen, in one case a miner beat his wife for leaving the house to attend a union meeting. Thus, the union's gender politics challenged many male workers' sense of their rights to control women's labor and sexuality and to demand their obedience, just as the union's articulation of moral codes of responsible and respectable behavior conflicted with the everyday cultural pursuits of miners.

The Miners' Strike and the Popular Front

Mobilized in increasingly combative community-based and workplace committees, the miners and their families were not inclined to depend on the government or on arbitration boards to solve the 1942 strike. Although union activists tried to get the government to intervene on behalf of the miners, most miners rejected the idea of state intervention altogether, preferring to rely on their own organizational force. The miners assented to the government proposal of arbitration with great reluctance. Despite speeches by the president of the FNM, labor minister Pradenas's secretary, and the president of the union, in which they appealed to the miners' patriotism and loyalty to the Popular Front, the workers repeatedly rejected the proposal in union assemblies, deeply suspicious of any kind of forced arbitration by the government.

During union assemblies, Communist Party politicians and union leaders urged the miners to accept arbitration as an important gesture of loyalty to the Democratic Alliance government. An indefinite strike, they argued, could do political damage and also hamper the government's economic program. They asked the miners to put the goals of the Popular Front's national program ahead of their own demands. Ultimately, they sought to convince workers that any significant changes in their lives would come from the political victories of the Alliance and reforms implemented from above, rather than from their own mobilizations.

Most miners, however, were unconvinced by these arguments and loudly booed, swore at, and even spit on union and PC leaders who urged them to bring the strike to an end. The strike had shown them the possibilities of direct action against the company, and they were unprepared to capitulate easily. Moreover, past experience had taught them to be wary of the labor courts. Only after days of meetings and speeches by union leaders, the union lawyer, and political figures did the union leadership manage to squeak out a narrow vote in favor of arbitration, despite the discontent of the bases. The miners agreed to go back to work, emphasizing that their decision had been made more as a gesture of support for the government than as a sign of confidence in the final decisions of the arbitration board. The vote of approval had been grudgingly wrung from the workers through the efforts of the PC deputies and leaders of the CTCH and the FNM, who had assisted and advised the union from the beginning of the conflict.[81]

The bitter and often violent debates in union assemblies about whether to accept arbitration or continue the strike revealed the tensions between the workers, the union leadership, and the political parties of the Democratic Alliance. The miners' strike depended on the support provided by the leftist parties, particularly the Communist Party. The leadership, material support, legal help, and political interventions of Communist politicians and militants gave the miners the necessary assistance with which to negotiate the complicated and often adversarial system of labor relations established by the Chilean state. Communist leaders, however, while actively supporting the strike, were also committed to maintaining the reformist program of the Popular Front and an alliance with the parties of the middle classes. Thus Communist militants were torn between conflicting pressures from the workers whom they had helped to mobilize and from the government whose fragile coalition the strike threatened to disrupt.

The final decision of the arbitration board was a significant victory for the workers. Of primary importance, the board granted them a wage increase of $6.50 pesos a day, $1.50 pesos more than the company's final offer and $1.50 pesos more than the smaller Socialist-led unions had settled for.[82] The board ruled that the union could have a representative on the Comité de Alimentación, which oversaw the cantinas and stores in the camps and could have the independent power to audit the stores in the camps. The arbitration board also agreed that the company would have to build new housing for workers and renovate the older buildings and that the new barracks could have rooms with a capacity of only six persons. The workers' demand to have the pay raise be retroactive was denied, as was their demand that the twenty-two days of the strike be considered days worked. Nor was their demand for pay for the hours spent in transportation to work sites within the mine recognized.

Most important, however, the miners had paralyzed El Teniente for three weeks, the longest strike in the mine's history, and had forced the company to agree to government arbitration. More than a material victory, the strike represented an important flexing of the miners' organizational muscle. It also demonstrated the possibilities for collective action with the support of a state apparatus, if not entirely sympathetic, at least not openly antagonistic to the workers' cause. For the first time, the workers had successfully challenged the almost total power exercised by the company. They had demonstrated that the days when the company could call in the armed forces to repress a strike, fire union leaders and activists, and break the union had finally come to an end. Braden's fear that the strike would reinforce the strength of the "red" unions had materialized. The miners emerged from the strike with a union which was far stronger and which had earned important legitimacy in the eyes of the vast majority of workers. In addition, the union enjoyed solid ties with the Communist Party and the national labor movement.

The 1942 strike revealed a significant change in the style of labor activism. Whereas labor conflicts before 1938 took the form of uprisings or rebellions, often accompanied by violence, that were put down with brutal military force, the new state-directed system of labor relations, the Popular Front government, and the support of the national labor movement and leftist parties at the level of the state created institutional channels for strikes. Miners' strikes now met with the legal imprimatur of the labor inspectorate, were organized with the help of activists and leaders from political parties, particularly the Communist Party, and followed the road map of bureaucratic protocols elaborated in the labor code. The state, and thus political parties, now played a central role in determining the course and outcomes of strikes. At the same time, older forms of worker militancy still fueled miners' confrontations with both the company and the state and, as debates during union assemblies indicated, led to clashes with union leaders, government officials, and Communist Party activists over strategy and tactics.

The Popular Front and Democratic Alliance governments thus marked a significant change for El Teniente's workers. After 1938, the provincial governor appointed by Pedro Aguirre Cerda and provincial labor inspectors began to implement the labor code and make the presence of the state felt in El Teniente. The enforcement of obligatory unionization laws by the Ministry of Labor made the miners' widespread organization and mobilization possible and limited Braden's policy of threatening and intimidating workers to prevent them from joining the union. The intervention of local labor inspectors in overseeing union elections; in guaranteeing that the company pay the Dirección General de Trabajo the required sums directed toward financing the unions; and in enforcing labor laws that provided security from firings for union leaders: these actions established the necessary conditions for building strong unions.

The arbitration board's decision in the 1942 strike handed the El Teniente workers an important victory over the issue of job classification. The decision gave workers the right to petition the company and then the labor inspector over problems of job classification. This alarmed the company almost as much as did the wage increases. In a memorandum to the president of Braden, General Manager W. J. Turner wrote that the decision "may cause us some trouble and annoyance, more particularly as I fear it is an opening wedge to attempt to reach the same situation as has caused so much trouble in the United States in the numerous jurisdictional disputes." Turner feared that this meant that "an electrician, for example, will not dig a hole in a plaster wall in order to insert a conduit, but that a plasterer must be called." He added that the company would refuse to accept such a situation and that he intended to put a clause in all workers' contracts "to the effect that work necessary to the completion of jobs in the various trades must be carried out."[83]

The arbitrator's decision satisfied the miners' long-standing complaint that, as the union's representative put it, "the contracts have not specified clearly the job that the worker is to do. . . . They force a miner, for example, to perform the labors of a timberman, cart worker, etc."[84] The classification of workers' jobs not only limited the freedom of supervisors to assign tasks but also created new openings for workers to seek higher wages commensurate with their classification and to seek reclassification. Following the 1942 strike, the company and the labor inspectorate in Rancagua were flooded with demands by workers for classification to higher categories. As the head of the Welfare Department noted, "Tradesmen's helpers want classification as tradesmen; the 4th., 3rd., 2nd. class men want to be jumped to 1st., not so much for the title but to get the wage difference."[85] Workers' many complaints to the labor court in Rancagua about job classification demonstrated the gradual erosion of the absolute control exercised by North American supervisors over the organization of work in the mine.[86]

With job classification, the union was able to bring to the attention of the company administration cases of unpaid bonuses, wages incommensurate with a worker's job, dangerous or onerous work conditions that required a special bonus, and dismissals and suspensions. The establishment of new commissions and appeals procedures over job classification provided the workers avenues through which they could restrict the power of foremen and supervisors to assign tasks, to set wages, and to transfer and fire workers.

Through the intervention of the president, the minister of labor, and labor inspectors, the miners were able to limit the Braden Copper Company's capacity to fire workers at will. Government support for the union and the growing strength of the union itself also allowed the miners to contest arbitrary firings and often to have firings changed to transfers or suspensions. In January 1941, for example, union leaders negotiated with company officials to rehire twenty-three workers dismissed for engaging in an illegal work stoppage.[87] Based on these negotiations, the union later forged an agreement with the company that workers fired for *graves faltas* would be suspended without pay, rather than fired permanently.[88] In another case, the company fired a former union leader and was then convinced by the union to transfer him instead to a different work section, where he received a salary of two pesos less daily.[89] The importance of the activities of labor inspectors and other government officials in limiting the company's capacity to fire workers was revealed in the company's complaint that "as for the workers who disturb production, the company has been eliminating them as much as the laws, contracts, and circumstances have permitted, but has met with serious obstacles to a broader action because of legal limitations and commitments made before the Labor Authorities."[90]

The lack of labor discipline in the copper mines during the Popular Front years was an important index of the shifting distribution of power between the workers and the company. A North American study of the Chilean copper industry noted in 1940 that "the labor courts almost invariably favor the workers and because of this wages are going up and the output of labor shows a marked decrease per man-shift; also because of the labor agitator the worker is becoming less disciplined."[91] In 1942, Braden Copper Company's paper, *El Teniente,* echoed this assessment, arguing that "a large part of the respect that before the miner had for his foreman or for his jefe has been lost and every worker wants to impose his own will."[92]

The balance of power between workers and jefes in the mine moved perceptibly in the workers' favor during these years. The company attributed increased lack of discipline and lowered productivity to the new political context provided by the Popular Front governments. The company also claimed that there "exists among the syndicalized workmen, a tacit agreement whereby individual attendance and efficiency is markedly reduced."[93] The company's manager declared to the union that "for some time we have seen a different atmosphere and it seems that they [union leaders] want to maintain a combative spirit among the workers against the company and their jefes. There is an effective and visible diminishment in services and individual force, there is aggressiveness by some sectors of the obreros and each worker seems to look for the way to get by with the least work possible."[94]

Company managers also looked with alarm on the miners' new public organizational presence in the mining camps and the governor's intervention to establish protected spaces where the miners could congregate to hold meetings and demonstrations. The Popular Front governor of O'Higgins oversaw the construction of an electoral post and a municipal government office building in the mining camps and defined public spaces in the camps where miners could hold meetings. These measures outraged company managers, who commented on the increasingly rebellious nature of miners' public meetings. In 1943, for example, the governor held a lengthy debate with Braden officials over the issue of public spaces in the camps. The debate was occasioned by a meeting held by the miners in which, according to Braden reports, "most of the speakers did little but throw mud at the Company officials." According to company managers, "as the meeting was held in an open court formed by camp buildings and walkways and the structures were used as galleries and forums by the crowd, we told the intendant [governor] who had authorized the meeting, that we thought this was going too far."[95] The incident revealed how much the company's power within the camps had been limited since 1939. The governor and the minister of the interior, after discussions with the company, came up with a set of regulations that provided public spaces for workers' meetings.[96]

The 1942 strike signified a transformation of the relationship between the miners, the Chilean state, and the North American copper companies. The Aguirre Cerda administration had already made some significant inroads in asserting the sovereignty of the Chilean government in the mining camps. It had increased the tax on copper revenues and insisted that the North American company follow the dictates of the labor code and Chilean law. The government's role in assigning an arbitration board to solve the strike and in pressuring both the workers and the company to accept arbitration indicated that it was no longer content to stand by and let the copper companies run their business without outside interference. By 1942, the role of copper in the national economy (and in the economic programs of the Popular Front and Democratic Alliance) was too important to leave decisions about production in the mines to the Braden Copper Company. Arbitration boards, committees to oversee the cost of living, and active national and provincial labor inspectorates all represented an extension of government control over labor relations and production in the copper mines.

The workers were able to exploit the government's nationalist inclinations and dependence on copper revenues as well as emergent conflicts between the government and the Braden Copper Company to their own ends. The El Teniente miners' mobilization had helped to drive a wedge between the North American company and the government, and the miners had succeeded in enlisting the state's support in their conflict with the company. Miners increasingly looked to the state to guarantee the rights inscribed in the constitution and the labor code. The new state apparatus of cost-of-living committees, arbitration boards, labor courts, and labor inspectors provided them a series of rights and protections. Thus, miners' radical nationalism was structured by their integration into the expanded, state-directed system of labor relations.

The government's dependence on copper revenues and U.S. aid to fuel its programs for economic development imposed limits, however, on the degree to which it would support workers' movements in the mines. Trapped in the contradictions of the Popular Front's populism, the government could go only so far in supporting the copper workers' demands, for it feared the company's threats to shut down the mine altogether and had to bow to the U.S. government's own insistence that copper production continue undisturbed. As a result, over the course of the next few years, the miners' dissatisfaction with the coalition governments grew, and the labor movement in El Teniente became increasingly militant in its opposition to both the company and the state.

9

The Radicalization of Working-Class Politics

United States Intervention, Miners' Strikes,

and the Crisis of Populism

On 9 July 1946 the workers in the morning shift left the El Teniente mine soaked to the skin and coated with mud. When the afternoon shift entered the mine, the workers quickly realized that the excessive amount of water in the tunnels would prevent them from working without completely drenching themselves. The workers resolved to stop work and to remain in the mine until the situation was resolved. As other afternoon shift workers began to go down into the mine, they encountered 150 miners who refused to leave "until the system of work was changed."[1] These workers left the mine and marched to the union hall.

While the miners stayed in the mine throughout the cold and wet winter night, union leaders discussed the situation with the company's assistant manager without arriving at an agreement. The following morning, the rest of the mine workers voted to join the stoppage in solidarity with the workers "who had to keep drilling in water and mud."[2] According to *El Rancagüino,* the workers also joined the stoppage to protest recent dismissals in the mine.[3] In the afternoon, the subinspector of labor, César Ojeda, went down into the mine, where he met with the striking miners and advised them to leave the mine, to eat something, and to get some sleep. Finally, after twenty-two hours, the miners abandoned the mine, and union leaders, the labor inspector, and officials from the company negotiated an end to the wildcat strike.[4]

The night following the settlement of the conflict, the mining camps were shaken by the noise of two explosions in the North American camp. Supervisors who ran outside to find out what was going on were forced to take cover from a rain of stones and earth. According to *El Rancagüino,* the explosions came from dynamite planted near the home of the company's assistant manager, Mr. Johnson, and constituted an attempted assassination. The captain of the police arrived and with the North Americans went to examine the area of the explosion, where they discovered that the cause had been two sticks of dynamite that had been planted so as to blow up Mr. Johnson's house.[5] The next day serenos and carabineros searched the workers leaving the mine and the miners' barracks for arms and dynamite. Interviewed in *El Rancagüino,* the captain of the carabineros declared that "for a long time now there have been acts of terrorism in the camp. Thus we have put a number of individuals at the disposition of the court for possession of cartridges of dynamite, fuses, and percussion caps. Also we sent one individual to Rancagua who was caught selling munitions and arms to the workers." According to the captain, the bombs were detonated "in the style of the Asturian miners in the Spanish Revolution."[6]

The union's version of these events differed radically. According to *Despertar Minero,* these were false accusations aimed at prejudicing the union during the tense process of negotiating a new contract. The explosions were not from dynamite but from fireworks placed on a pile of alum. Cherry bombs or dynamite, the gesture was a violent one. It marked an open violation of the symbolic and physical boundaries that separated workers from their North American bosses. In addition, the explosion was an act performed outside the union and conflicted with the efforts of union leaders to conduct an orderly negotiation of a new contract.

The explosion that rocked El Teniente's North American neighborhood signaled the growing effervescence and militancy of the miners and the expanding chasms that separated the miners from the union leadership, the parties of the Left, and the government. While the miners' unions had been effectively incorporated into the state-administered system of labor relations, the growing combativeness of miners expressed a basic dissatisfaction with the moderate policies of the coalition governments. Ultimately, the intensification of the mobilization of miners in El Teniente led to a confrontation with the North American company and the government of Gabriel González Videla. Forced to choose between the labor movement and pressures of the U.S. companies and the U.S. State Department, González Videla opted to bring the Popular Front's experiment with the politics of populism to an end. Although his government unleashed the military once again in the mining camps and quelled the activities of union activists and militants of the Communist party, the labor organizations and traditions of combativeness that had been built in El Teniente during the previous decade withstood the renewed repression and remained an important presence in the life of the mine and in the increasingly strained relationship between the Chilean state and North American capital.

The 1946–1947 Strike, the State, and Grassroots Militancy

Tensions between the company and its workers finally erupted in September 1946 following more than two months of fruitless negotiations through the Ministry of Labor. The 1946 strike bore many of the characteristics of the 1942 strike. The miners organized strike brigades to guard work sections from scabs, press committees, and women's committees. "These committees," wrote *Despertar Minero,* "are the transmission belts that aid the union leadership in the struggle and defense of the immediate demands: they work in consciousness raising among the workers, . . . orienting the workers, organizing and educating with the end of transforming the mentality of our men of work, of their women, and our youth."[7] The union also received economic aid from unions across the country—most important, from the coal miners, nitrate workers, the CTCh, and the FNM.[8]

As before, women organized support committees and played an active role in the strike movement. In October, a group of El Teniente women sent a petition to the president elect, Gabriel González Videla, asking him to intervene and provide a rapid solution to the conflict. *Despertar Minero* noted that "never as in the present occasion have the women compañeras, who suffer directly in the flesh the lashes of scarcity and misery, had so important a decisiveness and organization."[9] The workers' social and recreational clubs provided entertainment and diversion for the strikers and their families and helped to raise money for the strike fund, indicating how the official cultural and recreational institutions of the company provided the basis for forms of social solidarity among mining community members during labor conflicts. On one occasion, Communist Deputy Rosales led a parade of Boy Scouts with the union banner and later organized an athletic competition for the miners' children. Almost every night the miners put together variety shows and held dance contests in the union hall. They also organized basketball and soccer tournaments. Union leaders from the CTCh, which had split between Communist and

Socialist factions, also gave frequent talks to the miners and their families and organized programs on history and political education.[10]

During the 1946 conflict, the El Teniente workers received support and help in organizing the strike mostly from the Communist Party. Party officials such as Deputy Rosales and Regional Secretary José Mendoza helped to plan and organize the strike and bring material aid to the mining community. Their fiery speeches at meetings and rallies expressed the party's renewed vigor and militant postwar turn to the Left. Mendoza lambasted the "imperialist" companies which "robbed Chile's riches and which left behind in Chile only traces of the wealth they took at the cost of the sweat and sacrifice of the native Chilean" and demanded that the government intervene to restore the copper mines to Chilean sovereignty.[11]

Reflecting both the increasingly militant stance of the Communist Party following the end of the Second World War and workers' growing dissatisfaction with the coalition governments, workers became more and more angry and violent in their attacks on the North American company during union assemblies. Their speeches were filled with references to the "ignorant gringos . . . who for the sole fact of having blond hair believe themselves to be a superior caste," to "these criminal, vagabond, shameless gringos," and to the "soulless gringo theives."[12] The bitterness of these words both echoed and exceeded the more rhetorical and abstract anti-imperialist nationalism of the Left. The miners painted a picture of the North American administrators as uncultured, ignorant, and uncivilized, an image commonly used to describe the Chilean workers, and they expressed the virulence of this new hatred for "the gringo" and the force of their nationalist feeling in appeals for the expropriation of the mine.

In a meeting held before the strike, miners mobbed the union hall, and when the union leadership telephoned from Santiago, where they were negotiating at the labor ministry, with a request for a nine-day extension on the strike date, the miners shouted and whistled their rejection, demanding an immediate strike. When a former union leader made a speech arguing for a four-day postponement of the strike, he was whistled from the stage by the assembled workers. A Communist leader from the PC section of the CTCh also argued for a delay in the strike and was likewise roundly booed by workers. Similarly, onetime union leader and PC militant Teodoro Cid was whistled when he supported a delay to prolong the negotiations with the company. In the vote on whether to go on strike the following day, the workers voted yes and poured out of the union hall, shouting and cheering the strike.[13]

The following day at another packed assembly, union president Isaias Pardo informed the workers that he had accepted the delay in the strike because the labor inspector had failed to submit a necessary document to the labor bureau that would have made the strike legal. The infuriated workers whistled Pardo and demanded a strike. When the union lawyer took the stage to explain why a strike would be illegal, he too was booed and whistled. Representatives from the FNM, the CTCh, and the Communist Party pledged their support for a strike but urged that the miners accept the delay, and they were also vigorously assailed by the assembly.[14] The conflicts between the mass of miners and union and party leaders at the assemblies indicated that the tensions between the union leadership and grassroots which had emerged during wildcat strikes and protests had increased. As during previous conflicts since the beginning of the Popular Front, the level of militant action called for by miners surpassed what union leaders were willing or able to do. Unlike union leaders and party militants, the miners were restrained neither by commitments to the coalition government nor by the labor code.

Two days before the 4 September presidential elections and three weeks before the strike broke out, Gabriel González Videla, head of the Radical Party and candidate of a reconfigured coalition of the Radical, Communist, and Liberal Parties, had traveled to El Teniente to speak to the miners on one of his final campaign stops. In his speech he addressed the Braden Copper Company administration, assuring it that his government would support foreign capital that came to Chile "to collaborate in the progress of the nation until we succeed in obtaining our own economic independence." But, he continued:

> I want to tell you that I desire and demand for my countrymen who work in this mine the same treatment and the same considerations that you give to North American workers in your country. I will not permit you to mock, humiliate or inhumanly and cruelly exploit, as you do now, Chilean workers. And finally, I must tell you that in the case of a conflict between capital and the workers and confronted with the customary intransigence of the owners, my

government, the government of the people, will not sway or vacil-
late in placing itself at the workers' side to defend them and to aid
them to defeat their powerful and stubborn enemies.[15]

The presidential candidate's words bore nuances of the nationalism and
ethnic antagonism with which the workers defined their conflicts with
the company. González Videla had consciously attempted to revitalize the
old Popular Front coalition and rhetoric of the Aguirre Cerda government, relying on the electoral support mobilized by the Communist Party
among workers in Chile's industrial and mining zones. The use of militant
nationalist and pro-worker language in his speech signaled the candidate's
efforts to rekindle the radical populist appeal of the first Popular Front
government, following the conservative turn taken by the government of
Juan Antonio Ríos.

González Videla came from the left wing of the Radical Party and had
been one of the party's most flamboyant and combative leaders. Unlike
anti-Communist Radicals, such as Aguirre Cerda's successor, Juan Antonio
Ríos, who gravitated toward the Socialist Party and supported tight economic and political relations with the United States, González Videla
found support in the Communist Party and adopted a polemical anti-
imperialist stance. By 1946, despite his efforts to reassure the United States
that he supported U.S. investments in Chile, embassy officials had become
suspicious and regarded him as an unpredictable radical. González Videla's
nationalist language and open support of the PC helped win the miners'
allegiance. Communist Deputy Carlos Rosales expressed the miners' faith
in González Videla in a union assembly before the strike, at which he
told workers that "when González Videla is president his first decree will
be the expropriation of this Company, and then we'll see what kind of
face the gringos make."[16] Two days after the González Videla speech in El
Teniente, the miners lent the candidate their full electoral support.[17]

On 4 November a group of union leaders went to Santiago to attend
the new president's inauguration and to meet with him to discuss the
strike. González Videla promised them that "this problem merits my special interest. . . . The government will take energetic measures against
Braden Copper." González Videla told the union leaders to let the workers
know that his government would soon bring an end to the conflict.[18] For
the miners, according to *Despertar Minero,* González Videla was "their last

hope."[19] Already on 9 October two weeks into the strike, the miners had voted in a general assembly to petition the government to nationalize the El Teniente mine and "to recuperate for Chile the riches that [the company] has exploited for more than half a century."[20] The union's demand that the government expropriate the mine was echoed by other unions across the country and by the Communist Party. The Communist CTCh published a declaration demanding that the government nationalize the copper industry and look for new markets for Chilean copper in Europe and Latin America as an alternative to its actual dependence on exports to the United States.[21]

The call for nationalization of the mine was echoed in congress, where Carlos Rosales denounced the Braden Copper Company's intransigence and marshaled statistics to demonstrate the vast earnings of the company during the war. He was joined by Falange deputy and former minister of labor Bernardo Leighton, who blamed the company for the strike, stating that "the national economy is tied to the functioning of the El Teniente mine, and this normal functioning has been interrupted not by the workers, but by the company."[22] Right-wing deputies from the Liberal and Conservative Parties defended the company, invoking the conditions of the international copper market to support Braden's position. Raúl Yrarrázaval argued, for example, that "these conditions [of the copper market] are very precarious because the consumption of copper has greatly diminished and production in the United States and Canada has grown considerably as a consequence of the new mines put into operation during the war." Yrarrázaval, echoing Braden's own claims, concluded that because of this competition Chile ran the risk of incurring higher production costs and being "simply erased from the world market." He also promoted the positive benefits to the Chilean economy from the activities of foreign capital, repeating laissez-faire arguments made by the traditional parties of the Right since the beginning of the century.[23]

Braden also received support from the U.S. government. The U.S. embassy and State Department followed events in the Chilean copper mine carefully and held frequent conversations with Braden and Kennecott officials. In 1946, unlike in 1942 when the main goal of the United States had been to maintain copper production during the Second World War, both the embassy and the State Department were more willing to intervene on behalf of the company. The U.S. government, with much prodding from the Braden Copper Company, began to understand the conflict in the copper mine as a test of the future of United States–Chile relations in the new cold war era.

Despite the president's repeated insistence to U.S. embassy officials that he planned to remove Communist ministers from his cabinet, González Videla's initial threats to intervene to put an end to the strike and his insinuations that he would, if necessary, nationalize the copper mine seemed to represent the radical and nationalist possibilities of the new government. For the first few months of his administration, it seemed González Videla could go either way, embracing the Communist-led labor support that had helped bring him into office or distancing himself from labor and the Left and following social and economic policies based on the economic support of the United States and the political support of the Liberal Party.

The strike had become a test case for the new anti-Communist foreign policy of the United States in Latin America. For U.S. officials, González Videla was giving mixed signals that indicated he was an unreliable ally. At times he lapsed into virulently nationalist rhetoric, implying that he planned to nationalize the Braden Copper Company's holdings if the company did not comply with the government's decree to restart production. At other times, however, he promised the U.S. embassy that the inclusion of the Communist Party in his cabinet was temporary and a necessary inconvenience given the weak social base of his government. He pledged his own anti-Communism and his intentions of eventually removing the PC from the government.

During the strike, the U.S. embassy in Chile took active steps to place pressure on the wavering González Videla administration. Embassy officials met with cabinet members and tried to impress on them the importance of the outcome of the strike to United States–Chile relations. In a conversation with Minister of Finance Wachholtz, an embassy counselor for economic affairs stated that "we were not so much concerned with taking up the cudgels for the Braden Copper Company . . . as we were in avoiding an impasse which might prevent the close economic cooperation between the United States and Chile which we all hoped to see developed during the administration of President González Videla."[24] Assistant Secretary of State Spruille Braden was wary of threatening to refuse all credits, but he did "express concern to the President and to the Foreign

Minister lest it [the strike] increase the difficulty re credits and discourage capital investment here."[25] The message to the Chilean government was clear: either keep out of the strike or risk losing U.S. economic support.

The response of Chilean officials to the embassy's "inquiries" about the copper situation was reassuring. The minister of finance told embassy officials that he would vote against government intervention in the copper industry, as did Gustavo Vicuña, head of CORFO, and Senator Humberto Alvárez, a close friend of the president who promised to talk to González Videla. The president himself assured the U.S. ambassador that the Communists "would not linger in the government" and stated that he "was ashamed of having communists in at all but that he had told the communists himself that the point of view of his government will be that of a capitalist state." "I have a liberal government in a capitalist state," he told the ambassador.[26] He also emphasized that the economic future of Chile depended on "right relations" with the United States.[27]

González Videla did, however, insist to the ambassador that Braden accept outside arbitration of the strike, a proposal repeatedly rejected by Braden and Kennecott officials, who were already alarmed by the expansion of state intervention in the copper industry since 1938. González Videla further earned the mistrust of U.S. officials by stating on different occasions that while he wanted to expel the Communist ministers from his cabinet, he had to wait in order to avoid losing the electoral base the PC had provided during his presidential campaign. González Videla also displayed his mistrust of the Socialist faction of the CTCH headed by Bernardo Ibáñez, which was then sympathetic to the U.S. government, and he was equally wary of attempts by the American Federation of Labor (AFL) to promote an anti-Communist labor confederation in Latin America. González Videla even accused Socialist-led unions of attempting to destroy the Communist-led faction of the CTCH, which had supported him during the 1946 campaign. Thus González Videla was sending mixed messages: he insisted on his anti-Communism, yet he also used the threat of expropriation and a move to the Left to pressure the U.S. government and Kennecott to agree to arbitration and to bring an end to the strike.[28]

Finally, after González Videla threatened to appoint an "intervenor" to take control of the mine, an action that would have been a prelude to expropriation, the president of Kennecott, E. T. Stannard, agreed to arbitration by a justice of the Chilean Court of Appeals. Stannard had received support from the embassy in Santiago, which had warned González Videla "of the possible reactions of the United States to any action clearly unreasonable and unjust and illegal." In addition, the company and the U.S. embassy had received personal assurances from González Videla that they would have nothing to fear from the arbitration.[29]

The miners' dissatisfaction with the decision to pursue arbitration was exacerbated when they heard the decision of the government-appointed arbitrator, supreme court justice Franklin Quezada, a month after they had returned to work. In a widely attended union assembly held on 12 January, the miners voted to reject the decision and denounced reprisals taken by jefes against the workers in the mine and the company administration's refusal to meet with union leaders. During the months following the conclusion of the strike, workers in the mine continued to engage in illegal work stoppages, wildcats, and slowdowns to protest the company's efforts to break the union and undermine the union's Communist leadership.

The miners' discontent coincided with new initiatives within the congress and the González Videla administration to increase the government's role in the copper industry, particularly through the creation of a state copper corporation that would expand Chilean control of the marketing of copper. The stirrings within the Chilean government were provoked by the importance of copper revenues to the economy and the fact that during the war, while production had increased dramatically, the Chilean government's share of the wartime bonanza had been limited by a marketing agreement between the U.S. government and the copper companies that held the price of copper at 11.775 cents per pound between 1942 and 1945. In 1937, the average price had been 13.167 cents. Naturally, this United States–imposed price ceiling directly influenced the revenues accrued by the Chilean government and sparked new efforts to increase Chile's control of marketing.[30] The Chilean Copper Corporation was to provide the government the capacity to take advantage of favorable international market conditions. By 1947, copper prices had soared to 21 cents per pound.[31]

The government's announcement that it intended to revise its copper policy and the conflicts in the copper mines sparked a visit to Chile from the presidents of Anaconda and Kennecott to negotiate with the González Videla administration. In the meetings between government officials and the U.S. copper executives, Kennecott president Earl Stannard asked the

Chilean government to end the indirect taxation through the discriminatory exchange rate charged the company, to clamp down on labor unrest
in the copper mines, and to allow wage cuts in the mines as conditions for
the companies' increased production and investment. In a memorandum
to the Chilean finance minister, Stannard enumerated the North American companies' "concerns" about U.S. investments in the copper industry.
He complained that "copper production has been seriously interrupted
and curtailed of late by illegal strikes, walkouts, temporary suspensions
and slow-downs, accompanying demands for increased wages, bonuses,
changed working conditions, protests against management decisions, etc."
The Kennecott president decried the Chilean government's failure to support management during these labor conflicts and contended that the
Popular Front governments had "advocated concessions, thus aggravating
the situation." The huge increase in labor costs, due to wage hikes, minimum wage laws, and other "social legislation" passed after 1938, he argued,
had impaired Chilean copper's competitive position in the world market.[32]

Stannard also criticized the discriminatory exchange rate established
by the Chilean government, which served as an informal form of taxation. He argued that this drain on the company's profits was added to the
unjust and weighty 1941 copper tax that pushed taxes on the companies
above 30 percent. With other forms of taxation, he concluded, the North
American companies were paying over 70 percent in taxes, a sizable increase from the low taxes paid before 1938. He concluded that the Chilean
government's efforts to increase investment in the copper industry would
flounder because "it is evident that the outlook for a proportionate return
to the investor in the future is even more uninviting under present labor
conditions, exchange and taxes."[33]

Meanwhile, the government proposed a new hike in the copper tax and
an agreement with the companies in which they would reinvest a portion
of their profits in the development of a copper manufacturing industry in
Chile, a longtime aspiration of the Popular Front governments.[34] Government negotiators also demanded a greater Chilean role in the marketing
and sales of copper. The minister of finance stated Chile's desire to have
control of copper sales so that it could make international trade treaties
with other countries and have a say in fixing prices. The Chilean financial mission concluded that "it is not acceptable, from the point of view
of the higher interests and national dignity of Chile, that Chile, as the

second copper-producing country of the world, and that country which has the largest known reserves, greater than those of the United States, should not have a voice in sales policy."[35]

González Videla's meetings with Stannard also included efforts to obtain U.S. material assistance. The Chilean president asked Stannard to help Chile to obtain coal from the United States to ameliorate shortages and weaken the position of striking coal miners in the south. He also sought Stannard's help in obtaining a loan from the World Bank. In response, Stannard assured González Videla that he would do what he could if the Chilean president would "fight the Communists" and "prove his anticommunism." He also warned the president that until the Chilean government took a convincing anti-Communist stand and began fiscal reforms, he could expect little help from the copper companies. Secretly, Braden did, however, immediately ship two cargoes of coal to the Chilean government to help fight off a coal shortage caused by the miners' strike.[36]

In addition to meetings with Anaconda and Kennecott executives in June and July, Chilean officials also met with representatives from Standard Oil, Esso, City Bank, Chase National Bank, and the Coca Cola Company to discuss foreign investment in Chile. The government's search for foreign exchange to solve Chile's problems with its balance of payments and capacity to import also included Chilean commercial missions to the United States, in which Chilean representatives assured favorable treatment for U.S. investors in exchange for U.S. credits. In conversations with officials of the International Bank and the State Department, the Chilean delegations sought credits from the Export-Import Bank, the World Bank, and private U.S. banks.[37]

A major obstacle to the González Videla government's negotiations with these foreign corporations and the U.S. government was the labor unrest which had paralyzed the coal and copper mines for a good part of 1946 and which had spread to urban industries in Santiago, as well as to the countryside where the Communist Party had embarked on a campaign to organize campesino unions. The labor effervescence of 1946 and early 1947 reflected the PC's active attempt to exert its power through the labor movement by organizing new unions and supporting workers' strikes.

The Chilean Communist Party had seen its electoral strength grow rapidly after 1946 because of its central role in organizing rural and urban workers and through its participation in the González Videla government.

In the 1947 municipal elections, the PC increased its electoral support from the 10.2 percent it had won in the 1945 congressional elections to 16.5 percent. Participation in the government and an increasingly militant labor policy, combined with the decline of the fragmented Socialist Party, greatly strengthened the PC's political position. In congress, Communist Party representatives were vocal in their criticisms of González Videla's turn to the United States and to the Right. Communist congressmen argued that owing to the price ceiling placed on copper by the U.S. government during the Second World War, Chile had lost millions of dollars. In addition, they pointed out that when copper prices went up following the war, "the administration of Señor González, far from taking advantage of this favorable situation to capitalize the country, made new agreements for payments of the foreign debt to bond holders in the USA of nearly forty million dollars per annum, in barter to obtain new credits in machinery and equipment." They suggested loosening Chile's dependence on U.S. markets for copper and on U.S. credits by looking for new copper markets in Europe and Asia.[38]

Labor unrest and the PC's strength, both nationally and in the copper mines, created obstacles for the government in its attempts to convince Anaconda and Kennecott to increase investment in the copper industry and to attract credit from financial institutions in the United States.[39] In a 1946 meeting between the Chilean chargé d'affaires and Spruille Braden, Braden described "the Department's very serious concern with the El Teniente (Braden Copper Company) strike situation." Braden impressed on the Chilean representative "the possible averse effects on public opinion and Congress of precipitate action and subsequent settlement on terms that might prove tantamount to government intervention." In addition Braden, in a not so subtle threat, indicated that "should the situation develop to the point of irrevocably damaging this U.S. private investment in Chile, the Department, the Export-Import Bank, and the Government as a whole would be in a most embarrassing position for having simultaneously extended large loans to Chile."[40] Thus, the labor conflicts in El Teniente threatened not only the annual copper production and copper revenues but also future Kennecott investments, the investments of other private corporations, and loans from U.S. financial institutions.

This situation was exacerbated in 1947, when twelve hundred El Teniente empleados walked out on strike for the first time in the mine's history. They were supported by the mine's obreros as production was shut down completely. Almost simultaneously, empleados in Anaconda's northern Chuquicamata copper mine also went on strike. The empleados demanded a significant wage hike to keep up with the cost of living and denounced the fact that North American empleados were paid in dollars, whereas they were paid in Chilean currency for the same work. They asked for their pay in dollars, a month's indemnification for every year worked, and an increase in the family allowance.[41] As with the obreros' strike in 1946, both the minister of labor and the president stepped in to mediate the conflict. After labor inspectors informed the government that the empleados' strike was being fomented by the Communist Party, the government declared a state of emergency in the copper mining zones.

The final blow, as far as the company and the government were concerned, came when the unions for empleados and obreros constituted a single Unión de Empleados y Obreros de Braden Copper Company, O'Higgins.[42] This new union of empleados and obreros represented a serious threat to the company and to the government. In late October the new union sent a telegram to González Videla stating that "the empleados and obreros of Braden Copper in an assembly . . . agreed unanimously: 1. To defend our real wages in terms of the increase in the cost of living." The petition called on the government to support striking workers across the country, fix price ceilings on basic consumer goods, implement agrarian reform, and stimulate domestic industrialization.[43]

The union of obreros and empleados gave the El Teniente workers added organizational strength in their confrontations with Braden and seemed to augur a future in which the company could expect strikes not only from its blue-collar workers but from its white-collar workers as well. The empleados' strike and the new union thus represented the culmination of almost two years of constant labor conflicts, stoppages, and strikes in El Teniente and the workers' increased power to shut down production. It also revealed that clearly drawn ethnic conflicts between the Chilean workers and the North American company had helped to blur the long-established divisions between obrero and empleado.

The union of empleados and obreros in El Teniente eliminated the social and economic divisions that the legal separation of blue- and white-collar workers had originally intended. The labor code established separate legal rights and unions for empleados and obreros and the copper company used this legal distinction to promote divisions within its own workforce by holding out the promise of social mobility to its obreros. Laborers who worked obediently and efficiently and who went to vocational schools or who proved their skill and capacity for hard work could eventually hope to become crew chiefs, foremen, or even skilled technical workers and win classification as an empleado. As we have seen, the company's policy of fueling workers' aspirations for social mobility in order to co-opt them often backfired. Many workers who actively embraced the ideal of socioeconomic mobility through education, cultural improvement, and hard work also became militant unionists. The goal of becoming an empleado did not necessarily diminish workers' militancy and their antagonism to the company.

Empleados and obreros enjoyed basic, common experiences that joined them in a shared cause. Both were paid in Chilean pesos, which were subject to the constant, debilitating pressures of the steadily escalating cost of living in Chile, whereas North American administrators, supervisors, and technicians were paid in dollars. Although empleados and obreros lived in different barracks and empleados enjoyed more spacious and comfortable accommodations, neither group of Chilean workers had access to the North American camp with its gardens, swimming pools, tennis courts, and houses. A three-tier class system divided the El Teniente camps, with each social group separated from the other two spatially, socially, and economically. Empleados, for example, belonged to their own social and recreational clubs. The distance that separated Chilean white-collar workers from their North American supervisors was, however, considerably greater than the gulf that distinguished them from Chilean obreros.

In addition, by the 1940s, many empleados had begun work in the mine as obreros. They had friends, relatives, and former neighbors who worked as obreros and who belonged to the industrial, as opposed to professional, union. The collusion of foremen and workers in the practice of altering the marks in the mine was a concrete expression of the economic, social, and racial ties that bound empleados and obreros together in common antagonism to the North American copper company in spite of the legal and economic differences that separated them.

At the same time as empleados and obreros were consolidating their organizations in El Teniente, the Communist Party was making striking gains in winning union elections. In the May 1947 elections, the PC won control of the small Rancagua unions of warehouse workers and Coya electrical plant workers, as well as the major miners' union. In the Caletones foundry, the long-term Socialist union president was reelected, but the PC was able to win a significant number of votes and leadership posts in the union. Communists also held most of the posts in the new union of empleados and obreros. The PC's ascendancy in the El Teniente miners' organizations had grown as it increased its national profile and political power and through its prominent role in galvanizing national political support for the miners' strikes and in aiding the miners in their conflicts with the copper company.

The intense level of organization and conflict in the copper mines created profound problems for González Videla and tested the limits of his populist and nationalist inclinations. The labor conflicts in the mines were also accompanied by the organization of campesino unions in the countryside by the PC and strikes by the PC-led unions of coal miners. In response to the Communists' campaign to mobilize campesinos, the Liberal Party, which had a base among large landowners, withdrew its support for the coalition government and joined the Conservative and Socialist Parties in demanding that González Videla remove the Communist ministers from his cabinet. While the government began a process of negotiating new foreign loans, the Liberal and Conservative Parties embarked on a public campaign, arguing that foreign confidence could be won only by controlling both labor unrest and the PC. The Right's anti-Communist and antilabor campaign sowed distrust among foreign investors and effectively sabotaged the government's attempts to get new foreign credits.[44]

Political crisis and the atmosphere of widespread social upheaval turned González Videla to the right. Ultimately, the president remained wedded to the Radical Party's traditional conception of Chilean economic development. Industrial growth was to be achieved with foreign investment and loans that would supply the foreign exchange necessary to strengthen and expand Chile's industrial base. To appease U.S. corporations and financial institutions and the U.S. State Department, González Videla had to do something about a dynamic labor movement and an increasingly powerful Communist Party.

In late 1947, González Videla expelled the three Communist ministers from his cabinet and demanded extraordinary powers from congress to control strikes in the coal, copper, and nitrate mines. In October, according to a U.S. embassy report, the Chilean government "determined to take stringent measures to eliminate Communist domination of labor unions, particularly in industries producing vital raw materials."[45] The González Videla government declared states of emergency in and sent the army to control provinces in which nitrate, coal, and copper were produced. The military crackdown came as a response to an alleged plan by the PC to begin strikes of railroad workers and nitrate and copper miners. The government arrested Communist Party leaders, militants, and union leaders and sent them to military-controlled concentration camps and to distant parts of the country in internal exile.[46] A large number of El Teniente Communist Party activists and union leaders were detained and some sent to the Pisagua concentration camp in the northern desert. González Videla had brought the "populist" period of Popular Front governments to an abrupt end.

General Humberto Luco, the designated commander of O'Higgins Province, immediately traveled with a detachment of troops to El Teniente, where the miners had struck to protest the repressive measures taken by González Videla.[47] Upon his arrival in El Teniente, General Luco immediately informed the acting manager of the Braden Copper Company that he wanted to "clean out all Communists and 'agitators' who had been causing labor difficulties during the past few years." The general requested from the company a list of all "agitators, organizers, and union officials." The company also sent a copy of the list of discharged and arrested workers to the U.S. State Department to be included with lists of workers arrested in other mining centers.[48] Months later, in 1948, the González Videla government passed the "Law for the Defense of Democracy," which banned the Communist Party and established a new coalition government that included the Socialist, Conservative, and Liberal Parties.

The González Videla regime's repression of the labor movement and the Communist Party immediately bore fruit. Anaconda announced a plan to invest $130 million and expand production in the northern Chuquicamata copper mine. Kennecott president E. T. Stannard expressed his own satisfaction with González Videla's turn to the right. In Kennecott's yearly report for 1949, he noted that owing to the anti-Communist actions of the Chilean government, any noticeable activity of the Communist Party had been diminished, and as a result, work discipline had improved, as had the productivity of the labor force. He also reported that the government had not increased taxes on the copper company. In brief, he concluded, 1948 had been a year in which "the government solved many problems in a way that has inspired confidence with respect to the future."[49]

The head of the Welfare Department in El Teniente happily told reporters that "the respect and dedication to work has returned, coinciding with the measures taken by the Supreme Government to combat communism. The slow rhythm of work is beginning to disappear, and a new patriotic spirit among the obreros is observable." He condemned the "anarchy" and "violation of discipline" that had led to the erosion of "the hierarchies established by the company" since 1938. With the repression of the PC, however, he forecast a bright future for Chile, stating that "Chile will win a preponderant place in the progressive growth of production if it continues to follow this path."[50]

In addition to the U.S. copper companies' new plans for expanded investment and production, the U.S. Export-Import Bank offered the Chilean government new credits, as did the World Bank, which had rejected Chilean requests for loans in 1947. The Export-Import Bank credits were used to finance the creation or growth of major Chilean industries and assured U.S. influence in these industries. The bank loans required that Chile import U.S. capital goods and that private investors hold a majority of the stock of the United States–financed industries. Thus, the Kennecott Copper Corporation, in addition to owning the El Teniente copper mine, became a stockholder in three major, CORFO-funded and planned industries: the Pacific Steel Corporation, the National Petroleum Corporation, and the National Electric Corporation.[51]

González Videla's decision to turn on the PC and the labor movement resolved a fundamental tension that had underscored the coalition governments since the first Popular Front government of Pedro Aguirre Cerda. Ultimately, the reliance of these Radical Party–led governments on a form of economic growth that precluded any internal social structural change and relied on external financing, particularly from the U.S. government and United States–dominated lending institutions, clashed with the radical growth in the mobilization and organization of workers and campesinos unleashed by these same governments. While the coalition governments depended on the electoral support mobilized by the leftist parties and organized labor and won with promises of social and labor reform and political participation, the demands of workers and campesinos far exceeded what the Popular Front administrations were prepared to concede.

In El Teniente, this contradiction in the coalition government's policies meant that the mining community was able to organize on an unprecedented scale and resist the almost complete control the company exercised over the mine and its camps. As a result of expanded governmental intervention in labor relations, men and women in El Teniente increasingly looked to the state to secure their petitions and the rights mandated in the labor code and social welfare apparatus. Incorporation into the state-administered system of labor relations did not, however, erode miners' militancy. After 1938, the miners increased the strength of their unions and engaged in numerous work stoppages and strikes over both workplace and community issues. During these years, they were able to chip away at the foundations of what they called "the American empire in Sewell," often with the support of labor inspectors, the intendancy, congressmen, and even the president. The mining community's new organizational capacity allowed it to defend in increasingly effective ways demands about work conditions, wages, and the cost of living and to place pressure on both the company and the government. After 1938, the autonomy of the Braden Copper Company, both in its relations with its workers and in its relation with the Chilean state, was severely curtailed.

The concern of the Radical Party–led coalition governments with maintaining high levels of copper production and good relations with the U.S. private sector and government imposed limits on how far the government would go to support miners in their conflicts with the North American company and thus provoked the workers' growing discontent. Only now, workers were in a far better position to try themselves to wrest these changes from employers and the government. The Popular Front governments thus confronted a labor militancy in the copper mines that threatened their entire program of economic development. The El Teniente miners could now engage in work stoppages and strikes that threatened not only the well-being of the copper company but the entire national economy as well.

The repression unleashed by González Videla temporarily answered the government's need to reestablish political stability and social tranquility as conditions for future U.S. investments and loans. In El Teniente, the miners' rapidly growing mobilization was interrupted with the arrest and internal exile of union leaders and the dismissals of large numbers of workers. As the company cut back production during the 1949 economic recession, it continued to fire workers, thus further weakening the miners' position. For a short period, the government and the companies were able to enjoy labor peace in the copper mines.

The fundamental problems of copper policy, however, remained unresolved. During the 1950s, the Chilean state would once again try to increase its participation in the production and marketing of copper, while encouraging the North American copper companies to increase their investments in their Chilean mines. At the same time, as repression against labor and the Left diminished, the copper workers organized powerful strike movements against their U.S. adversary, threatening the government's efforts to increase its copper revenues. In 1951, three years after the repression unleashed by González Videla, the miners from Chile's three large, North American–run mines met in the town of Machalí, neighboring El Teniente, to organize a national union of obreros and empleados, the Confederación Nacional de los Trabajadores del Cobre (CTC), whose primary goal was the nationalization of the North American–owned copper mines.

The Miners, North American Capital, and the Chilean State

The repression of the Communist Party, the major political presence in the El Teniente copper mine until 1947, led neither to the elimination of the powerful union structures forged during the decade of Popular Front governments nor to the eradication or reformation of the militant working-class culture of the mining camps. Although hundreds of leftist workers were fired and detained by the military, the miners maintained their ties to the Left. Many entered militant factions of the fragmented Socialist Party, while others sustained informal and clandestine links to the Communist Party infrastructure. The miners' unions, now legally recognized by both the company and the state, also provided a space for the sustenance of the miners' radical political culture.

Chilean politics for the next decade and a half followed Gabriel González Videla's turn to the right and renunciation of populism. Despite an electoral campaign which played on the strains of the Popular Front's nationalism and populism and which won support from a faction of the splintered Socialist Party, former dictator Carlos Ibáñez ruled over a conservative regime between 1952 and 1958 that focused on liberalizing trade and fighting the chronic inflation that had plagued the Popular Front governments.[52] Ibáñez followed orthodox economic recipes that included cuts in public spending, monetary and credit restrictions, ceilings on wages, and reduced subsidies for public services. Rural and urban workers suffered the consequences of the attack on inflation with increased unemployment and declining real incomes.

Ibáñez's regime also marked a retreat from the interventionist stance of the Popular Front governments toward the North American–owned copper industry and a return to the sympathetic state policies of the 1920s and 1930s. In 1955, the Ibáñez administration signed "the New Deal" (Nuevo Trato del Cobre) with Kennecott and Anaconda, which was designed to increase investment and production in the mines. In exchange for reduced taxes and such other indirect benefits as favorable exchange controls, the U.S. companies agreed to invest in expanded production in the copper industry and to locate many of their processing activities in Chile. However, while Kennecott's and Anaconda's profits increased considerably during these years, investment in the mines remained low, copper exports failed to increase, and the percentage of copper refined in Chile actually decreased. The copper companies were also fortified by Ibáñez's repression of organized labor. Strikes were broken, and under the Law for the Permanent Defense of Democracy, union leaders and Communist activists were sent to detention camps. When the CTC declared an illegal general strike to protest the Nuevo Trato, a state of siege in the copper mines was declared once again, and Ibáñez sent in the military to induct El Teniente workers into the army forcibly.

Despite the repression of organized labor and the Communist Party, a number of crucial changes between 1952 and 1958 had a transformative effect on both national politics and the labor movement in the copper mines. First, before leaving office Ibáñez fulfilled an earlier campaign promise to eliminate the Law for the Permanent Defense of Democracy, which he himself had invoked to repress strikes, and legalized the Communist Party. Second, after the general strike in the copper mines in 1955, the CTC was given legal standing. Third, electoral reforms limited the possibility of fraud and abuse with the introduction of a single official ballot, made voting compulsory, and thus extended the franchise into the countryside, reducing the political dominance of the landed elite. Finally, the Socialist Party turned toward the left, established a political alliance with the Communist Party in the Frente de Acción Popular (Popular Action Front, FRAP), renounced political alliances with parties of the middle and upper classes, and declared a workers' front in a new leftist version of the Popular Front coalitions.

The 1958 elections revealed a redrawn Chilean political landscape. Rural and urban workers, disillusioned by the conservative rule of Ibáñez, threw their vote to the revitalized FRAP coalition candidate and Socialist Salvador Allende, who came within 33,000 votes of winning a plurality of the vote. The Radical Party, now running on its own, saw its electoral support decline and be eclipsed by the recently organized Christian Democratic Party (PDC), formerly the Falange Nacional, which laid claim to the votes of white-collar workers, the middle class, and the political center. The winner, rightist candidate Jorge Alessandri, managed only 31.2 percent of the vote.[53] As Socialists, Communists, and Christian Democrats flocked to the countryside to organize recently enfranchised rural workers, the leftist FRAP and social reformist PDC increased their political bases, and the Right continued its slow political demise. In 1961, the FRAP won 27.5 percent of the seats in the Chamber of Deputies and thirteen of forty-five seats in the Senate.[54]

The political rejuvenation and radicalization of the Socialist and Communist Parties were also reflected in a resurgence of leftist politics and militant unionism in the copper mines. In 1957, after a decade of state-backed repression, El Teniente miners engaged in a major legal strike. Over seven thousand obreros and empleados walked out on strike despite Ibáñez's threat that "they would have to suffer the consequences," his rejection of the workers' petition for government intervention, and his warning that any demands for a salary hike that violated anti-inflationary wage ceiling legislation would be illegal. While a military zone of emergency was declared around El Teniente, workers continued the strike and managed to wrest several important concessions from the company. In 1958, a strike was averted at the last minute when the company agreed to a 27 percent increase in salaries and a significant increase in the family allowance.[55] The next year, the El Teniente miners engaged in another major strike that won national attention. The FRAP organized demonstrations of unions and the CTC in Santiago, and FRAP presidential candidate and Socialist Party leader Salvador Allende spoke to the assembly of miners. Linking the miners' strike to the broader movement to nationalize the copper mines, he told a huge demonstration of workers that "the entire people of Chile, the unions, the progressive politicians, and the public in general must be on the strikers' side, because they are defending the cause of Chile." [56]

Between 1960 and 1970, the El Teniente miners, often in conjunction with miners from Chile's north, engaged in almost annual strikes and innumerable wildcats. In December 1960, for example, the miners voted almost unanimously for a strike (of 5,535 voters, only 29 voted against the strike) a month after a major copper miners' strike in Anaconda's Chuquicamata mine. The following five years were a period of intensified militancy in El Teniente. Miners engaged in a number of section wildcats; three legal strikes; a general strike in 1965 to demand nationalization of the copper industry; and another general strike in 1966, in which miners in Anaconda's Chuquicamata and El Salvador mines engaged in a solidarity strike with the El Teniente workers, who had gone on strike after failed contract negotiations. [57]

During these years the miners' union, the Sindicato Industrial de Sewell y Mina, was led almost entirely by militants of the leftist parties. In 1962, three Socialists, one Communist, and an independent leftist occupied leadership positions, and in 1965, three Socialists and two Communists. El Teniente's smaller, aboveground obreros' unions in the Caletones foundry, Coya electrical plant, and Rancagua warehouses were also led by Socialists and Communists. In 1969, the CTC, which represented unions of both empleados and obreros in Chile's copper industry, had a directorate composed of seven Socialists, four Communists, one Christian Democrat, and a Radical. Twelve out of thirteen national leaders belonged to Salvador Allende's Unidad Popular (Popular Unity) coalition, a redrawn version of the FRAP that included the Radical Party, as well as segments of the "Christian Left." The entrenchment of the leftist union leadership continued throughout the 1960s, as copper miners voted for militants of the parties that most clearly articulated opposition to the conservative administration of Jorge Alessandri (1958–1964) and the reformist government of Christian Democrat Eduardo Frei (1964–1970). Opposition to Alessandri and Frei, strong calls for the expropriation of the copper mines that played on decades of nationalist tradition in El Teniente, and the long-standing presence of the leftist parties in the camps made the Socialist and Communist Parties a hegemonic force among El Teniente obreros.

Whereas Jorge Alessandri's government continued the orthodox economic and alternating populist and repressive social policies of Ibáñez, Eduardo Frei sought a middle road between the rapidly polarizing politics that threatened to bring a revolutionary leftist government to power. Backed by the United States and reluctantly by Chile's traditional right-wing ruling class, Frei embarked on a dual program to engage in social reform to preempt more radical and revolutionary possibilities for change and to consolidate the PDC's support among peasants and workers, as well as among the middle classes. In the countryside, Frei pushed the unionization of peasants and agrarian reform. In the copper industry, he proposed the "Chileanization" of the North American–owned mines with the support of the North American companies and the United States. The Chilean state purchased 51 percent of the Braden Copper Company and joined Kennecott in a program of increased investment and expansion of production. In El Teniente, the Braden management continued to run the mine, and Kennecott reaped enormous profits from the arrangement.

The copper miners' unions and the Chilean Left rejected Frei's Chileanization plan and called for full-scale nationalization of the industry. In 1966, the Frei government responded to a general strike in the copper mines by jailing union leaders and imposing military rule in the northern mines. In Anaconda's El Salvador mine, eleven miners were killed in conflicts with the military, and the repudiation of Frei and the PDC by miners was confirmed. Despite Frei's efforts to court organized labor and to mobilize worker support behind his program of social reform and Chileanization and despite the growing popularity of the PDC among white-collar employees in the copper industry, events in the copper mines between 1964 and 1970 drove both the copper miners' unions and the national labor movement to the left. The Chileanization program was assailed by the Left and organized labor as selling out to North American capital.

During the 1960s, copper miners composed one of the most militant sectors of the labor movement. Their constant strikes and movements for nationalization of the copper industry propelled them into the national eye and linked their struggles to the growing social movements of urban and rural workers and the increasing power of the national labor federation (the Central Unica de Trabajadores, CUT) and the Left. The working-class militancy of copper miners was evident in their general strikes, calls for nationalization, and consistent voting for the parties of the UP in local, national, and union elections. During these years little was said of the miners' "privileged status and position." Rather, the CUT and the Left joined the CTC and the copper workers' unions in emphasizing that miners' material improvements were the result of hard struggle and the just rewards for the sacrifices of life and labor in the mines. For the Left and organized labor, the miners were pivotal to the national struggles for socialism and recuperation of Chile's most important resource.

The copper miners themselves constructed a number of arguments to make it clear that their wages and benefits did not make them a privileged sector of the labor movement. They emphasized that they had earned their standard of living both through the terrible sacrifices of living and working in the mines and through years of constant union struggle. As the Communist Party paper *El Siglo* pointed out during the 1959 El Teniente strike, "The working and living conditions of the striking obreros and empleados are hard and sacrificial."[58] The miners also argued repeatedly that their conflicts were with a North American company that paid its workers in the United States significantly higher wages. The CTC produced studies that demonstrated that Chilean copper workers earned less than a third of the salaries paid to U.S. copper workers.[59] Finally, the miners' unions maintained that their increased wages signified money earned by the North American companies that stayed in Chile and that benefited the Chilean economy. In the context of the 1959 strike, *El Siglo* invoked the mantle of nationalism to argue that "every cent that the El Teniente workers earn stays in our country and takes away from the enormous profits that the foreign company extracts from Chile."[60]

Most of the leftist activists and union militants who led the miners' strikes, like most miners during the 1960s, had grown up in El Teniente. Their fathers had been miners who migrated to the mine during the 1920s and 1930s, the years when the community's permanence was finally established and fixed. Their mothers were the housewives that the company had hoped to attract. In 1966, the company paper commented that "over the last years a large contingent of youngsters has been preferred by the company in its contracting since all are sons of workers . . . taking into account that this satisfies an aspiration shared in many homes, as much by the workers as by their families. . . . There are already innumerable cases of workers who have been replaced by their own children. . . . There are many families that have cultivated as a tradition working in El Teniente."[61] These workers' experiences of life in the camps had been defined by the bitter struggles of the 1930s and 1940s, the repression of 1947–1949, the powerful presence of both the company and the union in every aspect of their lives, and the activism of the Socialist and Communist Parties. In oral histories, union leaders and miners who participated in the movements of the 1960s constantly evoked the topography of class relations that was so starkly laid out in the mine's camps as crucial to their leftist politics and labor activism. They had grown up in a community that was shaped in every possible way by notions of class difference and antagonism. As many miners emphasize, their daily lives were permeated by the realities of labor in the mine, union movements, and the spatial and social hierarchy of the camps. As children they had walked the picket line with their mothers at their fathers' side, organized unions of students in the camps, and attended plays, concerts, and meetings in the union hall. From a young age they had expected that their future would be to work in the mine and participate in the union.

The miners' movements of the 1960s expressed the culmination of the processes that had been developing in El Teniente since the 1930s. The consolidation of a permanent workforce and community provided the company a stable and constant supply of labor as miners' male children took on jobs in the company. In addition, the company continued to provide numerous economic incentives to workers to marry and form families. The Braden Copper Company's family allowance increased regularly with each new session of collective bargaining and was significantly higher than the family allowance paid other workers by the national social security service. Whereas in other areas of the economy obreros earned a family allowance that constituted 37.1 percent of the allowance received by empleados in 1966, in El Teniente obreros received the same allowance as empleados.[62] Similarly, the company continued to pay wages that exceeded the wages of workers in other mining and industrial sectors. In 1965, a Braden Copper Company study analyzed the incomes and wages of obreros in various industries. While the monthly income of single copper workers came to 719.94 escudos, metalworkers earned 386.43 escudos; oil workers, 460.15 escudos; textile workers, 276.90 escudos; and construction workers, 254.84 escudos. Most important, these differences in earnings increased radically for married workers whose average monthly income in the copper industry was 1,173.60 escudos, compared with 476.97 escudos for metalworkers, 605.63 escudos for oil workers, 363.69 for textile workers, and 302.39 for construction workers.[63] El Teniente's high wages induced workers and then their children to settle in the mining camps, and the possibilities for significantly greater incomes for married workers provided the incentive for the establishment of families.

As during the 1940s, El Teniente's working-class community provided the basis for a militant class politics imbued with the ideology of the Left and the rhetoric of nationalism and anti-imperialism. The movements of the 1960s were community movements in which women and children participated, much as they had during the 1940s. Strikes and protests focused as much on housing conditions, schools, services, and the cost of living as on wages and other work-related demands. Women organized ollas comunes, formed women's committees, attended union meetings, marched with their husbands from the mine to Rancagua and Santiago during strikes, and voted for the Left.[64] Solidarity between the sexes and within the El Teniente community gave the annual struggles of the miners with the company added force.

For women in El Teniente, these years brought little change. Despite the radicalization of the Left and the state of labor militancy in the copper mines, the social movements of the 1960s did little to address the structure of patriarchy in workers' families. Women's interests and demands were linked directly to the struggles of their husbands and the miners' union. The success of El Teniente miners in winning material benefits during the late 1950s and 1960s made the structure of the nuclear family in the camps even more solid and permanent. Miners' high wages combined with the family allowance, bonuses for children, and other benefits to allow men to occupy the central role of breadwinner. Miners' economic situation made it unnecessary for women to work, husbands prohibited their wives from engaging in wage labor, and the camps continued to provide few jobs for women. As in other mining enclaves around the world, boys growing up in El Teniente were educated to take up careers in mining, whereas girls in El Teniente expected to marry an El Teniente miner and work as a housewife. These were years when fathers refused to let daughters work as empleadas because work for single women was equated with immorality, and single women's social lives were strictly regulated within miners' families. They were provided little education relative to men and enjoyed few opportunities to leave their homes and the mine's camps.

The construction of a community of male workers who lived in the mining camps, attended company schools, married, and had children they raised to be miners was an established fact by the 1960s. Unlike the 1940s, however, by the 1960s miners had begun to wrest significant material improvements from the North American copper company through annual collective bargaining and constant strikes and wildcats. During this decade they saw their standard of living rise significantly, despite the continued hardships of labor in the mine and life in the camps' crowded barracks. Improved material conditions further reinforced the stability of the nuclear family in the camps, the masculinization of work, and the relegation of women to the domestic sphere. Men's role as head of household and primary wage earner and their associated control over women's labor and sexuality were reaffirmed and enabled by their economic situation.

Members of the mining community perceived their high wages and benefits to be both the result of their history of collective struggle and the just reward of decades of deplorable living and working conditions. Miners expressed an occupational pride based on their hard work, onerous conditions in the mines, and sense that to be a miner was also to stand up to the company and to the state. This pride was also tied to their high earnings and capacity to fulfill the middle-class ideal of the wage-earning head of household who ruled with patriarchical authority over his wife and children. Male workers understood the dependability of their position at the head of families and their material well-being to be contingent on decades of strikes, work stoppages, and union activity, as well as on the hard sacrifices of mine labor. Women, in turn, had come to identify with the domestic sphere and the rights of the mother and wife. Economic security, education, and social services were rights, not privileges, guaranteed by the ideology of domesticity and backed by the state and the company. Thus, women saw their interests as tied to the security of their husbands and families and to the traditions of struggle associated with the broader El Teniente community. Their husbands had become reliable workers, and they had become housewives, but together, they confronted the copper company with the strength and solidarity of a community.

CONCLUSION

Until 1973, the Chilean labor movement distinguished itself from union movements throughout Latin America by its Marxist political identity. Unlike workers in Brazil, Argentina, and Mexico, Chilean workers built unions with close ties to the Communist and Socialist Parties and supported a socialist program of change that culminated in the election of Salvador Allende and the Popular Unity in 1970. Although traditional Chilean labor historiography focuses on the first decades of the century, particularly the experiences of nitrate miners, to explain the singular trajectory of Chilean labor, in this book I demonstrate that the period following the Great Depression and during the Radical Party–led coalition governments between 1938 and 1952 was crucial to the process of working-class formation and to the construction of a leftist political culture and radical anticapitalist labor movement in Chile.[1] The forces that contributed to the electoral victory of the Marxist Popular Unity government in 1970 were already in motion during the 1930s, and the tensions and contradictions that beset Chile's experiment with a peaceful and democratic socialist revolution were well in place during the Popular Front's efforts to establish programs of moderate social reform and capitalist national industrial development.

The 1930 world economic crisis initiated a new period of working-class formation both nationally and in Chile's export sector. The development of the copper industry introduced a new form of modern industrial enterprise that employed sophisticated technologies and methods of production for extracting, processing, and refining copper ore. Unlike the nitrate industry, the North American copper companies were capital-intensive and oligopolistic and required a permanent and trained labor force. Whereas the radical fluctuations and labor-intensive nature of nitrate production, combined with the unequal structure of land ownership in the countryside, created a mobile labor force that could migrate to other sectors of the economy to find work in agriculture, ports, and urban industries during the cyclical downswings of the late nineteenth and early twentieth centuries, the copper industry required a settled, full-time, and skilled labor force. Following the First World War, the Braden Copper Company introduced a set of new management practices that reshaped the nature of working-class formation in the mining export sector. The company implemented corporate welfare schemes for the first time in Chile in order to reform workers' disruptive forms of sociability, high levels of turnover, and lack of labor discipline. Thus, the growth of the copper industry after the First World War initiated the transformation of Chile's itinerant male mine laborers into a permanent industrial workforce.

This study also shows that the process of capitalist development and proletarianization in the modern copper industry was shaped by gender ideologies and, in turn, reshaped working-class gender relations. As Ava Baron has argued, in conflicts between labor and capital the strategies employed by management and male workers take place on a "field of gender" and are shaped by "concepts of gender."[2] Beginning in 1914, the North American copper company employed a gender ideology of female domesticity to restructure both the work and nonwork lives of men and women who migrated to the mining camps. In the copper industry, the gendered division of labor was redrawn to define wage labor as masculine and domestic activity as feminine. Both the company and the state engaged in the close surveillance of single women's social and sexual behavior and worked to train them to be skillful administrators of working-class households. Meanwhile, men too were encouraged to marry and assume the responsibilities of the head of household. Thus, I show that the process of working-class formation during this period in Chile involved the settlement of both male and female workers within stable nuclear families and the reformulation of gender identities. The male-headed family became the primary structure within which working-class men and women fashioned their masculinity and femininity.

After 1930, both men and women established a permanent working-class community in El Teniente, pushed by the crisis in the nitrate industry and agricultural sector and pulled by the Braden Copper Company's corporate welfare policies. New ideas about male respectability and citizenship and the moral virtues of female domesticity redefined the meanings of masculinity and femininity, shaped the nature and significance of work, and replaced earlier, more fluid forms of male and female working-class sociability. Yet, the transition to a new order of class and gender relations in the mining industry was not direct or free of conflict. As they adjusted to the disciplinary regimes of capital and the state, men and women continued to resist the reorganization of their labor, social habits, and values.

Male workers actively fought efforts to regulate their leisure time and labor by drawing on the traditions of itinerant peones. They participated in an oppositional work culture based on the expression of masculine pride in a challenging attitude toward company and state authority. Miners extended their masculinized work identity into illicit social practices in which they asserted control over their nonwork time and public space in the mining camps and rejected the company's efforts to restrict their sexual and social activity. Increasingly, however, male workers found affirmation in their capacity for hard labor, work skills, economic power, and patriarchical authority over women within their households. Miners located a new sense of masculine respectability in their capacity to fulfill the role of wage-earning head of household and rule over the social and economic lives of their families. By signifying their labor and earnings— and the authority over female sexuality and labor that economic power enabled—as a source of manhood and dignity, workers increasingly identified both with their work as miners and with the company's ideology of gender relations and thus conformed to the company's demand for a settled and married labor force, even as they lost control of their mobility, independence, and bodies owing to new forms of work and social discipline and the devastating effects of mine labor.

In El Teniente, both the resistance and the accommodation of workers to the initiatives of capital in the workplace were practiced on the fields of power surrounding sexuality. Drawing on Joan Scott's argument that labor historians examine the ways in which the social construction of the meanings of sexual difference are elaborated and shape different forms of social hierarchy, I show that sexuality and labor composed structures of power that shaped and reshaped men's and women's lives in articulation with one another.[3] For men, class alienation was linked to and signified by their sense of loss of control sexually, and it was expressed in anxieties about female adultery and the power of female sexuality. In turn, male workers defined the transcendence of estrangement in the labor process and broader system of class relations, molded as it was by gendered managerial practices in the modern mining industry, in terms of their capacity to exercise control over their own bodies and the bodies of women. Thus, I demonstrate the ways in which conflicts over the labor process and work identities were informed by gendered systems of meaning and social power.[4] Male workers figured their labor as the sexualized conquest of the feminized and threatening mine, subjected their wives and daughters to close social control, and asserted their right to expect women's services and social-sexual obedience. At the same time, they claimed their own sexual autonomy and freedom in opposition to the norms of behavior dictated by the company, building a masculine work identity based on a challenging posture toward company authority.

Like men, single women workers frequently opposed the efforts of the state and the copper company to regulate their social practices and male workers' attempts to assert their rights over women's bodies and behavior. Some women continued to engage in informal romantic/sexual liaisons or sex work, affirming control of their own activities during the 1940s. But the restriction of women's work and social lives exercised by the company and the state limited the capacity of single women to exercise social and economic independence. Single women's weak economic position, vulnerability to male violence, and social stigmatization rendered their assertions of autonomy increasingly difficult. By the 1940s, many women, as well as men, had come to define appropriate female activity in terms of the ideology of domesticity. Women sought respectability, social legitimacy, and economic security in marriage to a miner. The hegemony of this new arrangement of working-class gender relations was reinforced as married women in the mining camps looked to social welfare institutions to demand a new set of rights, encoded in the ideology of the nuclear family and companionate marriage, to male wages, the family allowance, and protection from domestic violence. Women defied the absolute patriarchical authority claimed by male workers by invoking their moral and legal rights as mothers and wives and men's new duties as husbands and fathers to their families in appeals to both the company and the state to intervene on their behalf in conflicts with their husbands.

Although married women were excluded from the labor force by both the company and male workers, their daily work was essential to the survival of mining families. Miners' wives accepted responsibility for their families' welfare; they took in boarders, prepared and sold baked goods, and even occasionally engaged in the contraband alcohol trade in addition to the daily routine of laundry, housecleaning, and preparing meals. As the company had intended, their work extended male workers' wages during a period in which the steady increase in the cost of living eroded real wages and rendered women's earnings and unremunerated domestic labor crucial to their families' subsistence. Thus, married women came to accept the duties and to claim the rights of mothers and wives dedicated to the household, adopting the moral codes of appropriate female behavior dictated by the gender ideology of domesticity. While they drew on the company's social welfare institutions and the judicial apparatus of the state to claim important securities and protections in their relationships with male workers, they increasingly identified their interests with those of their husbands and families.

During the 1930s a stable, working-class industrial community took shape in El Teniente. Although it provided the Braden Copper Company a permanent source of trained labor, the copper mining community also confronted the North American company with a powerful unity and strong class identity during labor conflicts after 1938. As Peter Winn has demonstrated for urban Santiago, a similar process occurred in neighborhoods developed around textile plants during the process of import substitution industrialization after 1930. Textile companies' paternalist management strategies and social welfare policies contributed to settling and disciplining migrants from the countryside in the city. These emergent communities provided the basis for the formation of a strong working-class identity in urban industrial neighborhoods.[5] In El Teniente, men's and women's ideas of what it meant to be working class were shaped by the close community ties they shared in the mining camps' barracks and informed by the structure of the nuclear family. Community in El Teniente did not arise from the shared traditions, "moral economy," or reinvented customs and cultural practices of peasant villages but was forged out of the process of proletarianization. The development of a community in El Teniente was inseparable from the process of class formation and proletarianization; capitalist development in the copper industry built a community out of a highly transient and diverse group of working-class men and women. Therefore class and community emerged as closely entwined spheres of social identity and cultural practice.[6]

In the mining camps, residence was directly linked to occupation and workplace. Issues related to consumption, household, and neighborhood life fell under the rubric of labor-capital relations, for the North American company provided workers and their families housing, schools, and cultural activities and oversaw the provision of daily necessities. Similarly, work-related demands and issues permeated the everyday culture of the camps, because the survival of every member of the El Teniente population depended on production inside the mine. The unity of these different domains of daily life in the camps brought the members of mining families, male workers, and single women workers together in a shared community whose class identity was defined relationally by their common antagonism to the North American company. Thus, I argue, the spaces of neighborhood and community were closely related to the world of the workplace and were important sites where working-class consciousness and politics were produced.

Although many male workers and their wives increasingly accepted elements of the company's paternalist ideology and strove to fulfill the company's promise of social mobility and middle-class domesticity, they compared the material hardships of life and labor in the camps with the company's ideal of middle-class domesticity and developed an oppositional stance, defined by national and ethnic hostility, to the power of the North American company. The social hierarchy and rigid boundaries laid out in the topography of the mining camps represented the material limits of workers' possibilities, exacerbated their antagonism toward North American supervisors, and solidified their sense of class and community. After 1938, this class identity was expressed in the mobilization of the entire mining community during labor conflicts. The miners' union came to represent both miners and their families as the El Teniente community's main political speaker. The union hall served as the central social space in which workers and their families gathered for cultural events, as well as for political meetings. In addition, the union organized miners' wives and daughters in a local chapter of the MEMCh and in several political groups for women, helping promote the establishment of a union of domestic servants in the camps.

The closely knit working-class community that developed in El Teniente during the 1930s and 1940s was based on the male-headed nuclear family and predicated on married women's economic dependence on men.

Women from mining families came to equate their interests with those of their husbands in conflicts with the copper company over wages and social benefits. Their political participation in community movements was structured by their economic reliance on male workers, acceptance of their own duties as wives and mothers, and identification with the ideology of female domesticity. Women participated in the MEMCh, cost-of-living committees, and women's committees to fulfill their responsibilities as managers of the domestic sphere and protectors of their families. Labor and the Left projected a role for women in the community's political and labor struggles as mothers and wives, locating the development of a proletarian "morality" and consciousness in the realm of the family and household. The miners' union urged women from miners' families to mobilize around issues specific to the life of the household, family, and consumption. Thus, the emergence of a robust, working-class community politics in El Teniente obscured the deepening structures of social and economic inequality between men and women within the labor market, the daily life of the camps, and mining households, occluding women's increased subordination to the power of male workers, capital, and the state.

This book also shows that the development of the El Teniente mining community was shaped by the formation of an activist and interventionist state after 1938. The election of the Popular Front in 1938 initiated a period of state formation and economic development that concluded in the UP electoral victory in 1970. The Popular Front and its successor coalition governments oversaw the implementation of a new system of state-directed labor relations, imposed the authority and sovereignty of the state in the copper industry, and provided the political space for the rejuvenation of the Left and the rebuilding of a national labor movement. The coalition governments established a series of social reforms that reproduced at the state level the corporate welfare schemes which the Braden Copper Company had introduced and which had drawn the interest of social reformers since the early 1920s. With the state supporting the institutionalization of the labor code, workers were able to organize independent unions and go on strike legally for the first time in the copper mine's history. Economic gains and social benefits won by miners in successful strikes and collective bargaining during these years consolidated the "family wage" in the mining camps and thus the dominant role of the male wage earner in miners' families. The capacity of miners to wrest concessions from the North American company after 1938 enabled the maintenance of a stable community of mining families.

While the center-left coalition governments sought to sponsor capitalist industrial development and implement moderate social welfare programs, they articulated a radical nationalism and ideology of citizenship that offered workers who toiled in the foreign-run enclave political languages with which to articulate and understand their conflicts with the copper company. For the first time, miners confronted the state not as an open antagonist but as a potential ally. They invoked the labor code and constitution, as well as the Popular Front's own nationalist rhetoric of citizenship, to press the coalition governments to intervene on their behalf in conflicts with the North American copper company. The period between 1938 and 1948 transformed workers' orientation toward the state and their style of labor politics. Until 1930, mine workers had viewed the state as an adversary, and their strikes and protests had taken the form of full-scale uprisings. As married women drew on rights and protections guaranteed by both capital and the state, male workers also began to look to the state during labor conflicts and to articulate a new sense of their rights as workers and citizens. Labor conflicts were now channeled through the bureaucratic institutional protocols established by the labor code and organized with the assistance and support of the national labor movement and the leftist parties at both the local and the national level. For the first time, mine workers and their unions requested that the state intervene in labor relations in El Teniente and demanded the nationalization of the mine in the name of all Chile. Thus, as the El Teniente mining community took shape, it was structured by the increasing integration of mine workers into a national system of labor relations and an "imagined community" of Chilean citizens.

Under the Popular Front governments, the Socialist and Communist Parties, although in competition and often fragmented by internal divisions, came to play an important role both in national politics and in the politics of the mining camps. The leftist parties provided a more radical and anticapitalist version of the coalition governments' protean, multiclass political rhetoric and thus enabled the copper miners to elaborate a class-specific rendering of the Front's ideology of nationalist development and citizenship. In the labor traditions disseminated by union activists from the FOCh and CTCh, militants of the Communist Party, and former nitrate miners, copper workers found a way of interpreting their experiences in the mine and defining their sense of class and community. After 1938, politicians from the Socialist and Communist Parties supplied important support for the miners' union during conflicts with the company, representing the miners at the level of the state. Rather than "discrediting" the Left, "incorporation" led to workers' increased identification with and ties to the Marxist parties. The link between miners' integration into the state-directed labor relations system and the development of strong ties to the leftist parties contradicts the common portrayal of this period as one in which workers sacrificed autonomy, militancy, and a revolutionary project, shackled by the moderate leaderships of both the PC and PS and constrained by the labor code.[7]

Incorporation into the new system of labor relations, the growing legitimacy of languages of rights and citizenship, and ties to the leftist political parties did not lead to the demobilization or quiescence of the mining community. Rather, miners continued to maintain informal forms of workplace combativeness that pushed union leaders and Communist Party activists to take more challenging stands and placed pressure on the coalition governments when they turned to the right, revealing the contradictions in their multiclass coalition and ideology of class cooperation in the name of national industrial growth. A number of writers argue that this period was one of diminished worker activism and relative weakness for organized labor. By shifting the focus from the level of national politics to the workplace and local community, I demonstrate that this period was one of widespread working-class mobilization and intensified militancy in which, at least in the copper industry, miners were able to wrest significant gains from Kennecott's Braden Copper Company, limit the power of foremen and supervisors, establish independent unions, and push the state to intervene in the administration of the copper mines. Ultimately, workers' success in establishing a powerful labor movement and the combative posture of the Communist Party in the copper mines contributed to González Videla's decision to turn on the Communists, repress labor, and bring an end in 1947–1948 to a decade of intermittent populist politics.[8]

Although the period of the Popular Unity government and the military dictatorship of Augusto Pinochet fall outside the scope of this study, copper miners' experiences under the Popular Front help explain developments under the UP and the military regime. In 1973, a strike over cost-of-living raises in El Teniente contributed to the destabilization of Allende's government and won the miners the reputation of composing a "labor aristocracy."[9] But this book shows that the category of labor aristocracy does not effectively explain miners' multilayered and contradictory forms of identity and consciousness. The shifting tensions between accommodation and resistance in the mine produced structures of feeling and formal ideologies that combined identification with the Left, a sense of the rights of citizenship, and a militant and untamed opposition to the state and capital. At the level of the everyday, the culture of the mining camps brought together a partial acceptance of many elements of Braden's gendered, paternalist ideology of social mobility and appropriate forms of masculine and feminine behavior with informal forms of opposition to the norms of middle-class morality and behavior.

Under the UP, the hybrid nature of miners' working-class consciousness became clear. During the 1960s, a majority of miners supported the UP's socialist project, voted for union leaders from the PS and PC, and frequently struck to demand the nationalization of the copper industry with the support of the Left. Miners' integration into the state-directed system of labor relations, while providing the basis for militant strikes and ties to the Left, had also cemented a relationship to the state based on a sense of rights. Copper workers were able to use their strategic position in the national economy and the fact of foreign control of the copper industry to define their labor conflicts in nationalist terms and to enlist state backing for their unions and limited support during labor conflicts. During the years leading up to 1970, miners' strikes and nationalist understanding of citizenship had radical meaning in the context of Chile's struggles to exert control over the copper industry. Following the nationalization of the copper industry in 1971, however, militant nationalism no longer held the same meaning in miners' conflicts with the state-run company, and a sense that the state was the guarantor of their rights to high wages and social benefits contradicted the Popular Unity's strategies for implementing a gradual socialist restructuring of the economy.

As the Popular Front governments had depended on copper revenues to underwrite policies designed to promote industrial growth and social reform, the UP relied on copper to help fund its program of socialist restructuring and thus sought to keep costs down, establish labor discipline, and maintain high levels of production. The socialist government depended on copper revenues to combat inflation, stimulate economic growth, and fund redistributionist economic policies and the socialization of key sectors of the economy. Under the UP, as between 1938 and 1948, labor conflicts in the copper mines threatened the process of reform. The El Teniente mining community's sense of rights to economic and social security placed it in an ambiguous position toward the state. Many workers sought to preserve state-enforced guarantees of social and economic benefits that they had won from the North American company in hard-fought strikes since 1938. Changes introduced by the socialist administration, particularly new institutional channels designed to promote worker participation in the management of the mine, appeared to undermine the autonomy and power of miners' unions, their traditional position of antagonism to company authority, systems of job classifications, and miners' rights to such benefits as the family allowance and automatic cost-of-living raises. In addition, the UP's emphasis on increasing production while decreasing costs echoed the managerial strategies of the North American company. Unlike the textile industry described in Winn's *Weavers of Revolution* in which independent unions were established only following the UP election, in the copper mines workers had built autonomous and militant labor organizations since 1938, and these unions had come to play a central role in the political life of the entire mining community. New forms of management and worker participation seemed to threaten and supersede the long-established position of miners' unions. Thus, when miners went on strike to demand an additional cost-of-living raise, their sense of rights—most important, to protections against inflation—won through years of struggle and traditional forms of union militancy clashed with the government's demands for discipline, sacrifice, and a reordering of company-worker relations in the name of socialist change.

Miners' informal styles of opposition to the authority of capital and the state also conflicted with the control demanded by the Left, the national labor movement, and the coalition government. The UP, like the Popular Front and parties of the Left during the 1930s and 1940s, called for moral moderation and labor restraint from workers. On taking power, Salvador Allende, who had been an outspoken supporter of miners' strikes from the 1940s through the 1960s, met with copper union leaders and called for miners to curb their wildcat strikes, lecturing them on the evils of excessive alcohol consumption and absenteeism. The state-run company, like the North American company, developed schemes to increase production, embarked on campaigns of moral and cultural reform, although with the ultimate goal of building a socialist and revolutionary consciousness, and sought to establish new forms of work discipline. As during the Popular Front era, labor leaders and activists from the leftist parties encountered workers in the mine who maintained their own culture of workplace militancy and "disorderly" patterns of sociability that did not conform to the demands of the UP's program. While workers' everyday activities had served as a means to resist the demands and authority of the North American company, they also conflicted with the Left's requirement of social discipline.

The 1973 strike revealed that despite miners' incorporation into the labor relations system, they continued to nurture a grassroots militancy that, as during the Popular Front era, was expressed in antagonism to and suspicion of the state. Many workers who initially participated in the strike, despite their consistent support for the Left, adhered to codes of workplace solidarity, honor, and manhood based on a challenging attitude toward authority that had shaped El Teniente's labor traditions since the 1920s. Miners' rebellious forms of masculine behavior were rooted in a transgressive attitude toward middle-class norms of behavior and contradicted the socialist Left's call for a revolutionary manhood based on discipline, responsibility, and sacrifice. Miners' everyday culture established the basis for an informal combativeness, expressed in "disruptive" forms of sociability, that conflicted with the demands of organized labor and the Left for moral reform and discipline.

Finally, the 1973 El Teniente strike reflects the gendered working-class culture and politics that had developed in the mining camps after 1930. During the conflict, both men and women participated in protests, strikes, marches, and meetings with the president. Christian Democratic workers who opposed the UP and sought to maintain the strike as an act of political sabotage organized women's committees. Their wives marched and petitioned Allende and drew on their moral authority as women to legitimize the strike. Similarly, women from the families of workers who supported the UP, largely from the mine's blue-collar unions, also marched in the streets and met with Allende to demand that he put an end to the strike, invoking their rights as mothers and wives as well. In both cases, the opposition and workers loyal to the Left sought to draw on women's moral authority as wives and mothers, as well as decades-long traditions of women's mobilization in El Teniente, to lend legitimacy to their position. The 1973 strike demonstrated women's centrality in political movements and labor mobilizations in the camps and the close ties between men and women within miners' families. Women organized in support of their husbands, whether they were Christian Democratic empleados or leftist obreros. In both cases, women invoked their rights and the legitimacy of their demands in terms of the gender ideology of domesticity. Women from both camps turned to the state to guarantee the security of their households and families. Regardless of their political orientation, the prominent role played by miners' wives during the strike illustrates the singular protagonism of women in mobilizations and the gendered structures that shaped political life in the mine.

Working-class men and women's sense of gendered rights also helps to explain the extraordinary militancy of the El Teniente community during protests against the military regime of Augusto Pinochet in the early 1980s.[10] The Pinochet regime dismantled the state social welfare apparatuses and the system of labor relations that had been established after 1938. In addition, by unleashing a wave of terror against working-class organizations, unions, and the Left, the military regime sought to eradicate the political arrangements that had shaped workers' integration into the national political system and ties to the Left after 1930. The regime's harsh, neoliberal economic policies also removed many of the social and economic guarantees that the miners had won during the 1940s. As unemployment grew, wages dropped, and union activity continued to meet with state repression, the stability of the working-class nuclear family in the mining community was eroded. Male workers could no longer count on a well-paying job, benefits, and guaranteed jobs in the mine for their children. Women began to enter the informal and the formal labor markets to help their families get by. A community created by the movements of North American capital after World War I was now disrupted by the restructuring of the international economic order and the readjustment of Chile's insertion into the world economy.

As copper miners and their families came together during three years of civil unrest and protest, they invoked rights that had become naturalized since the 1930s: for men, the right to a steady job, a decent wage, and such basic benefits as health care and social security that would allow them to maintain their families with a single wage; for women, the security of their families from the violence of employers and the state and economic and social protection for themselves and their children. The undermining of the economic pillars of the male-headed nuclear family moved both men and women in El Teniente to demand an end to the repression of organized labor and radical free-market economics in mobilizations that encompassed the entire mining community. Miners and their family members invoked the sense of rights to social and economic guarantees from the state developed during the 1930s and 1940s and drew on traditions of militant community and workplace-based labor activism that dated to the era of the Popular Front in protests in their neighborhoods, the union hall, and the mine. Through their mobilizations, men and women from El Teniente sought to rebuild a community decimated by the depredations of the market economy and to galvanize a national campaign for democracy, human rights, and social justice.

NOTES

Throughout the text all translations are my own.

Introduction

1 Manuel Barrera, "El conflicto obrero en el enclave cuprífero," paper presented at the Seminario Movimientos Laborales en América Latina, Mexico City, 1972; Francisco Zapata, "Enclaves y sistemas de relaciones industriales en América Latina," *Revista Mexicana de Sociología* 39 (April–June 1977); Francisco Zapata, "Los mineros de Chuquicamata: ¿Productores o proletarios?" (Mexico: Centro de Estudios Sociológicos, Colegio de México, 1975); Francisco Zapata, "The Chilean Labor Movement and the Problems of the Transition to Socialism," *Latin American Perspectives* 3 (Winter 1976).

2 Zapata, "Enclaves y sistemas de relaciones industriales"; Barrera, "El conflicto obrero en el enclave cuprífero"; Clark Kerr and Alan Siegel, "Interindustry Propensity to Strike," in *Collective Bargaining,* ed. Allan Flanders (New York: Penguin, 1969), pp. 141–143. Two classic expressions of the enclave literature applied to Chile are James Petras and Maurice Zeitlin, *El radicalismo político de la clase trabajadora chilena* (Buenos Aires, 1969), and Charles Bergquist, *Labor in Latin America: Comparative Essays on Chile, Argentina, Venezuela, and Colombia* (Stanford: Stanford University Press, 1986). Examining the results of national presidential and congressional elections in the late 1950s and early 1960s, Petras and Zeitlin found that copper miners provided the strongest and most cohesive base of support for the growing Socialist Party (PS) and the Communist Party (PC). Copper miners' history of strikes and political activity rendered them "the most active revolutionary force in Chilean society" (p. 75). Bergquist asserts that the copper miners uphold the radical traditions of the nitrate miners and, because of their strategic location in the export sector of the economy, have acted as the major force in the Chilean labor movement and the Left. Bergquist's emphasis on the export sector in the nitrate and copper mines draws on the traditional Marxist

labor historiography in Chile, which attributes the birth of labor and the Left to the nitrate miners. See Hernán Ramírez Necochea, *Historia del movimiento obrero en Chile, siglo xix* (Santiago: Ediciones LAR, 1956). This literature has been critiqued by Peter De Shazo in *Urban Workers and Labor Unions in Chile, 1902–1927* (Madison: University of Wisconsin Press, 1984). De Shazo argues that urban workers in Santiago and Valparaíso, organized into largely anarchist-led unions, were the major force of the early labor movement.

3   This is the argument of Sergio Bitar, minister of mining during the 1973 El Teniente strike, and sociologist Crisostomo Pizarro in their study of the strike, *La caída de Allende y la huelga de El Teniente* (Santiago: Ediciones del Ornitorrinco, 1986).

4   Alain Touraine and Daniel Pecaut, "Working-Class Consciousness and Economic Development in Latin America," in *Masses in Latin America,* ed. I. L. Horowitz (New York: Oxford University Press, 1970); Elizabeth Jelín and Juan Carlos Torre, "Los nuevos trabajadores en América Latina: Una reflexión sobre la tesis de la aristocracia obrera," *Desarrollo Económico* 85 (April–June 1982); Zapata, "Los mineros de Chuquicamata."

5   For a history of the concept of "labor aristocracy" and a summary of the debate that surrounds its use by historians of the British working class, see Eric Hobsbawm, "Debating the Labour Aristocracy" and "The Aristocracy of Labour Reconsidered," both in *Workers: Worlds of Labor* (New York: Pantheon, 1984). Hobsbawm argues that in Victorian England a labor aristocracy of skilled workers and artisans, distanced from laborers of the same proletarian class, was identified with a moderate and reformist labor movement. This labor aristocracy was defined both by a shared world of lifestyles, values, and attitudes and by the superior level of their wages. This stratum was highly organized—and thus composed "the nursery" of the Left—to protect its privileges and higher income, often from the encroachment of other workers. Writing about African struggles for independence in *The Wretched of the Earth* (New York: Grove Press, 1963), Frantz Fanon used the notion of a labor aristocracy to argue that the urban working class "is the nucleus of the colonized population which has been most pampered by the colonial regime." The colonial urban working class fails to organize around revolutionary flags because radical transformation threatens its privileged position (pp. 108–109). Fanon's analysis lays the basis for similar views about the Latin American working class.

6   Raymond Williams, *Marxism and Literature* (Oxford: Oxford University Press, 1977), p. 132; Pierre Bourdieu, *Outline of a Theory of Practice* (Cambridge: Cambridge University Press, 1977).

7   Williams, *Marxism and Literature*, p. 132.

8   Williams, *Marxism and Literature;* and Antonio Gramsci, *Selections from the Prison Notebooks* (New York: International Publishers, 1971). See also Ernesto Laclau and Chantal Mouffe, *Hegemony and Socialist Strategy: Towards a Radical Democratic Politics* (New York: Verso, 1985).

9   For a seminal work on gender and working-class history, see Joan Wallach Scott, *Gender and the Politics of History* (New York: Columbia University Press, 1988). For a critique of historians' use of gender-blind class analysis, see Sally Alexander, "Women, Class, and Sexual Difference in the 1830s and 1840s: Some Reflections on the Writing of a Feminist History," *History Workshop Journal* 17 (Autumn 1984). Three collections of essays on gender and working-class history in the United States, Europe, and Latin America have provided important new perspectives on the articulation of class and gender in history: Ava Baron, ed., *Work Engendered: Toward a New History of American Labor* (Ithaca: Cornell University Press, 1991); Laura L. Frader and Sonya O. Rose, eds., *Gender and Class in Modern Europe* (Ithaca: Cornell University Press, 1996); and John D. French and Daniel James, eds., *The Gendered Worlds of Latin American Women Workers: From Household and Factory to the Union Hall and Ballot Box* (Durham: Duke University Press, 1997).

10   Joan Wallach Scott, *Gender and the Politics of History.*

11   See Judith Butler, *Gender Trouble: Feminism and the Subversion of Identity* (New York: Routledge, Chapman, and Hill 1990); Donna Haraway, *Simians, Cyborgs, and Women: The Reinvention of Nature* (New York: Routledge, 1991); and Judith Butler and Joan W. Scott, eds., *Feminists Theorize the Political* (New York: Routledge, 1992).

12   June Nash, *We Eat the Mines and the Mines Eat Us: Dependency and Exploitation in Bolivian Tin Mines* (New York: Columbia University Press, 1979); Michael Taussig, *The Devil and Commodity Fetishism in South America* (Chapel Hill: University of North Carolina Press, 1980).

13   See Karin Rosemblatt's pioneering work on gender and the Popular Front, "Por un hogar bien constituido: El estado y los frentes populares," in *Disciplina y desacato: Construcción de identidad en Chile, siglos xix y xx,* ed. Lorena Godoy, Elizabeth Hutchison, Karin Rosemblatt, and M. Soledad Zárate (Santiago: SUR/CEDEM, 1995).

14   See Ernesto Laclau, *Politics and Ideology in Marxist Theory* (New York: Verso, 1977).

15   See Gramsci, *Selections from the Prison Notebooks,* pp. 323–327; Stuart Hall, "Gramsci's Relevance for the Study of Race and Ethnicity," *Journal of Communications Inquiry* 10 (1986); Williams, *Marxism and Literature.*

16   See, for example, Ranajit Guha, "The Prose of Counter-Insurgency," in *Selected Subaltern Studies,* ed. Ranajit Guha and Gayatri Chakravorty Spivak (New York: Oxford University Press, 1988).

17   For a discussion of this point, see Dipesh Chakrabarty, "Conditions for Knowledge of Working-Class Conditions: Employers, Government, and the Jute Workers of Calcutta, 1890–1940," in Guha and Spivak, *Selected Subaltern Studies.*

18   For discussions of the use of oral history, see Daniel James, "Tales Told Out on the Borderlands: Doña María's Story, Oral History, and Issues of Gender," paper presented at the Annual Meeting of the American Historical Association, New York, December 1990; Jeffrey L. Gould, *To Lead as Equals: Rural Protest and Political Consciousness in Chinandega, Nicaragua, 1912–1979* (Chapel Hill: University of North Carolina Press, 1990); Deborah Levenson-Estrada, *Trade Unionists against Terror: Guatemala City, 1954–1985* (Chapel Hill: University of North Carolina Press, 1994); Alessandro Portelli, *The Death of Luigi Trastulli and Other Stories: Form and Meaning in Oral History* (Albany: State University of New York, 1991); and Paul Thompson, *The Voice of the Past: Oral History* (Oxford: Oxford University Press, 1978).

1   *The Formation of a Modern Mining Enterprise: Capital, Labor Migration, and Early Forms of Worker Resistance*

1   Personnel Records, Mineral El Teniente, CODELCO-Chile.

2   Congreso Nacional de Chile, Senado, Oficina de Informaciones, "Antecedentes económicos y estadísticos relacionados con la gran minería del cobre," *Boletín de Información Económica* no. 157, 1969.

3   C. F. B. Head, *Rough Notes Taken during Some Rapid Journeys across the Pampas and among the Andes* (London, 1826), quoted in Gabriel Salazar, *Labradores, peones, y proletarios: Formación y crisis de la sociedad popular chilena del siglo xix* (Santiago: Ediciones SUR, 1985), p. 198.

4   Charles Darwin, *Journal of Researches into the Natural History and Geology of the Countries Visited during the Voyage of H.M.S. "Beagle" under the Command of Capt. Fitz Roy, R.N.* (New York: Heritage Press, 1957), p. 235.

5   Salazar, *Labradores, peones, y proletarios,* p. 199.

6   Darwin, *Journal of Researches,* p. 311.

7   Ibid., p. 235.

8   Markos Mamalakis and Clark Reynolds, *Essays on the Chilean Economy* (Homewood, Ill.: Richard D. Irwin, 1965), p. 213; Theodore H. Moran, *Multinational Corporations and the Politics of Dependence: Copper in Chile* (Princeton: Princeton University Press, 1974), p. 20.

9 CODELCO-Chile, *El cobre chileno* (Santiago: CODELCO, 1975), p. 27.

10 Salazar, *Labradores, peones, y proletarios*, p. 214.

11 Quoted in ibid., p. 215.

12 The early history of the El Teniente mine is recorded in a number of official histories located in the archives of the Braden Copper Company (henceforth referred to as ABCC): "Braden Copper Company: El Mineral de El Teniente" (1930); "History of the Development of the Braden Copper Company" (1938); and "The Formation of Braden Copper Company and Its Importance for the National Economy since Its Commencement of Operations: Historical Data" (1959). Also useful is Spruille Braden, *Diplomats and Demagogues: The Memoirs of Spruille Braden* (New York: Arlington House, 1971), p. 13. Luis Hiriart, *Braden: Historia de una mina* (Santiago: Editorial Andes, 1964), provides a helpful official company history of the mine's early years. A recent history of El Teniente written for the company also provides valuable background. See María Celia Baros Mansilla, *El Teniente: Los hombres del mineral, 1905–1945* (Rancagua: CODELCO-Chile, Mineral El Teniente, 1995).

13 Moran, *Multinational Corporations*, p. 20–23.

14 Ibid., pp. 28–46.

15 Norman Girvan, *Copper in Chile: A Study in Conflict between Corporate and National Economy* (Kingston: Institute of Social and Economic Research, University of the West Indies, 1972), p. 2; Mamalakis and Reynolds, *Essays on the Chilean Economy*, p. 214.

16 William W. Culver and Cornel J. Reinhart, "Capitalist Dream: Chile's Response to Nineteenth-Century World Copper Competition," in *Constructing Culture and Power in Latin America*, ed. Daniel H. Levine (Ann Arbor: University of Michigan Press, 1993), p. 46.

17 Braden, *Diplomats and Demagogues*.

18 Al Gedicks, *Kennecott Copper Corporation and Mining Development in Wisconsin* (Madison: Community Action on Latin America, 1973), p. 9; Girvan, *Copper in Chile*, p. 46. See also Harvey O'Connor, *The Guggenheims: The Making of an American Dynasty* (New York: Covici, 1937), pp. 346–378.

19 Brian Loveman, *Chile: The Legacy of Hispanic Capitalism* (New York: Oxford University Press, 1979), p. 238.

20 Gedicks, *Kennecott Copper Corporation*, p. 12.

21 Girvan, *Copper in Chile*, p. 49.

22 Pope Yeatman, "Report on <u>Braden Copper Company</u>," 1 September 1911, Kennecott Copper Company Reference Center (henceforth referred to as KRC).

23 Much of the following discussion is taken from a 1932 United States consu-

late report, "The Copper Industry in Chile." U.S. Department of State, General Records, RG 59, 825.6352/23, National Archives. See also Braden Copper Company, "Mineral El Teniente: Preguntas y Respuestas," undated pamphlet, ABCC, for a good description of the system of production in the mine.

24 Ibid.

25 See annual reports of the Braden Copper Company for the years 1915–1924, KRC.

26 Arthur Barrete Parsons, *The Porphyry Coppers* (New York: Rocky Mountain Fund Series, 1933), p. 159.

27 U.S. consulate report, 1932, U.S. Department of State, General Records, RG 59, 825.6352/23.

28 Ibid.

29 Parsons, *Porphyry Coppers*, p. 160.

30 Mamalakis and Reynolds, *Essays on the Chilean Economy*, p. 226.

31 Moran, *Multinational Corporations*, p. 22.

32 Mamalakis and Reynolds, *Essays on the Chilean Economy*, p. 218.

33 See Arnold Bauer, *Chilean Rural Society from the Spanish Conquest to 1930* (Cambridge: Cambridge University Press, 1975); Loveman, *Chile;* and Salazar, *Labradores, peones, y proletarios,* for descriptions of the mobile rural workforce in the Chilean countryside.

34 Salazar, *Labradores, peones, y proletarios* p. 44. For histories of the nitrate miners, see Arthur Lawrence Stickell, "Migration and Mining Labor in Northern Chile in the Nitrate Era, 1880–1930" (Ph.D. diss., Indiana University, 1979); Bergquist, *Labor in Latin America;* Ramírez Necochea, *Historia del movimiento obrero en Chile;* Elías Lafertte, *Vida de un comunista* (Santiago: Empresa Editorial Austral, 1971); Eduardo Devés, *Los que van a morir te saludan* (Santiago: Ediciones Documentas, 1988); and Thomas F. O'Brien, *The Nitrate Industry and Chile's Crucial Transition, 1870–1891* (New York: New York University Press, 1982).

35 Hiriart, *Braden.*

36 Santiago Macchiavello Varas, *El problema de la industria del cobre en Chile y sus proyecciones económicas y sociales* (Santiago: University of Chile, 1923), pp. 180–181.

37 Ibid., p. 204.

38 Letters from C. E. M. Michaels, Braden Copper Company, to Intendente, 25 June 1912, 8 July 1912, 18 July 1912, 21 July 1912, Documentación Relativa a la Braden Copper Company, Intendencia de O'Higgins, Archivo Nacional de Chile (henceforth referred to as ANC).

39 "Accidentes del Trabajo Minas del Teniente," Documentación Relativa a la Braden Copper Company, Intendencia de O'Higgins, ANC.

40   Macchiavello Varas, *El problema de la industria del cobre en Chile,* p. 190.

41   Ibid., p. 195.

42   José Pezoa Varas, *En el feudo: Impresiones sobre la vida obrera del mineral del Teniente* (Rancagua: Imprenta de "La Semana," 1919), pp. 80–85.

43   Ibid., p. 85; *La Igualdad,* 14 July 1912.

44   Personnel Records, Mineral El Teniente, CODELCO-Chile.

45   Ibid.

46   Documentación Relativa a la Braden Copper Company, Intendencia de O'Higgins, ANC.

47   Assistant Manager to C. M. Lewyn, acting superintendent, 20 November 1912, ABCC.

48   Annual Report, 1922, Welfare Department, ABCC.

49   Of sixty-six workers who married in El Teniente in 1922, eleven came from urban areas and ports. As in 1917, the bulk of these miners came from Chile's central valleys and, specifically, from rural towns around Rancagua. Only five of the fifty-five who were born in the countryside came from southern rural towns or regions—from Parral, Talca, and Chillán to Chiloé. Of the eleven with urban origins, most came from Santiago and Valparaíso. None came from the *norte grande.* One came from the northern port of Coquimbo. Until the 1930s, the composition of the El Teniente workforce changed little. In 1930, for example, of seventy-eight workers who married, only six had urban origins. Eleven had been born in the mining camps (a new development), and sixty-one came from rural areas. Again, almost all these workers came from towns around Rancagua and El Teniente. The six workers with nonrural roots came from the northern port of Iquique, the southern port of Valdivia, the central port of Valparaíso, and the coal mining towns of Lota and Concepción. Registro de Matrimonios, El Teniente, Rancagua, Registro Civil, Machalí (henceforth referred to as RCM).

50   Yeatman, "Report on <u>Braden Copper Company,</u>" and Annual Report, November 1915, Braden Copper Company, KRC.

51   Annual Report, 1922, Welfare Department.

52   This case was brought to my attention by Verónica Valdivia. Details of the event appear in the Partido Demócrata's publication in Coronel, *El Pueblo,* 8 February 1920.

53   Robert Haldeman, interview by author, Santiago, 1991.

54   Ibid.

55   *La historia del Sindicato Industrial Sewell y Mina, 1906–1925,* prepared by the directorate of the Sindicato Industrial Sewell y Mina, investigator Walter Pineda (Rancagua: Sindicato Industrial Sewell y Mina, 1989), p. 26.

56   Manuel Tapia, interview by author, Rancagua, March 1992.

57   Mine Superintendent to Julio Maldonado, Sewell district court judge, 22 August 1915, ABCC.

58   Personnel Records, Mineral El Teniente, CODELCO-Chile.

59   Mine Superintendent to Maldonado.

60   Ministerio de Industria i Obras Públicas, "Informe," 1912, copy in author's possession. I thank María Celia Baros Mansilla for bringing this report to my attention.

61   Harold Thomas, chief clerk, to W. Broadbridge, mill superintendent, 11 December 1913, ABCC.

62   Alejandro Fuenzalida Grandon, *El trabajo i la vida en el mineral "El Teniente"* (Santiago: Imprenta Barcelona, 1919), p. 46.

63   Ibid., p. 96.

64   Annual Report, 1922, Welfare Department.

65   H. Mackenzie Walker to L. E. Grant, 2 May 1923, ABCC.

66   Quoted in Fuenzalida Grandon, *El trabajo i la vida en el mineral "El Teniente,"* p. 96.

67   Annual Report, 1922, Welfare Department.

68   Mine Superintendent to Maldonado.

69   Ibid.

70   Letter from H. Mackenzie Walker to G. L. Helmrich, 10 March 1924, ABCC.

71   Personnel Records, Mineral El Teniente, CODELCO-Chile.

72   Macchiavello Varas, *El problema de la industria del cobre en Chile,* p. 202.

73   B. M. Paley to W. Broadbridge, mill superintendent, 11 December 1913, ABCC.

74   B. E. Casey to Frank Langford, general manager, 23 January 1911, ABCC.

75   S. Severin Sorensen to S. B. Williamson, 22 May 1917, ABCC.

76   Ibid.

77   Fragment of Annual Report, 1924, Braden Copper Company, ABCC.

78   Letter from L. E. Grant, general manager, to S. S. Sorensen, vice president, Braden Copper Company, 27 March 1924, ABCC.

79   General Manager's Annual Report—1925, draft, Braden Copper Company, ABCC.

80   Annual Report, 1922, Braden Copper Company, ABCC.

81   Elizabeth Q. Hutchison, "Working Women of Santiago: Gender and Social Transformation in Urban Chile, 1887–1927" (Ph.D. diss., University of California, Berkeley, 1995), p. 9. See also Alejandra Brito, "Del rancho al conventillo: Transformaciones en la identidad popular feminina, Santiago de Chile, 1850–1920," in *Disciplina y desacato,* ed. Godoy, Hutchison, Rosemblatt, and Zárate; and Gabriel Salazar, "La mujer de 'bajo pueblo' en Chile:

Bosquejo histórico," *Proposiciones* 21 (December 1992), and Salazar, *Labradores, peones, y proletarios.*

82 Hutchison, "Working Women of Santiago," p. 12. See also Brito, "Del rancho al conventillo," p. 31; and Salazar, *Labradores, peones, y proletarios,* pp. 256–257.

83 Brito, "Del rancho al conventillo," pp. 57–59.

84 Salazar, *Labradores, peones, y proletarios,* p. 195.

85 Ibid., p. 206.

86 *La Voz del Obrero,* 1 August 1916.

87 Pezoa Varas, *En el feudo,* pp. 29–30.

88 Baltazar Castro, *Un hombre por el camino* (Santiago: Editorial Cultura, 1950), p. 174.

89 H. Mackenzie Walker to W. J. Turner, general manager, 10 May 1940, ABCC.

90 *Teniente Topics,* July 1915.

91 Personnel Records, Mineral El Teniente, CODELCO-Chile.

92 "Men Dismissed during May 1922," Superintendent's Office Report, Mine; Mine dismissal reports, 1921–1922, ABCC.

93 Personnel Records, Mineral El Teniente, CODELCO-Chile.

94 Thomas F. O'Brien, *The Revolutionary Mission: American Enterprise in Latin America, 1900–1945* (Cambridge: Cambridge University Press, 1996), pp. 166–178. See also Bergquist, *Labor in Latin America;* Lafertte, *Vida de un comunista;* and Devés, *Los que van a morir.*

95 See O'Brien, *Revolutionary Mission,* p. 180.

96 Ibid.; Baltazar Castro, *Sewell* (Santiago: Editorial Zig-Zag, 1966).

97 "Un Testimonio Sacerdotal de Actualidad Don Oscar Larson, Cura de Machalí," in Fidel Araneda Bravo, "Oscar Larson, el Clero y la Política Chilena" (1981); copy in author's possession.

2 *Labor Strife, Social Welfare, and the Regulation of Working-Class Sexuality*

1 Frank Langford to Intendencia de O'Higgins, 18 February 1911, Documentación Relativa a la Braden Copper Company, Intendencia de O'Higgins, ANC.

2 Ibid.

3 Gerente General, Braden Copper Company, to S. S. Sorensen, 4 January 1916, Documentación Relativa a la Braden Copper Company, Intendencia de O'Higgins, ANC.

4 *Homenaje al 1 de Mayo* (Rancagua), 1 May 1917.

5 For accounts of these strikes see Documentación Relativa a la Braden Cop-

per Company, Intendencia de O'Higgins, ANC. Of particular interest are "Informe de Ramón Sazo, 26 November 1919, to Intendente de O'Higgins"; "Primera Asamblea de Delegados del Consejo Federal de los Operarios de El Teniente," 3 December 1919; "Circular de M. Annabalón, Coronel y Jefe de las Fuerzas," 26 November 1919; "Circular del Gerente General, S. Severin Sorensen," 26 November 1919 and 27 November 1919; "Peticiones de Consejo Federal no. 2 de Rancagua de la Federación Obrera de Chile"; reports by H. W. Jones, 30 October 1919, and L. E. Grant and H. R. Graham, 31 October 1919; "Acta," 9 November 1919; S. Severin Sorensen to Intendente, 28 November 1919. Accounts can also be found in similar documents in the archive of the Sindicato Industrial Sewell y Mina (henceforth referred to as ASISM) and in *La Provincia.*

6   "Strike at Company's Plant," General Manager to William C. Potter, president, Braden Copper Company, 6 November 1919, ASISM.

7   Stella Joanne Seibert Alphand, "La legislación del trabajo y previsión social en El Teniente" (thesis, University of Chile, 1936), p. 35.

8   See Reglamentos Internos, Braden Copper Company, ABCC.

9   See *La Semana,* 20 December 1920; Report of L. E. Grant, 13 December 1920, Documentación Relativa a la Braden Copper Company, Intendencia de O'Higgins, ANC.

10   L. E. Grant, general manager, Braden Copper Company, to Burr Wheeler, general manager, Chile Exploration Company, 11 August 1925, ABCC. See also similar letters from W. L. Joyce, welfare superintendent of the Andes Copper Mining Company, Potrerillos, to W. J. Turner, assistant general manager, Braden Copper Company, 4 February 1929, and Burr Wheeler to W. J. Turner, 24 November 1936, ABCC.

11   Personnel Records, Mineral El Teniente, CODELCO-Chile.

12   Lautaro Silva, "Yo Conozco la Braden Copper," *El Siglo,* 24 November 1936.

13   Copies of these reports on union meetings are located in the ABCC.

14   *La Tribuna,* 10 November 1938.

15   Mr. Sorensen to the Consejo de Operarios del Mineral El Teniente, 22 June 1920, ABCC.

16   In 1922, 50 percent of the serenos were former carabineros, and practically all had done military service. The company also paid carabineros to do patrols in the camps night and day (Annual Report, 1922, Welfare Department).

17   *Despertar Minero,* 6 April 1939. Personnel records of the Braden Copper Company also reveal that carabineros, after detaining workers for drinking, fighting, vagrancy, or smuggling union pamphlets into the camp, sent reports to the company that went into each worker's file. In 1944, for example, Sabino Abarca and some friends were arrested for consumption and

possession of *aguardiente* (hard liquor). These workers were fined and, after a report to the Welfare Department from carabineros, suspended for fifteen days (Personnel Records, Mineral El Teniente, CODELCO-Chile).

18 Copies of these criminal records and police files are located in Personnel Records, Mineral El Teniente, CODELCO-Chile.

19 See, for example, Juzgado de Letras de Menor Cuantía, Sewell, Causa no. 6115, 14 January 1941, in the Conservador de Bienes y Raíces, Rancagua (henceforth referred to as CBRR).

20 *La Igualdad,* 14 July 1912.

21 Pezoa Varas, *En el feudo,* pp. 78–79.

22 Quoted in Moran, *Multinational Corporations,* p. 24.

23 Alfred Houston to L. E. Grant, 25 July 1922, and L. E. Grant to Alfred Houston, 27 July 1922, ABCC.

24 After 1917, a number of North American and European industrial employers and mining companies began to construct social welfare systems and establish paternalist policies as part of a general strategy aimed at reforming workers' culture, building labor stability, and enforcing work discipline. This was as true in the coalfields of West Virginia and coal mines of Yorkshire as on the Northern Rhodesian copperbelt. See David Corbin, *Life, Work, and Rebellion in the Coal Fields: Southern West Virginia Miners, 1880–1922* (Urbana: University of Illinois Press, 1981); Jane Parpart, *Labor and Capital on the African Copperbelt* (Philadelphia: Temple University Press, 1983); Norman Dennis, Fernando Henriques, and Clifford Slaughter, *Coal Is Our Life: An Analysis of a Yorkshire Mining Community* (London: Tavistock Publishers, 1969). In Great Britain, the government implemented the Mining Industry Act of 1920, which set up a Miners' Welfare Fund and Miners' Welfare Committee. The fund and committee were designed for "the social well-being and recreation of miners" and established recreational clubs, billiards halls, boys clubs, boxing clubs, dances, plays, concerts, and theaters.

25 Annual Report, 1922, Welfare Department.

26 Walker to Grant, 2 May 1923; L. E. Grant to S. S. Sorensen, vice President, 24 May 1923, ABCC.

27 Personnel Records, Mineral El Teniente, CODELCO-Chile.

28 *El Teniente,* 1922–1944.

29 Guillermo Drago and Pedro Villagra, *Historia general del mineral El Teniente, 1823–1988* (Rancagua, 1989), p. 36.

30 Annual Report, 1922, Welfare Department.

31 Undated report located in ABCC.

32 Annual Report, 1924, Braden Copper Company.

33 See Annual Reports, 1923–1927, Braden Copper Company.

34   See *El Teniente*, 3 October 1922, for a description of these institutions. The Welfare Department provided a list of the social institutions in El Teniente in 1922, which included Club Social Mina, Club Social Sewell, Club Social Obrero El Teniente, Centro Social Recreativo Molino, Centro Recreativo y Instrucción El Bienestar, Círculo Atlético y Filarmónico A. Lincoln, Centro Sportivo y Filarmónico Aurora de los Andes, Centro Social Cordillera, Centro Instructivo y Recreativo La Democracia, Sociedad la Unión de Gasfitters, Sociedad de Socorros Mutuos Unión y Fraternidad, Asociación Deportiva de Sewell, Unión Cordillera Football Club, the Great Turner Football Club, Molino Boxing Club, Escuela y Biblioteca de Teniente C, Unión Deportiva Teniente C, Academia de Extensión Cultural, Centro Pro-Educación y Asistencia Social Sewell, the Sewell Athletic Club, the Braden Masonic Society, Club Caletones, Centro Social Caletones, Unión Caletones Football Club, Sport Turner Boxing Club, Centro Obrero Barahona, Unión Barahona Football Club, Centro Social Coya, and Social Coya Football Club. See also Annual Report, 1922, Welfare Department.

35   See Welfare Department reports on meetings with workers' representatives, 19 September 1922 and 31 May 1922, ABCC. See also reports in *El Teniente*, 1922–1927.

36   *El Teniente*, 13 November 1922.

37   Annual Report, 1924, Braden Copper Company.

38   For a fascinating discussion of the development of the companionate marriage in early-twentieth-century Brazil, see Susan K. Besse, *Restructuring Patriarchy: The Modernization of Gender Inequality in Brazil, 1914–1940* (Chapel Hill: University of North Carolina Press, 1996).

39   Fuenzalida Grandon, *El trabajo i la vida en el mineral "El Teniente,"* p. 101.

40   Ibid.

41   Ibid., p. 95.

42   *La Prensa*, 13 March 1912.

43   Fuenzalida Grandon, *El trabajo i la vida en el mineral "El Teniente,"* p. 95.

44   *Teniente Topics*, August 1916.

45   Ibid., June 1916.

46   Ibid., August 1917.

47   Filoberto Figueroa, interview by author, Rancagua, February 1992.

48   Braden Copper Company to Hernán Cousiño Tocornal, January 1946, ABCC.

49   Figueroa, interview.

50   *Despertar Minero*, 6 April 1939.

51   Javier Donoso, interview by author, Rancagua, July 1993.

52   Braden Copper Company to Hernán Cousiño Tocornal.

53   *El Teniente*, 11 October 1922.

54   *Tópicos del Teniente,* 15 March 1920.

55   Ibid., 1 May 1920.

56   *El Teniente,* 7 August 1941.

57   See, for example, "Concurso de Condiciones Higénicas," *Tópicos del Teniente,* July 1919.

58   Ibid.

59   Ibid., 15 March 1920.

60   Ibid., 1 May 1920.

61   Ibid., 15 March 1920.

62   Ibid., March 1920.

63   Ibid., 15 April 1920.

64   Ibid., 1 May 1920.

65   Ibid., March 1920.

66   Ibid., 1 May 1920.

67   *El Teniente,* 10 September 1941.

68   *Tópicos del Teniente,* April 1920.

69   *El Teniente,* 31 October 1922.

70   Undated report, ABCC.

71   *Tópicos del Teniente,* 1 June 1920.

72   Ibid., 1 June 1920, 14 October 1923.

73   *El Teniente,* 9 October 1922.

74   Seibert Alphand, *"La legislación del trabajo,"* p. 46.

75   Nélida Carrasco, interview by author, Rancagua, August 1996.

76   Rosa Silva, interview by author, Rancagua, August 1996.

77   *Tópicos del Teniente,* March 1920.

78   Ibid.

79   Ibid.; *Teniente Topics,* January 1917.

80   *Tópicos del Teniente,* January 1917.

81   *El Teniente,* 14 November 1922.

82   Ibid.

83   Ibid., 7 January 1923.

84   Ibid.

85   See, for example, "Dos Grandes Fechas Históricas: Batallas de Independencia," *Tópicos del Teniente,* 1 April 1920; "Héroes de Iquique, 1879," *Tópicos del Teniente,* 15 May 1920; "Batallas Históricas: La Batalla de Rancagua, 1 y 2 de Octubre, 1814," *Teniente Topics,* 15 October 1915; and "Anécdotas de Manuel Rodríguez," *Teniente Topics,* August 1917.

86   See *Teniente Topics,* June 1916, October 1916, November 1916, and January 1917; and *Tópicos del Teniente,* 1 October 1920.

87   *Tópicos del Teniente,* March 1920.

88 Ibid.

89 Ibid.

90 Ibid., 1 October 1920.

91 *El Teniente,* 27 October 1922.

92 *Tópicos del Teniente,* 1 December 1920.

93 Virgilio Figueroa, *Diccionario histórico, biográfico, y bibliográfico de Chile* (Santiago: Balcello, 1928), pp. 263–267.

94 L. E. Grant to Carlos Briones Luco, 6 December 1921, ABCC.

95 Alfred Houston to L. E. Grant, 12 January 1922, ABCC.

96 "La ley seca en los centros industriales: Sus ventajes vistas en la práctica en el mineral de El Teniente," ABCC; and "El Departamento de Bienestar," ABCC.

97 *El Teniente,* 17 October 1922.

98 *El Teniente,* 12 October 1922.

99 *El Teniente,* 14 November 1922.

100 Macchiavello Varas, *El problema de la industria del cobre en Chile,* p. 174.

101 Ibid.

102 Ibid., p. 202.

103 Seventh Annual Report of the Braden Copper Company, 1921, KRC.

104 *La Semana,* 13 February 1921, 18 February 1921.

105 Ibid., 8 November 1921.

106 Tapia, interview.

107 Annual Report, 1924, Braden Copper Company.

108 See the account of this incident in "Historia de los trabajadores del cobre, 1910–1930," *Informe del Cobre,* July 1982.

109 *La Semana,* 8 November 1924, 6 December 1924.

110 For a brief overview of this period, see Crisostomo Pizarro, *La huelga obrera en Chile* (Santiago: Ediciones SUR, 1986), and Paul Drake, *Socialism and Populism in Chile, 1932–1952* (Urbana: University of Illinois Press, 1978).

111 "Mr. Braden's Interview with Pres. Ibáñez, Nov. 29, 1927," internal document, Braden Copper Company, and Ministerio de Hacienda, Superintendencia de Salitres y Minas, "Ideas Cambiadas Entre S.E. el presidente Sr. Ibáñez, el Ministro de Hacienda, y el Señor Braden, el 29 de Noviembre de 1927," both in ABCC. See also Braden, *Diplomats and Demagogues,* pp. 50–51, for an account of this meeting.

112 Consulate Report, U.S. Department of State, General Records, RG 59, 825.6352/23.

113 *El Imparcial,* 17 July 1930.

3   *Community, Politics, and the Invention of a Labor Tradition*

1   Simon Collier and William F. Sater, *A History of Chile, 1808–1994* (Cambridge: Cambridge University Press, 1996), pp. 218–221.

2   "Braden Copper Company: El Mineral de El Teniente," 1930, ABCC.

3   Juzgado de Letras de Menor Cuantía, Sewell, Causa no. 2189, CBRR.

4   Ibid., Causa no. 2200, CBRR.

5   Registro de Matrimonios, El Teniente, Rancagua, 1917, RCM.

6   Ibid., 1922, RCM.

7   Ibid., 1935, RCM.

8   Memorandum to General Manager, 4 December 1935, Welfare Department, ABCC.

9   *Teniente Topics,* July 1915; Censuses, December 1937 and September 1952, Braden Copper Company, ABCC.

10 Eric Hobsbawm and Terence Ranger, eds., *The Invention of Tradition* (Cambridge: Cambridge University Press, 1983); James, "Tales Told Out on the Borderlands," p. 23.

11 Ninth Annual Report, 1923, Braden Copper Company, ABCC.

12 General Manager's Annual Report–1927, Braden Copper Company, ABCC.

13 Haldeman, interview. In 1936, El Teniente's "yellow" union paper echoed the North American supervisor's racially condescending perception that mine workers came from the most "backward" sectors of the population, "nitrate workers, miners, and campesinos" (*El Minero,* Segunda Quincena de Agosto, 1936.

14 Former Braden Copper Company employee, interview by author, Rancagua, August 1996.

15 Rosa Silva, interview.

16 Luis Herrera, interview by author, Rancagua, April 1991.

17 Tapia, interview.

18 Ibid.

19 For a description of Baltazar Castro's life and activities, see his autobiographical work *¿Me permite una interrupción?* (Santiago: Editorial Zig-Zag, 1962).

20 Baltazar Castro, *Mi camarada padre* (Santiago: Editorial Nacimiento, 1985), p. 18.

21 Ibid., p. 73.

22 Ibid., p. 161.

23 Gonzalo Drago, *Cobre: Cuentos mineros* (Santiago: Impresa el Esfuerzo, 1941), p. 128.

24 Ibid., p. 163.

25 Brian Loveman, *Struggle in the Countryside: Politics and Rural Labor in Chile, 1919–1973* (Bloomington: Indiana University Press, 1976), p. 145.

26 Domingo Quintero, interview by author, Rancagua, November 1991.

27 Herrera, interview.

28 Drake, *Socialism and Populism in Chile,* p. 166.

29 Congreso Nacional de Chile, Informe de las Comisiones de Hacienda y Minería, Sesiones de la Cámara de Diputados, 1965, Historia de la Ley 16.425, Chileanización del Cobre. The nitrate economy in Chile began to go into decline during World War I with the beginning of the fabrication of synthetic nitrates. In 1917–1918, between 115 and 124 nitrate oficinas were in operation, producing 2,977.1 tons of nitrate and exporting 2,913.0, whereas in 1921–1922, only between 31 and 45 oficinas produced 890.0 tons. The 1930 recession provided the final blow, and despite a small recovery after 1936, in 1938–1939, 17 oficinas produced 1,427.5 tons of nitrate. From a labor force of 56,378 employed in the nitrate oficinas in 1917–1918, only 21,062 workers labored in nitrates in 1938–1939. Meanwhile, the production of copper increased from 71,288,540 kilograms in 1916 to 413,283,275 kilograms in 1937 and to 351,482,483 in 1938 (Anuario Estadístico de Chile, Minería e Industria, 1938–1948, Dirección General de Estadísticas, Instituto Nacional de Estadísticas, Chile). By 1941, copper exports were worth $1.523.349.628 pesos, and nitrate exports were worth $512.642.224 pesos (Anuario Estadístico, Minería, 1940–1941, Dirección General de Estadísticas).

30 For an excellent analysis of the labor code, see Alan Angell, *Politics and the Labour Movement in Chile* (London: Oxford University Press, 1972). See also Pizarro, *La huelga obrera en Chile,* and Jorge Barría, *El movimiento obrero en Chile* (Santiago: Universidad Técnica del Estado, 1971).

31 See Angell, *Politics and the Labour Movement in Chile,* p. 95, and Julio César Jobet, *Historia del Partido Socialista de Chile* (Santiago: Ediciones Documentas, 1987).

32 See Drake, *Socialism and Populism in Chile,* p. 173; Loveman, *Chile,* p. 270; Adolfo Aldunate, Angel Flisfisch, and Tomás Moulian, *Estudios sobre el sistema de partidos en Chile* (Santiago: Facultad Latinoamericana de Ciencias Sociales [FLACSO], 1985), p. 47.

33 Traditional labor histories of Chile devote little space to the CTCH and its formation. The best account can be found in Pizarro, *La huelga obrera en Chile,* pp. 111–123. See also Angell, *Politics and the Labour Movement in Chile,* pp. 106–120.

34 Gabriel González Videla, *Memorias* (Santiago: Editora Nacional Gabriela Mistral, 1975), p. 165.

35 Drake, *Socialism and Populism in Chile,* p. 176. See also Jobet, *Historia del Partido Socialista de Chile.*

36 Loveman, *Chile,* pp. 267–270; Pizarro, *La huelga obrera en Chile,* pp. 101–102.

37 Letter to President, Sindicato Industrial B. C. Co., Caletones, 8 October 1934, ABCC.

38 For accounts of the activities of the O'Higgins Federation, see articles in *La Tribuna,* 1935–1936.

39 Ibid., 31 October 1935.

40 Ibid., 2 November 1935, 5 November 1935.

41 In 1939, for example, a CTCH organizer and Communist Party militant recalled in a speech to the miners' union that before 1938 he had covertly entered the mine's camps by foot to hold union meetings (*Despertar Minero,* 11 May 1939).

42 *La Tribuna,* 4 August 1936.

43 Ibid., 18 August 1936.

44 Ministerio del Trabajo, Inspección General del Trabajo, to Gerente General de la Braden Copper Company, 10 August 1937, ABCC.

45 Ministerio del Trabajo, Oficios no. 36, 8901–9200, 1938, ANC.

46 Juzgado de Letras de Menor Cuantía, Sewell, Causa no. 4700, 22 October 1938, CBRR.

47 *La Tribuna,* 27 October 1938.

48 Chile, Cámara de Diputados, Sesión Ordinaria, Diario de Sesiones, 4 July 1938.

49 J. Ignacio Vergara Ruiz, Tte. Coronel de Carabineros y Prefecto, Prefectura de O'Higgins no. 9, to the Contralor Local de Braden Copper Company, Saul M. Arriola, 1 July 1938, ABCC. See also Contralor Local S. M. Arriola to Prefecto de Carabineros, 28 June 1938, ABCC.

4 *Miners and Citizens: The State, the Popular Front, and Labor Politics*

1 For a description of Aguirre Cerda's visit, see *Despertar Minero,* 14 April 1939.

2 In the 1938 elections, 1,015 Sewell residents voted for Aguirre Cerda and only 481 for former Alessandri minister of finance Gustavo Ross. Nationally, Aguirre Cerda squeaked out a narrow victory with just over 50 percent of the votes, 222,720 to 218,609, a difference of only 4,111 votes. The miners' electoral support for the Popular Front was reaffirmed in the congressional elections of 1941, in which they gave 1,702 votes to the parties of the Popular Front and only 274 votes to the right-wing opposition and the Falange Nacional (Anuario Estadístico de Chile, Dirección General de Estadísticas, 1938, 1941).

3 The seminal work on the Popular Front is Drake, *Socialism and Populism in Chile.*

4 Benedict Anderson, *Imagined Communities* (New York: Verso, 1991).

5 Drake, *Socialism and Populism in Chile,* p. 177.

6 *La Hora,* 18 July 1938.

7 U.S. embassy report, Department of State, General Records, RG 59, 825.00/1085.

8 Drake, *Socialism and Populism in Chile,* pp. 201–213.

9 *La Hora,* 18 July 1938.

10 U.S. embassy report, 23 November 1938, Department of State, General Records, RG 59, 825.00/1097.

11 Popular Front program published in *La Nación,* 18 April 1938.

12 See "Programa del Frente Popular de Chile," in Confederación de Trabajadores de Chile, "Memoria del consejo directivo nacional," 1939, pp. 44–50.

13 *Despertar Minero,* 6 April 1939.

14 Ibid.

15 Ibid.

16 Ibid.

17 Ibid.

18 Ibid., 14 April 1939.

19 Ibid., 23 September 1939.

20 This account of the meeting is found in a "strictly confidential" memorandum sent by Mackenzie Walker to F. E. Turton, Braden's assistant general manager, 7 November 1939, ABCC.

21 Ibid.

22 Ibid.

23 *Despertar Minero,* 16 August 1939.

24 Ibid., 31 August 1939.

25 Ibid., 23 September 1939.

26 Ibid.

27 Ibid.

28 F. E. Turton to E. T. Stannard, 29 July 1940, ABCC.

29 Ibid.

30 *La Hora,* 18 July 1938.

31 *Despertar Minero,* 11 May 1939.

32 Ibid., 5 December 1940.

33 Ibid., 21 November 1940.

34 Ibid., 9 November 1940, and U.S. consulate report, 26 June 1940, U.S. Department of State, General Records, RG 59, 825.6374/1375. See also ibid., 30 April 1941.

35 *Despertar Minero,* 1 August 1941.

36 Ibid.

37 *El Teniente,* 1 May 1939.

38 Ibid., 4 April 1939.

39 Ibid., 5 April 1939.

40 Ibid., 1 May 1939.

41 Ibid.

42 Ibid.

43 See Rosemblatt, "Por un hogar bien constituido."

44 See ibid. For a brilliant discussion of working-class communities, welfare capitalism, and the development of the welfare state in the United States, see Lizabeth Cohen, *Making a New Deal: Industrial Workers in Chicago, 1919–1939* (Cambridge: Cambridge University Press, 1990). For feminist analyses of the family wage and state welfare policies, see Linda Gordon, "Social Insurance and Public Assistance: The Influence of Gender in Welfare Thought in the United States, 1890–1935," *American Historical Review* 97 (February 1992), and Gordon, ed., *Women, the State, and Welfare* (Madison: University of Wisconsin Press, 1990). For an excellent study of gender, class, and the development of the welfare state in Germany, see Kathleen Canning, "Social Policy, Body Politics: Recasting the Social Question in Germany, 1875–1900," in *Gender and Class in Modern Europe,* ed. Frader and Rose.

45 U.S. embassy report, U.S. Department of State, General Records, RG 59, 825.00/1085. Literature on state formation includes Phillip Corrigan and Derek Sayer, *The Great Arch: English State Formation as Cultural Revolution* (Oxford: Basil Blackwell, 1985); Gilbert M. Joseph and Daniel Nugent, eds., *Everyday Forms of State Formation: Revolution and the Negotiation of Rule in Modern Mexico* (Durham: Duke University Press, 1994); Florencia Mallon, *Peasant and Nation: The Making of Postcolonial Mexico and Peru* (Berkeley: University of California Press, 1995); and Rosemblatt, "Por un hogar bien constituido."

46 Rosemblatt, "Por un hogar bien constituido."

47 Ibid.

48 See Confederación de Trabajadores de Chile, "Memoria del Consejo Directivo Nacional," 1939.

49 *Despertar Minero,* 4 September 1941.

50 Ibid.

51 Ibid., 1 August 1941.

52 Ibid., 16 August 1941.

53 Ibid., 1 March 1941.

54 Ibid., 31 May 1939.

55 See *La Hora,* 9 March 1938, for a description of the CTCH campaign against

gambling, and *La Opinión*, 1 March 1938, for a description of the FNM congress.

56 *Despertar Minero*, 16 August 1941.

57 Ibid., 23 October 1941.

58 See, for example, Castro, *Mi camarada padre*.

59 Ibid., p. 43.

60 Ibid., p. 18.

61 Ibid., p. 78.

62 *Despertar Minero*, 25 April 1939.

63 Ibid.

64 Ibid., 4 September 1941.

65 Marguerite Guzmán Bouvard, *Revolutionizing Motherhood: The Mothers of the Plaza de Mayo* (Wilmington, Del.: Scholarly Resources Inc., 1994). For discussions of motherhood and mobilization see also Temma Kaplan, "Female Consciousness and Collective Action: The Case of Barcelona, 1910–1918," *Signs* 7 (Spring 1982) and Maxine Molyneux, "Mobilization without Emancipation: Women's Interest, the State, and Revolution in Nicaragua," *Feminist Studies* 11 (Summer 1985).

66 *Despertar Minero*, 16 August 1941, 4 September 1941.

5 *Conflict and Accommodation at Work: Masculinity and the Labor Process inside the Mine*

1 Michael Burawoy, *Manufacturing Consent: Changes in the Labor Process under Monopoly Capitalism* (Chicago: University of Chicago Press, 1979). Among pioneering works on the importance of the labor process and workplace culture are Harry Braverman, *Labor and Monopoly Capital: The Degradation of Work in the Twentieth Century* (New York: Monthly Review Press, 1974), and David Montgomery, *Workers' Control in America* (Cambridge: Cambridge University Press, 1979).

2 See, for example, Daniel James, *Resistance and Integration: Peronism and the Argentine Working Class, 1946–1976* (Cambridge: Cambridge University Press, 1988), and James P. Brennan, *The Labor Wars in Córdoba, 1955–1976: Ideology, Work, and Labor Politics in an Argentine Industrial City* (Cambridge: Harvard University Press, 1994).

3 *Despertar Minero*, 23 September 1939.

4 *El Siglo*, 7 March 1942.

5 Ibid., 15 March 1942.

6 This description of workers' jobs in El Teniente is drawn from Liliana Muñoz, *Estudio ocupacional de la minería del cobre* (Santiago: Servicio Nacional

del Empleo, 1971); Barrera, "El conflicto obrero en el enclave cuprífero"; the study *Así trabajo yo* (Santiago: Empresa Editora Nacional Quimentu, 1971); and oral histories.

7   Castro, *Mi camarada padre,* p. 268.

8   Ministerio del Trabajo, Inspección General del Trabajo to Gerente General, 10 August 1937.

9   See monthly accident reports for the late 1930s and 1940s, ABCC. In July 1943, for example, the mine alone reported 249 accidents, most of them involving fractures of some kind as a result of falls, falling rocks or planks, or accidents with the cars carrying the copper rock. In January of that same year, there were 288 accidents; in February, 280; in March, 292; in April, 221; in May, 217; and in June, 216, for a total of 1,514 accidents for the first half of the year. That same month of July 1943 registered 24 accidents in the mill, 38 in the smelter, 60 in the mechanical department, 11 in the electricity department, 3 in the railroad department, 2 in the warehouse, and 14 sundry accidents, for a monthly total of 401 accidents. The first seven months of 1943 registered 2,776 accidents in all of El Teniente (Informe Mensual de Accidentes, July 1943, Braden Copper Company, ABCC). Other monthly reports show that these figures were standard throughout the 1930s and 1940s.

10 Fatal accidents were usually caused by falling rocks, explosions when blasting, or falls. In one typical case in January 1939, a number of miners were killed when the dynamite they had placed in twenty-two perforations exploded prematurely. See Welfare Department Safety Division report, 20 January 1939, ABCC.

11 Letter, 16 August 1939, Antecedentes, Oficios, 1801–1980 (1939), no. 13, Ministerio del Trabajo, ANC.

12 For accounts of the accident, see *Despertar Minero, El Rancagüino, El Mercurio,* and *La Batalla* for June and July 1945, and debates in the congress. See also the Sindicato Industrial Sewell y Mina's own history of the accident, *19 de junio de 1945 . . . el humo,* written by Walter Pineda, in ASISM.

13 See Informe Mensual de Accidentes, July 1943.

14 Confidential memorandum from P. A. Seibert to F. E. Turton, 20 May 1935, ABCC.

15 Yearly Report, 1942, Medical Department, Braden Copper Company, ABCC.

16 Inspección General del Trabajo, Tribunal del Trabajo de Rancagua, no. 9014, 18 October 1939, CBRR.

17 In June 1942, for example, an average of 2,946 men were employed in the mine, whereas 821 were employed in the Caletones foundry, 492 in the Coya electrical plant, and 828 in the Rancagua railway, workshops, and warehouses. Another 2,062 men were employed in Sewell in activities of

support for the mine in warehouses or in the mill. In terms of wages, workers in the mine earned an average of $49.88 pesos per shift (U.S. $2.58); workers in Sewell in mine-related activities earned $49.50 pesos per shift (U.S. $2.56); and workers in Caletones earned $46.47 pesos per shift (U.S. $2.41).

Within the Mine Department, underground workers, or the actual miners involved in extracting the ore, were higher paid than were workers above ground. Above the ground, in 1939, peones earned between $21.50 pesos and $24.50 pesos per shift. Carpenters earned $26.50 pesos per shift. *Capataces* (foremen) or cuadrilla leaders earned between $35.00 and $41.00 pesos per shift.

In the mine's warehouses, peones also earned between $21.50 and $24.50 pesos per shift. Wages in the mine's workshops were higher because of the higher levels of skill required. Mechanics earned from $24.50 to $32.00 pesos per shift. Braziers (coppersmiths/boilermakers) earned similar wages.

18   Two former mine workers, Don Luis and Don Rubén, interview by author, Rancagua, January 1992. Quote from Don Rubén. Last names withheld to protect sources' confidentiality.

19   Manuel Troncoso, interview by author, Rancagua, February 1992.

20   Anuario Estadístico de Chile, Minería e Industria, 1938–1946, Dirección General de Estadísticas.

21   A good example of this practice was that of the three jornaleros, Armando Sánchez, Guillermo Dissett, and Carlos Moscoso, who were fired on 24 February 1940 after being surprised by a card checker (*tarjador*) marking the car worked by Sánchez. The checker found a difference of thirty cars that the workers had marked. That same day three other workers were fired for the same reason. All admitted having altered the mark. See A. F. Boyd, Sub-Jefe General de la Mina, Oficina General de la Mina, to J. S. Webb, 24 February 1940, ABCC.

22   For a more complete list of miners' terms, see the glossary of Castro, *Sewell*.

23   Don Rubén, interview.

24   For a description of these practices see Seibert Alphand, "La legislación del trabajo," p. 57.

25   Cited in *La Semana*, 12 November 1921.

26   Quintero, interview.

27   Castro, *Mi camarada padre*, p. 267.

28   Figueroa, interview.

29   Castro, *Sewell*, pp. 11–18.

30   Ibid., p. 25.

31   Ibid., p. 26.

32   Ibid., p. 39.

33   Ibid., p. 89.

34   *Página Abierta,* 12–25 October 1992.

35   Castro, *Un hombre por el camino,* p. 202.

36   Drago, *Cobre,* p. 18.

37   Ibid., p. 82.

38   Castro, *Sewell,* p. 126.

39   Oral sources.

40   Drago, *Cobre,* p. 99.

41   Barrera, "El conflicto obrero en el enclave cuprífero," p. 37.

42   Quintero, interview.

43   Montgomery, *Workers' Control in America,* pp. 13–14.

44   *Despertar Minero,* 6 April 1939.

45   Ibid., 11 May 1939.

46   Tadeo Alvarado, interview by author, Rancagua, April 1991.

47   *Despertar Minero,* 1 January 1943, 21 November 1940.

48   Ibid., 20 June 1939.

49   Ibid., 1 June 1941.

50   Informe de Ramón Sazo, 26 November 1919, Intendencia de O'Higgins, ANC.

51   *Despertar Minero,* 16 August 1939.

52   Ibid., 17 February 1942.

53   Ibid.

54   Ibid., 7 July 1942.

55   See Departamento de Bienestar Social, Oficina del Trabajo, Nómina de Obreros Despedidos Desde el 1 de Marzo al 31 de Mayo de 1940, Braden Copper Company, and other reports on dismissals for the 1940s, ABCC.

56   Mine dismissal reports, 1943. For cases of disobedience, see lists of firings and suspensions, 1922–1946, Braden Copper Company, ABCC.

57   Ibid.; mine dismissal reports, 1943, ABCC.

58   Fuenzalida Grandon, *El trabajo i la vida en el mineral "El Teniente,"* p. 112.

59   Ibid., p. 113.

60   Ibid., p. 114.

61   Castro, *Sewell,* p. 30.

62   Drago, *Cobre,* p. 11.

63   Oral sources.

64   Juzgado de Letras de Menor Cuantía, Sewell, Causa no. 1275, 17 April 1941, CBRR.

65 Mine dismissal reports, 1940, ABCC.

66 Juzgado de Letras de Menor Cuantía, Sewell, Causa no. 11.280, 10 April 1947, CBRR.

67 Ibid., Causa no. 4045, 21 September 1937.

68 Ibid., Causa no. 6037, 11 December 1940.

69 Ibid., Causa no. 11.280, 10 April 1947.

70 General Manager's Annual Report—1940, Braden Copper Company, ABCC.

71 Personnel Records, Mineral El Teniente, CODELCO-Chile.

72 Haldeman, interview.

73 Juzgado de Letras de Menor Cuantía, Sewell, Causa no. 11.142, 14 January 1947, CBRR.

74 Ibid., Causa no. 7824, 21 January 1942.

75 Ibid., Causa no. 11.014, 11 October 1946.

76 See, for example, ibid., causas no. 11.015, 14 October 1946; no. 11.027, 21 October 1946; and no. 10.918, 17 August 1946.

77 Ibid., Causa no. 6134, 3 November 1941.

78 *La Tribuna,* 5 March 1942.

79 Juzgado de Letras de Menor Cuantía, Sewell, Causa no. 6290, 29 April 1941, CBRR.

80 Ibid., Causa no. 10.546, 6 February 1946.

81 Ibid., Causa no. 5430, 15 January 1940.

82 Members of the Círculo Social Sewell, interview by author, Rancagua, August 1996.

83 Enrique Araneda, interview by author, Rancagua, August 1996.

84 Members of the Círculo Social Sewell, interview.

85 Ibid.; Haldeman, interview.

6 *"Rotos Macanudos" and Football Stars: Popular Culture, Working-Class Masculinity, and Opposition in the Mining Camps*

1 Terry Eagleton, *Ideology* (New York: Verso, 1991).

2 *El Teniente,* 25–27 October 1922.

3 Ibid.

4 Ibid.

5 Annual Report, 1922, Welfare Department, ABCC.

6 *La Semana,* 4 January 1928; *Despertar Minero,* 4 September 1941; Barrera, "El conflicto obrero en el enclave cuprífero," p. 35.

7 See, for example, Juzgado de Letras de Menor Cuantía, Sewell, Causa no. 2823, 16 July 1935, and Causa no. 2816, 15 July 1935, CBRR.

8 Carabineros de Chile, Prefectura de O'Higgins, Tercera Comisaría, Sewell,

to Welfare Department, 10 October 1934, Personnel Records, Mineral El Teniente, CODELCO-Chile.

9 Carabineros de Chile, Prefectura de O'Higgins, Tercera Comisaría, Sewell, to Welfare Department, 2 May 1937, Personnel Records, Mineral El Teniente, CODELCO-Chile.

10 Carabineros de Chile, Prefectura de O'Higgins, Tercera Comisaría, Sewell, to Welfare Department, 11 December 1935, Personnel Records, Mineral El Teniente, CODELCO-Chile.

11 Personnel Records, Mineral El Teniente, CODELCO-Chile.

12 Members of the Círculo Social Sewell, interview.

13 Fuenzalida Grandon, *El trabajo i la vida en el mineral "El Teniente,"* p. 89.

14 *Despertar Minero,* 6 April 1939.

15 Former El Teniente worker, interview by author, Coya, February 1992.

16 Castro, *Un hombre por el camino,* p. 34.

17 Eric Hobsbawm, *Bandits* (New York: Delacorte Press, 1969). See also Eric Hobsbawm, *Primitive Rebels: Archaic Forms of Social Movements in the Nineteenth and Twentieth Centuries* (New York: Norton, 1965).

18 For anecdotes and stories of guachucheros in the Sewell popular literature, see Castro, *Un hombre por el camino,* and Drago, *Cobre.*

19 Intendencia de O'Higgins, Documentación Relativa a la Braden Copper Company, ANC.

20 Braden, *Diplomats and Demagogues,* p. 15.

21 Fuenzalida Grandon, *El trabajo i la vida en el mineral "El Teniente,"* p. 88.

22 Personnel Records, Mineral El Teniente, CODELCO-Chile.

23 Intendencia de O'Higgins, Documentación Relativa a la Braden Copper Company.

24 Castro, *Un hombre por el camino,* p. 34.

25 Don Luis and Don Rubén, interview.

26 Castro, *Un hombre por el camino,* p. 98.

27 James C. Scott, *Domination and the Arts of Resistance: Hidden Transcripts* (New Haven: Yale University Press, 1990).

28 Drago, *Cobre,* p. 57.

29 Ibid., pp. 104–105.

30 Ibid., p. 193.

31 Personnel Records, Mineral El Teniente, CODELCO-Chile.

32 See dismissal reports of the Braden Copper Company, 1946, ABCC.

33 Jorge Emilio Achurra Achurra to F. E. Turton, Gerente General, Braden Copper Company, 22 June 1943, Personnel Records, Mineral El Teniente, CODELCO-Chile.

34 Fuenzalida Grandon, *El trabajo i la vida en el mineral "El Teniente,"* pp. 101–102.

35 Head of Welfare Department to Ana Pino Santibañez, 3 February 1939, ABCC.

36 Braden Copper Company to Hernán Cousiño Tocornal, ABCC.

37 Javier Donoso, interview.

38 Seibert Alphand, "La legislación del trabajo," p. 39.

39 H. Mackenzie Walker to W. J. Turner, 6 September 1939, ABCC.

40 Nélida Carrasco, interview by Paola Fernández, Rancagua, April 1992.

41 Castro, *Un hombre por el camino,* p. 73.

42 Welfare Department, "Indices on Costs of Living with Special Reference to Clothing," 17 May 1940, ABCC.

43 Daniel Silva, interview by author, Rancagua, March 1992.

44 Ibid.

45 Ibid.

46 Ibid.

47 Tapia, interview.

48 See William E. French, "*Progreso Forzado:* Workers and the Inculcation of the Capitalist Work Ethic in the Parral Mining District," in *Rituals of Rule, Rituals of Resistance: Public Celebrations and Popular Culture in Mexico,* ed. William H. Beezley, Cheryl English Martin, and William E. French (Wilmington, Del.: Scholarly Resources Books, 1994), pp. 199–200.

49 Quintero, interview.

50 Walker to Turner, 6 September 1939, ABCC.

51 Ministerio del Trabajo, Inspección General del Trabajo, to Gerente General de la Braden Copper Company, 10 August 1937, ABCC.

52 *Lircay,* 6 July 1938.

53 Julia Medel, interview by Paola Fernández, Rancagua, June 1992.

54 Flor Rocia, interview by Paola Fernández, Rancagua, June 1992.

55 Ibid.

56 *Despertar Minero,* 21 November 1940, 15 May 1941.

57 Markos J. Mamalakis, comp., *Historical Statistics of Chile,* vol. 4 (Westport, Conn.: Greenwood, 1983); Welfare Department, Braden Copper Company, ABCC.

58 *Despertar Minero,* 15 May 1941.

59 *Lircay,* 6 July 1938.

60 *Despertar Minero,* 14 April 1939.

61 *Despertar Minero,* Primera Quincena de Agosto, 1944.

62 Ibid., Primera Quincena de Agosto, 1945.

63 Haldeman, interview.

64 *Despertar Minero,* 21 November 1940.

65 Carlos Pérez, interview by author, Rancagua, March 1991. I have changed the interviewee's name to protect his confidentiality.

66 Araneda, interview.

67 Don Luis and Don Rubén, interview.

68 Members of the Círculo Social Sewell, interview.

69 Pérez, interview.

70 Members of the Círculo Social Sewell, interview.

71 Don Luis and Don Rubén, interview.

72 Pérez, interview.

73 Rosa Silva, interview.

74 Troncoso, interview.

75 Members of the Círculo Social Sewell, interview.

76 Rosa Silva, interview.

77 Members of the Círculo Social Sewell, interview.

78 Luis Vergara, interview by author, Rancagua, March 1992.

79 Orlando Moraga, interview by author, Rancagua, March 1992.

80 Manuel Ahumada, interview by author, Rancagua, March 1992.

81 *El Cobre,* 11 December 1936.

82 Ibid.

83 *El Siglo,* 2 March 1942.

84 *Despertar Minero,* 21 November 1940.

85 U.S. embassy report, 2 March 1942, Department of State, General Records, RG 59, 825.5045/114.

86 *El Cobre,* 11 December 1936.

87 *Despertar Minero,* 21 November 1940.

88 *El Siglo,* 12 February 1942.

89 *El Siglo,* 7 March 1942.

90 See H. Mackenzie Walker, superintendent, Welfare Department, to L. E. Grant, general manager, Braden Copper Company, 11 October 1923, ABCC.

91 Ibid.

92 Annual Report, 1922, Welfare Department.

93 See letters from Departamento de Bienestar, 8 September 1938, 26 August 1938, and 15 August 1938, ABCC.

94 Annual Report, 1922, Welfare Department.

95 Pezoa Varas, *En el feudo.*

96 *El Siglo,* 10 October 1946.

97 Figueroa, interview.

98 Castro, *Mi camarada padre,* p. 62.

99 Ibid.

7　*Women, Marriage, and the Organization of Sexuality*

1　For some writers in the Marxist-feminist tradition, the subordination of women within the family is a function of men's control of women's labor power. In this view, the marriage contract is a labor contract. This approach ignores, however, that the control of labor also involves the control of sexuality. Marriage implies a sexual contract, forms of exchange and domination based on sex, as well as work. For expressions of the Marxist-feminist theoretical perspective, see Heidi Hartmann, "Capitalism, Patriarchy, and Job Segregation by Sex," *Signs* 1 (Spring 1976), and Annette Kuhn and Ann-Marie Wolpe, eds., *Feminism and Materialism: Women and Modes of Production* (London: Routledge and Kegan Paul, 1978). Also see Joan Scott's discussion of "dual systems" theory in *Gender and the Politics of History,* and Michèle Barrett's discussions of Marxism and feminism in *Women's Oppression Today: The Marxist/Feminist Encounter* (New York: Verso, 1988).

2　See, for example, Scott, *Gender and the Politics of History;* Carole Pateman, *The Sexual Contract* (Stanford: Stanford University Press, 1988); and Alexander, "Women, Class, and Sexual Difference."

3　Juzgado de Letras de Menor Cuantía, Sewell, Causa no. 6036, 11 December 1940, CBRR.

4　Ibid., Causa no. 4947, 10 March 1939.

5　Ibid., Causa no. 10.093, 4 June 1945.

6　Ibid., Causa no. 2768, 24 June 1935.

7　Ibid., Causa no. 10.945, 28 August 1946.

8　Ibid., Causa no. 9701, 29 November 1944.

9　*Despertar Minero,* 31 August 1939, 30 January 1941.

10　Juzgado de Letras de Menor Cuantía, Sewell, Causa no. 8058, 9 May 1942, CBRR.

11　Ibid., Causa no. 8527, 14 December 1942.

12　Ibid., Causa no. 4835, 6 January 1938.

13　Ibid., Causa no. 8428, 26 October 1942.

14　Ibid., Causa no. 4879, 24 January 1938.

15　In a similar case, a married woman refused to press charges against her husband, who had beaten her because she "had behaved badly" by dancing with another man (ibid., Causa no. 6382, 17 June 1941).

16　Ibid., Causa no. 11.960, 31 May 1948.

17　Ibid., Causa no. 10.033, 3 May 1945.

18　Ibid., Causa no. 5136, 12 July 1939.

19　Ibid., Causa no. 11.082, 7 December 1946.

20　Haldeman, interview.

21   Robert Haldeman, quoted in Baros Mansilla, *El Teniente,* pp. 305, 307.

22   Juzgado de Letras de Menor Cuantía, Sewell, Causa no. 13.599, 26 July 1951, CBRR.

23   Ibid., Causa no. 11.082, 7 December 1946.

24   Castro, *¿Me permite una interrupción?* p. 43.

25   Nora Moncada, interview by author, Rancagua, August 1996.

26   Juzgado de Letras de Menor Cuantía, Sewell, Causa no. 4925, 21 February 1939, CBRR.

27   Welfare Department, letter to President, Sindicato Industrial Braden Copper Company, Sewell y Mina, 31 July 1943, ABCC.

28   Castro, *Un hombre por el camino,* p. 170.

29   Juzgado de Letras de Menor Cuantía, Sewell, Causa no. 6049, 14 July 1940.

30   Ibid., Causa no. 9926, 23 March 1945.

31   Welfare Department, "El Departamento de Bienestar," 1921, ABCC.

32   Pateman, *The Sexual Contract,* p. 132.

33   María Berrios, interview by Paola Fernández, Rancagua, June 1992; Julia Medel, interview.

34   Of these eight women, three were midwives, one sold "ladies novelties," two sold dry goods, one ran a restaurant, and one ran a hotel. "Taxes Payable on Concessions," Plant Comptroller's Office, 21 January 1925, ABCC.

35   "Concesionarios Autorizados por la Compañía," Departamento de Bienestar, 7 May 1952, ABCC.

36   Daniel Silva, interview.

37   Moncada, interview.

38   Don Luis, interview.

39   Berrios, interview.

40   Medel, interview.

41   Valentina Acosta, interview by Paola Fernández, Rancagua, May 1992; Carrasco, interview, 1992.

42   Don Rubén, interview.

43   Medel, interview.

44   Rocia, interview.

45   Registro de Matrimonios, El Teniente, 1930, 1935, 1940, and 1945, RCM.

46   Berrios, interview.

47   Tapia, interview.

48   Rocia, interview.

49   Moncada, interview.

50   Rosa Silva, interview.

51   That providing pensions to single workers or married workers without families was an important means to supplementing the income of the fami-

lies of miners is revealed in a company estimate that 40 percent of married and single workers who did not have lodgings in the camp lived in private pensions. Many families gave pensions to a number of workers at a time, even up to thirty-eight workers. This was a necessity because the number of cantinas and hotels was insufficient to serve the mine's workforce. In 1952, 502 miners took their pensions in private homes (Departamento de Bienestar Social, Informe, 29 January 1952, ABCC).

52   Ibid.

53   Juzgado de Letras de Menor Cuantía, Sewell, Causa no. 8374, 5 October 1942, CBRR; interview with former Sewell resident, Rancagua, 1991.

54   Don Rubén, interview.

55   Berrios, interview.

56   Ibid.

57   Medel, interview.

58   Rosa Silva, interview.

59   Rocia, interview.

60   Welfare Department, "Familias Obreras en Malas Condiciones Económicas," 3 May 1943, ABCC.

61   Confidential memorandum by Welfare Department, 28 July 1943, ABCC.

62   Welfare Department, letter to President, Sindicato Industrial Braden Copper Company, "Sewell y Mina," 4 September 1943, ABCC.

63   Letter to Ana Pinto Santibañez, 3 February 1939, ABCC.

64   Seibert Alphand, "La legislación del trabajo," p. 39.

65   Rocia, interview.

66   Carrasco, interview, 1992.

67   María de los Angeles Sanhueza Ruiz, interview by Paola Fernández, Rancagua, April 1992.

68   María Recabarren Cavieres, interview by Paola Fernández, Rancagua, April 1992.

69   Juzgado de Letras de Menor Cuantía, Sewell, Causa no. 12.047, 13 July 1948, CBRR.

70   Ibid., Causa no. 6266, 14 November 1941.

71   Ibid., Causa no. 8344, 15 September 1942.

72   Ibid., Causa no. 6146, 1 February 1941.

73   Ibid., Causa no. 2842, 26 July 1935.

74   Ibid., Causa no. 10.955, 2 September 1946.

75   Ibid., Causa no. 4742, 21 November 1938.

76   Ibid., Causa no. 11.342, 12 June 1947.

77   Ibid., Causa no. 11.334, 31 March 1947.

78   Ibid., Causa no. 10.770, 3 June 1946.

79 Ibid., Causa no. 11.342, 12 June 1947.

80 Welfare Department, letter to President, Sindicato Industrial Braden Copper Company, "Sewell y Mina," 4 September 1943, ABCC.

81 Rocia, interview.

82 Ibid.

83 Juzgado de Letras de Menor Cuantía, Sewell, Causa no. 12.047, 13 July 1948.

84 Ibid., Causa no. 5456, 3 November 1940.

85 Ibid., Causa no. 5458, 5 November 1940.

86 Ibid., Causa no. 5437, 19 January 1940.

87 Ibid., Causa no. 2820, 15 July 1935.

88 Ibid., Causa no. 6369, 13 June 1941.

89 Ibid., Causa no. 2841, 28 August 1946.

90 Ibid., Causa no. 2841, 22 July 1935.

91 Ibid., Causa no. 7769, 2 January 1942.

92 Ibid., Causa no. 10.764, 27 May 1946.

93 Ibid., Causa no. 11.237, 6 March 1947.

94 Ibid., Causa no. 5451, 31 January 1940.

95 Dirección General del Trabajo, Tribunal del Trabajo de Rancagua, no. 10.094, 1 November 1940, CBRR.

96 Ibid.

97 Rocia, interview.

98 Daniel Silva, interview.

99 Tapia, interview.

100 Carrasco, interview, 1992.

101 Rosa Silva, interview.

8 *Workers' Movements, Women's Mobilization, and Labor Politics*

1 Collier and Sater, *A History of Chile*, p. 274; Mamalakis, *Historical Statistics of Chile*, vol. 4, pp. 324–333.

2 *Despertar Minero*, 30 January 1941.

3 *La Tribuna*, 14 January 1941.

4 *Despertar Minero*, 17 February 1941.

5 Ibid., 15 March 1941.

6 Ibid., 4 October 1941.

7 Ibid., 25 November 1941.

8 Welfare Department, reports on cost of living, 1941, Braden Copper Company, ABCC.

9 *Despertar Minero*, 25 November 1941. The MEMCh was founded in 1935 by independents and militants of leftist parties, most notably the Communist

Party. The MEMch focused on the "economic, social, and legal emancipation of women," demanding equal salaries for men and women and the right of women to occupy any job. In addition, it petitioned the government to provide solutions to the problems of clandestine abortions and prostitution and to establish full civil and political rights for women. After 1936, the MEMch became "the female arm" of the Popular Front coalition. See Edda Gaviola, Ximena Jiles, Lorella Lopresti, and Claudia Rojas, *"Queremos votar en las próximas elecciones": Historia del movimiento femenino chileno, 1913–1952* (Santiago: La Morada, 1986).

10   *Despertar Minero,* 25 November 1941.

11   Ibid., 11 December 1941.

12   Ibid., 25 January 1942, 17 April 1942.

13   Ibid., 16 January 1941.

14   Ibid.

15   Ibid.

16   Quoted in Drake, *Socialism and Populism in Chile,* pp. 227–228.

17   Legation of the United States, 10 November 1941, U.S. Department of State, General Records, RG 59, 825.00/598.

18   Drake, *Socialism and Populism in Chile,* pp. 220–228.

19   Ibid.

20   See ibid.; Jobet, *Historia del Partido Socialista de Chile;* and Aldunate, Flisfisch, and Moulian, *Estudios sobre el sistema de partidos en Chile.*

21   Drake, *Socialism and Populism in Chile,* p. 258.

22   Loveman, *Struggle in the Countryside.*

23   Drake, *Socialism and Populism in Chile,* p. 257.

24   *Despertar Minero,* 5 June 1941.

25   Ibid.

26   *El Teniente,* 29 February 1942.

27   Memorandum from Advisor on Political Relations, 17 March 1942, U.S. Department of State, General Records, RG 59, 811.20 Defense (M) Chile/142.

28   Advisor on International Economic Affairs to E. T. Stannard, Kennecott Copper Company, U.S. Department of State, General Records, RG 59, 811.20 Defense (M) Chile/143.

29   U.S. Department of State, General Records, RG 59, 1940–1944, 825.5045/106.

30   Telegram, 28 February 1942, U.S. Department of State, General Records, RG 59, 825.5045/108.

31   *Despertar Minero,* 17 February 1942.

32   *El Siglo,* 12 February 1942.

33   Ibid., 16 January 1942.

34   Telegram, 28 February 1942.

35   *El Rancagüino,* 25 February 1942.

36   For statistics on copper production, see the *Boletín Minero,* published monthly by the Sociedad Nacional Minera, and *Minería,* published annually by the Dirección General de Estadísticas. In 1942 Chile produced 484,353,114 kilograms of copper, whereas in 1940 it had produced only 363,040,914 kilograms. The large increase was due largely to wartime demand.

37   Drake, *Socialism and Populism in Chile,* pp. 218–219.

38   Chile, Sesión Ordinaria de la Cámara de Senadores, 13 July 1938.

39   Chile, Sesiónes de la Cámara de Diputados, 12 July 1938.

40   William Turner to E. T. Stannard, 12 February 1942, ABCC.

41   *El Siglo,* 24 February 1942.

42   Ibid., 25 February 1942.

43   Ibid., 16 January 1942.

44   Ibid., 10 March 1942.

45   *El Rancagüino,* 6 March 1942.

46   *El Siglo,* 11 March 1942.

47   Ibid., 24 March 1942.

48   Ocampo had been elected secretary-general of the CTCH in its founding congress in 1936 by a narrow majority but had ceded to a Socialist candidate to preserve the unity of the confederation.

49   *El Siglo,* 5 March 1942.

50   Ibid., 10 March 1942.

51   *El Rancagüino,* 20 February 1942.

52   *La Opinión,* 20 February 1942.

53   U.S. consulate report, 20 February 1942, U.S. Department of State, General Records, RG 59, 825.5045/110.

54   Telegram, 4 March 1942, U.S. Department of State, General Records, RG 59, 825.5045/111.

55   Telegram, 5 March 1942, U.S. Department of State, General Records, RG 59, 825.5045/112.

56   *El Siglo,* 18 February 1942.

57   Ibid., 23–24 February 1942.

58   Ibid., 19 February 1942.

59   Ibid., 20 February 1942.

60   Ibid., 1 March 1942.

61   Ibid., 7 March 1942.

62   Ibid., 11 March 1942.

63   Ibid., 1 March 1942.

64   *Despertar Minero,* Segunda Quincena de Diciembre de 1942.

65   Ibid.

66   *Despertar Minero,* 4 September 1941.

67   Ibid., 3 October 1939.

68   Ibid., 31 August 1939.

69   Ibid., 30 January 1941.

70   *Mensaje Obrero,* 14 May 1939.

71   Ibid.

72   *Despertar Minero,* 30 January 1941.

73   *Despertar Minero,* Primera Quincena de Mayo de 1943 and Primera Quincena de Junio de 1943.

74   Departamento de Bienestar Social, "Circular a los Concecionarios de Hoteles y Cantinas," 23 June 1944, ABCC.

75   Memorandum to M. Fernández Greene, "Intervention of Syndicate Directors in Mere Details of Everyday Office Transactions," 25 October 1943, ABCC.

76   Welfare Department to President, Sindicato Industrial Braden Copper Company, "Sewell y Mina."

77   MEMch-Sewell declaration published in *Despertar Minero,* 5 March 1941.

78   *Despertar Minero,* 15 March 1941.

79   *Despertar Minero,* Segunda Quincena de Diciembre de 1942.

80   Acosta, interview.

81   *El Siglo,* 13 March 1942.

82   Text of the Decision of the Tribunal Arbitral, published in ibid., 24 March 1942.

83   W. J. Turner to E. T. Stannard, 20 April 1942, ABCC.

84   Segunda Sesión del Tribunal Arbitral, 19 March 1942, ABCC.

85   Memorandum from H. Mackenzie Walker to O. J. James, "Arbitral Decision with Reference to 'Classification of Workmen,'" 13 April 1942, ABCC.

86   See copies of workers' appeals to the labor inspectorate in the ABCC.

87   Untitled document, 24 January 1941, ABCC.

88   Inspección General del Trabajo, Inspección Provincial de O'Higgins, "Sobre reincorporación a las faenas obreros castigados," 17 October 1941, ABCC.

89   Confidential memorandum, 12 August 1943, Welfare Department, ABCC.

90   F. E. Turton to Enrique Bodecker Lara, 6 September 1949, ABCC.

91   Charles Will Wright, "The Mining Industries in Chile," U.S. Bureau of Mines, April 1940, U.S. Department of State, General Records, RG 59, 825.63/50.

92   *El Teniente,* 29 February 1942.

93   H. Mackenzie Walker, welfare superintendent, to W. J. Turner, general manager, 10 May 1940, ABCC.

94   W. J. Turner to Directores del Sindicato Industrial B.C.C. Sewell y Minas, 7 November 1940, ABCC.

95   Confidential memorandum from H. Mackenzie Walker, superintendent of the Welfare Department, to F. E. Turton, assistant general manager, 19 April 1943, ABCC.

96   See ibid., and H. Mackenzie Walker to Avelino Muñoz Moraga, 14 May 1943, and Controlar Local S. M. Arriola to F. E. Turton, 21 April 1943, ABCC.

9   *The Radicalization of Working-Class Politics: United States Intervention, Miners' Strikes, and the Crisis of Populism*

1   *Despertar Minero,* August 1946.

2   Ibid.

3   *El Rancagüino,* 10 July 1946.

4   Ibid.

5   Ibid., 12 July 1946.

6   Ibid., 13 July 1946.

7   *Despertar Minero,* September 1946.

8   *El Rancagüino,* 23 November 1946.

9   *Despertar Minero,* October 1946.

10   For descriptions of the workers' activities during the strike, see the reports of the Braden Copper Company's spies and the union's strike bulletins in the ABCC.

11   Informe sobre concentración llevada a efecto jueves, 26 de septiembre de 1946, ABCC.

12   Ibid.

13   Informe sobre reunión extraordinaria general, llevada a efecto . . . lunes, 16 de septiembre de 1946, ABCC.

14   Ibid.

15   Quoted in *El Siglo,* 4 October 1946.

16   Informe sobre reunión extraordinaria general . . . 16 de septiembre de 1946.

17   In El Teniente, González Videla won 1,211 votes and his opponent, Cruz Coke, only 306 votes in the 1946 elections. Former presidents Arturo Alessandri and Carlos Ibáñez won 226 and 155 votes, respectively (Instituto Nacional de Estadísticas, Chile).

18   *El Siglo,* 5 November 1946.

19   *Despertar Minero,* November 1946.

20   *El Siglo,* 10 October 1946.

21   Declaration of the Consejo Directivo Nacional of the CTCH (Communist-led faction) published in *El Siglo,* 23 November 1946.

22   Chile, Sesión Extraordinaria de la Cámara de Diputados, 27 November 1946.

23   Ibid.

24   Counselor of Embassy for Economic Affairs, memorandum, 8 November 1946, U.S. Department of State, General Records, RG 59, 825.5045/11–746.

25   Telegram to Secretary of State, 22 November 1946, U.S. Department of State, General Records, RG 59, 825.5045/11-2246.

26   Claude Bowers to Spruille Braden, Assistant Secretary of State, 18 November 1946, U.S. Department of State, General Records, RG 59, 825.5045/11-1846.

27   Claude Bowers to Spruille Braden, Assistant Secretary of State, 18 December 1946, U.S. Department of State, General Records, RG 59, 825.5045/12-1846.

28   At one point the U.S. ambassador was startled to observe "what appears to be an almost militant collaboration with the Communists," despite González Videla's professed distaste for his Communist ministers (Claude Bowers to Spruille Braden, Assistant Secretary of State, 4 December 1946, U.S. Department of State, General Records, RG 59, 825.5045/12-446).

29   Ibid.

30   Estimates of losses to the Chilean government in revenues were between $107 and $500 million according to Theodore Moran, *Multinational Corporations,* p. 61 and p. 47.

31   For Chile, each penny increase in copper prices signified a difference of $10 million in exports and $5 million in government revenues (ibid., p. 58).

32   Memorandums Regarding Current Negotiations between American Copper Companies and Chilean Government, U.S. Department of State, General Records, RG 59, 825.6352/7-1047.

33   Ibid.

34   Ibid.

35   Ibid.

36   Memorandum, 23 July 1947, U.S. Department of State General Records, RG 59, 1945–1949, 825.5045/8-1247.

37   Moran, *Multinational Corporations,* p. 65.

38   See Chile, Cámara de Diputados, Diario de Sesiones, 1948.

39   Ibid.

40   *Foreign Relations of the United States, 1946* (Washington, D.C.: U.S. Government Printing Office, 1969–1972), p. 613.

41   *El Siglo,* 28 July 1947.

42   Ibid., 1 October 1947.

43   Quoted in ibid., 29 October 1947.

44   Moran, *Multinational Corporations,* p. 177.

45   Dispatch no. 15772, 28 November 1947, U.S. Department of State, General Records, RG 59, 825.5045/11-2847.

46   *La Opinión,* 23 October 1947.

47   Ibid., 24 October 1947.

48   Dispatch no. 15772, 28 November 1947. Lists of Communist workers sent to the military commander by the company can be found in the ABCC. See also Informe sobre organizaciones del personal del mineral y situación general, 22 August 1949, ABCC, a company memorandum to the emergency zone commander that lauds "the opportune measures taken by the Supreme Government at the end of 1947 and the beginning of 1948 which eliminated the leaders and 'active' members of this group [the Communist party], bringing a little tranquility to the mine."

49   Quoted in *El Imparcial,* 19 March 1949; Annual Report, 1949, Kennecott Copper Company, ABCC.

50   *La Tribuna,* 3 June 1948.

51   Loveman, *Chile,* and Drake, *Socialism and Populism in Chile,* p. 289.

52   For discussions of Ibáñez's regime, see Paul Drake, "Chile, 1930–1958," in *Chile since Independence,* ed. Leslie Bethell (Cambridge: Cambridge University Press, 1993); Loveman, *Chile;* and Aldunate, Flisfisch, and Moulian, *Estudios sobre el sistema de partidos en Chile.*

53   Dirección del Registro Electoral, Instituto Nacional de Estadísticas, Chile.

54   For electoral data, see also Loveman, *Chile,* pp. 296–297, and Aldunate, Flisfisch, and Moulian, *Estudios sobre el sistema de partidos en Chile,* pp. 78–81.

55   See accounts of the conflicts in *El Rancagüino,* March and April 1957, and June and July 1958.

56   *El Rancagüino,* 15 August 1959.

57   Accounts of these strikes can be found in the local as well as in the national press. I have relied on *El Rancagüino, El Semanario de "El Teniente," El Comercio,* and *Crítica.* See also Jorge Barría, *Los sindicatos de la gran minería del cobre* (Santiago: INSORA, 1970), and Pizarro, *La huelga obrera en Chile.*

58   *El Siglo,* 5 October 1959, cited in Barrera, "El conflicto obrero en el enclave cuprífero," p. 96.

59   In 1965 the average North American copper miner brought home $3.15 an hour. In El Teniente, the average hourly wage for obreros and empleados combined was only $1.33, a figure that would be far smaller for just obreros. See Barrera, "El conflicto obrero en el enclave cuprífero," p. 95.

60   *El Siglo,* cited in ibid., p. 96.

61   *El Semanario de "El Teniente,"* 29 October 1966.

62   Barrera, "El conflicto obrero en el enclave cuprífero," p. 85.

63   Ibid., pp. 94–95.

64   Accounts of women's activities during strikes can be found in *Cobre,* the publication of the CTC.

Conclusion

1 Expressions of this traditional labor historiography can be found in Ramí-rez Necochea, *Historia del movimiento obrero en Chile,* and Bergquist, *Labor in Latin America.* For a critique of this focus on the export sector and miners during the first decades of the twentieth century, see Peter De Shazo's study of urban and port workers and the development of anarcho-syndicalist unionism in *Urban Workers and Labor Unions in Chile.*

2 Ava Baron, "Gender and Labor History: Learning from the Past, Looking to the Future," in *Work Engendered,* ed. Baron, p. 14.

3 Joan Wallach Scott, *Gender and the Politics of History.*

4 Here, I draw on Paul Willis's study of working-class masculinity in Britain, *Learning to Labour: How Working-Class Kids Get Working-Class Jobs* (Hampshire: Gower Publishing, 1981), and Nancy Hewitt, " 'The Voice of Virile Labor': Labor Militancy, Community Solidarity, and Gender among Tampa's Latin Workers, 1880–1921," in *Work Engendered,* ed. Baron.

5 Peter Winn, *Weavers of Revolution: The Yarur Workers and Chile's Road to Socialism* (New York: Oxford University Press, 1986).

6 For discussions of class and community, see Gould, *To Lead as Equals.* Gould's discussion of Craig Calhoun, *The Question of Class Struggle: Social Foundations of Popular Radicalism during the Industrial Revolution* (Chicago: University of Chicago Press, 1982), was quite useful for this book.

7 For the most recent expression of this argument, see Ruth Berins Collier and David Collier, *Shaping the Political Arena: Critical Junctures, the Labor Movement, and Regime Dynamics in Latin America* (Princeton: Princeton University Press, 1991), esp. pp. 390–401.

8 See ibid. While there are suggestions that working-class activism was quelled after 1946, hindered by integration into the new labor relations system, and constrained by the politics of the left and center parties, particularly the Socialist Party, in his *Socialism and Populism in Chile,* Drake presents a more nuanced analysis of the dialectic between incorporation and working-class mobilization during this period.

9 Although blue-collar workers initially supported the strike, after a short period many returned to work following the direction of leaders of the obreros' union, almost all of whom were identified with the Socialist and Communist Parties. The strike was led and maintained by militants of the Christian Democratic Party and supported largely by white-collar workers. In addition, the strike was given a wider national audience by the important role played by groups that sought to destabilize the UP, including the ultra-Right terrorist Patria y Libertad and the right-wing women's group

Poder Feminino. The strike was part of a national strategy of the Right and Christian Democratic opposition to undermine the UP. For an account of the strike, see Bitar and Pizarro, *La caída de Allende y la huelga de El Teniente*. For important critiques of the description of workers in modern industrial sectors of Latin American economies as composing a labor aristocracy, see Jelín and Torre, "Los nuevos trabajadores en América Latina." See also John Humphrey, *Capitalist Control and Workers' Struggle in the Brazilian Auto Industry* (Princeton: Princeton University Press, 1982).

10   For a more extensive discussion of miners' opposition to the Pinochet dictatorship, see Thomas Miller Klubock, "Copper Miners, Popular Protest, and Organized Labor in Pinochet's Chile," *International Labor and Working-Class History* 52 (Fall 1997).

BIBLIOGRAPHY

Archival Sources

Archive of the Sindicato Industrial Sewell y Mina, Rancagua, Chile (ASISM)
Archivo Nacional, Santiago, Chile (ANC)
    Dirección General del Trabajo
    Intendencia de O'Higgins. Documentación Relativa a la Braden Copper
        Company, 1908–1922
    Ministerio del Trabajo, Oficios, 1938–1948
    Oficina del Trabajo
Conservador de Bienes y Raíces, Rancagua, Chile (CBRR)
    Inspección General del Trabajo, Tribunal del Trabajo de Rancagua
    Juzgado de Letras de Menor Cuantía, Sewell
Kennecott Copper Company, Reference Center, Salt Lake City, Utah, United
    States (KRC)
Mineral El Teniente, CODELCO-Chile, Rancagua, Chile
    Archives of the Braden Copper Company (ABCC)
    Personnel Records
National Archives, Washington, D.C., United States
    United States Department of State, General Records, 1930–1949
Registro Civil, Machalí, Chile (RCM)

Newspapers

Cobre (1962–1973)
Crítica (1940–1973)
Despertar Minero (1939–1946)
El Cobre (1936)
El Comercio (1940–1973)
El Imparcial (1930–1949)
El Mercurio (1938–1983)
El Minero (1931–1936)

El Rancagüino (1938–1983)
El Semanario de "El Teniente" (1964–1983)
El Siglo (1936–1947)
El Teniente (1922–1944)
Homenaje al 1 de Mayo (1916–1919)
Informe del Cobre (1982–1983)
La Aurora (1912)
La Avanzada (1921)
La Batalla (1945)
La Defensa (1947)
La Hora (1938–1951)
La Igualdad (1912)
La Nación (1938–1951)
La Opinión (1938–1951)
La Prensa (1912)
La Provincia (1919)
La Semana (1921–1949)
La Tribuna (1935–1949)
La Voz del Obrero (1916–1918)
Lircay (1938)
Mensaje Obrero (1939)
Teniente Topics (1915–1917)
Tópicos del Teniente (1916–1920)

Published Documents and Reports

Braden Copper Company. Annual reports, 1915–1924.

Chile, Cámara de Diputados. Diario de Sesiones, 1938–1950.

Chile, Cámara de Senadores. Diario de Sesiones, 1938–1950.

Chile, Instituto Nacional de Estadísticas. Dirección General de Estadísticas, Anuario Estadístico de Chile, 1938–1952.

CODELCO-Chile. *El cobre chileno.* Santiago: CODELCO, 1975.

Confederación de Trabajadores de Chile. Bernardo Araya. "Una CTCh unida." 1946.

———. Bernardo Ibáñez. "Memoria." 1946.

———. "Memoria del consejo directivo nacional," 1939.

Congreso Nacional de Chile. Informe de las Comisiones de Hacienda y Minería, Sesiones de la Cámara de Diputados, 1965, "Historia de la ley 16.425, chileanización del cobre."

———. Senado, Oficina de Informaciones, "Antecedentes económicos y estadísticos relacionados con la gran minería del cobre," 1969.

————. Senado, Oficina de Informaciones, "Nacionalización del cobre," 1971.

————. Senado, Oficina de Informaciones, "Pertenencias mineras y estadísticas laborales de las empresas de la gran minería del cobre," 1969.

Kennecott Copper Company. Annual Reports, 1915–1951.

Oral History Interviews Cited

All interviews, unless otherwise indicated, were conducted by the author. PF indicates interviews by Paola Fernández under the direction of the author. I have not used or have changed the names of some interviewees to protect their confidentiality; these interviews are indicated in the notes and are not listed below.

Valentina Acosta, Rancagua, May 1992 (PF); Manuel Ahumada, Rancagua, March 1992; Tadeo Alvarado, Rancagua, April 1991; Enrique Araneda, Rancagua, August 1996; María Berrios, Rancagua, June 1992 (PF); Nélida Carrasco, Rancagua, April 1992 (PF) and August 1996; Javier Donoso, Rancagua, July 1993; Filoberto Figueroa, Rancagua, February 1992; Robert Haldeman, Santiago, 1991; Luis Herrera, Rancagua, April 1991; Julia Medel, Rancagua, June 1992 (PF); Nora Moncada, Rancagua, August 1996; Orlando Moraga, Rancagua, March 1992; Domingo Quintero, Rancagua, November 1991; María Recabarren Cavieres, Rancagua, April 1992 (PF); Antonia Rivas, Rancagua, August 1996; Flor Rocia, Rancagua, June 1992 (PF); María de los Angeles Sanhueza Ruiz, Rancagua, April 1992 (PF); Daniel Silva, Rancagua, March 1992; Rosa Silva, Rancagua, August 1996; Manuel Tapia, Rancagua, March 1992; Manuel Troncoso, Rancagua, February 1992; Luis Vergara, Rancagua, March 1992.

Published Sources

Aldunate, Adolfo, Angel Flisfisch, and Tomás Moulian. *Estudios sobre el sistema de partidos en Chile.* Santiago: Facultad Latinoamericana de Ciencias Sociales (FLACSO), 1985.

Alexander, Sally. "Women, Class, and Sexual Difference in the 1830s and 1840s: Some Reflections on the Writing of a Feminist History." *History Workshop Journal* 17 (Autumn 1984).

Anderson, Benedict. *Imagined Communities.* New York: Verso, 1991.

Angell, Alan. *Politics and the Labour Movement in Chile.* London: Oxford University Press, 1972.

Baron, Ava, ed. *Work Engendered: Toward a New History of American Labor.* Ithaca: Cornell University Press, 1991.

Baros Mansilla, María Celia. *El Teniente: Los hombres del mineral, 1905–1945.* Ranca-gua: CODELCO-Chile, Mineral El Teniente, 1995.

Barrera, Manuel. "El conflicto obrero en el enclave cuprífero." Paper presented at the Seminario Movimientos Laborales en América Latina, Mexico City, 1972.

Barrett, Michèle. *Women's Oppression Today: The Marxist/Feminist Encounter.* New York: Verso, 1988.

Barría, Jorge. *El movimiento obrero en Chile.* Santiago: Universidad Técnica del Es-tado, 1971.

———. *Los sindicatos de la gran minería del cobre.* Santiago: INSORA, 1970.

Bauer, Arnold. *Chilean Rural Society from the Spanish Conquest to 1930.* Cambridge: Cambridge University Press, 1975.

Bergquist, Charles. *Labor in Latin America: Comparative Essays on Chile, Argentina, Venezuela, and Colombia.* Stanford: Stanford University Press, 1986.

Besse, Susan K. *Restructuring Patriarchy: The Modernization of Gender Inequality in Brazil, 1914–1940.* Chapel Hill: University of North Carolina Press, 1996.

Bethell, Leslie, ed. *Chile since Independence.* Cambridge: Cambridge University Press, 1993.

Bitar, Sergio, and Crisostomo Pizarro. *La caída de Allende y la huelga de El Teniente.* Santiago: Ediciones del Ornitorrinco, 1986.

Bourdieu, Pierre. *Outline of a Theory of Practice.* Cambridge: Cambridge Univer-sity Press, 1977.

———. "Sport and Social Class." In *Rethinking Popular Culture,* ed. Chandra Mu-kerji and Michael Schudson. Berkeley: University of California Press, 1991.

Bowers, Claude. *Chile through Embassy Windows.* New York: Simon and Schuster, 1958.

Braden, Spruille. *Diplomats and Demagogues: The Memoirs of Spruille Braden.* New York: Arlington House, 1971.

Braverman, Harry. *Labor and Monopoly Capital: The Degradation of Work in the Twen-tieth Century.* New York: Monthly Review Press, 1974.

Brennan, James P. *The Labor Wars in Córdoba, 1955–1976: Ideology, Work, and Labor Politics in an Argentine Industrial City.* Cambridge: Harvard University Press, 1994.

Brito, Alejandra. "Del rancho al conventillo: Transformaciones en la identidad popular feminina, Santiago de Chile, 1850–1920." In *Disciplina y desacato: Con-strucción de identidad en Chile, siglos xix y xx,* ed. Lorena Godoy, Elizabeth Hutchison, Karin Rosemblatt, and M. Soledad Zárate. Santiago: SUR/CEDEM, 1995.

Burawoy, Michael. *Manufacturing Consent: Changes in the Labor Process under Mo-nopoly Capitalism.* Chicago: University of Chicago Press, 1979.

Butler, Judith. *Gender Trouble: Feminism and the Subversion of Identity.* New York: Routledge, Chapman and Hill, 1990.

Butler, Judith, and Joan W. Scott, eds. *Feminists Theorize the Political.* New York: Routledge, 1992.

Calhoun, Craig. *The Question of Class Struggle: Social Foundations of Popular Radicalism during the Industrial Revolution.* Chicago: University of Chicago Press, 1982.

Canning, Kathleen. "Social Policy, Body Politics: Recasting the Social Question in Germany, 1875–1900." In *Gender and Class in Modern Europe,* ed. Laura L. Frader and Sonya O. Rose. Ithaca: Cornell University Press, 1996.

Castro, Baltazar. *Un hombre por el camino.* Santiago: Editorial Cultura, 1950.

———. *¿Me permite una interrupción?* Santiago: Editorial Zig-Zag, 1962.

———. *Mi camarada padre.* Santiago: Editorial Nascimiento, 1985.

———. *Sewell.* Santiago: Editorial Zig-Zag, 1966.

Cohen, Lizabeth. *Making a New Deal: Industrial Workers in Chicago, 1919–1939.* Cambridge: Cambridge University Press, 1990.

Collier, Simon, and William F. Sater. *A History of Chile, 1808–1994.* Cambridge: Cambridge University Press, 1996.

Collier, Ruth Berins, and David Collier. *Shaping the Political Arena: Critical Junctures, the Labor Movement, and Regime Dynamics in Latin America.* Princeton: Princeton University Press, 1991.

Corbin, David. *Life, Work, and Rebellion in the Coal Fields: Southern West Virginia Miners, 1880–1922.* Urbana: University of Illinois Press, 1981.

Corporación del Cobre. *El cobre chileno.* Santiago: Editorial Universitaria, 1974.

Corrigan, Phillip, and Derek Sayer. *The Great Arch: English State Formation as Cultural Revolution.* Oxford: Basil Blackwell, 1985.

Culver, William W., and Cornel J. Reinhart. "Capitalist Dreams: Chile's Response to Nineteenth-Century World Copper Competition." In *Constructing Culture and Power in Latin America,* ed. Daniel H. Levine. Ann Arbor: University of Michigan Press, 1993.

Darwin, Charles. *Journal of Researches into the Natural History and Geology of the Countries Visited during the Voyage of H.M.S. "Beagle" under the Command of Capt. Fitz Roy, R.N.* New York: Heritage Press, 1957.

Dennis, Norman, Fernando Henriques, and Clifford Slaughter. *Coal Is Our Life: An Analysis of a Yorkshire Mining Community.* London: Tavistock Publishers, 1969.

De Shazo, Peter. *Urban Workers and Labor Unions in Chile, 1902–1927.* Madison: University of Wisconsin Press, 1984.

Devés, Eduardo. *Los que van a morir te saludan.* Santiago: Ediciones Documentas, 1988.

Drago, Gonzalo. *Cobre: Cuentos mineros.* Santiago: Impresa el Esfuerzo, 1941.

Drago, Guillermo, and Pedro Villagra. *Historia general del mineral El Teniente, 1823–1988.* Rancagua, 1989.

Drake, Paul. *Socialism and Populism in Chile, 1932–1952.* Urbana: University of Illinois Press, 1978.

Eagleton, Terry. *Ideology.* New York: Verso, 1991.

Engels, Friedrich. *The Origins of the Family, Private Property, and the State.* New York: International Publishers, 1972.

Fanon, Frantz. *The Wretched of the Earth.* New York: Grove, 1963.

Ffrench-Davis, Ricardo, and Ernesto Tironi. *El cobre en el desarrollo nacional.* Santiago: Ediciones Nueva Universidad, 1974.

Figueroa, Virgilio. *Diccionario histórico, biográfico, y bibliográfico de Chile.* Santiago: Balcello, 1928.

Frader, Laura L., and Sonya O. Rose, eds. *Gender and Class in Modern Europe.* Ithaca: Cornell University Press, 1996.

French, John D., and Daniel James, eds. *The Gendered Worlds of Latin American Women Workers: From Household and Factory to the Union Hall and Ballot Box.* Durham: Duke University Press, 1997.

French, William E. "*Progreso Forzado:* Workers and the Inculcation of the Capitalist Work Ethic in the Parral Mining District." In *Rituals of Rule, Rituals of Resistance: Public Celebrations and Popular Culture in Mexico,* ed. William H. Beezley, Cheryl English Martin, and William E. French. Wilmington, Del.: Scholarly Resources Books, 1994.

Fuenzalida Grandon, Alejandro. *El trabajo i la vida en el mineral "El Teniente."* Santiago: Imprenta Barcelona, 1919.

Gaviola, Edda, Ximena Jiles, Lorella Lopresti, and Claudia Rojas. "*Queremos votar en las próximas elecciones*": *Historia del movimiento feminino chileno, 1913–1952.* Santiago: La Morada, 1986.

Gedicks, Al. *Kennecott Copper Corporation and Mining Development in Wisconsin.* Madison: Community Action on Latin America, 1973.

Girvan, Norman. *Copper in Chile: A Study in Conflict between Corporate and National Economy.* Kingston: Institute of Social and Economic Research, University of the West Indies, 1972.

Godoy, Lorena, Elizabeth Hutchison, Karin Rosemblatt, and M. Soledad Zárate. *Disciplina y desacato: Construcción de identidad en Chile, siglos xix y xx.* Santiago: SUR/CEDEM, 1995.

González Videla, Gabriel. *Memorias.* Santiago: Editora Nacional Gabriela Mistral, 1975.

Gordon, Linda. "Social Insurance and Public Assistance: The Influence of Gender in Welfare Thought in the United States, 1890–1935." *American Historical Review* 97 (February 1992).

————, ed. *Women, the State, and Welfare.* Madison: University of Wisconsin Press, 1990.

Gould, Jeffrey L. *To Lead as Equals: Rural Protest and Political Consciousness in Chinandega, Nicaragua, 1912–1979.* Chapel Hill: University of North Carolina Press, 1990.

Gramsci, Antonio. *Selections from the Prison Notebooks.* New York: International Publishers, 1971.

Guha, Ranajit. "The Prose of Counter-Insurgency." In *Selected Subaltern Studies,* ed. Ranajit Guha and Gayatri Chakravorty Spivak. New York: Oxford University Press, 1988.

Guha, Ranajit, and Gayatri Chakravorty Spivak, eds. *Selected Subaltern Studies.* New York: Oxford University Press, 1988.

Guzmán Bouvard, Marguerite. *Revolutionizing Motherhood: The Mothers of the Plaza de Mayo.* Wilmington, Del.: Scholarly Resources Inc., 1994.

Hall, Stuart. "Gramsci's Relevance for the Study of Race and Ethnicity." *Journal of Communications Inquiry* 10 (1986).

Haraway, Donna. *Simians, Cyborgs, and Women: The Reinvention of Nature.* New York: Routledge, 1991.

Hartmann, Heidi. "Capitalism, Patriarchy, and Job Segregation by Sex." *Signs* 1 (Spring 1976).

Hewitt, Nancy. " 'The Voice of Virile Labor': Labor Militancy, Community Solidarity, and Gender among Tampa's Latin Workers, 1880–1921." In *Work Engendered: Toward a New History of American Labor,* ed. Ava Baron. Ithaca: Cornell University Press, 1991.

Hiriart, Luis. *Braden: Historia de una mina.* Santiago: Editorial Andes, 1964.

Hobsbawm, Eric. *Bandits.* New York: Delacorte Press, 1969.

————. *Primitive Rebels: Archaic Forms of Social Movements in the Nineteenth and Twentieth Centuries.* New York: Norton, 1965.

————. *Workers: Worlds of Labor.* New York: Pantheon Books, 1984.

Hobsbawm, Eric, and Terence Ranger. *The Invention of Tradition.* Cambridge: Cambridge University Press, 1983.

Humphrey, John. *Capitalist Control and Workers' Struggle in the Brazilian Auto Industry.* Princeton: Princeton University Press, 1982.

Hutchison, Elizabeth Q. "Working Women of Santiago: Gender and Social Transformation in Urban Chile, 1887–1927." Ph.D. diss., University of California, Berkeley, 1995.

James, Daniel. *Resistance and Integration: Peronism and the Argentine Working Class, 1946–1976.* Cambridge: Cambridge University Press, 1988.

————. "Tales Told Out on the Borderlands: Doña María's Story, Oral History, and Issues of Gender." Paper presented at the Annual Meeting of the American Historical Association, New York, December 1990.

Jelín, Elizabeth, and Juan Carlos Torre. "Los nuevos trabajadores en América Latina: Una reflexión sobre la tesis de la aristocracia obrera." *Desarrollo Económico* 85 (April–June 1982).

Jobet, Julio César. *Historia del Partido Socialista de Chile.* Santiago: Ediciones Documentas, 1987.

Joseph, Gilbert M., and Daniel Nugent, eds. *Everyday Forms of State Formation: Revolution and the Negotiation of Rule in Modern Mexico.* Durham: Duke University Press, 1994.

Kaplan, Temma. "Female Consciousness and Collective Action: The Case of Barcelona, 1910–1918." *Signs* 7 (Spring 1982).

Kuhn, Annette, and AnnMarie Wolpe, eds. *Feminism and Materialism: Women and Modes of Production.* London: Routledge and Kegan Paul, 1978.

Laclau, Ernesto. *Politics and Ideology in Marxist Theory.* New York: Verso, 1977.

Laclau, Ernesto, and Chantal Mouffe. *Hegemony and Socialist Strategy: Towards a Radical Democratic Politics.* New York: Verso, 1985.

Lafertte, Elías. *Vida de un comunista.* Santiago: Empresa Editorial Austral, 1971.

Levenson-Estrada, Deborah. *Trade Unionists against Terror: Guatemala City, 1954–1985.* Chapel Hill: University of North Carolina Press, 1994.

Loveman, Brian. *Chile: The Legacy of Hispanic Capitalism.* New York: Oxford University Press, 1979.

———. *Struggle in the Countryside: Politics and Rural Labor in Chile, 1919–1973.* Bloomington: Indiana University Press, 1976.

Macchiavello Varas, Santiago. *El problema de la industria del cobre en Chile y sus proyecciones económicas y sociales.* Santiago: University of Chile, 1923.

Mallon, Florencia. *Peasant and Nation: The Making of Postcolonial Mexico and Peru.* Berkeley: University of California Press, 1995.

Mamalakis, Markos J., comp. *Historical Statistics of Chile.* Vol. 4. Westport, Conn.: Greenwood, 1983.

Mamalakis, Markos, and Clark Reynolds. *Essays on the Chilean Economy.* Homewood, Ill.: Richard D. Irwin, 1965.

Molyneux, Maxine. "Mobilization without Emancipation: Women's Interests, the State, and Revolution in Nicaragua." *Feminist Studies* 11 (Summer 1985).

Montgomery, David. *Workers' Control in America.* Cambridge: Cambridge University Press, 1979.

Moran, Theodore H. *Multinational Corporations and the Politics of Dependence: Copper in Chile.* Princeton: Princeton University Press, 1974.

Mukerji, Chandra, and Michael Schudson, eds. *Rethinking Popular Culture.* Berkeley: University of California Press, 1991.

Muñoz, Liliana. *Estudio ocupacional de la minería del cobre*. Santiago: Servicio Nacional del Empleo, 1971.

Nash, June. *We Eat the Mines and the Mines Eat Us: Dependency and Exploitation in Bolivian Tin Mines*. New York: Columbia University Press, 1979.

O'Brien, Thomas F. *The Nitrate Industry and Chile's Crucial Transition, 1870–1891*. New York: New York University Press, 1982.

———. *The Revolutionary Mission: American Enterprise in Latin America, 1900–1945*. Cambridge: Cambridge University Press, 1996.

O'Connor, Harvey. *The Guggenheims: The Making of an American Dynasty*. New York: Covici, 1937.

Parpart, Jane. "Class and Gender on the Copperbelt: Women in Northern Rhodesian Copper Mining Areas." Working Paper no. 77. Boston: Boston University African Studies Center, 1983.

———. "Class Consciousness among Zambian Copper Miners, 1950–1966." Working Paper no. 53. Boston: Boston University African Studies Center, 1982.

———. *Labor and Capital on the African Copperbelt*. Philadelphia: Temple University Press, 1983.

Parsons, Arthur Barrete. *The Porphyry Coppers*. New York: Rocky Mountain Fund Series, 1933.

Pateman, Carole. *The Sexual Contract*. Stanford: Stanford University Press, 1988.

Petras, James, and Maurice Zeitlin. *El radicalismo político de la clase trabajadora Chilena*. Buenos Aires, 1969.

Pezoa Varas, José. *En el feudo: Impresiones sobre la vida obrera del mineral del Teniente*. Rancagua: Imprenta de "La Semana," 1919.

Pizarro, Crisostomo. *La huelga obrera en Chile*. Santiago: Ediciones SUR, 1986.

Portelli, Alessandro. *The Death of Luigi Trastulli and Other Stories: Form and Meaning in Oral History*. Albany: State University of New York, 1991.

Ramírez Necochea, Hernán. *Historia del movimiento obrero en Chile, siglo xix*. Santiago: Ediciones LAR, 1956.

Rosemblatt, Karin. "Por un hogar bien constituido: El estado y los frentes populares." In *Disciplina y desacato: Construcción de identidad en Chile, siglos xix y xx*, ed. Lorena Godoy, Elizabeth Hutchison, Karin Rosemblatt, and M. Soledad Zárate. Santiago: SUR/CEDEM, 1995.

Salazar, Gabriel. *Labradores, peones, y proletarios: Formación y crisis de la sociedad popular Chilena del siglo xix*. Santiago: Ediciones SUR, 1985.

———. "La mujer de 'bajo pueblo' en Chile: Bosquejo histórico." *Proposiciones* 21 (December 1992).

Scott, James C. *Domination and the Arts of Resistance: Hidden Transcripts*. New Haven: Yale University Press, 1990.

———. *The Moral Economy of the Peasant: Rebellion and Subsistence in Southeast Asia.* New Haven: Yale University Press, 1976.

Scott, Joan Wallach. *Gender and the Politics of History.* New York: Columbia University Press, 1988.

Seibert Alphand, Stella Joanne. "La legislación del trabajo y previsión social en El Teniente." Thesis, University of Chile, 1936.

Sindicato Industrial Sewell y Mina and Walter Pineda. *Historia del Sindicato Industrial Sewell y Mina, 1906–1925.* Rancagua: Sindicato Industrial Sewell y Mina, 1989.

Stickell, Arthur Lawrence. "Migration and Mining Labor in Northern Chile in the Nitrate Era, 1880–1930." Ph.D. diss., Indiana University, 1979.

Taussig, Michael. *The Devil and Commodity Fetishism in South America.* Chapel Hill: University of North Carolina Press, 1980.

Thompson, Paul. *The Voice of the Past: Oral History.* Oxford: Oxford University Press, 1978.

Tinsman, Heidi. "Unequal Uplift: The Sexual Politics of Gender, Work, and Community in the Chilean Agrarian Reform, 1950–1973." Ph.D. diss., Yale University, 1996.

Touraine, Alain, and Daniel Pecaut. "Working-Class Consciousness and Economic Development in Latin America." In *Masses in Latin America,* ed. I. L. Horowitz. New York: Oxford University Press, 1970.

van Onselen, Charles. *Chibaro: African Mine Labour in Southern Rhodesia, 1900–1933.* London: Pluto, 1976.

Vera Valenzuela, Mario. *La política económica del cobre en Chile.* Santiago: Ediciones de la Universidad de Chile, 1961.

Viotti da Costa, Emília. "Experience versus Structures: New Tendencies in the History of Labor and the Working Class in Latin America—What Do We Gain? What Do We Lose?" *International Labor and Working-Class History* 36 (Fall 1989).

Williams, Raymond. *Marxism and Literature.* Oxford: Oxford University Press, 1977.

Willis, Paul. *Learning to Labour: How Working-Class Kids Get Working-Class Jobs.* Hampshire: Gower Publishing, 1981.

Winn, Peter. *Weavers of Revolution: The Yarur Workers and Chile's Road to Socialism.* New York: Oxford University Press, 1986.

Zapata, Francisco. "The Chilean Labor Movement and the Problems of the Transition to Socialism." *Latin American Perspectives* 3 (Winter 1976).

———. "Enclaves y sistemas de relaciones industriales en América Latina." *Revista Mexicana de Sociología* 39 (April–June 1977).

———. "Los mineros de Chuquicamata: ¿Productores o proletarios?" Mexico: Centro de Estudios Sociológicos, Colegio de Mexico, 1975.

INDEX

Thomas Miller Klubock is Assistant Professor of History at
Ohio State University

Library of Congress Cataloging-in-Publication Data
Klubock, Thomas Miller.
Contested communities : class, gender, and politics in Chile's
El Teniente copper mine, 1904–1948 / Thomas Miller
Klubock.
p.   cm. — (Comparative and international working-class
history)
Includes bibliographical references and index.
ISBN 0-8223-2078-9 (cloth : alk. paper). —
ISBN 0-8223-2092-4 (pbk. : alk. paper)
1. Copper miners—Chile—History—20th century.
2. Copper mines and mining—Chile—History—20th century.
3. Sex role—Chile—History—20th century.   4. El Teniente
(Mine)—History.   I. Title.   II. Series.
HD8039.M72C55   1998
331.7′622343′098332—dc21   97-39535   CIP